The Canadian Party System

The Canadian Party System

An Analytic History

RICHARD JOHNSTON

UBCPress · Vancouver · Toronto

© UBC Press 2017

All rights reserved. No part of this publication may be reproduced, stored in a retrieval system, or transmitted, in any form or by any means, without prior written permission of the publisher, or, in Canada, in the case of photocopying or other reprographic copying, a licence from Access Copyright, www.accesscopyright.ca.

27 26 25 24 23 22 21 20 19 18 17   5 4 3 2 1

Printed in Canada on FSC-certified ancient-forest-free paper (100% post-consumer recycled) that is processed chlorine- and acid-free.

ISBN 978-0-7748-3607-4 (bound)
ISBN 978-0-7748-3608-1 (pbk)
ISBN 978-0-7748-3609-8 (epdf)

Cataloguing-in-Publication data is available from Library and Archives Canada.

Canada

UBC Press gratefully acknowledges the financial support for our publishing program of the Government of Canada (through the Canada Book Fund), the Canada Council for the Arts, and the British Columbia Arts Council.

This book has been published with the help of a grant from the Canadian Federation for the Humanities and Social Sciences, through the Awards to Scholarly Publications Program, using funds provided by the Social Sciences and Humanities Research Council of Canada.

Printed and bound in Canada by Friesens
Set in Univers Condensed, Zurich Condensed, and Minion
by Artegraphica Design Co. Ltd.
Copy editor: Dallas Harrison
Proofreader: Judith Earnshaw
Indexer: Lillian Ashworth

UBC Press
The University of British Columbia
2029 West Mall
Vancouver, BC V6T 1Z2
www.ubcpress.ca

To the memory of
George Chalmers Johnston and Agnes Jesse Blackbourn
Wilbert Harry Markle and Lily May Taggart
Joe Hilton and Jesse McNay

Contents

Tables and Figures / ix

Abbreviations / xiii

Acknowledgments / xv

1 Introduction / 3

2 Situating the Case / 13

3 Liberal Dominance, Conservative Interludes / 48

4 Liberal Centrism, Polarized Pluralism / 67

5 Catholics and Others / 101

6 The Life and Death of Insurgents / 133

7 Invasion from the Left / 163

8 System Dynamics, Coordination, and Fragmentation / 187

9 Federal-Provincial Discontinuity / 214

10 Conclusion / 239

Appendix: Data Sources / 263

Notes / 266

References / 283

Index / 300

Tables and Figures

Tables

2.1 The union movement and the party system: Canada, Great Britain, New Zealand, Australia, and the US / 41

2.2 Catholics and the party system: Canada, Great Britain, New Zealand, Australia, and the US / 42

3.1 Quebec as the pivot for government, 1878-1988 / 62

3.A1 Seats and votes by region, 1887-1988 / 66

6.1 Election timing, the price of wheat, and the Progressive/agrarian vote / 155

8.1 Electoral trade-offs among "old" and "new" parties: Historical patterns / 189

8.2 Vote shifts among parties, early campaign to election day, 1988, Canada outside Quebec / 192

8.3 Vote shifts among parties, early campaign to election day, 2011, Canada outside Quebec / 196

8.4 Vote shifts among parties, early campaign to election day, 1993, Canada outside Quebec / 199

8.5 Insurgents and the CCF-NDP as sources of fractionalization, 1908-2015 / 203

8.A1 Shifts in the relative contribution of support for insurgents and the CCF-NDP to federal fractionalization / 213

9.1 Insurgents and the CCF-NDP as major parties in provincial politics, 1900-2010 / 219

9.A1 Left threat and right consolidation, 1908-2011 / 236

9.A2 Joint effect of insurgents and the CCF-NDP on ENP, 1908-2011 / 237

9.A3 Impact of insurgent votes, CCF-NDP votes, and provincial ENP on federal-provincial dissimilarity, 1930-2011 / 238

Figures

2.1 Conservative and Liberal seats and votes, 1878-2015 / 17

2.2 Insurgents and CCF-NDP seats and votes, 1878-2015 / 20

2.3 Trajectories for specific insurgents, 1878-2015 / 21

2.4 Federal and provincial trajectories for Conservatives, Liberals, CCF-NDP, and insurgents, 1908-2011 / 24

2.5 Effective number of electoral parties: Anglo-American single-member district systems, twentieth century / 27

2.6 Components of electoral fractionalization, 1878-2015 / 29

2.7 Electoral volatility: Anglo-American single-member district systems, twentieth century / 32

2.8 Electoral divergence between arenas: Canada, Australia, Germany, Spain, and the US / 36

2.9 Left-right locations of Canadian parties, 2000 and 2004 / 44

3.1 Regions as brokers of government, 1878-2015 / 51

3.2 Popular vote distributions by region, 1887-1988 / 55

3.3 Seats and votes by region, 1887-1988 / 57

3.4 Seat-share distributions within regions, 1887-1988 / 58

3.5 Regional blocs in Parliament, 1887-1988: Liberals versus Conservatives and first versus second place / 59

4.1 Postwar evolution of left-right party positions / 70

4.2 Perceptions of parties' orientations to Quebec, 1988-97 / 72

4.3 Party supporters' orientations to Quebec, 1988-2011 / 73

4.4 Impact of language inside and outside Quebec, 1940-2011 / 76

4.5	Impact of language inside and outside Quebec, 1878-2006 / 78	
4.6	Vote shares: Quebec and the rest of Canada, 1878-2015 / 80	
4.7	Episodes of Conservative surge and decline: Quebec and the rest of Canada / 84	
4.8	Quebec/rest-of-Canada differences in non-partisanship / 87	
4.9	Turnout and the Liberal share, 1908-88 / 89	
4.10	Geographic breadth of Liberal and Conservative electoral coalitions, 1908-88 / 96	
4.11	Geographic breadth of Liberal and Conservative electoral coalitions, post-1993 / 100	
5.1	Geography of religion and language: Rest of Canada and Quebec / 105	
5.2	Emergence of the Catholic-Liberal alignment, 1878-1921 / 111	
5.3	The religious cleavage in the Liberal vote, 1949-2011 / 121	
5.4	Unpacking the cleavage: Impact of controls for region and ethnicity, 1949-2011 / 124	
5.5	Impact of French language or ancestry: Non-Quebec samples, 1949-2011 / 127	
5.6	Impact of ancestry: Non-Quebec samples, 1965-2011 / 129	
6.1	Federal and provincial insurgent dynamics by province, 1908-2011 / 135	
6.2	Dynamics for specific insurgents: Federal elections outside Quebec, 1908-2011 / 137	
6.3	Dynamics for specific insurgents: Provincial elections outside Quebec, 1908-2011 / 138	
6.4	Dynamics for specific insurgents: Federal and provincial elections in Quebec, 1908-2011 / 142	
7.1	Federal and provincial CCF-NDP dynamics by province, 1908-2011 / 166	
7.2	Labour mobilization and the CCF-NDP vote: The national picture / 170	
7.3	Labour mobilization and the CCF-NDP vote, by province and decade / 172	

7.4 Impact of union membership, 1940-2011/ 176
7.5 Impact on the NDP vote of excluding Quebec residents and Catholics, 1949-2011 / 179
7.6 The provincial "counterfactual," I: Official returns / 182
7.7 The provincial "counterfactual," II: Conditional impact of religious context, 1965-2011 / 184
8.1 Dynamics of vote intention, 1988, rest of Canada / 191
8.2 Dynamics of vote intention, 2011, rest of Canada / 195
8.3 Dynamics of vote intention, 1993, rest of Canada / 198
8.4 Common dynamics and divergent outcomes: Coordination failure on the left and right / 201
8.5 Sources of federal fractionalization: National level data, 1904-2015 / 204
8.6 Sources of federal fractionalization: Province-level data, 1904-2015 / 206
9.1 Federal-provincial dissimilarity, by province and year, 1908-2011 / 216
9.2 Variation of party shares across provinces, 1908-2011 / 218
9.3 Effective number of parties: Provincial versus federal arenas, 1908-2011 / 221
9.4 CCF-NDP strength and centre-right consolidation: Provincial versus federal patterns, 1908-2011 / 223
9.5 Covariance between NDP and insurgent shares: Provincial versus federal patterns, 1908-2011 / 225
9.6 Insurgents, the CCF-NDP, and ENP in the province: Provincial versus federal patterns, 1908-2011 / 227
9.7 Sources of federal-provincial dissimilarity, 1931-2011 / 229

Abbreviations

ALN	Action Libérale Nationale
CALURA	Corporations and Labour Unions Returns Act
CCF	Co-operative Commonwealth Federation
CCL	Canadian Congress of Labour
CES	Canadian Election Study
CIO	Congress of Industrial Organizations
CIPO	Canadian Institute of Public Opinion
CLC	Canadian Labour Congress
CMP	Campaign Manifesto Project
CSES	Comparative Study of Electoral Systems
ENP	effective number of parties
FPP	first past the post
FTA	Free Trade Agreement
FTF	face to face
GLS	Generalized Least Squares
ILP	Independent Labour Party
LFS	Labour Force Survey
MAR	Missing at Random
MMP	mixed-member proportional
NAFTA	North American Free Trade Agreement
NDP	New Democratic Party
PR	proportional representation
QCA	qualitative comparative analysis
SD	standard deviation

SF ratio	second-to-first ratio
SMD	single-member districts
STV	single transferable vote
SUR	seemingly unrelated regressions
TLC	Trades and Labour Congress
UFA	United Farmers of Alberta
UN	Union Nationale

Acknowledgments

This book has taken me somewhere between ten years and an entire career to write. Fortunately, I had an army of helpers and supporters, ranging from UBC undergraduates to heads of departments at other universities (some individuals occupy both categories), not to mention UBC mentors and colleagues who are now *sub specie aeternitatis*, as one of them was fond of saying.

Research assistants include Neil Sutherland, Brenda O'Neill, Mark Pickup, Amanda Bittner, Janine Van Vliet, John McAndrews, Grace Lore, Andrea Nuesser, Sule Yaylaçi, and Megan Dias.

Many colleagues have been implicated, not always to their knowledge. First I must mention the late Jean Laponce, who pioneered survey analysis in Canada. Not only did Jean set much of the intellectual agenda, but also he began compiling the dataset that underpins much of this book. The other critical survey dataset is the cumulative Canadian Election Study (CES). The father of the CES is Jean's great friend John Meisel. The CES collaborators are too numerous to mention, so I will single out those who worked with me on the 1988 and 1992-93 studies: André Blais, Henry Brady, Jean Crête, Elisabeth Gidengil, and Neil Nevitte. Without the design choices that we made in those years, this book would not have been possible. I must especially mention Henry Brady. A central trope in this book is the claim that the Liberal Party occupies contrasting poles inside and outside Quebec. Thinking of the party in precisely this way was enabled by a flash of graphical insight that is entirely Henry's and appeared in our book on the 1988 election. Whether they realize it or not, Chris Achen,

Chris Cochrane, Tom Flanagan, Aina Gallego, Simon Hug, Karen Long Jusko, Matt Shugart, and John Zaller materially influenced my thinking. Scott Matthews was persistent in his support and criticism of the text as it evolved. Finally, I must mention the two people who share almost as much responsibility for this book as I do: Pradeep Chhibber and Ken Kollman. A large part of my book is a critique of their magisterial volume on the formation of party systems. A visit by Pradeep to UBC nurtured the first inklings of my project, and he and Ken never ceased to be supportive. They epitomize the scholarly ideal.

Parts of the manuscript were presented in seminars and workshops at Temple, Calgary, University of British Columbia (Vancouver and Okanagan), Toronto, Alberta, Carleton, Berkeley, Michigan, Wisconsin, the Australian National University, and Griffith (Brisbane). I am grateful to these institutions for making the events possible and to the participants for pushing me hard on the weak points.

My thanks also go to the professionals at UBC Press. Randy Schmidt and Holly Keller brought the book to print, always with good sense. My deepest editorial debt, however, is to Emily Andrew. Emily kept up the chase for ten years, with no slackening of enthusiasm or insight. What a shock, then, to discover that the delivery of my final manuscript preceded her departure to a rival press by only a few weeks. I still think of it as her book. I hope she does too.

Data collection and analysis were funded by the Social Sciences and Humanities Research Council of Canada, the University of British Columbia, and the University of Pennsylvania.

The forbearance of my family was absolutely critical to the enterprise. I thank them all, since the project began when all were still at home (more or less). But the greater burden has fallen on my wife, Kathryn Fowler, especially in the past year as the pace of production seemed to be somehow both frenetic and glacial. Miraculously, she still *is* my wife.

The dedication of this volume lies elsewhere in biography and family history, however. My adult life covers many of the years described in the book, and my genealogy is a compendium of North American settler history. Accordingly, this volume is dedicated to three couples whose lives encapsulate key themes in it. My grandfather Johnston commanded the 2nd Canadian Mounted Rifles from 1916 to 1919. My grandmother

Blackbourn was born beside Nicola Lake, a daughter of the ranch. Grandfather Markle was an observant Catholic and one of many siblings (among them two nuns), but he did not conform to Catholic stereotypes. The eponymous Markle was a German Pietist, and the family came from New York to what is now Canada as United Empire Loyalists, always an awkward fact for my anti-imperialist mother. Grandmother Taggart was a non-observing Protestant and also a multi-generational North American. Their marriage was the third in a succession of interfaith unions. Joe Hilton was in rough chronological order a coal miner, a trapper, a park warden, and a firefighter – and all along a mountain man. It was my privilege to work with him deep in the mountains building trails. On snowshoes, Jess was even faster than Joe.

# The Canadian Party System

1

Introduction

The Canadian party system is unruly yet inscrutable. For one thing, it defies the most powerful generalization in empirical political theory, Duverger's Law. That law states that a strongly majoritarian institutional context such as Canada's induces voters to concentrate on two and only two parties. Instead, Canada has a multiparty system. Moreover, although the system's dominant parties date back to the mid-nineteenth century, each has been to death's door and back. The same citizens vote differently in provincial elections than in national ones. Although a party of labour exists, the system's class basis is weak. Party competition has been sustained by cultural politics, but most observers find the cultural patterns mystifying. Unlike most systems – and unlike all other systems with single-member districts – the Canadian system is dominated by a party of the centre.

Although some Canadian peculiarities have been used to make general points in comparative politics, such work tends to over-stylize the case, misstate its explanatory relevance, and understate its true peculiarity. I too present Canada as a deviant case and argue that its discharge is essential to a full understanding of more conventional cases. Likewise, comparison is essential to understand fully the Canadian case itself. A major virtue of the case is its disjointedness: a party system dating back to the mid-nineteenth century coexists with a mixed cast of newer parties. Because the institutional context is majoritarian, the coexistence is uneasy. In one sense, the Canadian system exhibits dynamics typical of general Anglo-American patterns. In other countries, however, the dynamics operated quickly, replacing one system of simple competition with another one. Because the dynamics were quick and took place nearly a century ago, the genealogy is obscured. In Canada, these dynamics have occupied the better part of a century, are geographically differentiated, and are still under way; the genealogy is continuously visible.

This book is historical not only because it mines long periods for data on dynamic processes but also because it appeals to history to account for certain patterns that otherwise seem to be locked in mystery. Even more to the point, it argues that certain critical features are historical accidents. The electoral framework was disruptive in amplifying the initial effects of those accidents and then was conservative in discouraging further assaults on the accidentally generated pattern.

This book is analytical not in seeking to reduce the system's complexity to a handful of theorems but in holding up a mirror to analytically based claims by others. It presents theoretically motivated chronologies to assist the causal process analysis. The chronologies do not purport to be comprehensive but are as balanced as possible in relation to particular questions. Most important, I test the empirical reach of what might be called the Neo-Duvergerian Synthesis, notably Cox (1997) and Chhibber and Kollman (2004). In this work, Canada is already recognized as a critical deviant case. But that literature gets Canada less than half right and, in doing so, risks being misleading for patterns in other countries. In particular, I argue that the stipulation in the synthesis that Duverger's Law operates only at the district level overlooks plain facts. The most reasonable interpretation of those facts is that many voters look beyond their particular district – indeed to the other side of the continent – for strategic cues about how to behave. Meanwhile, focusing on observable implications of the neo-Duvergerian theorems distracts us from lessons in the rest of the data. Those lessons are far-reaching. They extend from the competing logics of parliamentary and electoral majoritarianism to the party politics of federations. They require us to look at parties as organizations whose motives cannot be boiled down to short-term electoral advantage.

For understanding the totality of the case, my pivotal claim is that explaining most of the system's anomalies requires one simple fact: its domination by a party of the centre. Canadian parties can be ordered from left to right, as is true everywhere. The gap between the Conservatives on the right and the New Democrats on the left is wide and easy to interpret.

But standing between these parties is the historically dominant Liberal Party. This fact is pivotal to Canadian multipartism and to the weakness of class politics. Canadian parties also sit on a second axis of choice, which I refer to as the "national" dimension. Its content varies over the decades but always reflects the fact that Canada is a binational state. Such a second dimension with identity politics content is also not unusual. What is unusual is that on this second dimension the Liberals also command the centre. This control is critical to the system's volatility, to its geography, and to the gap inside Canadian voters' heads between their federal and provincial selves. In sum, the Canadian party system exhibits a pattern – "polarized pluralism" – normally associated with systems emerging from a crisis or heading toward one. If polarized pluralism explains so much, then it too begs to be explained. This is the other main task of the book.

The Argument in Brief
Canada combines low-detail Westminster institutions with the sociology of deep division. Among rich industrial countries, Canada is the most diverse (Fearon 2003). In particular, French Canada constitutes a nation within the nation, an island in an English-speaking sea, so to speak. For French Canada, survival has been the overarching preoccupation. To that end, francophones, although a national minority, have been well served by the country's majoritarian institutions. By any electoral standard, the francophone vote, especially in Quebec, has been remarkably coordinated, both in concentration on one party at a time and in mobility between parties. Concentration and mobility are then amplified by the electoral system. The upshot of this coordination was that, for nearly 150 years, Quebec alone could put one party halfway to a parliamentary majority. The rest of the country rarely matched Quebec in electoral coherence, however, so the province was the de facto pivot for the government. Quebec's history of coordinated mobility is a major contributor to the electorate's overall volatility.

Most of the time, the party that Quebec kept in power was the Liberals. Typically, this was because the Liberals were the only acceptable alternative, sometimes barely so. There was usually plenty of room on the Quebec nationalist side of the Liberals, but most of the time no party filled the space. Outside Quebec, the Liberals were the most pro-Quebec party, so there was also plenty of room on the anti-Quebec side. Taking both parts of the electorate together on this existential dimension, the Liberals occupied the centre. Since they were not just centrist but also dominant, the Canadian system exhibited the dynamics that Sartori (1966, 1976) called "polarized pluralism." This condition is normally associated with systems under challenge for their democratic character – postwar Italy or Weimar Germany – or for the integrity of the very community – India. Canada has been an example of the latter. In the electoral sphere, this has meant that, when cultural questions heated up, the Liberals have been vulnerable to invasion on both flanks, anti-Canadian forces in Quebec and anti-Quebec forces elsewhere in Canada. This has been a further contributor to electoral volatility.

Canada outside Quebec (and outside the handful of other francophone strongholds) is a classic Anglo-American settler society. Its identity is both plastic and susceptible to cultural and geostrategic influences from elsewhere in the Anglosphere. Canada has also undergone urbanization, industrialization, and labour mobilization on lines parallel to those of its main comparators, if sometimes at a slower pace. These forces have raised the dimensionality of policy debate. What is more, the economy is open and resource based and thus experiences the full weight of global business cycles. At first glance, it seems to be reasonable to suppose that these changes and vulnerabilities account for the party system's fragmentation. But other Anglo-American systems also feature roughly orthogonal cultural and economic policy dimensions, yet their party systems have absorbed these pressures without surrendering to enduring fragmentation. The absorption was often painful, with fragmentation and volatility in the short run. But the other systems reconsolidated along new lines. Older cultural divisions might persist but are normally subsumed by the now dominant economic dimension. In Canada, however, old and new divisions coexist in disjointed pluralism, like Europe.

They coexist, I argue, not in spite of the majoritarian institutional framework but because of it. Thanks to the framework, the presence of Quebec has ramifications throughout the rest of the country. In a system of proportional representation, Quebec would be a stand-alone factor, important in function of its size but not out of proportion to that size. In the majoritarian context, Quebec can empower certain other groups, typically culturally kindred ones, and thus strengthen the cultural agenda at the expense of the economic one. It can also provoke countermobilization by hostile forces, which simply reinforces the point. But coexistence is a two-way street. Much – probably most – of the rest of Canada feels the same pressures that the outside world does. And, crudely speaking, the further west one goes, the less immediately relevant a cultural agenda seems to be. Westerners are repeatedly tempted to try to reshape the Canada-wide issue agenda through the medium of a new party. The division of power in the federal system also shelters a big fraction of partisan contestation from transcontinental influences, such that provincial politics in places that do not mirror the Canada-wide cultural debate can resemble the world outside Canada. And forces originating in the provincial arena can bubble up into the federal one. A party system predicated on divisions in central Canada usually prevails federally. But its reach is never total, not all the way across the continent nor all the way down to the provincial arena. From time to time, pushback from outside central Canada threatens to undermine the system.

Among new parties, one is qualitatively different from the others. This is the New Democratic Party. The NDP and its precursors represent a universal force like that in almost all of the comparable systems, indeed in almost all systems in the rich capitalist world: a party of social democracy and organized labour. Its growth has generally been gradual, and it has experienced setbacks. It might never overturn the pattern of national politics, although it has come close. But it is securely ensconced in the Canada-wide system, and in certain provinces it is one of the dominant players. Its presence imparts a structure and a dynamic to elections that stand somewhat aside from both abiding cultural divisions and spasmodic geographically specific intrusions. Its presence is assisted by the forces of geography and federalism that create space for third parties. But its weakness, I argue, is not – or not mainly – the product of its own flaws or mistakes (of which there have been many). Rather, NDP weakness is the complement to Liberal strength. The strength of the Liberal Party means that consolidation on the centre-right to block the NDP has never been necessary. Similarly, the historical inability of the Conservatives to form governments means that NDP supporters can afford – most of the time – to stay put without risking coordination failure on the centre-left.

Coordination between NDP and Conservative supporters never makes sense, not on a left-right dimension at least. Here, too, the party system exhibits polarized pluralism.

At many points, the argument requires that we take seriously a force that seems to defy one logic of rational choice. The standing claim in the study of electoral coordination is that the critical arena is the local district. Strategic pressure operates at that level, and from this follow certain predictions for local equilibria. In showing how the predictions routinely fail, I find myself resorting to parastrategic arguments at a much higher level of aggregation, one at which voters have an even smaller chance of making a difference than the already infinitesimal one in the local district. I argue that actors respond to information about whole electorates, including ones to which they do not belong. This intuition travels beyond the explanation of local electoral fragmentation. Part of my substantiation of the case involves treating provincial electorates as counterfactuals for federal ones. In doing so, I also wind up accounting for a large fraction of Canada's massive federal-provincial discontinuity. Complementarily, this exercise holds up a mirror to party strategy. If parties focus only on winning the immediate election, then none of my arguments work. By indirection, we must conclude that parties think about the long run. As they do, they challenge much of the neo-Duvergerian apparatus.

Plan of the Book

An integrated account requires three main elements: the foundations of Liberal and Conservative electoral politics, the conditions for and patterns of third-party entry and exit, and interaction across federal and provincial arenas and between old and new parties. The majoritarian logic of Westminster parliamentarism privileges first movers, and this exerts downward pressure on later entrants. However, if a later entrant offers a programmatic alternative to the others and finds the means to survive, then at least some of the old parties will collaborate in opening up the new policy dimension. As this happens, at least one of the old parties might find itself at risk, especially to the extent that the majoritarian logic of the electoral system turns the party's initial strategic advantage on its head. The plan of the book follows from these elements.

Chapter 2 supplies a stylized introduction to the players and to critical dependent variables. The chapter is not just taxonomic but also underscores the inadequacy of some key analytical claims. It draws distinctions among the system's smaller parties. "Insurgents" appear suddenly and typically have rather short lives. The social democratic and labour left, culminating in the formation of the NDP in 1961, grew gradually and has staying power. The critical dependent variables are represented by indicators of fragmentation, volatility, and federal-provincial discontinuity. The indicators enable cross-national comparison. The chapter emphasizes that flux in the dependent variables and relations among them are not accounted for by the comparative elections arguments currently in play. In particular, fragmentation of the vote is as much the product of multiparty competition within electoral districts as it is of sectional conflict. What is more, the sectional pattern exhibits an episodic dynamic critical to understanding electoral volatility. The ebb and flow of regionalism complements cycles of Conservative boom and bust. The chapter also establishes the system's weak class foundations, its historically strong but now nearly defunct cultural bases, and the fact of Liberal centrism.

How the Liberals dominated the politics of the twentieth century is the topic of Chapter 3. The key was control of Quebec, the necessary and sufficient condition for Liberal victory in the country as a whole. The Quebec electorate exhibited a remarkable degree of electoral self-discipline: one-sided majorities in votes that produced even more one-sided majorities in seats. Eighty percent of the time between 1896 and 1988, majorities in Quebec were conferred on the Liberal Party, and almost every time this happened the Liberals formed the government. The few times that Quebeckers declined to give the Liberals a solid bloc the party fell from power. Occasionally, the Quebec electorate went all the way and gave a near-monolithic bloc to the Conservatives.

Chapter 4 substantiates how the Liberal Party is in fact centrist on both of the dimensions that dominate electors' choices: the left-right one that organizes party politics practically worldwide and a Canada-specific "national question," the existential issue forced by the presence of Quebec. It is not that the Liberals sustained a centrist position on one dimension by controlling a pole on the other one, as analytical accounts normally claim

(Chappell and Keech 1986). I show that Liberal centrism on the national question is made possible by segmentation of the electorate between Quebec and the rest of Canada, such that the Liberals do control a pole of debate in both Quebec and the rest of Canada – but the opposite pole in each place, pro-Canada inside Quebec and pro-Quebec outside the province.

In the twentieth century, the Liberal combination of control of Quebec and centrism on the national question meant that a Canada-wide Conservative victory required an ends-against-the-middle coalition of francophones and francophobes. Occasionally, the Conservatives succeeded in building such a coalition. Building it helped to fuel a boom in the party's Canada-wide vote. But the coalition was unsustainable, and the boom was always followed by a bust. Amplitudes of boom and bust increased over the century and ultimately blew up the old system.

Quebec was critical, but the Liberals required additional support elsewhere. For most of the twentieth century, this support emerged from a group – Catholics – whose interests often aligned with those of Quebeckers and whose geography was strategically helpful. This is the argument of Chapter 5. In late-twentieth-century terms, the Catholic-Liberal connection was something of a mystery. I argue that the mystery can be resolved only by examining the historical record. In the nineteenth century, when substantive religious controversy was most acute, the parties did not divide along denominational lines. It was only in the twentieth century, with Canada's engagement in great-power diplomacy and war, that the divide increased. The temporal pattern reveals that the religious divide was in fact over national identity. After 1965, as Canada's relationship with Britain faded, Catholics became less distinctively Liberal, and identity politics shifted to an internal, group-specific basis. As this happened, the Liberals' overall position weakened.

Chapter 6 documents the life and death of parties with geographically focused appeals, parties that I call – somewhat imprecisely – "insurgents." These parties supply a significant component of electoral fractionalization. Such parties defy simple explanation, however, since provinces with similar circumstances exhibit sharply divergent patterns. No less ubiquitous than third-party entry is third-party exit, sometimes as one third party displaces another, more often as old parties soak up sectional tension. The chapter shows that explanations of entry and exit and of variation across provinces must incorporate path dependence.

The puzzle of the NDP is addressed in Chapter 7. Why has the NDP historically been weak? If it is so weak, then why does it exist at all? The chapter argues that for a party to survive in the long run under Westminster rules, it must be present itself, even if only vestigially, everywhere. A corresponding logic is that voters respond not just to a party's local chances but also to its Canada-wide ones. I substantiate this claim in two ways. First, I show that focusing on cultural groups most favourable to the NDP still leaves the party short of the support that its labour counterparts receive from culturally similar groups in other countries. Second, I use provincial elections as counterfactuals for federal ones. In provinces culturally open to class politics, the NDP is a major party provincially if not federally. In provinces less amenable to class politics, the opposite pattern holds.

Chapter 8 shows that the dynamics of interaction among the parties are asymmetrical. Conservative support ebbs and flows mainly in counterpoint to insurgents. The Liberal vote moves contrary to the NDP vote, with a long-run trend toward the NDP. Asymmetry extends to the relationship between "new" party invasion and fractionalization of the vote. Insurgents disproportionately produce sectional discrepancies and thus boost the extra-local component in system breakdown. Entry from the left was also somewhat concentrated geographically, but the federal CCF and NDP grew as much by spreading their vote as by deepening it. This spreading produced three-party competition within individual electoral districts. Such competition bespeaks coordination failure. The chapter documents specific instances of such failure with evidence from three campaigns.

This takes us to federal-provincial discontinuities in Chapter 9. Two basic forces are in play. One is the appearance of insurgents. They are especially strong in provincial elections and in the provinces that sit uneasily in a Canada-wide partisan framework: Quebec and certain western ones. The second process reveals both the power and the limit of Duverger's Law. After an initial surge of multipartism in provincial elections, provincial party systems remain consolidated, as Duverger predicts, even as the federal electorate is fractionalized. This discrepancy is especially marked where the CCF-NDP has made inroads. Growth in the left vote induces strategic consolidation on the centre-right and does so much more efficiently in the provincial arena than in the federal arena. The identity of the centre-right beneficiary varies over time and place, however, reflecting historical accident and path dependency. Divergence is further enhanced where the provincial-level beneficiary of anti-socialist consolidation is a local insurgent with no enduring federal equivalent.

Chapter 10 recapitulates and integrates the findings, draws lessons that apply beyond the case, and identifies issues highlighted by the book but not directly addressed, much less resolved. One issue is the tension between parliamentary and electoral logics. Where the Westminster propensity for single-party governments creates pressure for geographically inclusive coalitions, the electoral system can create the opposite pressure. This observation comes out of the episodic dynamics that link Conservatives and insurgents. Another issue is the role of historical sequences in the evolution of the system. Only by such sequences can we make sense of certain patterns, especially for new parties. In this, Canada is a microcosm for processes and outcomes already part of the canon for the comparative study of elections. The patterns illustrate the various forms of path dependence. They also reinforce a message from the scholarship on party organization: parties do not always seek to maximize their vote share. Other goals can be worth pursuing, and the most basic goal of all is simple survival. The book's last theoretical point challenges us to become serious about how voters incorporate strategic information into their choices. The book then concludes with observations about the limits of its overall scope.

It is important to say what this book is not. It is not an exercise in thick description. Although my uses of history are balanced and inclusive (at least I have tried to make them so), they are no more detailed than required by theory. Information appears to the extent that it is probative and not otherwise. Similarly, the book does not try to explain everything about Canada's party system. It focuses instead on the features that can be explained by a modest number of central propositions. The focus is augmented where those central propositions signally fail or where they throw a sharp light on anomalies that fairly beg to be explored. Although the book has many implications for understanding the present state of the party system, it is not designed to that end. Indeed, the book is better at explaining the twentieth century than the twenty-first.

2

Situating the Case

In this chapter, I review Canadian electoral history to show how the system does – and does not – differ from its appropriate comparators. The chapter also serves as an agenda for the rest of the book.

I start by introducing the parties individually and typologically. The typology is not airtight, but it underscores that different parties have distinctive dynamics. The account is not blow by blow, nor does it plumb the depths. The point, rather, is to provide just enough narrative to motivate cross-national comparison.

I begin that comparison by moving up to the highest level of aggregation, with index numbers for fragmentation, volatility, and federal-provincial discontinuity in whole electorates. I show that fragmentation of the system does not correspond to predictions from the neo-Duvergerian model of electoral coordination. Indeed, it flat out controverts them. The Canadian system is more volatile than the others but not in a chronic sense. Rather, the volatility is episodic, startling punctuations of what is usually a stable system. Discontinuity between federal and provincial arenas is stunning.

I then move down the aggregation ladder to differences among groups, as captured by survey evidence from individual voters. Although the patterns here reflect observations already on the record, I bring the evidence up to date and present it in a way that enables cross-national comparison. The setup also highlights how puzzling these patterns were and are.

I conclude the empirical section by returning to the individual party as the analytical unit. The point is simple: all renderings of Canadian party locations on a left-right scale confirm that the Liberal Party stands between its chief competitors. That a large – indeed dominant – party occupies such a position is highly unusual. As the rest of the book argues, this anomaly is the system's pivotal feature.

The Players and the Stakes

The Canadian party system is an uneasy amalgam of parties competing to form the government and of parties invading on the flanks. The oldest parties predate the federation of 1867 and rival US parties for longevity. But for most of the twentieth century their very existence was contested. The first serious invasion by a new party occurred in 1921, and multipartism became a regular feature in 1935. Because of the majoritarian logic of the electoral system, old and new parties do not merely coexist; they compete across a porous and moving boundary.

For my purposes here, the Liberal and Conservative Parties are "old." All others are "new," even though many of them are quite old and some are now defunct. Old parties simply got there first. Getting there first was important: given the persistence of first past the post (FPP) throughout the period, a new party could get close to power only by pushing an old one aside. All new parties want to shift the agenda, and some work hard at breaking into the inner circle. A distinction rather like that between old and new is a standard feature in the "textbook theory" of the Canadian party system (Sniderman, Forbes, and Melzer 1974).[1]

But new parties are not all of a piece. A central proposition of this book is that one new party, the New Democratic Party, is unlike all other new ones, or at least it has become so. Although its origins are complex, it is basically a party of organized labour, like Labour parties in other Westminster systems. The NDP aspires to "mainstream" status in that it accepts the prevailing Westminster model: a majoritarian electoral formula,[2] disciplined parliamentary delegations, an imperative to build a broad electoral base, and single-party government. In this, it might be classified with the old parties.

The other new entrants might be thought of as "anti-system," "niche," or "insurgent" parties in being focused on a single policy dimension, in forswearing the bundling of considerations that would be necessary to expand their bases (Meguid 2005), and in exhibiting distinctive dynamics

(Adams et al. 2006). Such parties typically contest only a limited number of seats. Now and again, old parties exhibit niche characteristics even as some niche parties aspire to enter the mainstream. But all newcomers aside from the NDP exhibit distinctive dynamics, so I distinguish them collectively from the Liberals, Conservatives, and NDP. Using a shorthand, I call them "insurgents," a term that carries less normative freight than the term "niche" or "anti-system" and focuses on electoral dynamics: all such parties appear suddenly and, commonly, disappear suddenly.

Old Parties, Old System

The Canadian federation developed sequentially, and the old parties originated at an early stage in the sequence. As in the United States, 300 years elapsed between the first European settlements, on the one hand, and the organization of the newest states or provinces, on the other. Until the first decade of the twentieth century, the four western provinces were somewhat fictional: Manitoba and British Columbia had tiny electorates and were fiscal wards of the central government; Alberta and Saskatchewan did not exist until 1905. But the region came of age suddenly, such that by 1911 Saskatchewan was Canada's third largest province.

The old Canadian pattern of Liberal-versus-Conservative contestation originated in the 1840s and largely congealed in the 1850s (Cornell 1962). Notwithstanding some flux in each party's nomenclature, many of the foundational patterns persist to this day. By 1878, the name of the Liberals had stabilized, but there was still an occasional tendency to refer back to their roots as "Reform" in pre-Confederation Ontario (strictly speaking Canada West) and as "Rouges" in Quebec (formerly Canada East). At its origins, the party resembled its European namesakes: anti-clerical and with a Whiggish emphasis on legislative, as opposed to executive, prerogatives. On the other side, a significant fraction of Conservatives still called themselves "Liberal-Conservatives," including the first leader, Sir John A. Macdonald. This was a relic of Macdonald's ambition to encompass the entire political landscape, and in 1867 the first government of the new federation included individuals who had earlier associated themselves with the Reform tendency.

The parties competed on a politically dangerous landscape and coped mainly by suppressing divisions (Crunican 1974; Miller 1979; Siegfried

1966). Especially dangerous were cultural divisions, a compound of language and religion. Political economy differentiated the old parties, with the Liberals the party of export-oriented farmers and the Conservatives the champions of import-substituting manufacturers. Even here differences were muted. The Conservatives had a clear advantage since each time commercial policy (basically the tariff) became the central question – 1878, 1891, and 1911 – the free-trade Liberals lost. The party eventually drew the obvious conclusion.

Figure 2.1, which plots Liberal and Conservative votes and seats from 1878 to the present,[3] shows that the old parties' domination prevailed until 1921. Before then, each party hovered around 50 percent of the vote, and together they controlled almost all votes and seats. But their grip on potentially explosive underlying forces began to loosen in the early twentieth century, and the Great War irretrievably compromised it.[4] In 1917, Conservatives and many English-speaking Liberals coalesced to adopt conscription for overseas service (Granatstein and Hitsman 1977; Willms 1956). The coalition styled itself as Unionist, and this remained the name of the Conservative Party until 1940. In that year, it presented itself as the "National Government" on the ground that it alone had the requisite patriotic fervour to conduct Canada's war effort properly; by analogy to 1917, the name indicated openness to coalition. Such openness also reflected the party's weakness: its vote and seat shares in these years were often desperately small for what was still the system's second-place party. In 1942, in a further gesture of outreach, the party was renamed the Progressive Conservatives, a condition imposed by John Bracken, the new leader and former Progressive premier of Manitoba.

The 1917 election was a disaster for the Liberals, and 1921 signalled only a weak recovery. Liberals who stayed out of the coalition campaigned against conscription. This certainly helped them in Quebec, but the party could not entirely fill the vacuum left by the delegitimation of the Conservatives in the province. The vacuum made the province a potential site for nationalist third-party entry.[5]

Just as the crisis delegitimated the Conservatives in Quebec, so too it compromised the Liberals in the West. The region had been a battleground in earlier cultural conflicts. A prelude to large-scale post-1896 European

Situating the Case 17

FIGURE 2.1 Conservative and Liberal seats and votes, 1878-2015

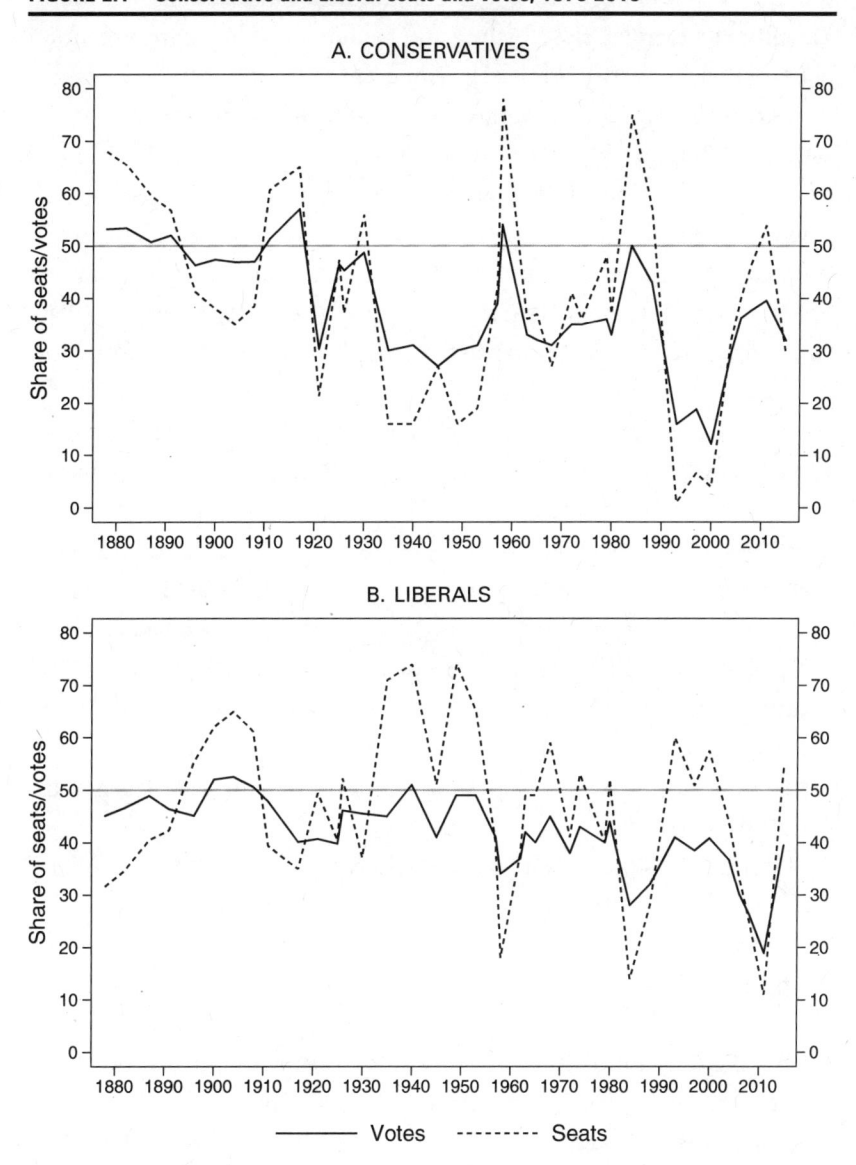

A. CONSERVATIVES

B. LIBERALS

——— Votes   --------- Seats

Note: Plots show each party's percentage of the national popular vote and of seats in the House of Commons.

settlement in the West was armed conflict with First Nations and Métis. The ultimate conflict, the Northwest Rebellion, ended with the execution of Louis Riel, its charismatic leader. This event roiled the waters everywhere in the country, and the resulting tensions persisted. In these early years, a significant fraction of the population in the West was French speaking, and a larger fraction still was Catholic. Because the federal government ruled the region directly and set the terms for creating provinces, it could not avoid hard choices. Among them were bilingualism in government operations and educational rights for Catholics (Lupul 1974; Thomas 1978). In the first decades of the twentieth century, Ontario and the West grew increasingly discontented with old-style party politics, and some of this discontent was driven by the very cultural tensions that the old parties tried to quell (English 1977). In this, the Canadian pattern was like that in the American Midwest and West. In contrast to the United States, however, the same forces that drove antipathy to party politics also drove conscriptionist sentiment. Sitting on top of these tensions as the dominant party in the region were the Liberals. As mentioned, many western Liberal MPs joined the 1917 coalition. The economic crisis that followed the 1918 armistice was felt with special force in the West. The coalition government was not sympathetic, such that its Liberal adherents were delegitimated. Some had already jumped ship to join the first great insurgency, the Progressive movement.

This insurgency produced the weakness of the collective old-party vote that began in 1921. Aside from trending generally downward, however, each party's subsequent trajectory was distinct. The most dramatic shifts involved the Conservatives, who in a sense never recovered from the 1921 cataclysm.[6] In the 1990s, they nearly disappeared. Only once since 1935 have they returned a winning share in the garden-variety 40-45 percent range; instead, the pattern has been boom or bust. That pattern also describes their seat shares. They returned over 75 percent of all seats in 1958 and 1984. Unsurprisingly, neither majority could be sustained on that scale, and only once in the twentieth century (1988) was a Conservative Party governing by itself able to return a second consecutive majority of any size. The party was exceptionally weak from 1935 to 1957, and in the 1990s it was barely visible in Parliament. The apparent recovery in 2004 was not an electoral phenomenon. Rather, it resulted from the party's merger with an insurgent, the Alliance (formerly the Reform Party).

Looked at another way, however, the party is no worse off now than it was in 1921. In the 1960s and 1970s, its vote was slightly higher than in the 1930s, 1940s, and 1950s, and its seat shares were dramatically higher. Conservative governments might have been rare, but their 1958 and 1984 victories were the only post-1940 ones based upon an outright majority of the popular vote. The distinctive fact about Conservative support post-1921 is not its trend – there is none – but its short-term flux.

The Liberal pattern is simpler but arguably more dire: the party's share has been eroding since 1911. No single setback has been as great as several of those visited on the Conservatives, but neither has any Liberal recovery restored all the lost ground. Although the party was in government for an unbroken 22 years after 1935, its vote share was slightly smaller than in its winning years from 1896 to 1911. In its extended period of power from 1963 to 1984, the party typically won shares in the low 40 percent range. Its return to power in 1993 was based upon shares around 40 percent. After 2000, the downward trajectory quickened, until 2015 at least.

The twentieth-century rot was masked by the seemingly endless enjoyment of power. Four of the five Liberal majorities between 1935 and 1957 were overwhelming – three of them over 70 percent of all seats. Although majorities were weaker, indeed hard to come by, in the 1963-84 interval, the Liberals won six of seven elections. And the 1990s brought parliamentary majorities that, notwithstanding the weak popular vote, were *more* secure than those in the 1960s and 1970s. At the time of writing, the party has returned to government, although with a modest vote plurality.

Insurgent Parties: Surge and Decline

The electoral shock of 1921 was produced by a mainly agrarian insurgency.[7] Over the following 70 years, three other high points merit notice: 1935, in the middle of the Depression; 1945, a retrospective plebiscite on the Second World War; and 1962, a recession year when the Diefenbaker Conservatives lost their majority. The high point came in 1993, when insurgents received more than one-third of all votes (Figure 2.2).

20 The Canadian Party System

FIGURE 2.2   Insurgents and CCF-NDP seats and votes, 1878-2015

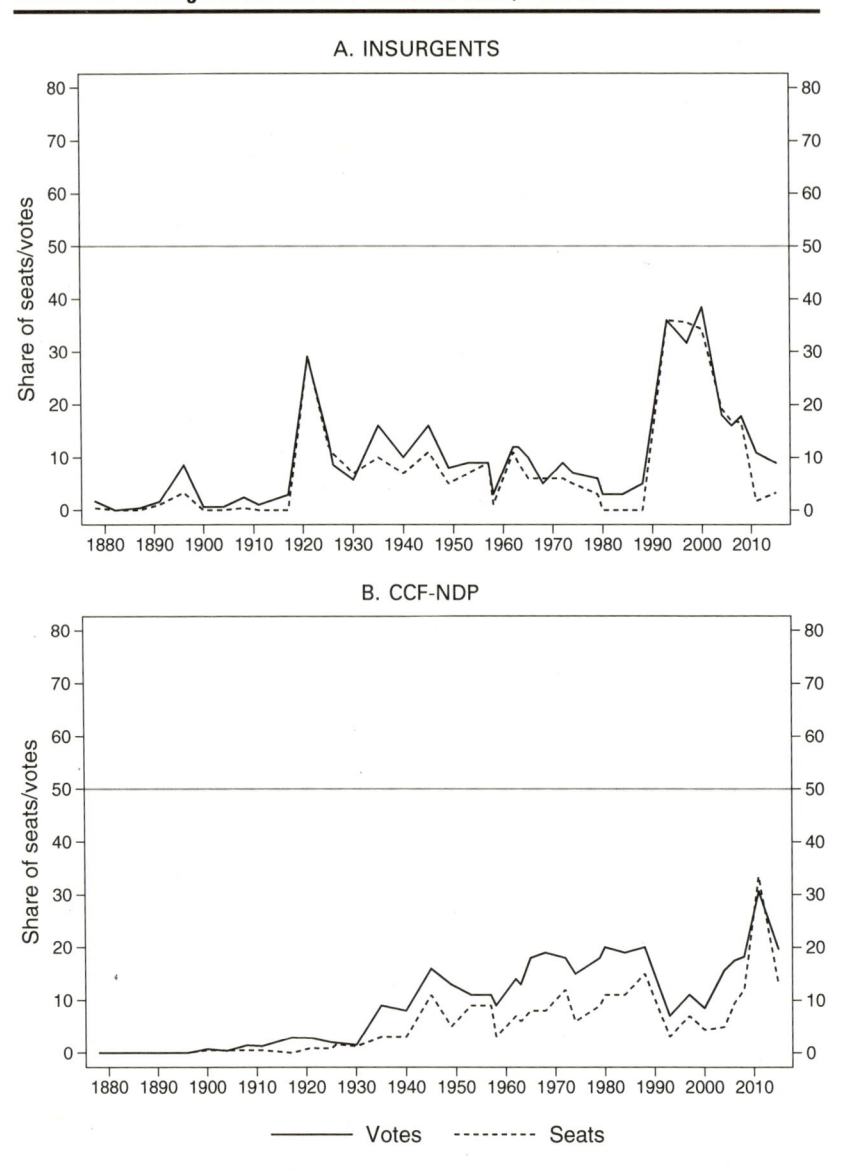

Note: Plots show each party's percentage of the national popular vote and of seats in the House of Commons.

Because insurgents typically concentrate their votes geographically, they are often proportionately rewarded in seats. At the highest points, 1921 and the 1990s, insurgent vote and seat shares were almost identical. As Figure 2.3 (which names names) shows, the 1921 result was mostly the work of the agrarian Progressive movement, strong in the prairie provinces and rural Ontario and weak everywhere else in the country. The pattern in the 1990s was driven by the mainly western Reform Party and the exclusively Quebec-based Bloc Québécois.

But the insurgent line drops as much as it rises. The post-1921 decline was almost as swift as the surge, although insurgents hung on at a higher level than before 1921. The trend from 1935 to 1993 was negative, with particular low points in 1958 and the 1980s, when the total insurgent vote was scarcely higher than in the 1910s, and such parties were basically shut out of Parliament. The impressive level reached in the 1990s was cut more than in half in 2004 and cut still further in 2011. This last year produced the biggest gap between insurgent seats and votes.

By glossing over distinctions among insurgents, Figure 2.2 understates the case for the brevity of their lives. Figure 2.3 remedies this and shows that specific insurgents' shelf life tends to be short, a few decades at most.[8] A few times the succession has involved the replacement of one insurgent

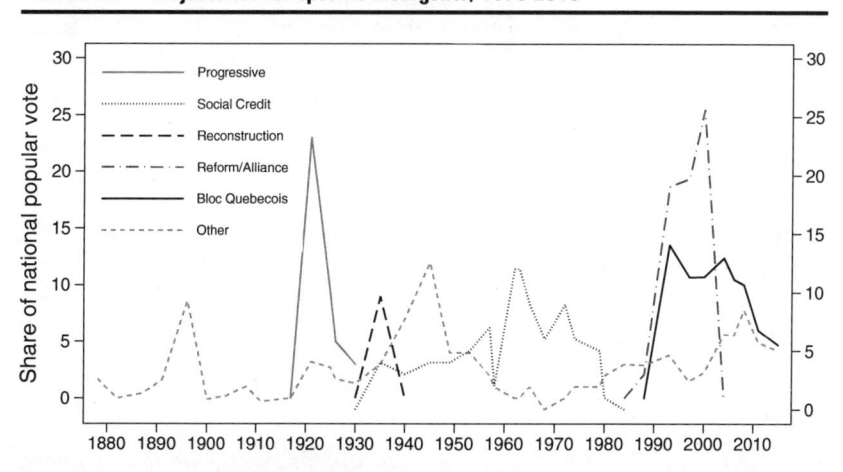

FIGURE 2.3   Trajectories for specific insurgents, 1878-2015

Note: Plots show each party's percentage share of the national popular vote from the last election before to the first election after it offered candidates.

by another. But theories of party insurgency typically focus on strategic interaction between the new party and one or more of the big, old ones (Hug 2001), and Canadian insurgents typically do gain at the expense of an old party. Figure 2.1 suggests that this is most often the Conservative Party, but the Liberal Party is not immune. The opposite is also mainly true: when an insurgent disappears, it is typically absorbed by an old party. On party disappearance, theory has little to say.

The CCF-NDP: Secular Growth

One new line of division did endure, however; the class division, embodied in the CCF-NDP, whose electoral history is plotted in Panel B of Figure 2.2. The hyphenated acronym refers to two separate parties with non-overlapping histories but strong continuities in ethos, membership, and electoral foundations. The older party is the Cooperative Commonwealth Federation, and the newer one is the New Democratic Party. Although the CCF was formally founded in 1932 and contested its first federal election in 1935, Figure 2.2 indicates activity before then. These earlier points are the aggregate of votes won by candidates for small, weakly coordinated socialist, social democratic, and labour parties. After its founding in 1932 as a party with a comprehensive program, the CCF required additional decades to consolidate fully as a party of labour. The culmination was the transformation of the CCF into the NDP in 1961, whereupon the party moved to contest every seat (Johnston and Cutler 2009). The vote trajectory corresponds to this history of programmatic commitment and institutional maturation. The party started out in single digits, moved into the low to mid-teens in the 1940s, and reached the upper teens after 1960. The 1990s were dire, a reversion to the 1930s. But the 2000s restored the party to the upper teens. It was never able to return seats commensurate with votes, again consistent with the logic of FPP. But this inability was compounded by the party's ambition to spread geographically, "wasting" votes in unwinnable seats. The 2011 election looked like a breakthrough, but 2015 undid all the NDP gains.

The Provincial Arena

Centrifugal pressures in federal politics also produced wedges between arenas within provinces. As the federal party system lost its continent-wide grip, it also broke down as a unitary career path and integrative force between federal and provincial politics. Just as Conservatives and insurgents supply much of the short-term dynamics in the federal arena, so too they provide most of the discrepancies between arenas. The tip of the iceberg appears in Figure 2.4, which plots all-Canada means for federal elections and for adjacent provincial elections.[9]

The disruptions of the 1920s left the Conservatives significantly worse off provincially than federally, and then things got even worse at both levels. The party's federal recovery in the late 1950s was followed by a provincial recovery, and that recovery continued even as further federal growth moderated. The Conservatives' federal collapse in the 1990s was anticipated provincially in the late 1980s but not on its ultimate scale. After 1993, the federal party ran some 15 points behind its typical provincial counterpart. All along, complements to the Conservative Party were mainly insurgents. Although insurgent support is volatile, provincial surges generally outstrip federal ones, and provincial insurgents have more staying power. The reverse was true in the 1990s, when insurgents were a federal phenomenon.

For the Liberals and CCF-NDP, federal and provincial values tend to move together. With only rare exceptions, the Liberals are stronger federally than provincially, and the dominant Liberal pattern in both arenas is a slow downward trend. The opposite is basically true for the NDP: provincial values are (slightly) higher than federal ones, and the trend is basically upward. Masked by the figure is the fact that the Liberals and CCF-NDP are also geographic complements. For most of the twentieth century, Liberal support was bigger, and NDP support was smaller as one went east, but as the NDP slowly closed the overall gap this regional pattern also weakened (Johnston 2013).

Yet there are also forces promoting cross-arena integration. The decline of the federal Conservatives in the 1920s and 1930s was eventually mirrored in provincial elections, as was the party's recovery in later decades. Similarly, history has not been kind to insurgents at either level. When and where they are important in provincial elections, they hang on longer and at higher levels than they do federally. But even in provincial elections they are less important now than they were in the first half of the twentieth century.[10]

FIGURE 2.4 Federal and provincial trajectories for Conservatives, Liberals, CCF-NDP, and insurgents, 1908-2011

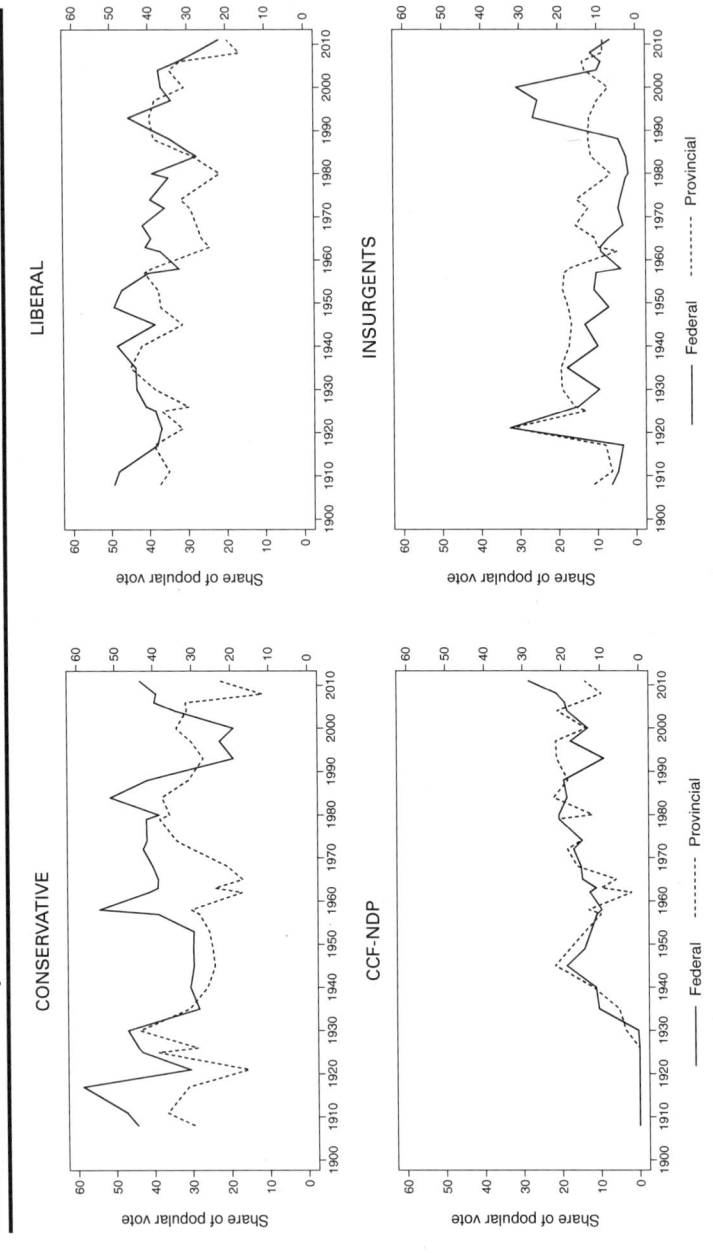

Notes: Plots show the mean of each party's percentage of the popular vote in the province for federal elections and for the provincial election temporally closest to the federal election year. Means are not weighted by the size of the province.

The Aggregate Patterns in Context

From a global perspective, Canada does not seem to be that unusual. Most systems have multiple parties. Large electoral swings have been common and are becoming more so. Most systems feature some form of cultural division, be it religious, ethnic, or linguistic. But Canada's electoral institutions are supposed to suppress these patterns. The proper comparison is with systems that have the same basic institutional endowment, most critically systems in which votes are counted in single-member districts. Against these comparators, basically the Anglo-American countries, the contrasts are sharp.

Fragmentation

Although all Anglo-American systems use single-member districts (SMD),[11] the five countries vary in three particulars of relevance. First is the separation of powers: the United States is presidential, whereas all others are parliamentary. Presidentialism creates extra pressure for electoral consolidation (Amorim Neto and Cox 1997; Shugart and Carey 1992), while the requirement for discipline in parliamentary systems creates pressure for party splits (Carey and Shugart 1995). Second is the electoral formula, plurality versus majority. Four systems use FPP, whereas Australia uses a majority formula. FPP makes no concession to coordination failure and thus is said to force voters into two camps. Australia's formula is more accommodating: its preferential ballot allows first preferences to be less consolidated than the single non-transferable preferences elicited by FPP. Third is the presence or absence of federalism. The United States, Australia, and Canada are federal, whereas Britain (for most of the twentieth century at least) and New Zealand are unitary states. According to Gerring (2005), federalism is an additional force for fragmentation. Adding all these things together, Australian first preferences ought to set the upper limit for fragmentation, and the United States should occupy the opposite pole. Britain and New Zealand are unitary states, so they should not experience fragmentation pressure from subnational units. But as parliamentary systems, both are more susceptible than the United States to pressure from within the national party system. Canada as a federation but with FPP should lie somewhere between Britain and New Zealand, on the one hand, and Australia, on the other.

For most of the twentieth century, in fact, Canada was the Anglo-American leader in electoral fragmentation. The facts appear in Figure 2.5, which contains raw and smoothed plots of the "effective number of parties" or ENP (Laakso and Taagepera 1979). In the first half of the twentieth century, values peaked for the United States in the 1910s, for New Zealand and Britain in the 1920s, and for Australia in the 1930s. In all of these countries, the fragmentation was transitional, reflecting the shift to class politics. In the United States, this meant the marginalization of socialist parties and the eventual reorientation of the Democrats to a privileged relationship with organized labour.[12] In New Zealand and Britain, this meant the emergence of a Labour Party as a serious force, which in turn induced rivals on the centre-right to jockey for strategic advantage and ultimately consolidate into a single party of the moderate right, with a concomitant drop in ENP values. Australia is a slightly more complicated story but with the same ultimate result. First, the disparate pre-1901 party systems of the formerly separate Australian colonies consolidated. Then, as in Britain and New Zealand, the advent of a Labour Party induced a sequence of fractionalization/defractionalization. A temporary breakdown on the labour side prolonged the crisis into the 1930s, but things finally settled down.

In Canada, the pattern has been altogether different. Fractionalization first appeared in 1921 but was not the result of labour mobilization. Rather, it reflected short-lived agrarian insurgency (the Progressives in Figure 2.3). Fractionalization recurred in 1935, and this time it never left. Part of the 1935 story is the appearance of the CCF, somewhat in imitation of the labour pattern elsewhere. But the CCF did not pose a coordination challenge on the UK or antipodean scale. At the same time, as Figure 2.2 shows, about half of the total new-party gain came from insurgents. Whatever the sources, the Canadian system thereafter featured nearly one extra "equivalent" party relative to the early years. This was a composite, of course, of the CCF-NDP and the rotating cast of insurgents.

In 1935, relative to the United States, Canada gained a full extra party. The United States is the extreme case, however, and the gap with the Westminster comparators is smaller: an extra 0.6 equivalent party. This deviance is all the more striking when Australia is brought into the comparison. When the Australian system settled down in the 1940s, its ENP

FIGURE 2.5 Effective number of electoral parties: Anglo-American single-member district systems, twentieth century

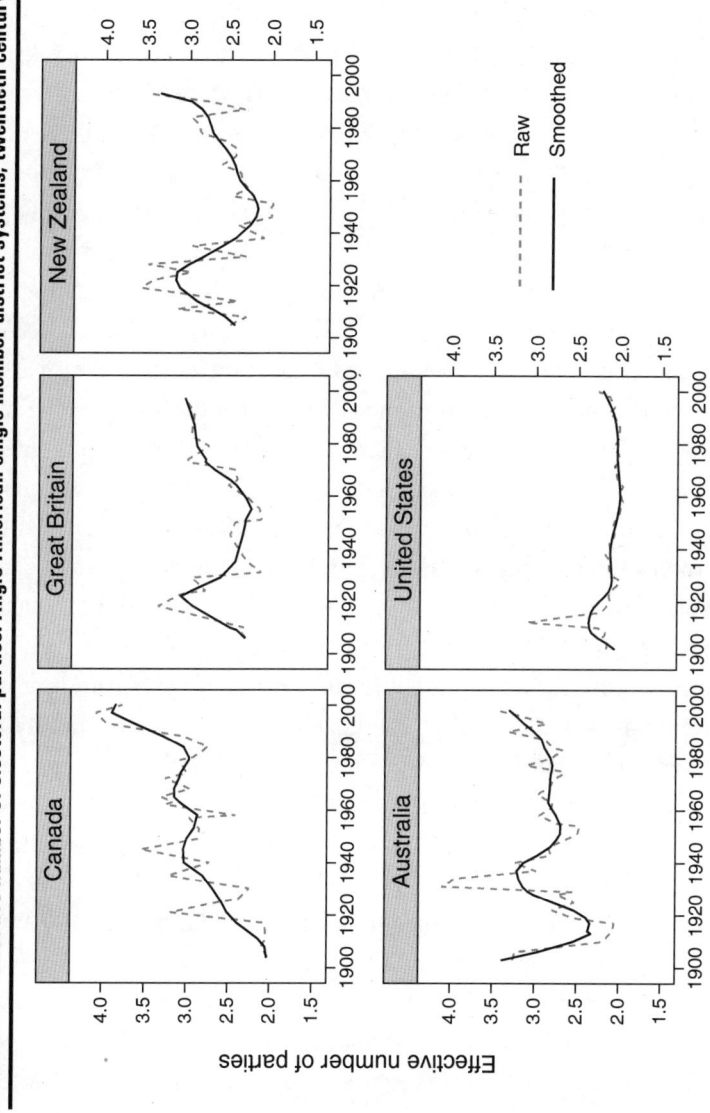

Notes: Entries are ENP values (Laakso and Taagepera 1979). Smoothed plots are by loess, bandwidth = 0.30. US values are for House elections. NZ series terminates in 1993.

was 2.8. If the contrast between Australia, on the one hand, and the United States, New Zealand, and Britain, on the other, is interpretable analytically, the contrast with Canada is not. In this period, notwithstanding Canada's persistence in FPP, the Canadian system was *more* fractionalized than the Australian one.

Canada and Australia are both federal polities, and perhaps federalism is the most powerful of the disruptive forces even as presidentialism trumps everything else. There remains, however, the problem of mechanism. The logic of Gerring's (2005) argument seems to be that certain parties appear in some subnational units but not others. The argument dovetails with the standing reformulation of Duverger's Law. Canada's mid-century multipartism was a matter of record and helped to inspire the rethinking of Duverger by Rae (1969) and Riker (1982) that culminated in Cox (1997). In this rethinking, Duverger's Law applies at the local level, whereas party coordination across locales requires another logic. For the latter, an obvious place to look is the growth of a unified national agenda that, combined with the requirements of parliamentary confidence, forced polarization in Parliament of the government versus the opposition. This in turn led to parallel mobilization across districts (Cox 1987). Canada is presented as the exception that proves the new rule: Chhibber and Kollman (2004) argue that Canada is one place where the role of the national government has shrunk. Accordingly, the imperative to coordinate party labels across federal units has also shrunk. Duvergerian logic continues to prevail at the district level, such that Canada-wide multipartism is the composite of locally varying bipartisan competitions.

However, as Figure 2.6 shows, this argument understates the complexity of the case. The logic of this figure originates with Cox (1997) and Chhibber and Kollman (2004) and is designed to partition total fragmentation into local and extra-local components. The *total* component is the raw plot from Figure 2.5 extended back to 1878. The *local* component is the average ENP within constituencies and is the index number that should reflect neo-Duvergerian forces. Party transitions might fragment local competition temporarily, but as the new alignment supplants the old one the effective number of district-level parties should settle back to near 2.0. The *extra-local* line is simply the difference between the local line and the total one. This is where the ebb and flow of central government power should

FIGURE 2.6 Components of electoral fractionalization, 1878-2015

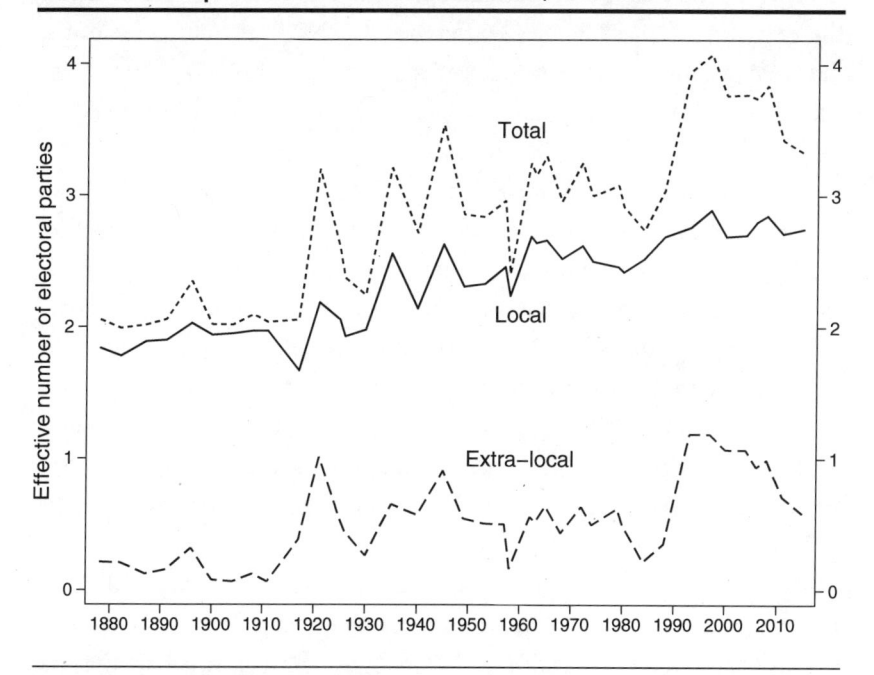

Notes: "Total" is the ENP based on the national popular vote; "local" is the average ENP at the electoral district level; "extra-local" is the difference between "total" and "local."

generate an observable implication: as central power wanes, different parties can gain prominence in different regions.

Contra Cox (1997) and Chhibber and Kollman (2004), the most powerful engine of fragmentation is within districts, not across them. In 1921, local values began a secular climb: from a pre-1921 average of 1.9 to a 1930s-40s-50s average of 2.4, to 2.6 in the 1960s-70s, to 2.7 since 1980. That is, the typical riding now features something like *three*-party competition. In principle, an ENP number like this could be produced by many small parties, none well positioned to affect the contest between the frontrunners (Dunleavy and Boucek 2003). Alternatively, there could be what Cox (1997) calls a "non-Duvergerian equilibrium," in which three contestants are just too close for voters or elites to discern which pair is strategically privileged. In Canada, however, as Johnston and Cutler (2009, Fig. 6.6) show, the third-place party is typically more than large enough to cover the margin between the first- and second-place finishers but is not itself positioned to displace either of them. The local line roughly tracks the growth pattern in Figure 2.2 for the CCF-NDP. The closeness of the fit remains to be demonstrated, and a persuasive case requires less aggregated information, but the basic parallelism between the lines needs to be emphasized.

Extra-local fragmentation, the component that Chhibber and Kollman (2004) emphasize, is also important and unquestionably supplies the fireworks. It erupted in bursts, an anticipatory breakthrough in 1921, a spasm in 1945, and – most critically – enduring lifts of roughly 0.5 "effective" parties each in 1935 and 1993. Broadly speaking, the extra-local line corresponds to the insurgent plot in Figure 2.2. This is doubly important since insurgents often win seats in proportion to their votes, such that these parties disrupt the smooth exercise of majority government. As with the parallel between the CCF-NDP and local fragmentation, the details remain to be nailed down.

In a crude sense, the correspondence between insurgency and extra-local breakdown seems to be consistent with the Chhibber-Kollman emphasis on the importance of the national government. It is true that the federal government's share of taxing and spending is lower now than it was a century ago. But this is no more than a "straw in the wind" (Bennett 2010, 208-11). It would be more persuasive if critical electoral moments somehow reflected jurisdictional conflicts. If anything, the opposite is true. The key pulses in fragmentation – 1921, 1935, 1945, and 1993 – came in moments of crisis when Ottawa was a critical actor. In no sense can they be characterized as initiating periods of federal government irrelevance. The 1921 surge, the breakthrough by the agrarian Progressives, had as its primary target the content of federal commercial policy, not the fact of federal jurisdiction. The 1935 pulse was a product of global economic distress, saw many parties win votes, and produced Social Credit as an insurgent with an above-average shelf life. This was also the breakthrough year for the CCF, sectional in its support but not in its program; the CCF favoured a more active central government. The 1945 pulse saw Liberal losses on its pro- and anti-conscription flanks even as the CCF grew. The Liberals themselves tabled a program that became the blueprint for a nationally directed welfare state. The 1993 shifts had an anti-Ottawa element that presupposed not that Ottawa was weak but that it was too strong.

Also troubling for the argument are four moments of regression to the pre-1921 baseline: 1930, 1958, 1984, and 1988. And, although the extra-local component is currently above the pre-1921 level, it has been shrinking since 1993. Given that the federation remains decentralized, why would a sectionally concentrated party lose ground?

Whatever the mechanism, each reversion accompanies another empirical regularity, which can be seen by triangulation with Figure 2.1: each of these elections returned a Conservative majority government, two of them as landslides. In the twentieth century, Conservative accession to majority status involved soaking up the sectional tension of the preceding years. Once every generation a grand consolidation occurs, the effective number of parties shrinks, and the Liberals are chased from office. Superficially, this looks like Duvergerian equilibration in that chronically deconsolidated opposition forces overcome their differences and successfully coordinate. However, if this is equilibration, then it takes place at the wrong level. Local consolidation in these episodes was always a small fraction of the total, and that fraction has been diminishing.

And now the distinction between Canada and the other systems is evaporating. Over the 1970s and 1980s, Britain and New Zealand closed the ENP gap, so much so that New Zealand went to a proportional electoral system, yielding to the logic of a new situation. Canada widened the gap with Britain further in the 1990s, but then the gap closed again. The Australian trend echoed the British one. With hindsight, Canada's status as a deviant case might be oversold, and the true deviant might be the United States. Deviant or not, Canada still confounds the Neo-Duvergerian Synthesis – but so might the other Westminster systems.

Episodic Volatility

Multipartism facilitates volatility (Mainwaring and Zoco 2007), possibly because the multiplication of parties crowds the policy space and reduces the average ideological distance among parties (Pederson 1983). The fact that Canada is thought of as an outlier in relation to both variables might simply be testimony to this functional link.

In one sense, however, the Canadian system is distinctively volatile only as a matter of degree. The histograms in Figure 2.7A indicate that most Canadian elections are alike, as is true elsewhere. Here the indicator

FIGURE 2.7 Electoral volatility: Anglo-American single-member district systems, twentieth century

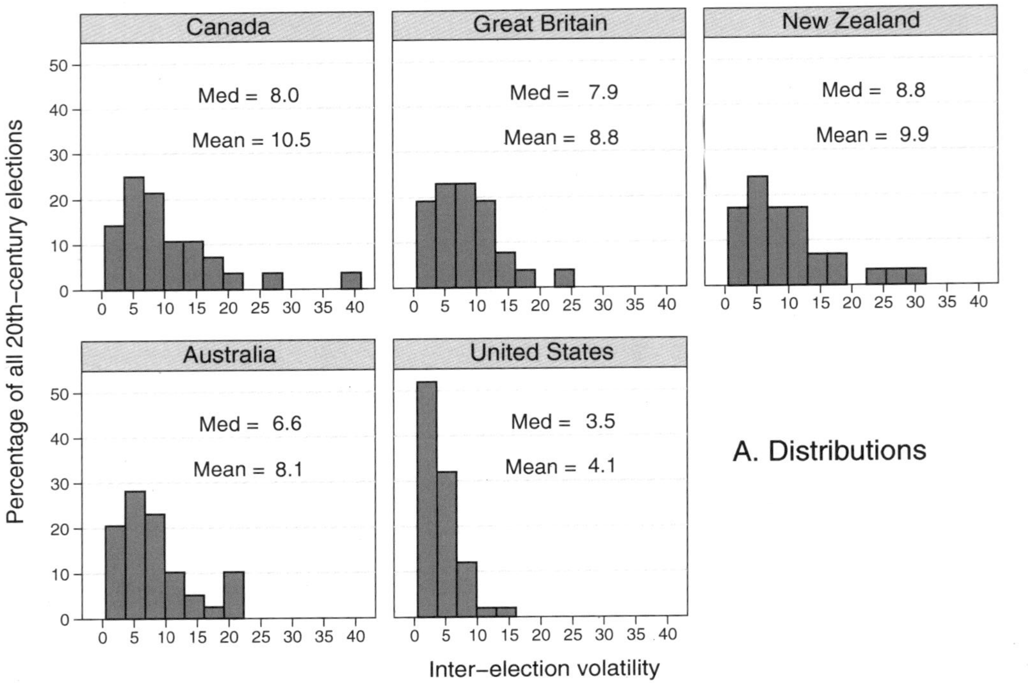
Canada
Med = 8.0
Mean = 10.5
Great Britain
Med = 7.9
Mean = 8.8
New Zealand
Med = 8.8
Mean = 9.9
Australia
Med = 6.6
Mean = 8.1
United States
Med = 3.5
Mean = 4.1
A. Distributions
Percentage of all 20th–century elections
Inter–election volatility
0
10
20
30
40
50
0 5 10 15 20 25 30 35 40

B. Sequences

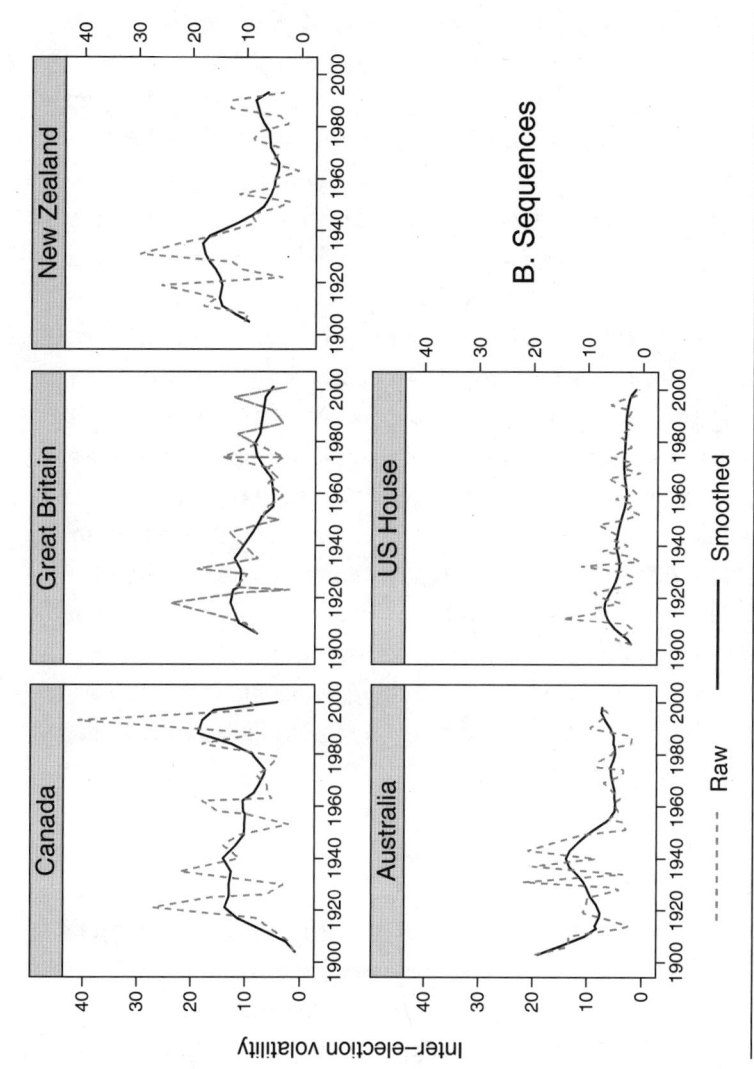

---- Raw —— Smoothed

Notes: Panel A shows the distribution of volatility values (Pedersen 1979), i.e., net shifts among all parties for pairs of consecutive elections. NZ series terminates in 1993. Panel B shows the temporal sequence of volatility values. Smoothing by loess, bandwidth = 0.30. NZ series terminates in 1993.

is Pederson's (1979) "volatility index," most easily interpreted as the minimum percentage of the electorate needed to transform one result into the other.[13] To sharpen the comparison, the dataset is confined to the twentieth century. For each Westminster system, the mode is about five points. The Canadian median is smaller than that for New Zealand and almost indistinguishable from that for Britain. Australia and the United States are strikingly stable cases. Canada stands out because of its outliers: the upper teens are relatively densely populated, three values sit at 20 or more, and the extreme value, remarkably, is in the 40s. Again, though, Canada is not absolutely alone. Each of the other Westminster systems has at least one value around 20 or greater; New Zealand has three. Thanks to its outliers, however, Canada has the highest mean.

But the true distinctiveness of Canadian volatility lies in its episodic and reversionary character. Figure 2.7B brings out the episodic element by plotting volatility values election by election, along with a smoothed series to facilitate visual comparison. In all other systems, volatility peaked in the 1930s or before. This was true even for the generally stable US House. As with fractionalization, volatility was a symptom of strain from the transition to class politics. Post-1945 values never approached the prewar peak. Canada also saw high volatility in the 1920s and 1930s on about the same scale as elsewhere and for somewhat parallel reasons. But flux did not stop there: there were more eye-catching swings *after* 1945 than *before*. The 1993 reading was arguably the single most volatile result among all old democracies outside the immediate aftermath of global war (Bartolini and Mair 1990).

Elsewhere, volatility values such as these mark enduring changes in the bases of party competition (Bartolini and Mair 1990, Tables 3.1 and 3.2). In Canada, extreme elections are stages in cycles of Conservative boom and bust. They either bring the Conservatives to power, often with an overwhelming majority, or they punish them proportionally (or more than proportionally) to their earlier gains. One postwar episode centred on 1958, the rise and fall of John Diefenbaker. The other occurred in 1984, a Conservative breakthrough on the scale of 1958, reversed with a vengeance in 1993. The pattern can also be discerned through the other end of the figurative telescope. The 1921 election was a disaster for the Conservative Party, but by 1930 almost all of the damage had been undone. If this only set the Conservatives up for a fall in 1935, then the 1953-57-58 sequence could be seen as undoing the damage of 1935. And the Conservative recovery of 2004-6 (off the screen for Figure 2.7B) repaired much of the damage of 1993.[14]

Conservative gains come disproportionately from absorbing support from sectionally concentrated smaller parties. Conservative losses reverse this sequence yielding yet more third-party insurgency (Johnston 2008, 2013). Figure 2.1 showed that Liberal and Conservative time paths are not strictly complementary. Figure 2.2 showed a similar divergence between CCF-NDP and insurgent dynamics. The complementarity was not within figures but between them: the NDP is linked to the Liberal vote, and the Conservatives commonly move against insurgents. This is the dynamic that underlies the extra-local component in Figure 2.6: its disappearance coincides with Conservative surges, its recrudescence with Conservative declines. The dynamic is one of the central paradoxes of the Canadian party system and a major preoccupation of the rest of the book.[15]

Federal-Provincial Discontinuity

As the federal party system fragments, federal and provincial electorates – the same people – diverge. In some provinces, there is almost no overlap between patterns in each arena. In no comparable system is discontinuity so stark. The box plots in Figure 2.8 depict "dissimilarity" between adjacent federal and provincial elections and compare it to that in other federations: Australia, Germany, Spain, and the United States. Australia permits a full twentieth-century comparison. Germany is available for postwar elections and Spain for the years since the restoration of democracy in the 1970s. Although Spain is nominally unitary, it has been acquiring federal characteristics quickly yet at different rates in different subnational units. Among the units are three proto-ethnonational jurisdictions – Catalonia, the Basque Country, and Galicia – and they make Spain an especially telling comparator. The United States is an awkward case. It is the prototype of federalism, but only with the civil rights revolution and federal attention to voting rights in state elections, especially in the South, did there appear a satisfactory comprehensive accounting for that arena. Accordingly, the US series begins only in the 1960s.[16] Dissimilarity here means the same thing numerically as volatility, as described in the previous section. Here

FIGURE 2.8 Electoral divergence between arenas: Canada, Australia, Germany, Spain, and the US

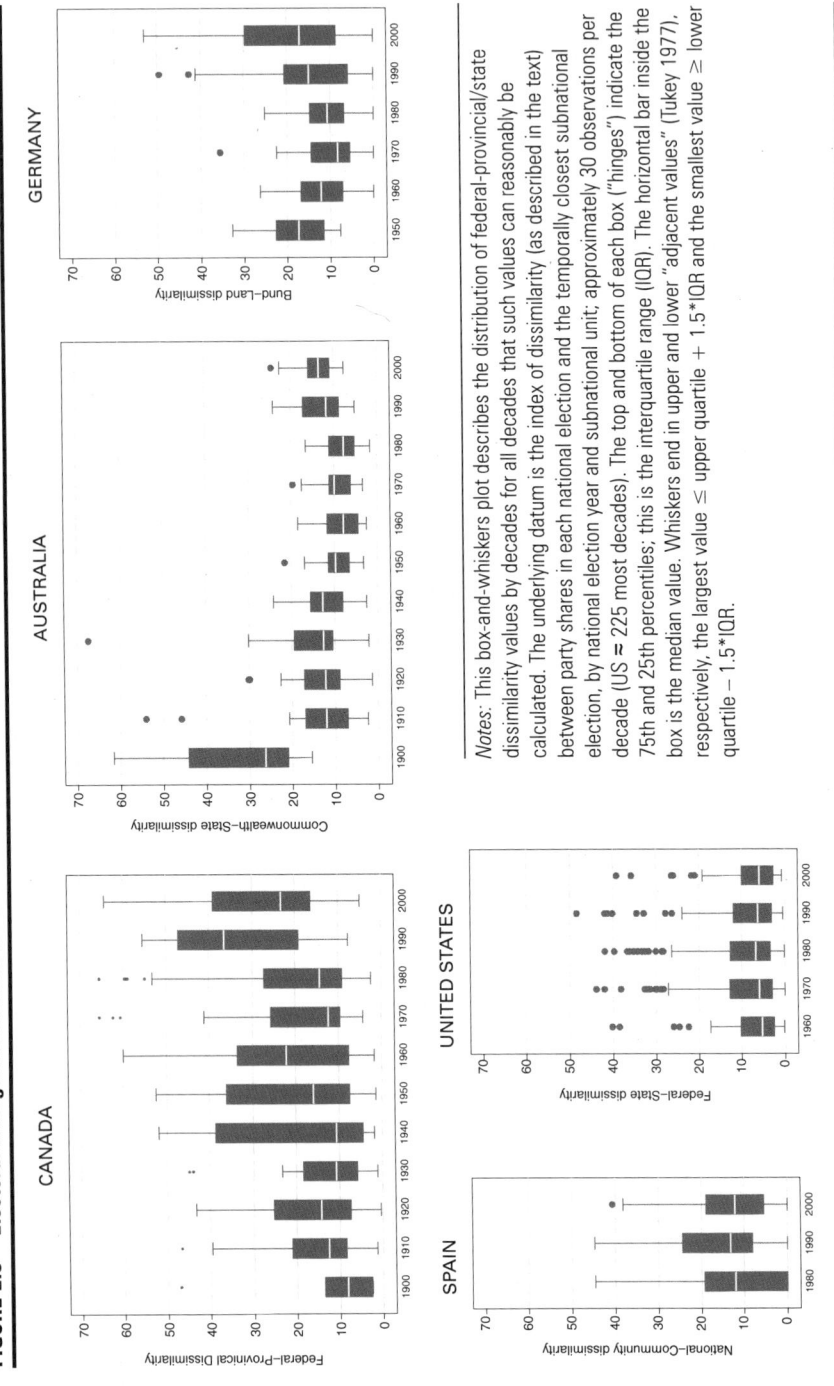

Notes: This box-and-whiskers plot describes the distribution of federal-provincial/state dissimilarity values by decades for all decades that such values can reasonably be calculated. The underlying datum is the index of dissimilarity (as described in the text) between party shares in each national election and the temporally closest subnational election, by national election year and subnational unit; approximately 30 observations per decade (US ≈ 225 most decades). The top and bottom of each box ("hinges") indicate the 75th and 25th percentiles; this is the interquartile range (IQR). The horizontal bar inside the box is the median value. Whiskers end in upper and lower "adjacent values" (Tukey 1977), respectively, the largest value ≤ upper quartile + 1.5*IQR and the smallest value ≥ lower quartile − 1.5*IQR.

the temporally closest provincial election is substituted for the previous federal one, on the logic of Johnston (1980). Like volatility, dissimilarity can range from 0 to 100. Data are grouped by decade.

Early in the twentieth century, most Canadian provinces remained closely aligned across arenas. Median values picked up modestly in the 1920s, but from the 1920s to the 1980s the median exhibited no further upward trend. In the 1990s and 2000s, the median surged, with the 1990s – the decade of Reform – as the extreme case. But medians hardly tell the full story; more striking is the top end. In the 1920s, the 75th percentile surged to 25 percentage points, with outside values over 40 percentage points. In the 1990s, the 75th percentile value was close to 50 percentage points; by implication, 25 percent of all scores were larger still. In four of the past five decades, outside values were over 60: in such cases, the federal and provincial party systems had very little overlap.

The contrasts with Australia and the United States are especially stark. After a decade of electoral consolidation, Australian federalism settled into a century of remarkable similarity across arenas. No trend was visible, and at the turn of the twenty-first century the highest values were lower than the Canadian median. The United States looks like an amalgam of the Canadian and Australian cases. As in Canada, there are striking outside values in the United States. But as in Australia, US median values are very low, the lowest of all in fact. Most states, then, have closely aligned state and federal electorates. But some states have strikingly disparate ones. The latter are mainly, but not exclusively, in the South. The essence of the matter is that since 1960 the US party system has undergone a regional realignment as striking as that in Canada. Although the US shift unfolded gradually, the pace was quicker in federal than in state elections. More like the Canadian case are the shorter series for Germany and Spain. Germany in the 2000s – 10 years after reunification – looks rather like Canada in the 1920s. But this is the high point in the German series. The Spanish plot looks like the German one, and its high values are the product mainly of Catalonia and Galicia. Even so, no Spanish province comes close to Canada's extreme values.

The Canadian pattern has been a matter of record for many years. For example, Canada was one of the first places thought to exhibit "balancing" dynamics (Wrong 1957), a claim that has been reiterated recently (Erikson and Filippov 2001). Balancing is one of several possible mechanisms said to operate in "second-order" elections, those in which behaviour is oriented to a more important arena (Reif and Schmitt 1980). But the sheer scale of Canadian discontinuity is far greater than necessary for any conceivable second-order mechanism. As FPP amplifies vote-to-seat translations, small vote shifts suffice to change the party in power, all that balancing requires. The Canadian pattern indicates outright divergence in some provinces between federal and provincial systems.

It is natural to ask if the heart of the matter is Canada's deep division. Such an interpretation appears to hold for the European scene, in which the biggest gaps are produced by national minorities with autonomist tendencies (Jeffery and Hough 2003; Pallarés and Keating 2003). But even the clearest European cases, Galicia and Catalonia, cannot rival the Canadian ones (Jeffery and Hough 2003, Table 1), and, as I will show in Chapter 9, not all extreme Canadian examples are generated by Quebec, the national minority jurisdiction. Interpretations currently on the table do not help much. Filippov, Ordeshook, and Shvetsova (2004, 247), for instance, recognize the importance of western Canada and emphasize constitutional conflict in the run-up to the Statute of Westminster, 1931. But it is already clear from Figure 2.4 that federal-provincial gaps opened before the late 1920s. And focus on the Statute of Westminster seems to be eccentric. The leverage that it gave the prairie provinces over the question of continuing federal control of lands was an aggravating factor, but the Progressive electoral disruption was driven mainly by economic distress (Morton 1950). The 1920s also featured intense conflict over water and power, pitting Ottawa against both Ontario and Quebec (Oliver 1977, 292 ff.). In later decades, the amending formula was a difficult issue but rarely the most pressing one.

Moreover, the trend in discontinuity was not uniformly upward. Until the 1990s, median values did not rise relative to those of the 1920s; if anything, they dropped. Relative to the 1940s-50s-60s, the 75th percentile dropped dramatically, such that it was lower than that in the 1920s. Discontinuity expanded again in the 1990s, with median values higher than 75th percentile ones in the preceding decade. The 2000s brought a modest reversion. In other words, discontinuity exhibits a cyclical dynamic, rather like that for insurgent parties. The correspondence is not an accident.

Foundations

The susceptibility of the Canadian party system to recurring massive swings and the complexity of the total federal-provincial party system suggest that the social anchoring of the system is weak. So does the tendency for insurgencies to appear and disappear, rather like the "flash" parties of the French Fourth Republic. The claim usually has two parts. On the one hand, class divisions, which ought to matter for a large fraction of the policy space, are weak. On the other, wide differences among religious denominations have almost no contemporary relevance, and when they do such differences run against the grain of differences among parties.[17]

The Weakness of Class

Alford (1963) identified this weakness in an early comparative survey analysis. He stipulated that the statistical representation of class impact was the arithmetic gap between manual and non-manual workers in support for the party or parties of the left. For Canada, in contrast to the rest of the Anglosphere, this gap was essentially non-existent. Almost every facet of his claim has been criticized, and the Canadian critiques parallel those in the cross-national literature. First, not all scholars agree that an arithmetic gap is the best representation of an electoral cleavage. Second, Alford's exclusive focus on the manual/non-manual distinction is said to obscure variation within each occupational group (Erikson and Goldthorpe 1992; Goldthorpe 1980; Manza and Brooks 1999). Third, a specifically Canadian issue is the identity of the "left." For Alford, this party group includes the CCF-NDP, naturally, but also the Liberal Party. Eventually, the Canadian literature settled on the NDP only. That literature was initially driven by denial, the hope that the right combination of independent variable, dependent variable, and impact measure would find the sweet spot. By degrees, denial yielded to acceptance, and the weakness of occupational differences in Canada is confirmed by comparative work, notably that by Nieuwbeerta and de Graaf (1999). For Canada, the only indicator that does any work is membership in the union movement (Archer 1985; Brym, Gillespie, and Lenton 1989). To give Canada its best shot, then, I focus on union/non-union difference.

Table 2.1 scales the Canadian pattern. Evidence comes from National Election Studies in Anglo-American systems, back to the 1960s or 1970s where possible. Because the demonstration in this chapter is merely exemplary, I present data from years that typify periods. We know that postwar party alignments began to go awry in many countries in the 1970s, hence my resort to data from the 1960s where possible. For the 2000s, by analogy to the 1960s, I use data from mid-decade. For the United States, data are from off-year House elections to minimize disruption from tides in presidential elections. The most recent available reading is from 2002. The target parties for union families are the NDP in Canada, the Democrats in the United States, and labour elsewhere. Cleavage strength is indicated in two ways: the arithmetic difference, the "Alford" index; and the log odds ratio, the "Thomsen" index (Thomsen 1987). The former is readily interpretable but has been criticized for its oversensitivity to the marginal distribution of the dependent variable. The latter, it is claimed, shows the intrinsic strength of the factor, but its meaning is less obvious to the naked eye.

In the 1960s and 1970s, the union/non-union gap in Britain and Australia was over 20 points. Even in the United States, the gap was in double figures. In Canada, the gap was just eight points. The 1965 Canadian Election Study (CES) sample also reported the smallest share of union families. So in the 1960s, class effects in Canada were weak twice over: a small union movement and a weak marginal effect from union membership. Four decades later the union effect had weakened slightly in Australia, weakened massively in Britain, but weakened hardly at all in the United States and Canada; indeed, in the United States, it might have strengthened. New Zealand, for which no data from the 1960s or 1970s are available, looks quite like Australia and the US. The Canadian gap was still a single digit, however, notwithstanding the fact that among these countries Canada now had the highest percentage of survey respondents in union households.

The Thomsen index yields roughly the same story, with Canada and Australia as polar cases. But cross-national differences are weaker on this criterion: Canada and the United States are similar, and the gap between these two laggards and the more polarized systems is smaller. By implication, some of the apparent variation in union impact is artifactual, a by-product of the target party's size. The union/non-union gap might be small in Canada because the NDP is weak, not the other way around.

TABLE 2.1 The union movement and the party system: Canada, Great Britain, New Zealand, Australia, and the US

	Non-union	Union	Alford (difference)	Thomsen (log odds)	% union
Canada: NDP					
1965	13	21	8	0.70	20
2006	14	23	9	0.59	32
Great Britain: Labour					
1974 (Oct)*	31	57	26	1.05	44
2005	38	45	7	0.27	23
New Zealand: Labour					
2005	39	54		0.62	25
Australia: Labor					
1967	30	53	23	1.00	39
2004	31	50	19	0.80	31
US: House Democrats					
1966	53	68	15	0.63	28
2002	45	64	19	0.76	16

Notes: Entries are for parties' shares of vote recall in each group, along with indicators of strength of relationship. Non-voters are excluded from the calculations. Union percentage is of the survey sample.
* Full election-year cross-sections for Britain are not accessible online before 1974. On the choice of the October survey, see the notes to Table 2.2.
Sources: National Election Studies for the indicated years.

The Strength of Religion

At its widest, the denominational gap in Liberal (and Conservative) Party preference was as great as any in the Anglosphere. Yet, as I write this, the gap has disappeared or possibly gone into reverse. Table 2.2 scales the cleavage for cross-national comparison. For each system, the contrast is between Roman Catholics and all others. This is not necessarily the sharpest contrast; usually, the polarization is Catholics against Protestants or Protestants against all others, since non-Christians and people with no religion commonly fall between the big Christian groups or outflank Catholics. But Catholics are the easiest of the big battalions to identify, while Protestant is an aggregation of denominations. Moreover, to many survey respondents, the meaning of the word *Protestant* might have

TABLE 2.2 Catholics and the party system: Canada, Great Britain, New Zealand, Australia, and the US

	Non-Catholic	Catholic	Alford (difference)	Thomsen (log odds)	% Catholic
Canada: Liberals					
1965	35	63	28	1.13	44
2006	27	28	1	0.03	40
Great Britain: Labour					
1974*	41	60	19	0.80	9
2005	38	49	11	0.45	10
New Zealand: Labour					
2005	42	46	4	0.17	14
Australia: Labor					
1967	37	46	9	0.39	25
2004	36	40	4	0.21	25
US: House Democrats					
1966	55	67	12	0.53	23
2002	49	45	−1	−†	27

Notes: Entries are for parties' shares of vote recall in each group, along with indicators of strength of relationship. Non-voters are excluded from the calculations. Catholic percentage is of the survey sample.
* Full election-year cross-sections for Britain are not accessible online before 1974. As religious denomination was not queried in the February 1972 sample, the data are from the October survey.
† Sign reversal. Catholic share smaller among Democrats than among Republicans.
Sources: National Election Studies for the indicated years.

changed, since the centre of gravity for Protestant practice shifted from strongly institutionalized, historically continuous entities to more supple forms in which identification is a by-product of current attendance and practice. In contrast, even though attendance at Catholic services has plummeted, the essential identity of the Catholic Church has not changed. Many non-practising Catholics still claim a basic identification with the church. For Canada, the target is the Liberal Party. Elsewhere, the targets are as given in Table 2.1.

For the 1960s, the pattern is clear. The Catholic/non-Catholic gap is wider in Canada than in any of the other countries. Indeed, it is impressively wide by the standard of any group difference, religious or otherwise, in the majoritarian world. The Thomsen index value is off the charts, so much so that it dwarfs all the union/non-union differences in Table 2.1. The closest rival is Great Britain, with the United States next in line.[18] By the 2000s, however, the Canadian variant of the cleavage had disappeared. This also happened in the United States and Australia. The country with the sharpest denominational difference is now Britain, although even there the gap has shrunk.

On this evidence, the Canadian system is – or was – as deeply rooted as any in the Anglosphere. In itself, a prominent role for religious denomination is not unusual. Lijphart (1999, Table 5.3) shows that religious cleavages are second in importance only to socio-economic ones. The typical European case of cultural politics is a country predominantly Catholic or with a large Catholic minority. In this, Canada, where Catholics are close to half of the total population, is squarely like Germany and the Netherlands. The difficulty is that on no matter of faith or morals were the Liberals the obvious choice of Catholics, not even in the 1960s. The Liberal Party occasionally champions the institutional interests of the Catholic Church, but so do the other parties. In any case, these interests are mostly questions for the provinces. Nor does a contemporary cultural or policy ethos account for the link (Blais 2005). Tellingly, Lijphart (1999) does not include Canada among the countries with an active religious dimension.

Even as the scholarly community continues to profess bafflement at the Catholic-Liberal connection, that connection has snapped and did so no later than 2006.

Centrist Domination

Notwithstanding its slow decline in the popular vote and the general volatility in Canadian elections, the Liberal Party was one of the most successful political operations of the twentieth century (Blais 2005, 821; Carty 2015). Liberals governed for more years than any other Westminster comparator,[19] and their stints in opposition were shorter. Not once were they forced to lead a coalition, and they never had to change their name. They governed for 70 years of the twentieth century, and if we extend the century by a decade, 1896 to 2006, they governed for 80 of 110 years.

Differences in longevity among the dominant Westminster parties are ones of degree, however, not of kind. What really sets the Canadian Liberals apart is that they exercised their domination from the ideological centre

44 The Canadian Party System

FIGURE 2.9 Left-right locations of Canadian parties, 2000 and 2004

A. BENOIT-LAVER 2000 (expert judgements)

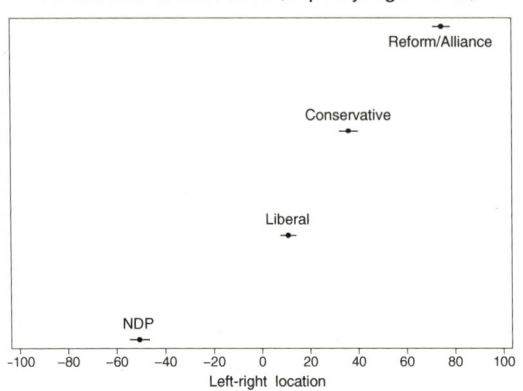

B. CMP 2004 (manifesto coding)

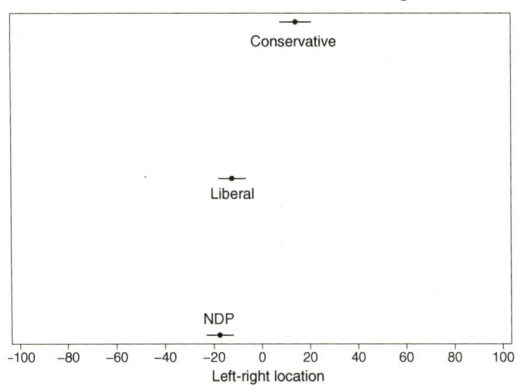

C. CES 2004 (respondent amputations)

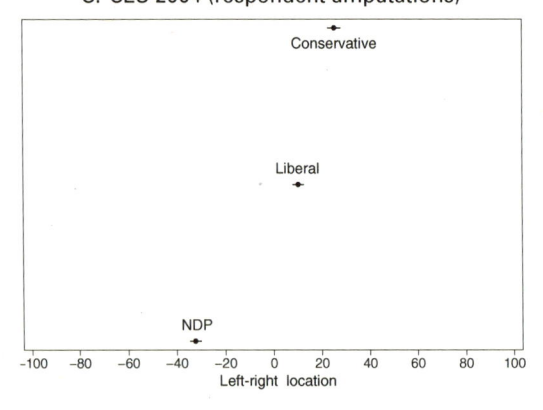

Note: Horizontal bars indicate 95 percent confidence intervals.
Source: See text and notes 20, 21, and 22 on page 268.

(Cochrane 2010; Johnston 2008). Although alternative readings differ in detail, all agree on this essential point. Figure 2.9 confirms this with data from three sources:

- *Panel A:* Left-right judgments from an expert survey conducted by Benoit and Laver (2006).[20]
- *Panel B:* Summary left-right scale readings from the 2004 iteration of the Campaign Manifesto Project (CMP). The project imputes positions in several specific issue domains on the basis of the frequency and valence of mentions in party platforms. Several domains are then aggregated into the left-right scale scored on a −100 to +100 range, and a confidence interval is imputed.[21]
- *Panel C:* Left-right imputations by respondents in the 2004 CES.[22]

To enable comparison, all indicators are scaled to the CMP's −100 to +100 range.

In every case, the Liberals command the centre. In the CMP data, the Liberal position is very close to that of the NDP. Indeed, the confidence intervals for these parties overlap considerably. No such overlap occurs between the Liberals' and the Conservatives' intervals. Liberal centrism is even clearer in the expert data. Here the gap with the NDP is larger and with the Conservatives smaller, although experts do not vary much in their judgments, and none of the confidence intervals overlap. CES respondents also see the Liberals as closer to the Conservatives than to the NDP, but here too confidence intervals do not overlap. Notwithstanding the mobility of the Liberals' position, all sources place the Liberals in the middle, and none fails to distinguish them from the Conservatives.

Moving Forward

In sum, the Canadian party system exhibits several distinctive features. Relative to standing theories of party competition, these features are outright anomalies. One anomaly, the domination of the system by a party of the centre, is critical to explaining most of the other ones.

The Canadian system has a history of multipartism that sets it apart from its comparators in the Anglosphere. Where the other systems settled down to roughly two-party competition after their realignment along class lines, the Canadian system embarked on a trajectory of permanent and, by stages, growing multipartism. Just as the system's overall fragmentation grew, so too did it grow within districts (contrary to strong predictions from theory). The relative importance of local and extra-local breakdown also shifted, on the same rhythm as electoral flux.

And that flux sometimes takes on massive proportions, such that the Canadian extremes dwarf those elsewhere. Where high-volatility elections in the comparator countries predate the Second World War, in Canada they are as frequent after the war as before it. In the other countries, such elections signal a change in the identities of the system's key parties. In Canada, the old parties remain as firmly in control as ever. Permanent displacements of old parties do occur in provincial elections, however, and the resultant gaps between federal and provincial electoral arenas within the same province can be wide and enduring.

The sociological foundations of Canadian party competition seem to be weak, inane, or both. None of the standard markers for class politics gives much purchase on Canadian party preference. The only one with any power is union membership. Fifty years ago, however, the system was strongly rooted. The roots lay in religious denomination – in essence Catholic versus Protestant – but a substantive religious basis for the link was not visible to the naked eye. In the years since, the denominational difference has evaporated.

For the entire twentieth century, the Liberals dominated the system and did so more completely than any party elsewhere in the Anglosphere. This difference is one of degree, however. What is qualitatively distinctive about Canada is the location of this dominant party – at the ideological centre. Elsewhere the middle party, where it exists, crowds one flank or the other, leaving the centre effectively empty (Johnston 2013, Fig. 13.5). In election campaigns in most countries, to be sure, the centre typically does exert a gravitational pull. But the centripetal pull is felt by parties whose starting point is off centre and whose sociological foundation and organizational logic exert a countervailing centrifugal force. In Canada, the dominant party is privileged to start in the centre; no further gravitation is required.

The rest of the book attempts to make sense of the system's distinctive features. For some features, the primary explanation lies in competition between the old parties. Others cannot be understood without reference to new parties, with important qualitative distinctions among them. Compartmentalization of the system is next to impossible, however, given the logic of FPP. To the extent that FPP amplifies differences and shifts among parties, outcomes rooted in one part of the system or in one place have implications for the rest of the system. To unlock the box, we must start with the anomaly that explains most of the others, the system's domination by a party of the centre. I start, then, with the competitive position of the Liberal Party and that of its ancient rival, the Conservative Party. New parties intrude on this early narrative but not as pivotal actors. Later I turn to the new entrants, insurgents and the CCF-NDP. Finally, I bring the new and the old parts of the system together to account for the system-level anomalies in fragmentation, volatility, and federal-provincial discontinuities.

3

Liberal Dominance, Conservative Interludes

> Les élections ne se font pas avec les prières.
>
> – PIERRE LAPORTE[1]

The secret of the Liberal Party's historical dominance was its stranglehold on seats from Quebec. Liberals could regularly roll out 80 to 100 percent of the province's seats. These seats in turn would represent 20 to 25 percent of all seats in the House of Commons, almost halfway to a single-party majority. As long as the Liberals had these seats in their pocket, voters outside Quebec were forced either to beat the Liberals or to join them. Really, the only way to beat them was to steal their Quebec bloc or at least make a big enough inroad to limit their head start. This the Conservatives occasionally did, but each time they paid a heavy price. All this made Quebec the pivot for government and a critical arbiter of party system transitions.

Quebec's pivotal status cannot be understood in isolation. It is equally critical that other regions were *not* coherent blocs, neither highly consolidated nor distinctively mobile. The partial exception to this claim is western Canada, which at certain periods rivalled – or sought to rival – Quebec as a regional pole. But the West rarely succeeded in this endeavour. Indeed, it has also been the prime site for third-party politics, hardly the route to pivotal status.

The starting point is that Quebec owns a lot of seats, more than any other province except Ontario. No less important, Quebeckers were able to capitalize on this advantage. The Quebec electorate was both consolidated and mobile, delivering seats *en bloc* in any given election but to more than one party across elections. Controlling Quebec was both necessary and sufficient for Liberal success. For Conservatives, the link was never so tight, but Quebec also mattered to their story. After a century as the system's pivot, Quebeckers abruptly stopped playing this role. When they did, the old system collapsed.

Preliminary Empirics

Although I focus mainly on Quebec, I look more generally at the broad correspondences – or lack of them – among the regions and the country as a whole. In Figure 3.1, the datum is the percentage of seats in the House of Commons. To be clear, this is not a party's share of seats in each region. Rather, it is the party's number of seats in the region expressed as a share of all House seats Canada-wide. For a given party, the "Overall" line is the same from picture to picture since it is always the Canada-wide share. Each graph also has a horizontal reference line at 50 percent, the threshold for majority government.[2] A vertical reference line appears in 1993, which marks the end of the bloc-pivotal system. First I will present the narrative of the old system for Liberals and Conservatives respectively; then I will turn to a capsule account of the events of 1993 and after.

The Liberal Party

The place to start is with Liberals, the "natural" party of government:

- The Liberals rose to dominance by riding a trend from 1882 to 1896. Of their total net gain in seats, 20 percent of the House, 17 percent came from Quebec alone. The shift from 1882 to 1887 was huge and reflected the reaction to the 1885 execution of Louis Riel that also powered the rise of the Liberals in Quebec provincial politics.[3] The 1887-91 gain was modest, notwithstanding the accession of Quebec francophone Wilfrid Laurier to the party's leadership. Most likely this was because the party's unexpected commitment to "Unrestricted Reciprocity" (free trade) with the United States was hardly calculated to win favour with the province's business interests. The full effect of his leadership was achieved in 1896.

- Further Liberal gains, post-1896, came basically from the West, mainly in Alberta and Saskatchewan. The Quebec bloc had little room to grow, and meanwhile the party reaped the benefit of rapid demographic growth in the West. Over the same period, the Liberal Party *lost* ground in Ontario.
- The 1911 election initiated a period of weakness that lasted until 1935. The substance of the election repeated that of 1891, reciprocity with the United States. In this case, the Liberal government went into the election defending an actual deal for free trade in natural products. The party was already weak in Ontario, but 1911 brought a catastrophic further drop, such that for more than two decades the party brought less than 10 percent of all seats in the House from the biggest region. The 1917 election brought losses in the West as most sitting Liberals joined the pro-conscription Unionist coalition and took their votes with them (although they were generally opposed by new Liberal candidates). The 1921 election saw the Progressive insurgency, which blocked any possible western rebound by the Liberals. Later in the 1920s, however, the Liberal bloc in the West returned to its pre-1911 level. For all its weakness in Ontario and the West, the Liberal Party governed for 9 of 19 years between 1911 and 1930. At the low point, what sustained the party was the bloc from Quebec.
- The 1935 election made the Liberals strong everywhere, strong enough at least to benefit from fragmentation of the rest of the vote. One could argue that their strength in Quebec was a by-product of their pan-Canadian appeal. But Liberal strength in the province was consistent with the earlier pattern, so the Quebec electorate's behaviour was more likely predicated on the traditional appeal. Besides, in every election in the Liberals' 22-year grip on power, withdrawal of the Quebec bloc would have denied the Liberals their majority. For Ontario, this was true only twice. The 1945 election, in which the electorate polarized once again over conscription and the Liberal majority was tiny, revealed the centrality of Quebec.
- After 1960, Quebec remained critical but so now was Ontario. The Liberals rebuilt their Quebec bloc and kept it intact – indeed grew it – until the collapse in 1984. Ontario was now the complement, for between 1963 and 1980 the province gave the Liberals blocs comparable

Liberal Dominance, Conservative Interludes 51

FIGURE 3.1   Regions as brokers of government, 1878-2015

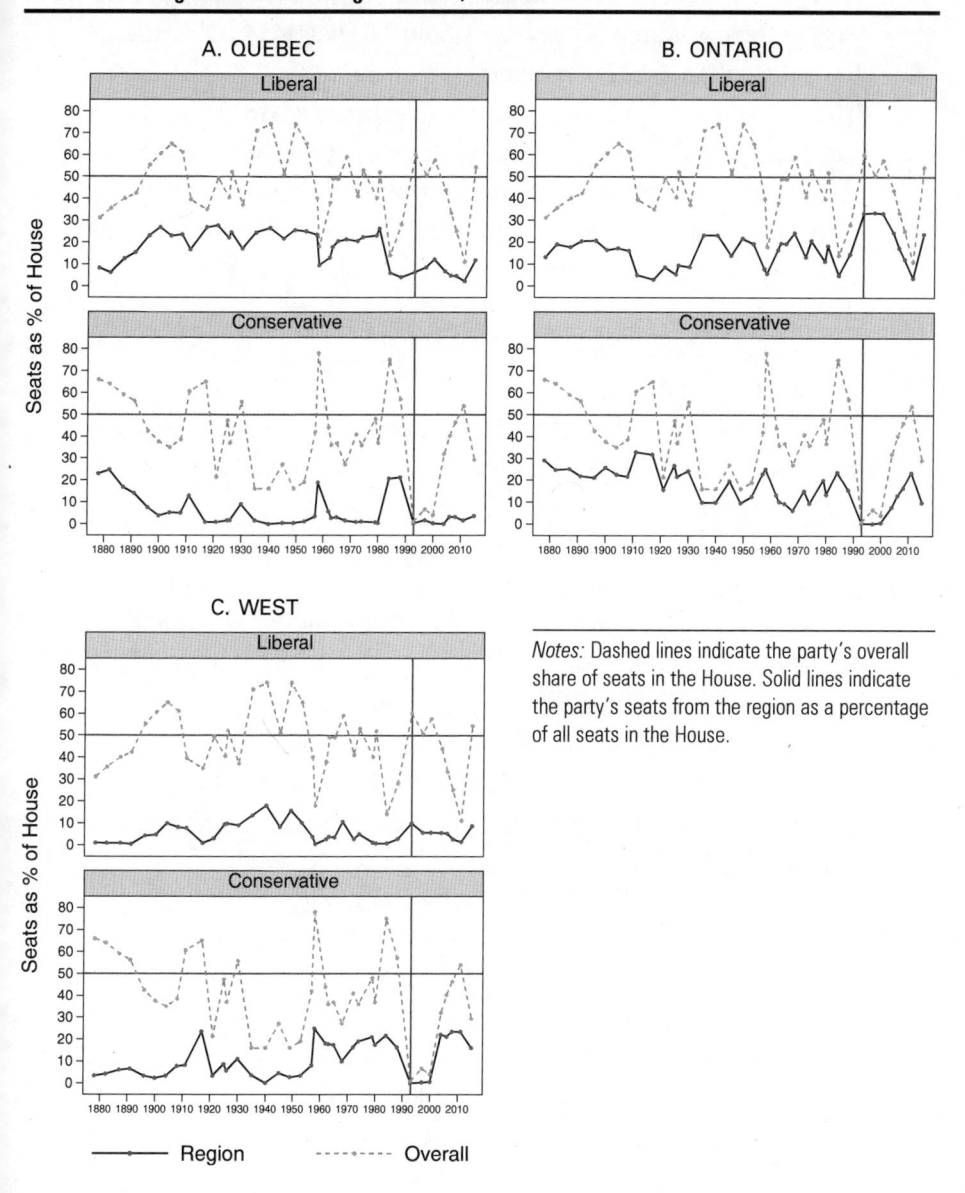

A. QUEBEC

B. ONTARIO

C. WEST

Notes: Dashed lines indicate the party's overall share of seats in the House. Solid lines indicate the party's seats from the region as a percentage of all seats in the House.

——— Region   - - - - - Overall

to those from Quebec. And Ontario became critical at the margin. After 1968, its trend was basically downward and the Ontario trend effectively drove the national one; the Liberal seat majority in 1980 was Pierre Trudeau's smallest, and the second smallest in Canadian history. Over the same span, Ontario's flux was the primary factor in determining whether or not the party returned a majority or even won the election. Movement in the West was basically a pale echo of that in Ontario but always at a level so low that the region was all but irrelevant to the Liberals' standing.

The Conservative Party

For the Conservatives, much of the story was the mirror image of that for the Liberals, so little elaboration is necessary. The following points deserve emphasis, however.

- The Conservatives' late-nineteenth-century losses in Quebec mirrored the Liberals' gains. From 1896 on, the Conservatives were chronically weak in Quebec until 1984.
- In the first decade of the twentieth century, the party held on to its Ontario bloc and extracted modest seat gains in western Canada as the region grew. Although the Liberals were usually slightly stronger in the region as a whole, the Conservatives were the dominant party in British Columbia and Manitoba.
- In the 1911-30 stretch, the Conservatives were distinctively the party of Ontario: in 1911 and 1917, about one-third of the House was composed of Conservatives from the province. Although in the 1920s the Conservatives' Ontario bloc was smaller, it still constituted about 25 percent of all seats. Apart from the exceptional result of 1917, the Conservatives were no stronger in the West than they had been before 1911.
- From 1935 until the Diefenbaker years, the Conservatives were weak everywhere.
- The 1960s saw a Conservative renaissance in the West, and the 1970s witnessed the party's growth in Ontario.
- In 1984 and 1988, the party was strong everywhere, replicating an earlier pattern in Conservative victories, the creation of geographically inclusive coalitions.

- Conservative weakness in Quebec, although chronic, was not unbroken. Every so often the Conservatives returned Quebec votes and seats in numbers ranging from substantial to overwhelming. Figure 3.1 renders these moments highly visible: bumps in 1911, 1930, 1958, and 1984, with the 1984 surge sustained to 1988. Each election returned a Canada-wide Conservative majority, and these five represent all twentieth-century Conservative majorities but one. The exception proves the rule: 1917, the year of extreme cultural polarization and coalition. In the four swings toward the Conservatives, seat gains in Quebec rivalled those in the rest of Canada. In 1911 and 1930, subtraction of the Quebec delegation would have denied the Conservatives a majority. In 1958 and 1984, each landslide was such that the Conservatives would have held an all-Canada majority without the Quebec contingent. But in both years the contingent was critical to turning a comfortable majority into an overwhelming one, and in 1988 Quebec saved the Conservatives from defeat.

The 1993 Landslide and Its Aftermath

The 1993 election ended all this. Each big region played a distinct role, but the region of outstanding importance, in contrast to earlier decades, was Ontario.

- Quebec opted out of being the pivot, essentially shunning the Conservatives while no longer producing an all-Liberal bloc. By giving the bulk of its seats to the Bloc Québécois, it also reduced the Canada-wide pool available for supporting a government, any government. This was a major factor in the renewed frequency of minority governments.
- If there was a new pivot for government, it was Ontario. In the 1990s, the province rallied so completely to the Liberals that it brought the party two-thirds of the way to a majority. In every year from 1993 to 2004, Ontario MPs occupied at least 55 percent of the governing party's seats. In 1997, Ontario played the role historically assigned to Quebec: backstopping the party against severe reverses elsewhere. Relative to the 2000 high point, Liberal losses in Ontario accounted for about two-thirds of the party's Canada-wide loss in each subsequent election. Once

the Conservative vote was reconstituted in 2004, gains in Ontario accounted for similar or greater proportions of the party's rise to power and eventual parliamentary majority.
- Notwithstanding its role as a prime source of insurgency, the West played an oddly passive role. The Reform breakthrough erased any chance of Conservative recovery, and only an outright merger restored the possibility. This sequence of insurgency and recovery registers in the Conservative seat lines in Figure 3.1C. But if we scan the Conservative line before and after the Reform interlude, the pattern is almost undisturbed, apart from a slight upward trend. So the West was vital to the Conservatives' overall position, but it was not the arbiter of the party's fortune. And, although the region routinely gave the party 20 percent or so of House seats, it was never cohesive enough – compared with Ontario from 1993 to 2004 or Quebec in earlier decades (both for the Liberals) – to give the party a lock on office, not even as a minority government.

One upshot of this was the end of party dominance. Since 1993 at least, and possibly since 1984, the alternation of power has been routine.

Although seats are the currency of Parliament, we need to get beneath raw totals and visual correspondences. The data underlying Figure 3.1 are a compound of within-region coordination and the region's sheer scale. These elements need to be separated. The logic of FPP, in augmenting differences and changes, overstates both the degree of homogeneity within a region and the extent of change when it occurs. We thus need to get to the votes that underlie the seats. And we need to pull all of this together to assess whether control of any region can be said to be necessary and sufficient for winning a Canada-wide election. Figure 3.1 already tells us that no such relationship exists now; 1993 put an end to that. The years before 1993 are more promising, however, and the obvious focal point is Quebec. In the sections that follow, I build from the ground up, starting with one-sidedness and mobility in the vote.

Votes

For more than a century, the Quebec electorate was peculiarly coordinated in that the vote was both consolidated and variable. Figure 3.2 portrays

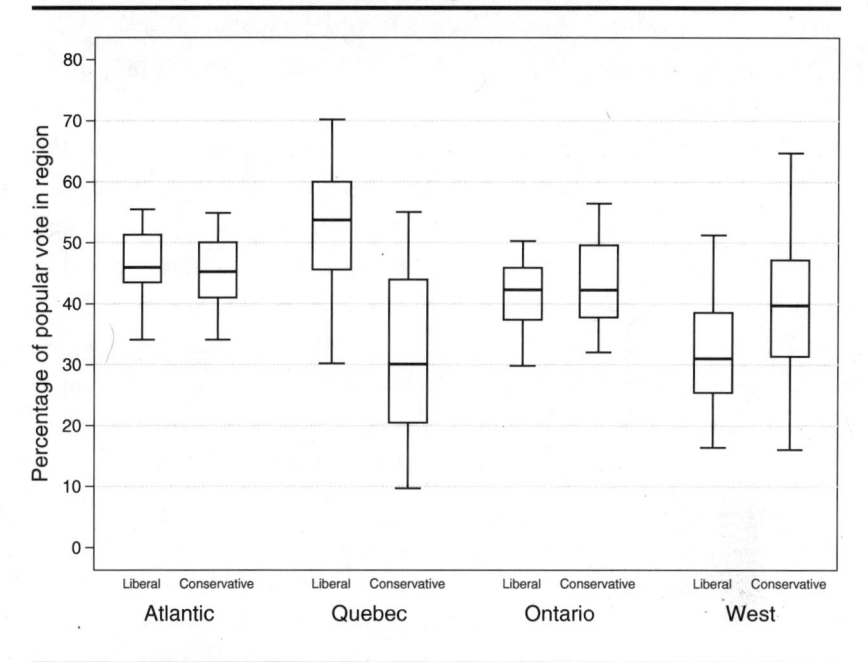

FIGURE 3.2 Popular vote distributions by region, 1887-1988

Notes: This figure shows the distribution of Liberal and Conservative percentage shares of the federal popular vote in each province or region. The figure is a box plot (see note on box plots in Figure 2.8). The dataset does not include the 1917 conscription election.

the situation from 1887 to 1988, with box plots on the model of Figure 2.8.[4] The starting point is the within-region gap between party medians. In Quebec, the median Liberal share is 24 points larger than the median Conservative share. Nowhere else does a gap like this appear. In Ontario and Atlantic Canada, there is essentially no gap; both parties have been reasonably competitive most of the time. The gap in the West is nine points in the Conservatives' favour. This reflects a transformation around 1960 and faithfully captures the recent importance of that region to the Conservative base. But it distracts us from the fact that Conservatives and Liberals were rarely major parties in the region at the same time. Instead, the West has been the least bipartisan region, the most vulnerable to invasion by new parties.

But the Quebec electorate is also more mobile than any other. The inter-quartile range is greater in Quebec than in either Ontario or the

Atlantic provinces. The Quebec range is especially great for the Conservatives: a 24-point span. The range for the Liberals is also relatively great, just not as spectacular as that for the Conservatives. The only other similarly volatile history is for the Conservative Party in the West. The western flux is qualitatively different from that in Quebec, however. In the West, most of the variance is the result of two massive but widely separated realignments, the Conservatives' drop after the First World War and their rise around 1960. In Quebec, the flux has an additional episodic feature, sudden Conservative surges followed shortly by sudden declines. Whatever their qualitative differences, the West and Quebec have supplied most of the system's dynamic juice. Not only are the inter-quartile ranges greater than those in Ontario and the Atlantic region, but also the upper and lower adjacent values are much further apart than elsewhere.

Seats

Quebec is big, historically controlling 25-30 percent of all seats in the House. The only single province of comparable size is Ontario, larger than Quebec but not always by a great margin. The West rivals Quebec only as a composite of four distinct provinces. In the years since 1867, Quebec's relative size has shifted only modestly and not always downward. Before the twentieth century, the West carried virtually no electoral weight. As it expanded by pulling in a disproportionate share of early-twentieth-century immigration, Quebec offset it with a high birth rate. The place that lost ground, relatively speaking, was Ontario. Quebec is now losing ground, and the near future might see a dramatic reordering of provincial weights. For the translation of votes into seats, Quebec is *un*remarkable. Indeed, if it is distinctive for the vote-seat translation, it is for inefficiency, not the opposite. The Quebec framework, according to Figure 3.3, over the critical middle range, is the least responsive.[5] This is just embellishment, however. The four regions, in truth, are remarkably similar.[6]

If the mechanics of Quebec's electoral system are like those elsewhere in Canada, the underlying vote dynamics are not. When the vote flux of Figure 3.2 is processed through the mechanisms in Figure 3.3, the result is the seat pattern in Figure 3.4. The figure gives box plots for Liberals and Conservatives for seat shares *within* regions. This elides differences across regions in relative size, an omission that I will redress in a moment.

FIGURE 3.3 Seats and votes by region, 1887-1988

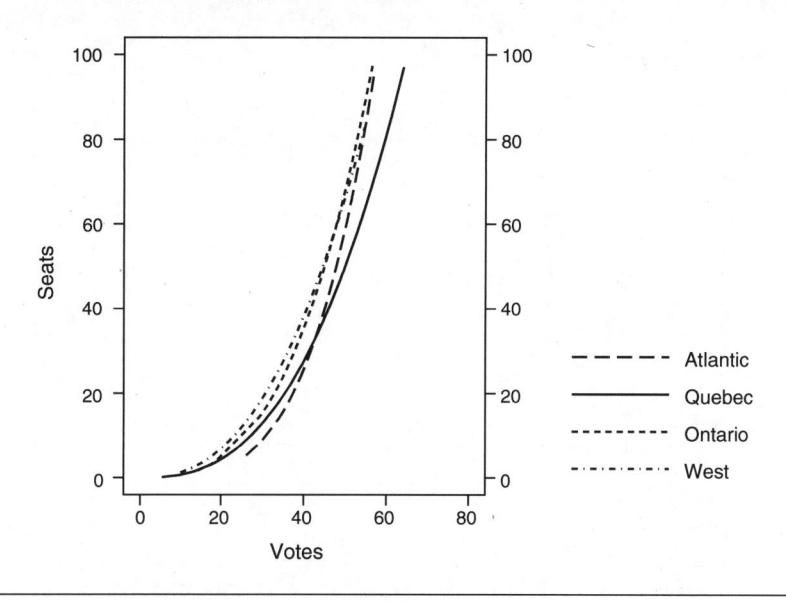

Notes: This figure shows the relationship between each party's vote percentage and its seat percentage, region by region. The underlying estimation uses the natural logarithms of vote and seat shares on the logic of King (1990) and includes shares for both Liberals and Conservatives. The figure is based on estimations in Table 3.A1.

Variability, of course, is much higher everywhere for seats than votes, exactly as implied by the swing ratios in Figure 3.3. Ironically, this expansion is least impressive for Quebec, where the inter-quartile ranges are barely larger than those for vote shares. This is a purely mechanical phenomenon, however, reflecting the fact that vote shares in Quebec are usually one-sided. What really counts is the difference between party medians. In Atlantic Canada and Ontario, the gap is less than 10 points. In the West, it is 22 points. *In Quebec, it is 68 points.* For the Liberal Party, the *median* share of seats in Quebec is almost four seats in five. Half the time the Liberals get even more seats. For the Conservative Party, the median share is 1 seat in 10. Half the time the party wins even fewer than that.

How these patterns cash out as regional blocs is shown in Figure 3.5. Here the datum is each party's seats from the region as a share of the whole House, election by election, exactly as in Figure 3.1. The top panel names parties, contrasting Liberals and Conservatives. The most basic point is

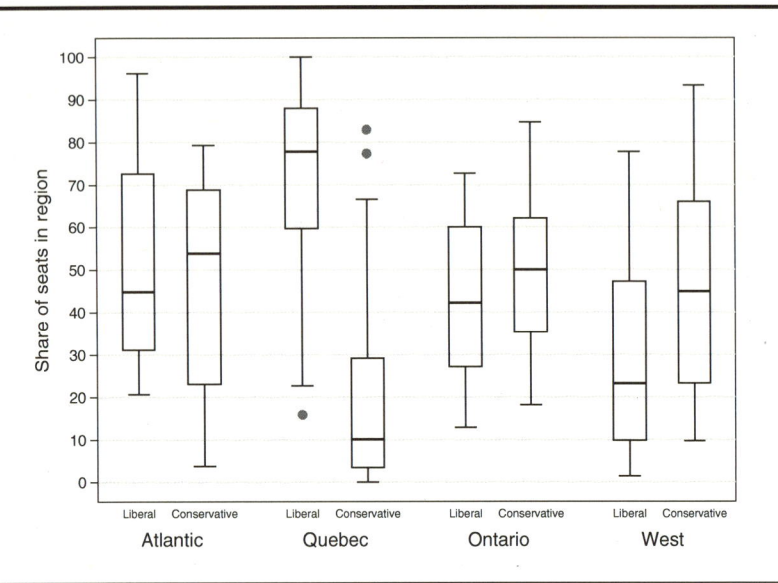

FIGURE 3.4 Seat-share distributions within regions, 1887-1988

Notes: This figure shows the distribution of Liberal and Conservative percentage shares of federal seats in each province or region. The figure is a box plot (see note on box plots in Figure 2.8). The dataset does not include the 1917 conscription election.

this: *the Liberal median in Quebec is higher than that for any party in any region.* In the typical election from 1887 to 1988, the Liberal Party brought 22 percent of all seats in the House from Quebec alone. That is, the Liberals positioned themselves almost halfway to a single-party majority before any other region checked in. Some of this reflects the sheer size of Quebec, of course, but this is more than just a matter of size. It is also a matter of concentration. For Conservatives, the median Quebec share of all seats in the House is 3 percent.

We might expect comparable blocs from Ontario, and indeed we find them. For instance, the second highest median value, a robust 20 percent of all seats in the House, is from Ontario. But note the identity of the beneficiary: the Conservative Party. Note further the third-place value among all region-party combinations: also in Ontario, this time the Liberals. Ontario can give big blocs to individual parties simply because it is big, but giving a big bloc to one party does not preclude a similarly big bloc for its principal rival. In Quebec, in contrast, there is room for only one big bloc

FIGURE 3.5 Regional blocs in Parliament, 1887-1988: Liberals versus Conservatives and first versus second place

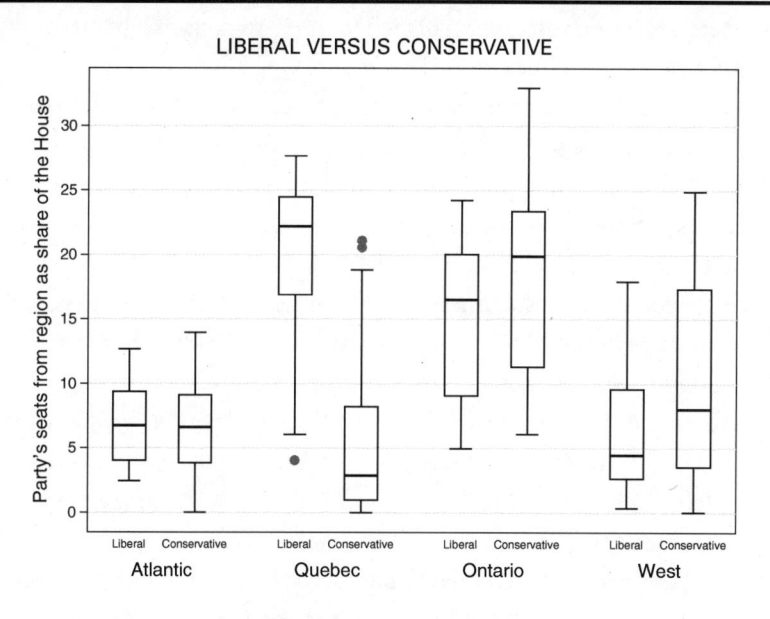

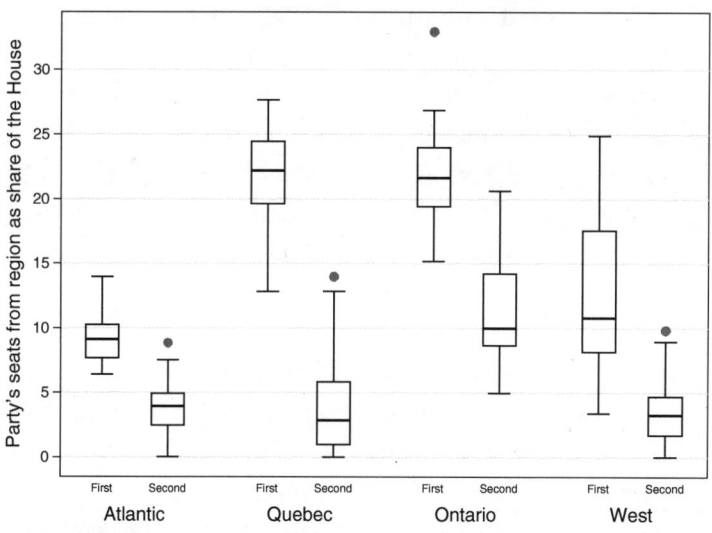

Notes: This figure shows the distribution of the percentage share of seats in the House of Commons that each party brings from each province or region (as in Figure 3.1 and Table 3.1). In the top panel, distributions are organized by the name of the party. In the bottom panel, the distributions are organized according to which party finishes first or second in the region. The figure is a box plot (see note on box plots in Figure 2.8). The dataset does not include the 1917 conscription election.

at a time, and for most of the twentieth century a large Quebec bloc was the Liberal norm.

There are, to be sure, moments when other regions exhibit seemingly massive bloc-like behaviour. The operative word is *seemingly*. The Conservatives, for example, have occasionally returned more than 30 percent of all House seats from Ontario alone and 25 percent from western Canada. For Ontario, some of these values are products of the nineteenth century, when the province held more than 40 percent of all House seats by itself. Others are the product of the Conservatives' propensity for Canada-wide sweeps, documented in Chapter 2. It does not make sense to speak of regional blocs when a party carries 75-80 percent of seats Canada-wide. Such results are exceptional, of course.

The picture is sharpened further by dropping parties' proper names and reordering them by standing, first or second place; the evidence is presented in the bottom panel of Figure 3.5. By first place and second place is meant the seat-share winner and runner-up, respectively, among the parties of government, Liberal or Conservative. At times, one party or the other is not – and even both are not – the runner-up or plurality holder, which can be a regional insurgent or the NDP. But for winning the overall race, ordering the parties by their relative standing makes the distinctiveness of Quebec even clearer. The first place/second place gap averaged across all years and all regions is 13 points. The gap is smallest in the smallest region, Atlantic Canada. In the West, the median gap is 7.5 points, and in Ontario it is 11.5 points. In Quebec, the gap is just over 19 points. The winner in the province typically brings 22 percent of all House seats from that province alone. The runner-up brings less than 3 percent.

Necessary and Sufficient Conditions for Power

For the Liberals over most of the twentieth century, securing a Quebec bloc was both a necessary and a sufficient condition for winning an election. Almost without fail, when the party carried Quebec *en bloc*, it carried the country. Conversely, if the Liberal Party failed to carry Quebec, then it was practically guaranteed to lose the election. To substantiate these claims, I use a simplified form of qualitative comparative analysis (QCA). Before getting to the analysis, though, I provide some definitional preliminaries.

What does it mean to carry Quebec *en bloc*? I propose as the basic datum whether or not a party returns 20 percent or more of seats in the House from a given region. The 20 percent threshold is frankly inductive. Figure 3.5 indicates that in 75 percent of cases the Quebec winner exceeded the 20 percent threshold, whereas the runner-up returned a much smaller number. The distributions for Quebec are highly discontinuous in contrast to other provinces.

By winning an election, I mean forming the government. Most of the time, but not always, this means forming a majority government. A minority government is usually formed by the party with the largest number of seats. In 1925-26, however, Liberal Prime Minister Mackenzie King held on to power for several months despite winning fewer seats than his Conservative rival, Arthur Meighen. The King government eventually fell, and Meighen, not King, was the incumbent in the 1926 election. But King's government lasted longer than Meighen's – indeed most of Meighen's time in office was spent fighting the election – so it seems reasonable to assign the victory to King. In keeping with the spirit of QCA, winning and losing also comprise a dichotomy.

Finally, a few words on why I employ a QCA-like analysis, aside from the fact that I estimate the impact of one qualitative state on another. It seems to be unreasonable intuitively that a Quebec bloc by itself would be the determining regional factor. So it is useful to gauge the impact from bloc-like success or failure in other provinces or regions. By setting up the data as input to QCA, it is easy to see how often a party clears the 20 percent threshold in a region and what happens when it does. The results appear in Table 3.1, a "truth table" with annotations to sort out thorny issues.[7]

The analysis begins by declaring the 20-plus share as a dummy variable for each region where it appears. As such, a share never appears in Atlantic Canada, and the region simply exits the analysis. Likewise, the Liberals never returned such a bloc from the West, so it also does not appear in the Liberal analysis. Only for the Conservatives is the West relevant. The table is then ordered by party and, within each party, into necessary and sufficient parts. If a Quebec bloc is a *necessary* condition, then a party should *never* form the government in the *absence* of such a bloc. If it is *sufficient*, then the party should *always* form the government in the *presence* of such a bloc. We can ask the same questions of the other relevant regions. The patterns for one party need not be the mirror image for the other party. In 31 elections from 1878 to 1988,[8] the Liberals failed to return 20 percent or more of seats in the House from Quebec 11 times. Only once

TABLE 3.1 Quebec as the pivot for government, 1878-1988

Seats from region: upper case: ≥ 20 lower case: < 20	Quebec bloc	Probability of forming government	Remarks
Liberal			
qo (N = 10)	Necessary?	0.10	1963 (minority government)
q0 (N = 1)		0.00	1891
Qo (N = 14)	Sufficient?	0.79	Majority governments: 1900, 1904, 1908, 1926,* 1945, 1953, 1980 Minority governments: 1921, 1925, 1965, 1972 Losses: 1917 to Unionist coalition; 1957, 1979 Conservative minorities
Q0 (N = 6)		1.00	1896, 1935-40, 1949, 1968, 1974
Conservative			
qow (N = 13)		0.08	1962 (minority)
q0w (N = 11)	Necessary?	0.46	Victories: 1887-91, 1911, 1930, 1957 (minority) Defeats: 1896-1908, 1925,[†] 1926
q0W (N = 3)		1.00	1917 (coalition), 1958 (landslide), 1979 (minority)
Qow (N = 1)		1.00	1988
Q0w (N = 2)	Sufficient?	1.00	1878, 1882[‡]
Q0W (N = 1)		1.00	1984

* Strictly speaking, a minority government; see the text in Chapter 2.
† Popular vote and seat plurality won by the Conservatives, but the Liberals retained office with Progressive support. The Conservatives acceded to office briefly in mid-1926.
‡ Precedes mass settlement of the West.

when this happened did they win the overall election. The exception was 1963, when they just missed the cut: the Liberals' Quebec bloc was 18 percent of seats in the House, and the result was a Liberal minority government. So carrying Quebec is de facto a necessary condition.

It is also close to a sufficient condition. Of the 14 elections in which Quebec and only Quebec gave the Liberals a 20-plus share, the party won 11, 7 of which were majority results. One of the losses was the conscription election in 1917, the extreme case of cultural polarization. The other two times yielded Conservative minority governments. Six times the Liberals returned 20-plus blocs from both Ontario and Quebec, and each time yielded – unsurprisingly given the arithmetic – a victory. Of these six, three (1935, 1940, and 1949[9]) were Canada-wide landslides, so in a sense Quebec and especially Ontario were not really acting as blocs on an otherwise deconsolidated field; they were swept along in a tide. Still, of all elections in which the Liberals swept Quebec, 85 percent yielded Canada-wide victories.

The pattern for Ontario is instructive – in the negative – for just how distinctive Quebec is. The Liberals failed to extract 20-plus blocs from Ontario 24 of 31 times. They nonetheless won 15 of these elections, 14 because they swept Quebec and one because they almost did so. When they exceeded the threshold in Ontario, they won six of seven. But the seventh instance is telling: this was an election, in 1891, in which they did not sweep Quebec (even though this was also an election in which Ontario controlled nearly 45 percent of all seats).

The pattern for the Conservatives is more complex. As noted, the West is relevant, so I consider bloc possibilities for three regions. As a result, the number of alternative routes to power is also greater. Of the 31 elections, the Conservatives failed to sweep Quebec in 27 of them,[10] and of these 27 elections they won 9. So sweeping Quebec was not an absolutely necessary condition for Conservative success, but failure to carry the province was a great inhibitor. Two of the nine victories came before 1900: that is, before the West became relevant. Of the other seven, three were minority results. A fourth was the Unionist victory of 1917. The other outright majority victories without a Quebec sweep came in 1911, 1930, and 1958. Even in these cases, Quebec delivered an important boost to the Conservatives, as Figure 3.1 shows. To be sure, the largest subset in these elections (13 observations) comprises occasions when the Conservatives were weak everywhere, so in many years the story of Conservative weakness is not just a story of Quebec.

A case could be made that sweeping Quebec is at least a sufficient condition for Conservative all-Canada success. On all four occasions in which the party swept the province, it won majorities. One was the landslide of 1984, for which Quebec was useful but not necessary. Two were in the nineteenth century and part of a sequence that indicates Quebec's pivotal status. In the fourth election, in 1988, Quebec definitely was pivotal: its seats kept the Conservatives in power.

Again Ontario is instructive. The pattern is not as negative as that for the Liberals, but neither is it one of resounding pivotal status. For the Conservatives, carrying Ontario is not quite a necessary condition, although it helps mightily. Of the 14 elections in which the Conservatives fell short in the province, they carried the country in only 2. One was in 1962, which yielded a weak and short-lived Conservative minority government. The other was in 1988, when Quebec stepped into the breach. But carrying Ontario is hardly sufficient for a Conservative victory. The party extracted 20-plus seat blocs from Ontario 17 times, only 10 of which resulted in Canada-wide victories, a 59 percent success rate. In 6 of these 10 times, the party extracted a big bloc from at least one other region. Of these six victories, three were landslides, including in 1917, so no region was pivotal.

Discussion

In the government game of the nineteenth and twentieth centuries, Quebec played a role out of proportion to its size. Voters in Quebec did this the hard way by consolidating their votes to an extraordinary extent around one party, the Liberals. On the occasions that they abandoned the Liberals, they went a long way toward the other side. Thus, they managed to be both more consolidated and more variable than any other electorate in the country. The electoral system compounded this behaviour, such that seats from Quebec came *en bloc*. For the Liberals, the Quebec bloc was almost the necessary condition and the sufficient condition for government, and the Liberals governed most of the time. In the probabilistic world of mass elections, this is well-nigh deterministic. The relationship is not so close for the Conservative Party, which usually found its way to power by a geographically inclusive route. But if Quebec was not absolutely pivotal to Conservative success, it was important.

These facts are relevant to normative arguments about the electoral system and the party system. The most widely cited article in the history of the *Canadian Journal of Political Science* (Cairns 1968) is commonly read as an attack on the appropriateness of FPP for a country with so much geography. One part of the argument is that the electoral system makes Quebec, in particular, seem to be more cohesive than it really is: "It is only at the level of seats, not votes, that Quebec became a Liberal stronghold, a Canadian 'solid South,' and a one-party monopoly. The Canadian 'solid South,' like its American counterpart, is a contrivance of the electoral system, not an autonomous social fact which exists independent of it" (Cairns 1968, 67). Strictly speaking, this must be true. Figure 3.3 is eloquent testimony to the amplification of magnitudes and differences, in which Quebec (notwithstanding subtle differences in swing ratio in the middle of the distribution) is a province like the others. But historically the Quebec electorate was *un*like the others in its strategically powerful combination of concentration and mobility.[11]

At some deep level, concentration and mobility might also have been electoral system artifacts. The potential for amplification embedded in FPP might be an incentive for some additional measure of electoral consolidation, to the extent that the arithmetic of Parliament dangles the possibility of one province alone being the pivot. And one province being such a pivot can itself be normatively problematic. But if we concede that francophone Quebeckers have a distinct quasi-national interest, it is hard to fault Quebeckers for exploiting the logic of a majoritarian system when they themselves can never be the majority.

But how did that coordination work? What were the issues? How or why did it end? These are matters for the next two chapters.

APPENDIX

The estimation underlying Figure 3.3 is as follows:

$$S_{it} = \beta \, V_{it}^{\,\rho},$$

where S_{it} is the i-th party's seat share at election t;
V_{it} is the corresponding vote share;
β is a "bias" parameter; and
ρ is a "representation" parameter.

The nomenclature of "bias" and "representation" originates with King and Browning (1987), who focus on fair division of the vote between parties. In a pure two-party situation, in which each party's vote share and seat share are just the complements of the other party's values, β estimates bias as the departure from equal treatment or the tilt off the 45 degree line. Bias is more easily grasped as the natural log of β, which centres the parameter at zero. The King-Browning framework can be adapted to estimate party-specific bias in a multiparty context (King 1990). Bias as such is not the issue in this chapter, however, since a given estimation incorporates data from both major parties. Instead, the coefficient of central interest is ρ. A ρ of one would indicate a purely linear relationship, as with a proportional formula. In general, the larger the value of ρ, the steeper the line in the middle of the vote-share distribution.

TABLE 3.A1   Seats and votes by region, 1887-1988

Region (N = 59)	ln (β)		ρ		Adjusted R^2
Atlantic	−10.53	(1.40)	3.74	(0.37)	0.64
Quebec	−6.52	(0.53)	2.67	(0.14)	0.86
Ontario	−7.29	(0.84)	2.94	(0.22)	0.74
West	−5.50	(0.71)	2.48	(0.20)	0.72

Wald tests for ρ		
	F	p
Quebec vs. Atlantic	4.99	0.03
Quebec vs. Ontario	0.79	0.37
Quebec vs. West	0.82	0.37
Ontario vs. West	1.99	0.16

4

Liberal Centrism, Polarized Pluralism

> We had no shape
> Because he never took sides,
> And no sides
> Because he never allowed them to take shape.
>
> — F.R. SCOTT, "W.L.M.K."

Intuitively, the centre seems like a good place to be. In the classic formulation by Downs (1957), the dominant strategy for both parties in a two-party system is convergence on the median voter. Even with more than two parties, Downsian logic still argues that the centre will be occupied (Cox 1990). But such conjectures are confuted by reality. Divergence is more common than convergence (Macdonald, Listhaug, and Rabinowitz 1991; Rabinowitz and Macdonald 1989), and so is differentiation in parties' social bases (Lipset and Rokkan 1967). Centripetal logic might operate during campaigns, but it operates on actors whose starting point is off centre. Duverger (1963, 215) states the case in stark terms:

> Political choice takes the form of a choice between two alternatives. A duality of parties does not always exist, but there is almost always a duality of tendencies ... This is equivalent to saying that the center does not exist in politics ... The term "center" is applied to the geometrical spot at which the moderates of opposed tendencies meet ... Every Center is divided against itself and remains separated into two halves, Left-Center and

Right-Center. For the Center is nothing more than the artificial grouping of the right wing of the Left and the left wing of the Right. The fate of the Center is to be torn asunder.

For a party to occupy the centre on one dimension, it must be plausibly off centre on another (Chappell and Keech 1986). But if reality confutes Downs, the Canadian party system seems to confute reality. It stands as an exception to the centripetal rule. The historically dominant Liberal Party controls the centre on both key axes of Canadians' political choices.

I argue in this chapter that, on the classic left-right axis captured in Figure 2.9, the centrism of the Liberal Party is a product of the years since 1970. Before then, Conservatives and Liberals hardly differed and together anchored a pole with the CCF-NDP on the other side. After 1970, however, the Conservatives took sole possession of the right wing, leaving the Liberals in the centre by default.

The other dimension underlying the system is the "national" question. Since 1960, this dimension has been mainly concerned with the place of Quebec in Canada. Before 1960, the question was more often about the place of Canada in the world. Whatever the specifics, the national question reflects the country's deep division. On this dimension, Liberal centrism is of long standing. To explain Liberals' survival at the centre, the critical electoral fact is that Canada comprises the two electorates described in Chapter 3, Quebec versus the rest. This segmentation enables the Liberals to control contrasting poles on the "national" axis, the pro-Canada one inside Quebec and the pro-Quebec one outside the province. In this sense, the pattern reflects the electoral logic in Chappell and Keech (1986). But the two electorates must come together on election day, such that the Liberals' contrasting segment-specific appeals stand revealed as a single appeal, at the centre.

The Canadian pattern is an example of "polarized pluralism" (Sartori 1966, 1976),[1] and from it flows a dynamic that is explosive in two senses. First, the centre shrank as the Liberal Party declined. This is consistent with the record in other polarized pluralist systems. Second, to unseat the Liberals, the Conservatives were forced to adopt an ends-against-the-middle strategy. If such strategies are difficult when they involve coalitions among ideologically disconnected parties (Axelrod 1970), the Conservatives achieved the seemingly impossible by building the disconnected coalition inside their own ranks. Such a coalition was hard to build and hard to sustain. The resulting pattern was boom and bust, sometimes in Quebec, sometimes in the rest of Canada, often in both. The ultimate result was collapse of the old system.

Liberal positioning on the national question was critical to the party's ability to survive at the centre of the left-right axis. As the system's most plausible champion of national unity, the Liberals blocked the growth of the NDP. This was critical to the system's other great anomaly, its early fractionalization. I state this here simply for the record; detailed exploration of multipartism is a task for later chapters.

Left and Right

In the "textbook theory" of Canadian parties and elections (Sniderman et al. 1974), the old parties are indistinguishable. When the theory was laid down, the description was essentially correct and remained so until the mid-1970s, as Figure 4.1 shows. It plots postwar left-right values from the Campaign Manifesto Project (CMP).[2] For the first 30 years, the left-right element in the system pitted the CCF-NDP against both old parties. They in turn hugged the centre. As often as not, the Conservatives were slightly to the left of the Liberals, although at every point the old parties' confidence intervals overlapped. Then in the 1970s the Conservatives pulled to the right. Reform's emergence in the 1990s pulled the system even further right and expanded the overall left-right range. The transformation of Reform into Alliance in 2000 might have signalled a desire for centrist reconciliation, but the Alliance-Conservative merger yielded a clearly rightist outcome. The Liberals tacked back and forth, often against the flow. After 1975, they generally moved left, relatively speaking, and their confidence intervals more often overlapped those of the NDP than those of the Conservatives. Never, however, did the point estimate for the Liberals place them anywhere but the centre.

The National Question

Some other axis must be in play, and it is the national question, Canada's particular form of identity politics. In recent years, the focus has been the place of Quebec in (or out of) Canada. Over the years, however, the

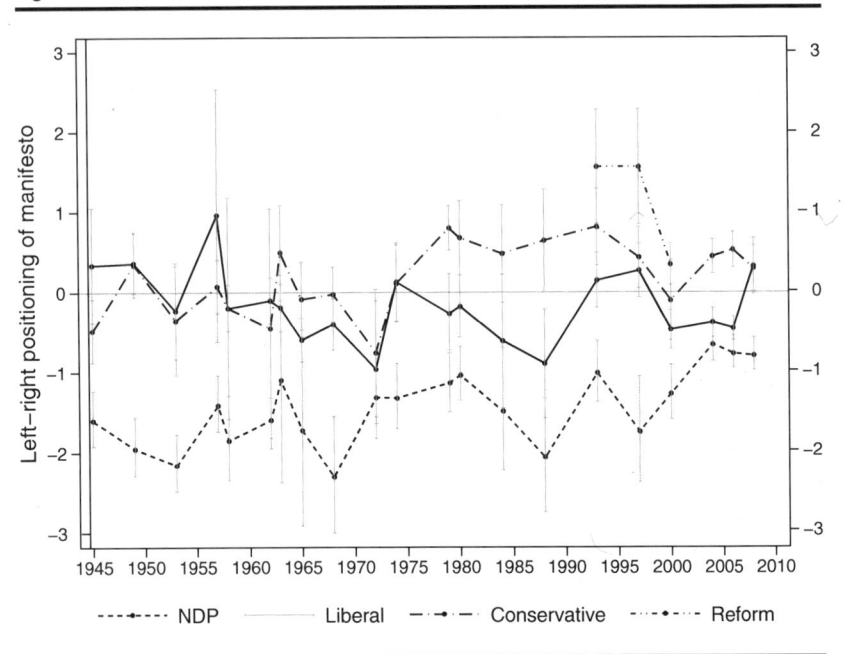

Figure 4.1 Postwar evolution of left-right party positions

Notes: This figure presents the overall position of each party on the left-right issue dimension, according to the Campaign Manifesto Project. High scores indicate positions on the right and low scores, positions on the left. Vertical bars plot 95 percent confidence intervals.
Source: See text and note 2.

dimension's issue content has taken different forms, as has its sociology and geography. To back my claims, however, I must look beyond the CMP. Even though identity politics produces most of the divergence and idiosyncrasy among party systems (Lipset and Rokkan 1967), such politics does not fit comfortably into the CMP coding scheme. Instead, I resort to a mix of data sources, not all of them measuring party policy directly. And I run history in reverse, so to speak, to bridge from finely grained recent survey data all the way back to coarse aggregate data in the nineteenth century.

Survey Evidence on Quebec in Canada

Canadian parties are routinely forced to consider how much to do for Quebec, and voters might ask themselves the same question. Starting in 1988, the CES posed this question to Canada-wide survey samples, and the survey item has appeared ever since.[3] From 1988 to 1997, respondents were additionally asked to place each party on the same scale. For presentational clarity, I recast values to the −1, +1 interval.

For party placement, the situation is ambiguous. The Liberal Party is certainly seen as centrist, according to Figure 4.2, but so are its chief rivals. The NDP stands a little apart but is hardly seen as anti-Quebec. Between 1988 and 1997, both the NDP and the Conservatives are seen as becoming slightly less pro-Quebec, whereas perceptions of the Liberals do not budge. Although the parties do not seem to be very different, there is a strong consensus on the location of each, as the tight confidence intervals testify. Panel B indicates that Quebeckers and non-Quebeckers see almost the same picture. (For this panel, confidence intervals have been dropped to reduce clutter.) In 1993 and 1997, the mainstream parties are flanked by strongly pro- and anti-Quebec alternatives. These placements reflect the fact that both the Conservatives and the NDP made special efforts in Quebec in the 1980s and that the Conservatives enjoyed great success. For the Conservatives in particular, this was action contrary to type, and its eventual effect was to give birth to both the Bloc Québécois and Reform.

The secret, in any case, lies *inside* each party for supporters' positions on the question. If we divide supporters by region, then two things become clear: the centrism of the Liberals and the vulnerability of the Conservatives. Figure 4.3 shows this by presenting mean values by year for respondents' positions on how much to do for Quebec, with respondents sorted by party and region.[4] The critical comparisons are among parties within each region and within each party among regions.

Without exception, Liberal supporters outside Quebec are the most pro-Quebec. Occasionally, NDP supporters match them. In 1988, the outliers were Conservative supporters, clearly the most anti-Quebec group. In the 1990s, this group seemed to converge on Liberal supporters, but this is deceptive. The 1988 Conservative base did not collectively become centrist. Rather, most of it deserted to Reform, such that the centrist Conservatives of 1993 were residual, a rump. Merger of the parties in 2003 yielded a Conservative bloc as fully anti-Quebec as Reform had been. In sum, the ordering is clear: year in, year out, Liberals are the most sympathetic to Quebec and Conservatives – or their wingmen – the least sympathetic.

72   *The Canadian Party System*

FIGURE 4.2   Perceptions of parties' orientations to Quebec, 1988-97

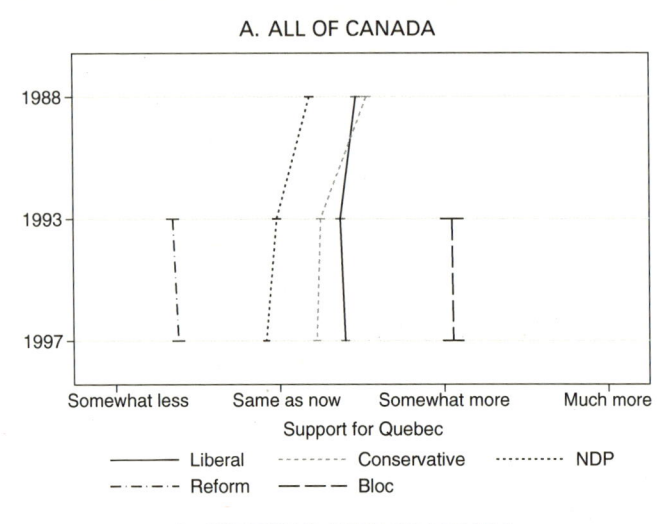

A. ALL OF CANADA

B. QUEBEC VS. REST OF CANADA

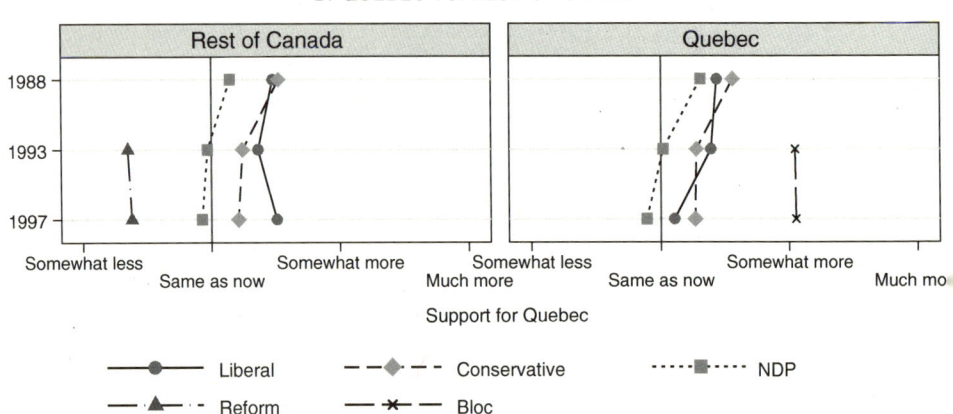

Notes: These figures show the average perception of each party on support for Quebec. Panel A refers to respondents from all of Canada. Panel B divides the sample between Quebec and the rest of Canada. For wording of survey items, see page 263n3.

In Quebec in 1988, the reverse was true. Liberal voters there were the least supportive of Quebec's claims, and Conservative voters there were the most supportive. Liberal positioning hardly changed in later years. But from 1993 on, the pro-Quebec pole was controlled by the Bloc Québécois. As a counterpoint to Reform in the rest of Canada, many Blocistes had voted Conservative in 1988. The NDP appears only twice, as between 1988

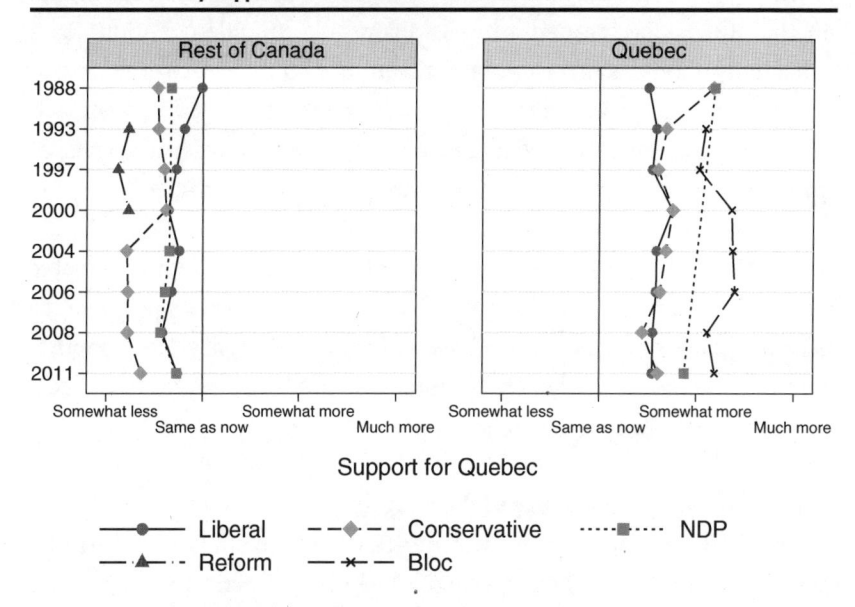

FIGURE 4.3 Party supporters' orientations to Quebec, 1988-2011

[Chart with two panels: "Rest of Canada" and "Quebec", showing years 1988, 1993, 1997, 2000, 2004, 2006, 2008, 2011 on the y-axis, and a scale from "Somewhat less / Same as now / Somewhat more / Much more" on the x-axis, labeled "Support for Quebec".]

Legend: Liberal — Conservative — Reform — Bloc — NDP

Notes: This figure plots support for Quebec among supporters of each party, where party preference is indicated by the vote in the current election. The sample is divided between Quebec and the rest of Canada. For wording of survey items, see page 269n3.

and 2011 their Quebec vote was risible. When New Democrats do appear, they pop up on the pro-Quebec flank; unlike in the rest of Canada, Quebec New Democrats never resemble Quebec Liberals. And Liberals, to sum up, were always to the pro-Canada side of whichever party was the chief rival in Quebec.

Now consider Quebec/rest-of-Canada gaps *within* the parties that run candidates Canada-wide. Gaps always appear: averaged across all the years and all the parties, their Quebec supporters are 0.54 (of a possible 2.0) points more pro-Quebec than their non-Quebec supporters. But the gap is always smallest for the Liberals, averaging about 0.42. For the Conservatives and NDP, the average difference is 0.65 to 0.70. Summary numbers understate the Liberal/Conservative contrast, however. The evidence most diagnostic of the twentieth century is from 1988. In that year, the Quebec/rest-of-Canada gap for the Liberals was 0.26; for the Conservatives, it was 0.82. On the national question, the Liberals' electoral coalition is compact and coherent. Sitting at opposite poles inside and outside Quebec does not require them to be untrue to themselves. The Conservatives in the 1980s, on the other hand, crafted an ends-against-the-middle coalition. As a collectivity, Conservative supporters were not so different from Liberal supporters. But the Conservative parts were sharply at odds with each other: as Johnston et al. (1992) put it, they were an uneasy amalgam of francophones and francophobes. The coalition was powerful but – as 1993 proved – fragile.

The Liberals' centrism on the national question yields an observable implication: certain sociological indicators should carry opposite signs between Quebec and the rest of Canada. Testing the implication is important for validation of the general proposition, but it also serves to indicate how far back in history the logic travels.

Survey Evidence on Sociology of the Vote, 1940-2011
Quebec is the one place in North America where francophones constitute a majority, and most other aspects of Quebec's distinctiveness flow from that fact. So at one level promoting the distinct interests of Quebec also promotes the interests of the language group. But not entirely. Inside Quebec resides a large non-francophone population. Indeed, this group is larger than the populations of most other provinces. At the same time, a comparably large fraction of Canada's francophone population lives outside Quebec. As a minority in the rest of Canada, this group needs a powerful federal government to vindicate its rights. It also needs the country to hang together, for without Quebec its position as a special national minority would be fatally weakened.

In relation to the Liberal Party, francophones inside and outside Quebec should react oppositely. Outside Quebec, the Liberals have been their champions, and francophones should be disproportionately likely to support them. Inside Quebec, the party has historically been strong, such that over the years most of the province's francophones have supported it as well. But as the party of official language minorities, the Liberals get even more support from Quebec's *non*-francophones. This should be especially true after 1960, when language politics came to the fore and this group was forced to see itself as a minority rather than the local beachhead of a continent-wide anglophone majority.

Broadly speaking, the story of the Conservative Party should be the opposite, although with election-specific variation in Quebec. Outside Quebec, both the Liberal Party and the Conservative Party have been continuously present and compete with each other on roughly similar terms.[5] Inside Quebec, however, the pattern must be somewhat election-specific. For long stretches, the Conservative Party was anti-Quebec and anti-French, so support for the party inside Quebec was basically non-existent. Occasionally, however, the party mounted a serious campaign in the province. When it did so, its obvious allies were located on the pro-Quebec side of the Liberals. The coalition of opposites visible in Figure 4.3 testifies to this. When they occur, support in Quebec for Conservatives would be greater among francophones than among non-francophones – in contrast to the case elsewhere.

Figure 4.4 presents the survey evidence. The data come from two sources: the Canadian Election Study, with readings for each election from 1965 to 2011 (except 1972), and the Canadian Institute of Public Opinion (CIPO), the official name of the Canadian Gallup Poll, which extends back to the 1940s. In most of its polls, Gallup asked about behaviour in the previous election, such that in some intervals respondents number in five figures.[6] Marginal distributions for retrospective reports resemble official returns reasonably closely and remain stable notwithstanding the widening temporal gap since the previous election. Thanks to this retrospection, I have been able to extend the survey series back to 1940.[7] The Canadian Gallup Poll disappeared in 2000, but its troubles were evident almost a decade earlier. Because of a serious decline in sample quality, especially in Quebec, I did not feel comfortable extending the series past the 1988 election. For the years that the CES and Gallup Poll overlap, the correspondence between the series is reassuring. The figure reports *differences* (as indicated by marginal impacts derived from underlying bivariate probit estimations) between French Canadians and others, inside and outside Quebec,[8] in support for the Liberal Party and Conservative Party in each election.

Without fail, francophones outside Quebec are pro-Liberal and anti-Conservative. At the peak, around 1980 in the Gallup series, the cleavage is 25-35 points. The 1980 value caps more than a decade of effective advocacy

FIGURE 4.4 Impact of language inside and outside Quebec, 1940-2011

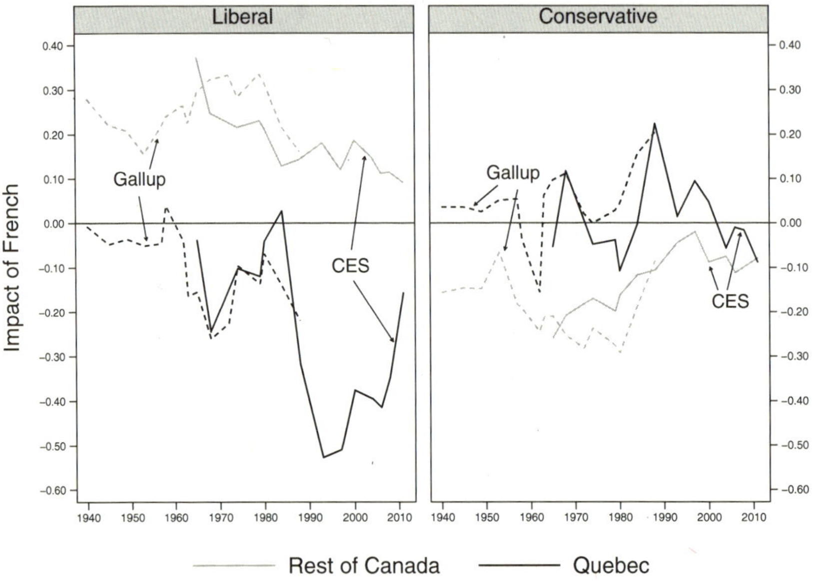

[Figure: Two panels (Liberal, Conservative) plotting Impact of French over time, 1940-2010, for Rest of Canada and Quebec, with Gallup and CES series labeled.]

Notes: This figure plots the difference in support between francophones and non-francophones for the Conservative and Liberal Parties inside and outside Quebec, election by election. Where the line lies above zero, francophones are more likely to support the party. Where the line lies below zero, they are less likely to support the party. These are marginal effects estimates derived from underlying bivariate probit estimations in Gallup and Canadian Election Studies survey data. Non-voters are excluded. Confidence intervals are suppressed for visual clarity.

of official language minority interests by Pierre Trudeau. The Quebec side is less consistent, but it never mimics the rest of Canada. Almost without fail, francophones inside Quebec are less supportive than others of the Liberal Party. The gap widened in the 1960s, reflecting the group-specific drawing power of the Ralliement Créditiste and, probably, the Conservatives' flirtation with a "two nations" plank in their 1968 platform (Black 1975, Chap. 7). Trudeau was especially hostile to this venture. The Liberals' recovery among Quebec francophones in the 1970s reflected the marginalization of Social Credit. The bottom fell out of the Liberals' Quebec francophone support in 1988 and 1993. The apparent recovery in the 2000s mostly reflected shrinkage of the Liberal share among non-francophones.

The Conservative pattern in Quebec is highly variable but, as with the Liberals, rarely the same as outside the province. Most years the

Conservative coefficient in Quebec is positive: although the Conservatives are usually weak in the province, the support that they do receive is disproportionately francophone. Their most negative moment was in 1962, the breakthrough year for the Créditistes. Their high point was 1988; not only did they carry the province overall, but also their share among francophones was 22 points higher than among non-francophones. This was the apex of the party's ends-against-the-middle strategy. The Conservatives swept francophone Quebec yet continued to repel francophones elsewhere. When the Conservatives retreated in Quebec in 1993, they still drew more francophone than non-francophone votes. Only in 2004, after the reverse takeover by Reform, did the Conservatives begin a streak of negative values.

Aggregate Evidence on Sociology of the Vote, 1878-2011

To go back further than 1940, I resort to data organized by parliamentary constituency. The strategy mirrors that for surveys, a bivariate estimation of impact from the percentage of French in a constituency on the vote share for an old party. Estimates appear in Figure 4.5. The figure divides the estimates into four periods: the late nineteenth century, before the massive peopling of western Canada; 1900-11 inclusive, elections that the Liberals entered as incumbents; 1917 and 1921, the two convulsive elections that initiated breakdown of the old party system; and elections after the Second World War. After 1921, census data ceased to be captured by riding and did not become available again until the 1953 election.[9] The estimate for a given period is based upon all contested constituencies in every election year.

The starting point is to validate the correspondence between aggregate and individual patterns. The results are reassuring since the aggregate postwar pattern in Figure 4.5 echoes the survey pattern in Figure 4.4.[10] Signs on the coefficients are opposed: for the Liberals, positive outside Quebec and negative inside it; for the Conservatives, the opposite pattern. But something changed between the 1920s and the 1940s. Things also changed between the nineteenth century and the twentieth century. I will consider the earlier transition in detail in Chapter 5, but suffice it to say here that 1900 marked a transition in the fundaments of choice. In the nineteenth century, the two parties struggled mightily to suppress linguistic

FIGURE 4.5 Impact of language inside and outside Quebec, 1878-2006

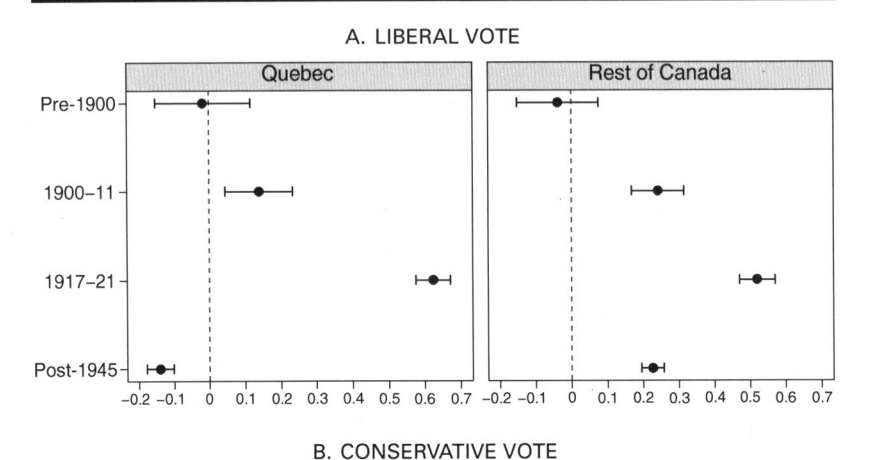

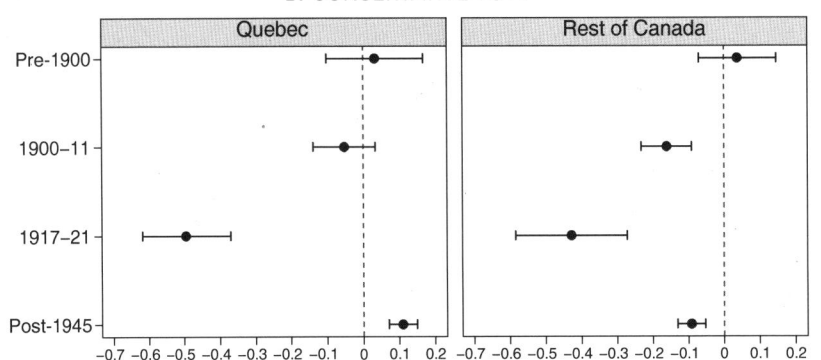

A. LIBERAL VOTE

B. CONSERVATIVE VOTE

Impact of % French in riding

Notes: This figure plots coefficients and confidence intervals for the impact of the percentage French in the riding on the percentage vote for each party, based on ecological regressions for certain periods. The coefficients can be interpreted as estimating the francophone/non-francophone difference in party support. Where the marker lies to the left of zero, francophones are less likely to support the party. Where the marker lies to the right of zero, they are more likely to support the party.

and religious tensions. On the language front, their success is indicated by the pre-1900 coefficients in Figure 4.5. Neither inside nor outside Quebec is the language coefficient strictly distinguishable from zero (although it is interesting that it sits slightly on the negative side for the Liberals and on the positive side for the Conservatives and does so in both regions).

It was in the twentieth century that identity politics divided the parties, and the issue (as I will argue at length in the next chapter) was the claim of empire in a period of great power tension and global war. The 1900-11 coefficients are now larger than the nineteenth-century ones and with the signs reversed. The Liberals are clearly the pro-French party and the Conservatives the anti-French one. The forces operative in the first decade of the century were magnified in 1917, with coefficients increasing manyfold, especially in Quebec. The 1917 election was fought on the issue of conscription for overseas service, and francophones strongly resisted the idea. Critically, in this period, the electoral meaning of being a francophone was similar both inside and outside Quebec.

That said, the early years of Liberal dominance – before the conscription crisis – exhibit fault lines that anticipate later fractures. Most importantly, coefficients are smaller inside Quebec than outside it, a difference of about 0.10. On the Conservative side, the confidence interval on the negative Quebec coefficient overlaps zero. This overlap reflects the fact that subsets of the Conservative coalition in Quebec were moving in opposite directions. The party continued to hold the allegiance of the anglophone business community in Montreal, even as the francophone business community went over to the Liberals (Neatby 1973). With the latter group subtracted, the Conservatives' francophone residual became increasingly dominated by the ultramontane Catholic and cultural nationalist elements, known as Castors. The coexistence of these opposites accounts for the weak coefficient in Figure 4.5.

By 1940, however, the structure in Quebec had clarified. The language coefficient in Quebec in most elections has the opposite sign of its non-Quebec counterpart. In absolute terms, Quebec coefficients are small, not surprising considering that the Conservative Party was at one of its low points in the early postwar years. The real point is not that French and English were so distinctively different in Quebec but that the simple and enduring pattern outside Quebec was no longer the same as the one inside Quebec.

Segmented Dynamics

In the peculiarly Canadian form of polarized pluralism, on the left-right dimension the Liberals are clearly centrist and flanked by the Conservatives on the right and the New Democrats on the left. On the national dimension, things are more complicated. The Liberals were the natural custodians of

80   *The Canadian Party System*

Figure 4.6   Vote shares: Quebec and the rest of Canada, 1878-2015

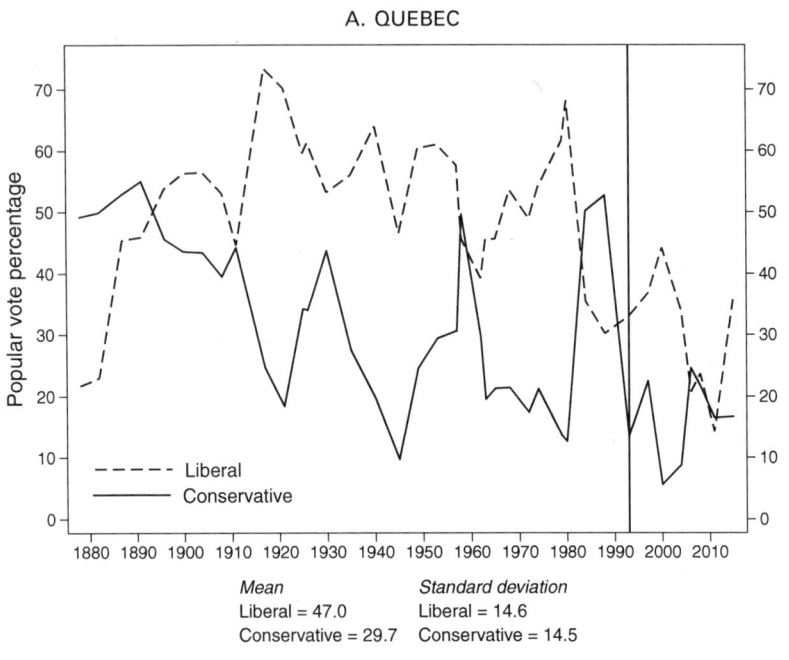

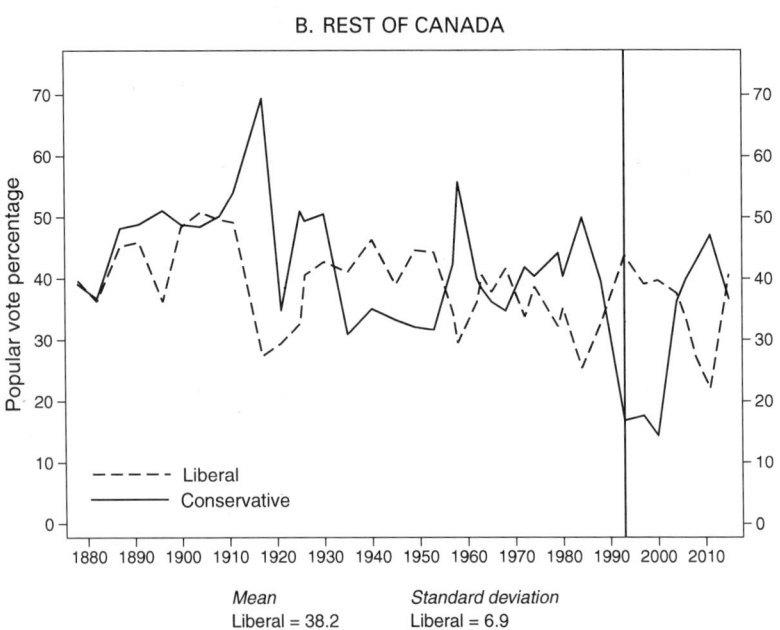

A. QUEBEC

Mean
Liberal = 47.0
Conservative = 29.7

Standard deviation
Liberal = 14.6
Conservative = 14.5

B. REST OF CANADA

Mean
Liberal = 38.2
Conservative = 40.9

Standard deviation
Liberal = 6.9
Conservative = 10.7

the centre, but the logic of the Westminster system combined with Quebec's distinctive historical pattern of consolidation and mobility tempted other parties to usurp that place. The usual usurper, the Conservative Party, was intermittently tempted to construct an ends-against-the-middle coalition. The result has been dynamics compartmentalized between Quebec and the rest of Canada and between Liberals and Conservatives. Figure 4.6 contrasts the time paths of old-party votes on each side of the Quebec/rest-of-Canada divide. It also presents summary statistics for each party and place.

Quebec

Quebec is a distinct electorate for both parties. In Quebec, the parties are alike in having seemingly erratic trajectories and almost indistinguishable standard deviations. These standard deviations in turn are much larger than the corresponding ones in the rest of Canada.[11] But the meaning and significance of Quebec volatility differ between the parties.

The Liberal Party

For the Liberals, the most important component was a long-term one, a two-decade rise and a sudden, permanent drop. Between 1878 and 1896, the party more than doubled its Quebec share of votes. Early vote gains followed the appearance of Liberal candidates: before 1887, only one seat in three featured an identifiable Liberal candidate; after 1887, the party climbed to universal nominations and to domination of the province. From 1896 to 1980, the Liberals averaged 56 percent of the Quebec vote. Their share exceeded 60 percent more often than it dropped below 50 percent. Between 1980 and 1984, their share dropped nearly in half, and in only one year since then – 2000 – did the party win more than 40 percent of the vote.

The Liberal vote also exhibits considerable short-term movement – a range greater than 30 points. For one thing, the party has lost occasionally. As for the rest of the flux in the Liberals' Quebec vote, the main logic is simple: when the party was led by a Quebec francophone, it benefited. The Liberals' choice of Wilfrid Laurier before the 1891 election was a brilliant example of "casting against type" in the Hollywood sense (Johnston et al.

1992, 169). Choosing him was a tangible signal of the party's seriousness in wooing Quebeckers. Since then the party has unfailingly alternated between French- and English-speaking leaders. Doing so has boosted its general credibility in Quebec but also affected its standing, leader by leader. Choosing a Quebecker boosted the share within the province by about 11 percent.[12] This obviously has a downside: when it is an anglophone's turn, the party can be at extreme risk.

The Conservative Party

For the Conservative Party between 1896 and 1980, the Quebec story was desperate. The party's average share was only 29 percent, and its median share was slightly smaller. The post-1896 marginalization of Conservatives in Quebec was not instant, however. Including 1896, the record reveals four stages of the decline, each stage with an "equilibrium" share about 10 points lower than the preceding one. The cumulative drop was dire, about 40 points. But startling punctuations also occurred.

The Rest of Canada

The Liberal Party

The Liberals never really recovered from the 1911 election. Their return to power in 1921 came with a weak base outside Quebec. From 1896 to 1980, the party's average vote share was 39 percent, nearly 20 points behind the average share inside Quebec. It was smaller than the Conservative share in all but eight elections. In the 1920s, the party was hostage to Quebec and in the 1970s nearly so.[13] Moreover, Liberal support followed a slow downward trajectory, a cumulative post-1921 loss of about seven points. At critical points, the Liberal share dropped suddenly and was then quickly reversed, with each reversal leaving the Liberals modestly worse off than before.

The Conservative Party

The Conservatives' vote share also dropped after the Great War and never fully recovered. Even so, the Conservatives remained stronger than the Liberals. For the Conservatives, the truly striking pattern was massive bidirectional short-term flux. The spectacular drop in 1921 was essentially reversed in 1925, and the recovery persisted until 1930. Then followed a 20-point drop, such that Conservative support from 1935 to the mid-1950s averaged just over 30 percent. The 1953-58 sequence raised the Conservative share dramatically, only to see support drop back below 40 percent in 1962-63. The later 1960s and the 1970s brought gradual growth, such that 1984 matched the pre-1911 level. Yet again support collapsed, this time to unprecedented lows. Only with the party's merger with the Alliance in 2003 did the Conservative share reclaim earlier heights.

Conservative Boom and Bust

Governmental succession in Canada in the twentieth century was not an orderly procession of ins and outs, of modest course corrections. Rather, the Liberals would govern for multiple decades – not always with robust majorities – and then suffer a devastating defeat. Put another way, the Conservatives did not win often, but they usually won big, more so as the century advanced. Yet victory was a poisoned chalice. Majorities tended to evaporate as quickly as they materialized, usually leaving the party worse off.

The pattern is stylized in Figure 4.7, which isolates key moments of Conservative surge and decline. Each moment requires identification of a *baseline*, a *peak* for the surge, and the moment of *decline*. I define each as follows:

- The baseline is usually the election before the initial Conservative majority victory. The exception is for the Diefenbaker surge of 1957-58. Outside Quebec, the 1957 election, which returned a Conservative minority government, was a shocking result and delivered almost half of the total 1953-58 surge. For Quebec, 1957 and 1953 were almost identical results, so nothing is lost by using the earlier year.
- The peak is always the first majority result.[14]
- The terminal elections are those that drove the Conservatives from power.

Every twentieth-century Conservative surge was accompanied by a breakthrough in Quebec. Each Quebec surge was larger than the preceding one by a factor of about two: the gain in 1911 was 5 points; 1930, 10 points;

FIGURE 4.7 Episodes of Conservative surge and decline: Quebec and the rest of Canada

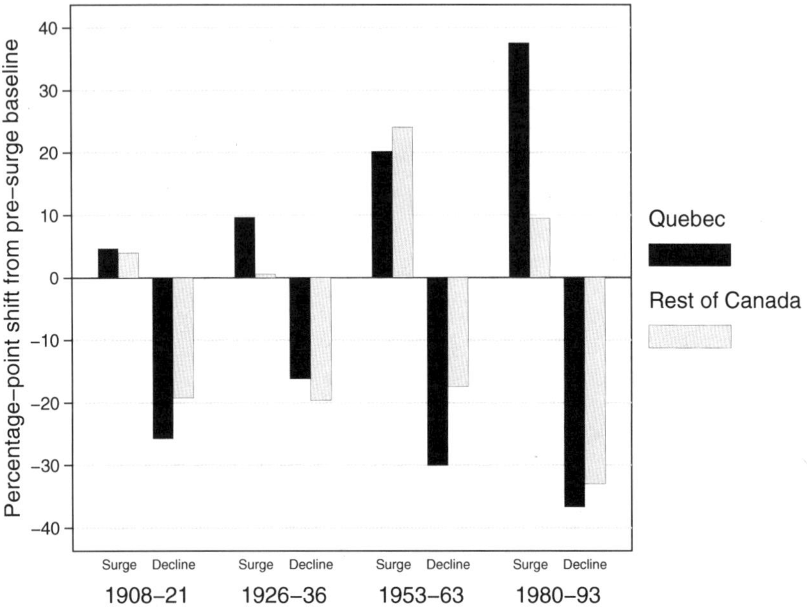

Notes: Black bars in this figure show the scale of Conservative gains relative to earlier elections, when the party wins a majority of seats. Grey bars show the scale of losses relative to the year in which the majority was won. Surges are 1908-11, 1926-30, 1953-58, and 1980-84. Declines are 1911-21, 1930-35, 1958-63, and 1984-93. For a detailed justification, see text.

1958, 20 points; and 1984, 38 points. In three of the four cases, the Conservatives also gained in the rest of Canada; the only exception was 1930. Only in 1958 did a gain outside Quebec rival that inside the province.

Declines were also generally bigger after the Second World War than before it and all along generally bigger in Quebec than in the rest of Canada. The exception was 1935, when the downturn was slightly bigger outside Quebec. The sharpest discrepancy was in the 1958-63 drop: in Quebec, this was the biggest drop to that date and the second largest overall; outside Quebec, the drop was the smallest of all. The 1921 and 1993 collapses were massive in both places. For this chapter, however, the critical questions are about Quebec. The patterns outside it require attention to new parties, so I postpone further exploration to later chapters.

Underlying Mechanisms

There are two parts to the Quebec story, and each has its own mechanism. For the Liberals, the question is how they sustained such one-sided coalitions for so many years. The answer is that they were *faute de mieux*, usually better than the alternatives but not much more. For the Conservatives, the question is how, in spite of extended episodes of hostility to Quebec or to French Canada, they were able to effect breakthroughs in Quebec – and sometimes stampedes. For the Liberals, the evidence rests on patterns of partisan commitment and turnout. For the Conservatives, I need to do process tracing to reconstruct the history of each surge.

Liberals: Demobilization and the Lack of Alternatives

The sheer scale of Conservative surges indicates the fragility of the Liberal position. Liberals rarely delivered everything that Quebeckers wanted. As the "party of Canada," they were also the chief advocate of the federal government's jurisdictional interests. And sometimes Liberal governments made compromises with unsympathetic forces to minimize the damage or do what seemed to be necessary, as with the late and reluctant adoption of conscription for overseas service in 1945. As the century progressed, the Liberal base inside Quebec became increasingly weighted toward the non-francophone minority in the province. This was philosophically consistent with their record of advocacy for the francophone minority in the rest of Canada. Before 1960, however, there was rarely any sense that their anglophone counterparts inside Quebec needed help. English-speaking Quebeckers controlled the high ground of the economy in an ethnic division of labour (Hechter 1987). Unilingual anglophones enjoyed incomes higher not just than unilingual francophones but also than bilingual persons (Lieberson 1970). In Montreal, control of the professions was so complete that francophones usually had to consult unilingual anglophones if they required specialist help (Lieberson 1970). With the increased emphasis on French in public life and the economy, the minority began its retreat. Its alliance with the Liberals put the party on a direct collision course with Quebec nationalism.

Politically, tectonic shifts began earlier in the century. Even before 1930, Liberals were vulnerable to attacks on the nationalist flank, by Henri Bourassa for instance. Emergence of the Union Nationale, in 1935-36, put

Quebec nationalism squarely on the table. Mostly, this was confined to the provincial arena, but twice before 1993 it broke through to federal politics. The short-lived Bloc Populaire confirmed that the Liberals faced pressure on both flanks in the 1945 conscription crisis. The Social Credit insurgency of 1962, although protean and confused, had clerico-nationalist elements (Pinard 1975). Then came the explicitly secessionist Bloc Québécois in 1993. Critically, for other parts of my argument, Quebec nationalism was sometimes expressed through the Conservative Party. This was so in 1911, when the Conservative surge in that province was an expression in part of nationalist resentment against the 1910 Naval Bill, and in 1984, when Brian Mulroney reached out to supporters of the yes side in the 1980 referendum. It was also part of the story of 1958.

If this interpretation is correct, then apparent Liberal success in Quebec reflects chronic *demobilization* of the province's most pro-Quebec elements. The Liberals win in Quebec because their potential nationalist opponents do not feel threatened or because no plausible alternative presents itself. For the Liberals to lose Quebec, nationalists need to be mobilized. This line of argument yields two observable implications. One avenue is for party identification in sample surveys; the other concerns the link between turnout and party shares.

Partisanship

To identify with a party is to express an ongoing preference. One might abandon the party from time to time, but this should be rare. Where short-term forces are weak or offsetting, the party should be the default choice. In Canada, these claims are contested, for example by Clarke et al. (1996). But no observer of the Canadian scene claims that party identification counts for nothing. In any case, the implication that I examine turns not on specifics of choice among parties but on willingness to express an identification-like choice in the first place. The key contingency is the presence or absence of an organized and enduring nationalist alternative on the federal election menu in Quebec. Before the emergence of the Bloc Québécois, no federal party was relevant for sovereignists. Thus, Quebec respondents as a group should be less likely than non-Quebec ones to claim party identification as such. Of course, many respondents in other

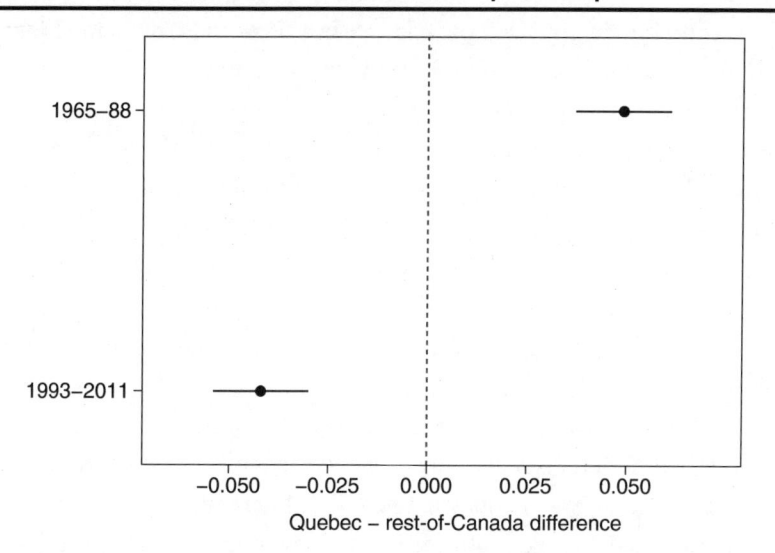

FIGURE 4.8 Quebec/rest-of-Canada differences in non-partisanship

[Figure: Dot plot showing Quebec – rest-of-Canada difference on x-axis (-0.050 to 0.050). 1965–88 period shows positive difference (~0.035). 1993–2011 period shows negative difference (~-0.030).]

Notes: This figure shows the differences between Quebec francophones and all respondents in the rest of Canada in the probability of claiming to identify with no party. Markers to the right of zero indicate that Quebec respondents are more likely to be non-partisan. Markers to the left of zero indicate that they are less likely to be non-partisan. Entries are differences of proportions with 95 percent confidence intervals. This figure is based on underlying probit estimations.

provinces have reasons not to identify with a federal party. But in no other province has there been an anti-federal force as powerful as Quebec nationalism. The Bloc Québécois provides the counterfactual for the earlier pattern. Once it appears, the difference between regions should shrink or even reverse. Expectations are confirmed in Figure 4.8. Entries are Quebec/ rest-of-Canada differences in non-partisan proportions and their associated confidence intervals.[15] The polarity of the difference reverses: before 1993, Quebeckers were significantly more likely than other Canadians to claim no party identification; after 1993, Quebeckers were less likely than other Canadians to claim no party identification: the Bloc Québécois filled the void. Relative to the rest of Canada, the positional shift for Quebec spans about 10 points. Before 1993, then, the Quebec electorate had a lot of partisan slack, so to speak. The shift in and after 1993 provides at least circumstantial evidence that the pattern before that year reflects the absence of a full-on nationalist alternative.[16]

Turnout

The second implication is in the relationship between turnout and Liberal vote share. If the Liberals are tolerated without enthusiasm in low-threat times but vulnerable to anti-Liberal mobilization at other times, then the turnout–Liberal vote relationship should be negative. On this argument, the Liberals benefit from relative indifference but remain vulnerable to mobilization on the nationalist flank. If, as Figure 4.8 suggests, indifference to all federal parties is more common in the absence of a Quebec nationalist alternative, then Quebec abstainers should be disproportionately nationalist. There might be critical moments – the 1917 conscription election, for example – in which the Liberals themselves control the relevant pole. Most of the time, however, the cultural-political temperature might be low enough that nationalists just stay home. But should the temperature rise – with the Liberals still clinging to the middle but now facing an alternative on the nationalist flank – citizens formerly demobilized would spill into the electorate.

To test this hypothesis, I estimate the Liberal-turnout relationship in four Canadian regions. In Quebec and Ontario, this requires a time series setup. In the multi-province regions of Atlantic Canada and western Canada, I use Generalized Least Squares (GLS) with fixed effects for each component province. Estimations are for the classic period of two-party contestation, before 1993. Estimation starts in 1908, the first election with nine provinces coast to coast and one of the earliest with de facto universal male suffrage. By stopping in 1988, I also ensure that the estimation is not overwhelmed by the most successful insurgent, the Bloc Québécois.[17] Evidence is presented in Figure 4.9.

The negative relationship appears everywhere, in fact, but most distinctively in Quebec. The only other region in which the relationship is unequivocally not zero is the West. But the Quebec coefficient is over twice as large as that in the West and three times as great as that in Ontario. The Quebec relationship is one to one: a percentage point gain in turnout is associated with a percentage point drop in the Liberal share.[18]

Conservatives: Mobilization of the Quebec Flank

The evidence for partisanship and turnout is for the psychological entailments of patterns in history: that is, for the end of a causal chain. Something

FIGURE 4.9 Turnout and the Liberal share, 1908-88

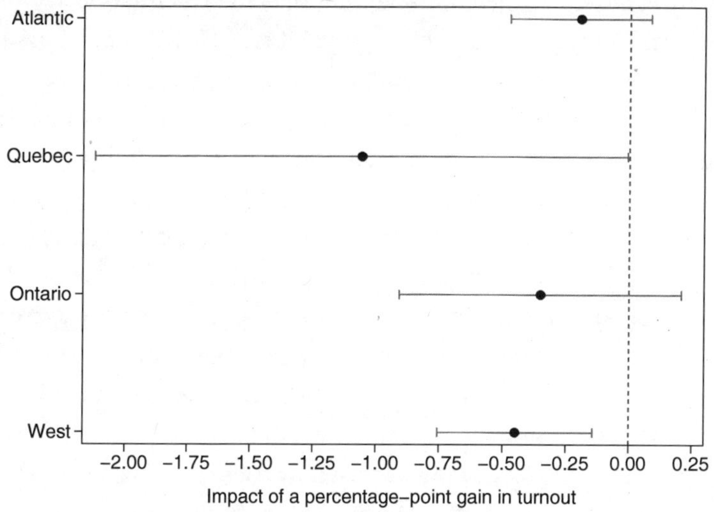

[Figure: dot-and-whisker plot showing impact of a percentage-point gain in turnout on Liberal vote share by region (Atlantic, Quebec, Ontario, West), with x-axis ranging from -2.00 to 0.25.]

Notes: This figure shows the negative impact of turnout on the Liberal vote, by region. Entries are coefficients for bivariate regression of Liberal share of federal votes on turnout, by region. Estimations in Atlantic and western Canada are GLS with fixed effects (Ns = 85 and 96 respectively), for Ontario and Quebec, Prais-Winsten, AR1 (Ns = 25).

must be said about the intermediate steps, the translation of nationalist tension into votes. Substantive accounts are thin on the ground. Political biographies permit some triangulation, but the ideal – almost never realized – is thematic comparison of multiple elections. What follows is a thin outline synthesized from both kinds of sources.

1911: Reciprocity and the Naval Bill

In 1911, the Conservative Party's position in Quebec was not as desperate as it later became, and operatives on the ground could still be found. Although the party's decline in the late nineteenth century might have been driven by reaction to the execution of Louis Riel and growing imperial sentiment in English Canada, the peeling away of support on the ground came disproportionately from its commercially minded wing, the so-called Bleus (Neatby 1973). Left behind were the Castors, clericalists allied with powerful Ultramontane forces in the Quebec church. For Castors, the Liberals, still harbouring an anti-clerical Rouge element, were simply unacceptable.

The 1911 election created a moment for nationalist mobilization with the Conservatives as the coordination pole. The chief nationalist of the period was Henri Bourassa, a breakaway Liberal. He led opposition to the Laurier government's bill to found a naval service. British pressure was mounting for Canadian assistance in the naval arms race. By analogy to certain colonies and other dominions, one idea was that Canada should pay for one or more dreadnoughts and possibly contemplate contributions of personnel. Laurier responded with a small Canadian naval service. Unsurprisingly, this did not satisfy imperialists. This group was even more exercised about the government's conclusion of a reciprocity agreement with the United States, seen as the thin edge of the wedge for dissolution of the British Empire. This point of view overlapped that of the business community, which saw a long-term threat to the protective tariff. Once it became clear that Bourassa was successfully energizing anti-Liberal sentiment with the Naval Bill, the Montreal community poured money into nationalist candidacies (Rumilly 1953, 75). Focusing on the Naval Bill was critical since not all nationalists were reflexively anti-American. The large Franco-American diaspora exerted a southward gravitational pull, and reciprocity might be styled as facilitating closer ties with that community, not least to defend it against Irish Americans (Rumilly 1953, Chap. 20). Reciprocity might even have been perceived as a ploy to divide their vote, as Ernest Guimont, candidate for Saint-Hyacinthe, put it: "On amène la question de la réciprocité et l'on tente d'en faire la seule question à considérer. Eh bien! Le piège ne prendra pas!" (cited in Jones 1980, 105). The result, of course, was a devil's bargain: the Conservative victory entailed an aggressively imperialist prewar naval policy and, most likely, a more forward policy in the Great War than a Laurier government would have contemplated.

1930: Butter Not Guns

The Conservative position in Quebec was weaker in the 1920s than in 1911. According to Figure 4.6, the party bounced back from the depths of 1917 and 1921, but it was still some 10 points below the level of the early 1900s. But the Liberal position in the rest of Canada was also weak, and, for Quebec to bring the Conservatives to a Canada-wide majority, not much was required. Cohen (1965, 60 and Table 7) hints that Quebec elites saw evidence of Liberal senescence, basically as Liberal provincial governments fell by the wayside in the late 1920s, so a bandwagon psychology set in. The economy was the main catalyst, however. The Great Depression did not pass Quebec by, and the Conservatives attacked the increase in imperial preference, which threatened to flood the market with New Zealand butter: "Le beurre de la Nouvelle-Zélande joue un plus grande rôle que la conscription aux élections canadiennes de 1930" (Rumilly 1953, 722).[19] Tellingly, of the 15 rural seats won by the Conservatives, 13 were in the predominantly dairy-producing St. Lawrence valley (Cohen 1965, 119n8). More generally, the party's growth built out organically from its Montreal base. Of the 24 new Conservative MPs, eight had British surnames. Three with French names benefited from splits in the Liberal vote. Of the Liberals' 51 winners, in contrast, only 4 had British surnames. Of ridings that had the same names as in 1921, those won by Conservatives in 1930 contained on average 8 percent fewer francophones than the province-wide median.

1958: Revenge for 1939

The sweep of 1958 required more active intervention by nationalist forces. Unquestionably, efforts by the Union Nationale provincial machine were important. Black (1977, 404-5) sees 1958 as Maurice Duplessis's revenge on the Liberals for his defeat in 1939, which resulted from the unprecedented intensity of the federal intervention in that year's provincial election. No election in the intervening decades presented circumstances as favourable to nationalists as 1958. In that year, the Liberals replaced a Quebec francophone with Lester Pearson, a unilingual anglophone from Ontario. Pearson had no Quebec lieutenant of real stature, and the Conservatives already controlled the federal government.[20] Duplessis turned up the heat: "Duplessis himself selected the candidates, authorized the contributions, and oversaw the effort. They would concentrate on 50 ridings of the province's 75, the others being conceded to the Liberals. Duplessis authorized $15,000 for each of the constituencies, the extraordinary sum of $750,000 in total" (Black 1958, 406).

Duplessis's commitment probably amplified things, but there also seems to have been an independent groundswell. The Conservatives started building riding-level muscle on their own account right after the 1957 election. Under Charles-Guy Paré, 21 associations were organized in Montreal before Parliament was dissolved. Although some nomination meetings showed signs of manipulation, genuine enthusiasm was evident and abetted by above-the-table resource commitments from the federal party (Beck 1968, 320-21). Finally, there might have been a bandwagon, an echo of 1930. Polls signalled a sweep outside Quebec,[21] and Conservative ads emphasized it. Most notable was an ad that put it all on the line: beside the image of an axe cleaving the country at the Quebec-Ontario border were the words "on prédit un triomphe éclatant à Diefenbaker. N'isolons pas Québec."[22] But Quebec was isolated anyway: "Le succès conservateur est encore plus prononcé dans les provinces anglaises. Diefenbaker pourrait gouverner sans le moindre concours de Québec. Cela se sent, et Duplessis en est presque déçu" (Rumilly 1973, 633). Not only did Diefenbaker not need Quebec, he did not much care about it. The result was a 1962-63 drop in Quebec bigger even than in 1917.

1984: "Honour and Enthusiasm"

The flight from Diefenbaker makes the recovery of 1984 all the more remarkable, at least on the bare numbers. In at least three ways, 1984 repeated features of 1958, and this time each feature was enhanced.

First, the Liberal Party replaced a Quebec francophone with an English speaker from outside the province.[23] This compounded the effect of the Conservatives' 1983 choice of a leader from Quebec, a move that was the mirror image of the Liberals' choice a century before of Laurier. Although Brian Mulroney is not a native French speaker, he is fluently bilingual and a graduate of Laval University Law School, and he was already a public figure in the province.

Second, the theatre of federal-provincial relations made the Liberal Party even more the opponent of provincial autonomy than it had been in the 1950s. Although the federal government did not bestride the fiscal landscape as formidably as it had in the 1950s, conflict over energy and, most importantly, the battle for entrenchment of the Canadian Charter of Rights and Freedoms raised the stakes.[24] The case could be made that, for the first time since the nineteenth century, the Conservatives were intrinsically the more acceptable party to Quebeckers. Getting to that point required passage through language politics that reflected the complexity of the policy domain. Twice in his first months as an MP the Liberals tried to trap Mulroney into opposing a resolution reaffirming French language rights in Manitoba, and each time he escaped by rallying his party to the resolution. Given the historical animus against French of many of his MPs, this required real deftness (Sawatsky 1991, 506 ff.). Mulroney was helped by Turner, who early in his 1984 leadership campaign expressed public doubts about the very line of Liberal policy that Mulroney had earlier affirmed. Although Turner back-pedalled, Mulroney could now proclaim in Quebec media that the parties' historical positions had reversed (518-19). In the 1984 campaign, however, he forecast his later alignment with the majoritarian view that animates Quebec's own language policy. In his nomination speech in Sept-Îles, Mulroney emphasized Quebec's exclusion from the constitutional deal of 1981 and expressed his determination to bring Quebec inside the constitutional tent "with honour and enthusiasm" (cited on 545). Among his candidates were supporters of the yes side in the 1980 referendum.

Third, the intensification of commercial polling meant that information conveyed over nine months in 1957-58 could be transmitted in 1984 in a matter of days. By the end of July, with five weeks remaining in the campaign, it was already clear that the Conservatives were going to win handsomely. With a week and a half to go, all indications were for a landslide (Frizzell and Westell 1985, 82, Table 3).

Taken all together, these conditions arguably more than offset the fact that in other ways the Parti Québécois, the new Quebec nationalist party, was a much less natural partner for the federal Conservatives than the Union Nationale had been.

If 1984 ended Liberal claims to hegemonic domination of Quebec, it also set the stage for blowing up the system. If it seemed to come apart so definitively in 1993, why did it take so long? Early on, nationalists were blocked by two things: the self-inflicted inaccessibility of the Conservative Party and the time required for robustly nationalist alternatives to define themselves. The Conservatives' position is well known and occupies many pages in this book.

On the nationalist side, the picture could be stylized as one in which actors struggled to find both a defining issue and a coordination point. Henri Bourassa, notwithstanding his eloquence, did not always see a clear path: "Quebec sought more than understanding and sensitivity from its leaders. The province cried for direction, specific direction, a responsibility Bourassa chose to neglect" (Cohen 1965, 32). The nation to which he was devoted was French Canada, which arguably included New England, not to mention New Brunswick, Ontario, and the Prairies. Concern for francophones outside Quebec combined with his intense clericalism blocked him from aligning with people such as Lionel Groulx, for whom "race" arguably trumped religion and whose focus was the ancestral Laurentian basin. Indeed, Bourassa's corporatist engagement with Catholic social doctrine as it was elaborated by Pius XI and ultimately expressed in *Quadragesimo Anno* made Bourassa a regular interlocutor with J.S. Woodsworth of the CCF.

By mid-century, the key figure was Maurice Duplessis, founder of the Union Nationale and a major thorn in the side of successive federal governments. Even he argued for an alternative reading of the 1867 constitutional bargain, not for breaking it. He was willing to work with Conservatives outside the province even before John Diefenbaker's accession to leadership. While Duplessis was fighting conscription, his hand-picked successor and co-founder of the party, Paul Sauvé, was fighting overseas. Sauvé ended the war as commanding officer of Les Fusiliers Mont-Royal.

The shift of nationalism toward secession made cooperation with outside forces harder but not impossible. All along, versions of sovereignty that included continuing close association with the rest of Canada trumped bolder options (Cloutier, Guay, and Latouche 1992, Graphiques 5, 6, and 7; Pinard 1997a). For ambivalent voters in Quebec, the critical factor is recognition or respect. They care deeply about what the rest of Canada thinks or feels about them (Mendelsohn 2003). This makes intentions "febrile," to quote Cloutier et al. (1992, 150 ff.) and variably subject to external forces (Pinard 1997b).

Whatever the objective, there was also the question of which political vehicle, if any, could express it. Bourassa's peregrinations are a case in point. So is 1945, when feeling ran high in the aftermath of the second conscription crisis. Coordination failure among potential nationalist candidates was massive: 190 insurgents contested 65 seats (Cohen 1965, 80, Table 7). A useful contrast is Réal Caouette and the Ralliement Créditiste in 1962. Caouette was ambiguous on constitutional matters but emotionally nationalist and not much concerned with anglophone opinion. His appeal was also populist and socially conservative (Pinard 1966, 1975). The critical thing, however, is that – unlike 1945 – there was no surplus of insurgent candidates. The modal 1962 contest featured three candidates only: a Liberal, a Conservative, and a Créditiste.[25] Social Credit subsequently declined, especially after Pierre Trudeau succeeded to the Liberal leadership. Consistent with the pattern in Figure 4.9, Liberal growth and Social Credit decline tracked closely a decline in turnout. But if Social Credit in Quebec was ultimately a misfire, it was diagnostic of further insurgent potential, ultimately realized by the Bloc Québécois.

Regional Coalitions

Figures 4.6 and 4.7 mask both the complexity of the rest of Canada and the full asymmetry between the Liberal Party and the Conservative Party. To extract these patterns, further stylization is helpful. To this end, Figure 4.10 shows how cyclical sectionalism maps onto the history of Conservative success and failure. It does so by portraying the geographic basis of party coalitions in three parliamentary situations. The horizontal axis arrays the provinces from west to east. The vertical axis gives average values of the federal vote within each province. The portrayal is for all years from 1908 to 1988. The nuance washed over by such draconian pooling is not central to my argument. Besides, surprisingly little nuance is lost: the picture remains remarkably stable over many temporal groupings.

To underscore just how remarkable the Conservative pattern is, consider first the unremarkable Liberal one. The popular basis of Liberal governments has always been highly differentiated geographically. The east-west gradient steepened in the second half of the twentieth century, but changes since 1921 have been modest. When the Liberals retreated from power, differences sharpened only at the margin. When they lost their majority but held on as a minority government, losses were all outside Quebec, and Quebec sustained them in power. Only when they suffered a reverse in Quebec did they actually lose power. Although this pattern might not indicate healthy, broad support for a purportedly national government, its dynamics were at least moderate and contained.

The Conservative Party, in contrast, constantly flirted with the edge. When the party was in opposition, its support outside Quebec followed an east-west gradient altogether like that for the Liberals. The gradient was

96 *The Canadian Party System*

FIGURE 4.10   Geographic breadth of Liberal and Conservative electoral coalitions, 1908-88

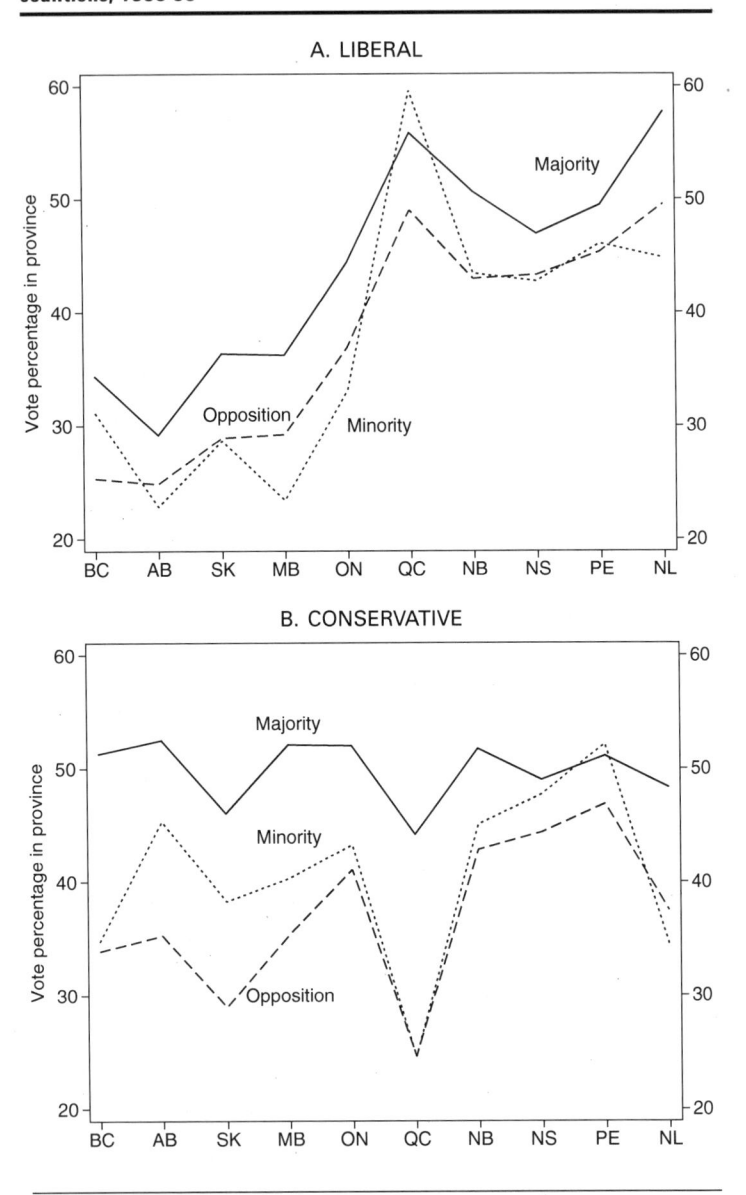

Note: This figure shows the average vote percentage for each party in each province from 1908 to 1988 inclusive, according to whether the party formed a majority or a minority government, or lost the election.

shallowest from 1963 to 1984, although even in those years Conservative support was lower in Manitoba, Saskatchewan, and British Columbia than in Atlantic Canada. Conservative support seems to be more uniform when the party forms minority governments. This reflects the fact that all Conservative minorities postdate 1957, the year that began the party's rebirth in the West. Indeed, Conservative strength in the West seems to be a necessary condition for the party even to approach power. In taking the next step, to majority status, the party's further gains were proportional to former weakness. Gains in the West did not suffice to give Conservatives parliamentary majorities, however. For that, capturing Quebec was the necessary final step. As Figure 4.10 shows, this transition was always stunning. The figures portray losses as well as gains, however, and the flip side of stunning growth is sudden collapse.

Polarized Pluralism and Electoral Dynamics

To recapitulate, the Canadian party system exhibits polarized pluralism on two dimensions. Since 1970, the Liberal Party has stood alone at the centre of the classic left-right spectrum. On the national question, the Liberals have also been the natural party of the middle. The centre has been contested occasionally, and before 1993 the extreme pro-Quebec side of the spectrum was usually dormant. These locational facts are critical to the divergent dynamics of each old party and to the peculiar place of Canada among SMD-based party systems.

The Ebb and Flow of Sectionalism

Weakness in Quebec was critical to the Conservatives' absence from power. Overcoming that weakness, as the party did once per generation, was always helpful – and occasionally critical – to giving the party a parliamentary majority. Quebec was not the whole story, however, for the West was also crucial. Although the Conservative Party never dominated the region before 1917, its pre-1917 western base was not minuscule. After 1917, however, the party hit bottom, a situation reaffirmed in 1935. Although it was not impressively strong anywhere, it was almost non-existent in the West (outside parts of British Columbia), such that overall the Conservative Party of these decades provided the numerically weakest opposition in the history of Canada or of any other Westminster system. Restoration in the West was critical to making it a strong opposition party after 1960. The persistence of this pattern into the 1980s meant that when the Conservatives detached almost all of Quebec from the Liberals, the resultant majority was large, more durable than any previous Conservative one since 1896, and authentically representative of the whole country.

This is a story of overcoming sectionalism yet of drowning in it. The ebb and flow of Conservative fortunes explain one of the most striking elements of Figure 2.6. Recall that the time path for the extra-local component in the total fractionalization of the party system is punctuated. Each time a Conservative majority government materializes, the extra-local component retreats to its pre-1921 value. Put another way, all of the sectionalism of the decades since the Great War washes away, and the system seems to be fully integrated. The largest single part of this integration is incorporation of Quebec into the winning coalition. Sometimes Quebec is the pivot for that coalition. Another part is the Conservative recovery in the West. As mentioned, without the West, the Conservatives would not be poised to govern.

The Electoral System and the Party System

These two elements are difficult to square with the account of the electoral system and the party system in Cairns (1968). Although his account of centrifugal incentives in the electoral system is most explicit for small parties, there is more than a hint that it is meant to apply to large ones as well. This puts him at odds with, among others, Lipset (1960) and Calvo and Rodden (2015) and, for the Canadian case in particular, Johnston and Ballantyne (1977) and Bakvis and Macpherson (1995). Unquestionably, as Chapter 2 reaffirms, the electoral system over-rewards small parties content with sectionalist appeals, even as it punishes small parties that represent broadly based interests. But if a party seeks to govern, it cannot simply remain bottled up in one place. Conservative processions to power are absolutely on point.

Yet, in the twentieth century, Conservative electoral coalitions repeatedly blew up, with consequences that persist into the new millennium. The size of each explosion was a product of the very inclusiveness that returned the Conservatives to power in the first place. So, although the electoral system might not be a culprit in creating these dynamics, it is an accessory to the crime.

Envoi

If the explosion of 1993 ended the old system, it did not end the long Liberal twentieth century. The party governed for an additional dozen years. The east-west gradient in Liberal support bequeathed by the First World War remained largely intact. But two features distinguish the current period. One is the party's position in Quebec: not desperate but not hegemonic. Quebec was not the key to the party's success in 1993 or to its loss of power in 2006. For the first time in Canadian history, the pivot was Ontario.

No less significant was division on the right. Figure 4.11B shows it by implication. Crudely speaking, the 1990s also restored the east-west gradient in Conservative support. Quebec was no longer the gash in the middle, as it was in earlier decades. But otherwise the gap between extremes was much the same as in earlier periods of opposition, about 20 points. The overall level was at a historical low, however, and the party was on the sidelines. Only some of the vacuum was filled by the Liberals. The rest was occupied by third parties, most significantly Reform/Alliance.

The transition to the twenty-first century was a mixture of old and new. The Liberal Party embodied the old. Figure 4.11A shows that, Quebec aside, the 1920s are still with us: the Liberals fell from power simply by retreating a little further everywhere, with only a tiny increase in the overall east-west gradient. In contrast, according to Figure 4.11B, the new Conservative Party presented a face never seen before: a major party with the opposite gradient, west-east. Although John Diefenbaker bequeathed a Conservative Party stronger in the West than it had been for decades, it still had serious strength in Atlantic Canada. And his western legacy was not as strong as the current one. Only when the Conservatives returned Canada-wide landslides did they gain western support on the scale that has regularly accrued in the twenty-first century to a party that, although successful, could hardly be called a juggernaut.

FIGURE 4.11 Geographic breadth of Liberal and Conservative electoral coalitions, post-1993

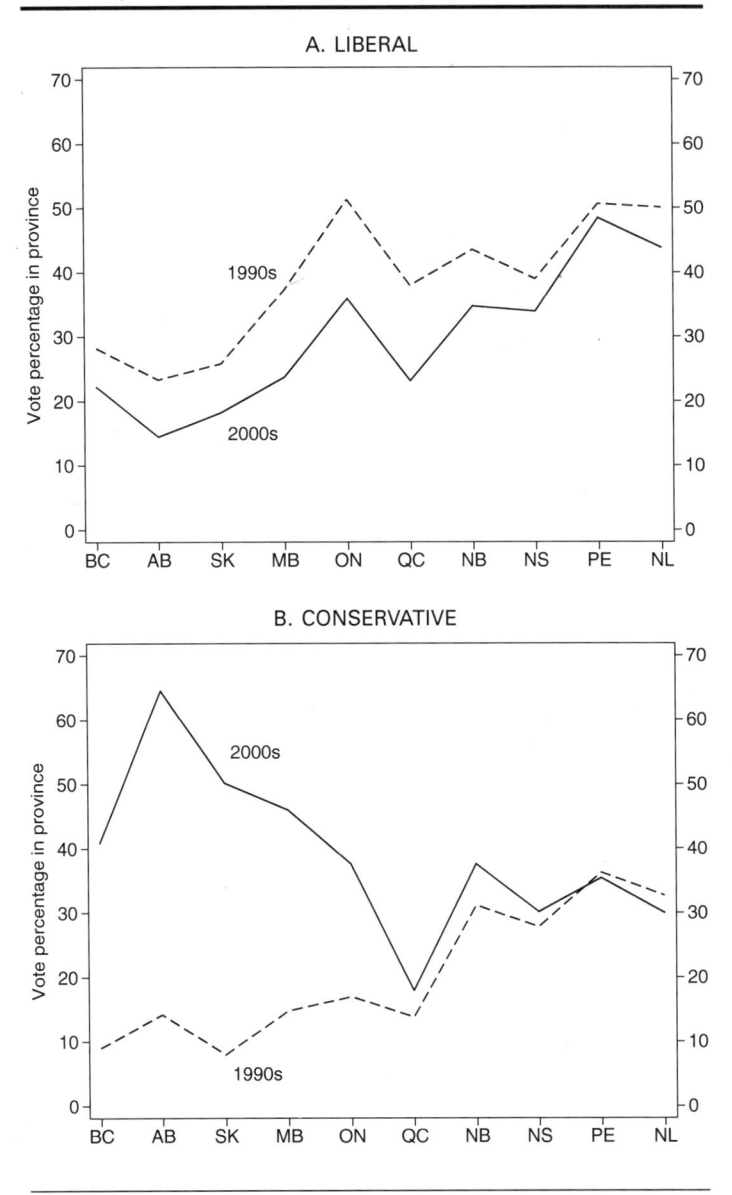

A. LIBERAL

B. CONSERVATIVE

Note: This figure shows the average vote percentage for each party in each province for the elections of 1993–2000 inclusive ("1990s") and 2004–11 inclusive ("2000s").

5

Catholics and Others

For I dipt into the future, far as human eye could see,
Saw the Vision of the world, and all the wonder that would be;
Saw the heavens fill with commerce, argosies of magic sails,
Pilots of the purple twilight, dropping down with costly bales;
Heard the heavens fill with shouting, and there rain'd a ghastly dew
From the nations' airy navies grappling in the central blue;
Far along the world-wide whisper of the south-wind rushing warm,
With the standards of the peoples plunging thro' the thunder-storm;
Till the war-drum throbb'd no longer, and the battle-flags were furl'd
In the Parliament of man, the Federation of the world.

– ALFRED TENNYSON, *LOCKSLEY HALL*

Ab amicis nostris, libera nos Dne.

– ALBERT LACOMBE, OMI[1]

For years, Quebeckers and francophones had an army of fellow travellers. These were Catholics, and apart from shared religious orientation few had any tie to French Canada. Indeed, the Catholic community itself was occasionally riven by ethnic conflict. Even so, for much of the twentieth century, the best single predictor of major-party support in Canadian elections was religious denomination, with Catholics much more likely than non-Catholics to support the Liberals and shun the Conservatives.

But the effect was as elusive in its origins as in its persistence. And from 1965 on, as hinted in Table 2.2, it died a lingering death.

This chapter argues that the essential source of the relationship had little to do with faith, morals, ecclesiology, or institutional interest. Nor was it the effect of a simple composite of the distinctive ethnic or immigrant/native makeup of Protestant and Catholic followings. In fact, as ethnically specific considerations were primed late in the twentieth century, the heterogeneous Catholic coalition unravelled. Yet, I argue, the religious effect *was* ethnic, just not in a compositional sense – not a summing up of Catholicism's distinctive ethnicities. Rather, the effect was contextual. The critical mediator was the ethnic conception of the Canadian nationality, as distinct from the ethnicity of its individual members. For most of the twentieth century, the focus of identity politics was Canada's connection to Britain, primarily for its foreign policy implications but also for the symbolism of nationality. Catholicism as an overarching identity was commonly at odds with the British connection. One implication is that as the connection diminished in importance, so did the religious cleavage. Concomitantly, as the focus of identity politics shifted to official language policy and multiculturalism, the system's ethnic bases followed suit.

Much of the case involves an interweaving of narrative and evidence, each driving the other at critical points. The case illustrates an admission about the study of identity politics that Fearon (1999, 14) was forced to make: "What determines the pattern of coordination in the first place may be idiosyncratic factors particular to the time, place and interplay of political strategies. So understanding how a pattern of political coalitions and identities came about may often be a matter of historical narrative rather than the finding of general factors."

I begin with geography and demography to show that the Catholic community was both useful electorally and heterogeneous demographically. Then I interleave historical and quantitative passages. One feature of the quantitative exhibits is the appearance and disappearance of effects in historical time. The other is the unpacking of the denominational effect as it waxes and wanes. Doing so shows when the denominational effect is the essential one – and when it is not. The account of the unravelling of the effect is not just interesting in its own right but also critical, I submit, to interpreting the effect at its peak.

Geography and Demography

For francophones inside and outside Quebec, Catholics are a politically useful ally. Their distribution across the country is strategically helpful and has grown only more so. They span more than just a narrow ethnic core and have become more heterogeneous. This heterogeneity is not just a matter of adding new ethnic groups – although that has certainly happened. No less important is net absorption into the Catholic fold of people with backgrounds that do not fit the stereotypes.

Catholics have always been a big battalion, usually constituting more than 40 percent of the population. In the early years, francophones were the community's centre of gravity, averaging about 70 percent of the Catholic total. Concomitantly, a majority of Catholics lived in Quebec. Even so, a significant fraction of the community lived in other regions, and francophones were usually only a small fraction of the non-Quebec total. As the overall Catholic share advanced, both Quebeckers and francophones retreated in proportion. By the turn of the millennium, francophones made up only half of the Catholic total even as the Catholic share of the total population exceeded 45 percent.

How this maps onto electoral districts is shown in Figure 5.1, which presents box plots for distributions of Catholics and francophones inside and outside Quebec.[2] On the Quebec side, the picture is one of linguistic and, even more, religious homogeneity. Until recently, the median percentage Catholic share of a Quebec riding was about 95 percent. One riding in four contained essentially no Protestants.

Outside Quebec, the story is one of growth and diversification. From the start to the end of the twentieth century, the median percentage of Catholics doubled – from 14 percent to 29 percent. By the millennium, one riding in four was more than 40 percent Catholic. Accompanying these shifts was a regional transformation (not shown in Figure 5.1) that brought Ontario to the fore. Before the Second World War, Ontario was the least Catholic region. But between 1941 and 1971, the Ontario Catholic share surged 11 percent, half again more growth than over the preceding century.[3]

Now roughly one Ontarian in three is a Catholic. All along, the most Catholic region outside Quebec has been Atlantic Canada, but this region has lost electoral clout.[4] Before 1941, the West was more Catholic (and more French) than Ontario, but thereafter the Catholic community lost ground, relatively speaking.

As Figure 5.1 hints, the Catholic community was ethnically complex even in the nineteenth century. The francophone community in Quebec included substantial numbers of people with Scottish or Irish surnames, a pattern that persists and whose diversity has been augmented by postwar immigration. In the combined 1965-2011 CES, for instance, about 30 percent of Quebec francophones claim a primary ancestral origin other than in France. Catholics also constitute nearly half of the province's non-francophone population. A token of this is that the median value for the percentage of French in Quebec ridings in Figure 5.1 is consistently four points smaller than the median value for the percentage of Catholics.

Outside Quebec, the picture, not surprisingly, is even more complex. Figure 5.1 indicates that the median percentage of French has always been low, 2-3 percent. This is 12-14 points smaller than the Catholic median. Even in the nineteenth century, the overwhelming majority of Catholics were not French. To be sure, there have always been ridings with francophone centres of gravity, with outside values that trail up to 100 percent. Still, the big numbers then – as now – come from other ethnolinguistic sources.

Irish descent was important, especially in the nineteenth century. As early as the 1820s, Ireland was the largest single source of migrants to British North America. People of Irish origin outnumbered those with English ancestry as late as the 1881 census. This preponderance was such that, given the median values in Figure 5.1, people of Irish descent must have dominated the Catholic populations in most of the country. This would have been so even though Scottish Canadians were prominent in the Catholic hierarchy in the nineteenth century and early twentieth century and are still important in the Catholic populations of Atlantic Canada and eastern Ontario.

As time passed, the Catholic community was augmented in three ways: differential birth rates, migration from abroad, and interfaith marriages. The differential birth rate enabled Quebec, despite its relatively low rate of

FIGURE 5.1 Geography of religion and language: Rest of Canada and Quebec

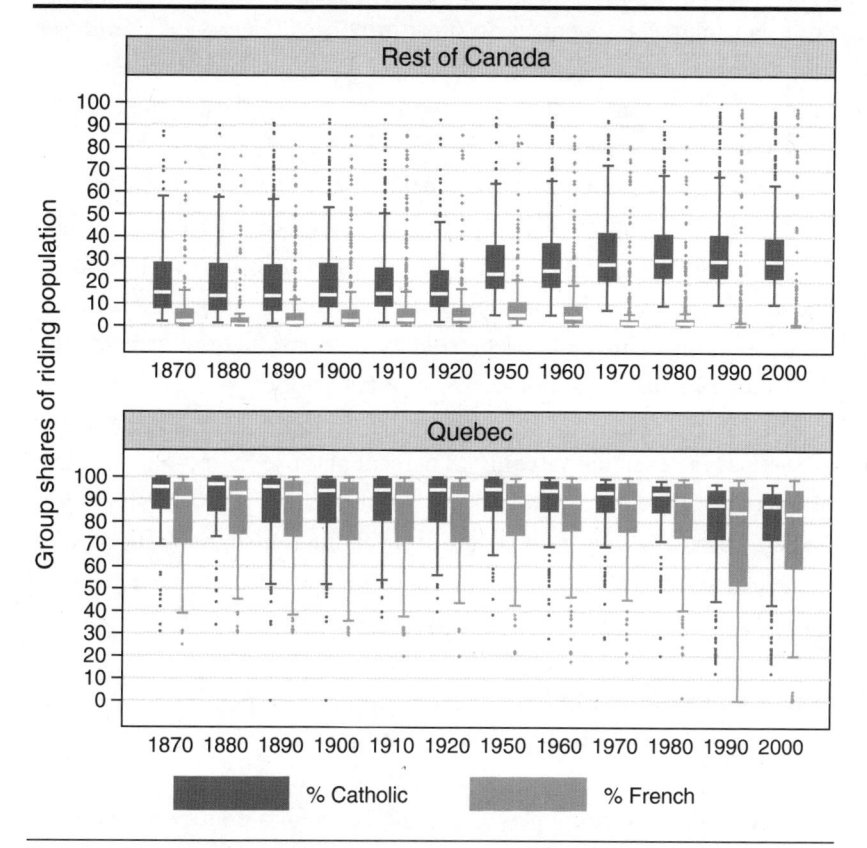

[Box plot figure showing percentage Catholic and percentage French in ridings by decade, for Rest of Canada (top panel) and Quebec (bottom panel), from 1870 to 2000.]

Notes: Data show percentage Catholic and percentage French in the riding, by decade. Riding level data are unavailable for the 1930s and 1940s. The figure is a box plot (see note on box plots in Figure 2.8).

in-migration, to keep pace with the rest of Canada. This was probably also a major factor in Catholic growth in Atlantic Canada and must be part of the twentieth-century story in Ontario. Migration played a different role early than it did late. Early-twentieth-century immigrants were less Catholic than the native born, and this partly offset the birth-rate differential. After 1945, however, immigration was critical to the dramatic augmentation of Catholic numbers. This reflected flows from predominantly Catholic southern Europe but also from northern European countries with large Catholic minorities, notably the Netherlands and Germany, and from eastern Europe. Finally, Catholic numbers were augmented by interfaith marriages. Over the twentieth century, the rate of Catholic-Protestant marriages went up in most provinces (Heer 1962). Children from these marriages were more likely to follow the Catholic parent than the non-Catholic one, such that, even in a closed population, the Catholic share would have grown.

So the Catholic community outside Quebec was ethnically diverse and has become only more so. According to the combined 1965-2011 CES, people of French or southern European ancestry are predominantly Catholic, and the non-Catholics in those groups are mostly post-religious. These two groups make up about 30 percent of the non-Quebec Catholic total. A further 19 percent claim eastern or northern European origin. For all that, the largest single source, roughly one-third of the total, is the British Isles. This is so even though only 18 percent of those claiming British Isles origins are Catholic. Of Catholics claiming British Isles ancestry, about half are Irish, and they in turn constitute about one-sixth of all Catholics outside Quebec.[5] This leaves 35 percent unaccounted for, so by implication many Catholics do not have stereotypical Catholic ancestry, a testament to the importance of interfaith marriages.

This, then, is a community with potentially great political power. Outside Quebec, it now constitutes about one-third of the electorate. If most Catholics can be mobilized for one party, then they can, together with Quebec, control electoral play. The temptation for a political party is obvious. The cohesiveness of the Catholic community is not a given, however, and has become more problematic as the community has grown. Its ethnic complexity represents a potential for internal rifts. An early example is Ontario's Regulation 17 (issued in 1912), which limited the use of French in schools. The measure was a concession to Irish Catholics in a power struggle within the province's separate school system (Oliver 1977; Prang 1960). Catholics outside Quebec did not necessarily identify their interests with those inside Quebec, even if the voice from Quebec was the church's hierarchy. These divisions became especially important after 1965.

Finally, reading ancestry totals from the census and assigning all members of a given group to one or the other side of the Catholic/Protestant divide misstates the issue. Irish Canadians are a case in point: 60 percent or so of Irish Canadians are Protestant, most descended from families that immigrated before the famine in the late 1840s. Although Catholics predominate among the Irish in Quebec and Newfoundland and constitute narrow majorities in Nova Scotia and Prince Edward Island (Houston and Smyth 1990, 227, Fig. 7.10), the Irish populations of these provinces are massively outnumbered by descendants of the Protestant Irish immigration to Upper Canada. Although the famine induced a massive surge in Catholic immigration, which peaked in 1847 (ibid., 22, Fig. 2.3; see also the discussion at 200), Catholics were more likely than Protestants to move on to the United States, such that some of the surge was effaced (73). For most of the period covered by this book, an Irish Protestant identity was, to say the least, vivid. It is not so much that Irishness is a common way of being Catholic as that Catholicism is one of two competing ways of being Irish. The same division applies to other ancestry groups with serious Catholic and non-Catholic subsets and to Canadians who claim no distinctive ancestry but are cleaved by religious identity.

The interleaving of narrative and evidence begins in the next section. Evidence and analysis come in two forms. Emergence of the religious cleavage in the early twentieth century is captured and interpreted with evidence from ecological regression, plots of the relationship between the religious composition of a riding and the Liberal share of the vote. Evidence of the continuation of the cleavage into the decades after the Second World War and its disappearance comes from sample surveys, the same surveys as in Chapter 4. With survey data, I can show when the religious cleavage subsumes differences among component ethnicities on each side of the cleavage and when it does not. The riding-level and survey analyses are similar in spirit – each involves time plots of regression coefficients – but necessarily different in detail. I return to the details when I get to the data.

Religion, Identity, and the Party System

Historically, Catholics and non-Catholics differed on a wide range of public questions that transcended mere group interest: observance of the Sabbath; temperance and the regulation of alcohol; and marriage to a deceased wife's sister. Added in the twentieth century were differences over social doctrine, divorce, and abortion. But these issues never mapped easily onto the party system. Before 1900, religion (and language) divided parties internally but did not polarize them against each other. Siegfried (1966, 113-14) captured the parties' usual *modus operandi* with precision:

Aware of the sharpness of certain rivalries, they know that if these are let loose without any counter-balance, the unity of the Dominion may be endangered. That is why they persistently apply themselves to prevent the formation of homogeneous parties, divided according to race, religion or class – a French party, for instance, or a Catholic party, or a Labour party. The clarity of political life suffers from this, but perhaps the existence of the federation can be preserved only at this price.

Federal party leaders strove to contain the passions since each electoral coalition embodied conflicting forces. Provincial politicians and provincially minded federal ones rubbed at sectarian sores, as did extra-parliamentary groups. The Conservative coalition included people happy to support sectarian schools, whether out of principle or out of convenience. But the party was also the only one that Orangemen, who opposed any concessions to Catholics or the French, could realistically support. The Liberal coalition included people who resisted overt Britishness in Canadian life and were anti-imperial. But some in the ranks wanted to substitute for Britishness a home-grown monoculturalism, and the party included legatees of Whiggism, who wished to keep church and state separate.

The divisions are illustrated by five intense and protracted controversies. Two involved ethnic minority rights, which had denominational differences as by-products: the execution of Louis Riel and language rights in the North-West Territories. Three were directly on religious questions and pitted Protestants against Catholics: the disposition of Jesuits' estates in Quebec, the Manitoba schools controversy, and North-West schools.[6]

The execution of Riel in 1885 was a factor in the decade-long realignment of federal forces in Quebec, captured in Figure 4.6. The parties had to survive a motion in the House of Commons expressing regret for the execution. The intention was to force a split along language lines inside the government, which partly succeeded. It also forced out the two leading figures in the Liberal opposition, Edward Blake and Wilfrid Laurier. Both supported the motion, but not all of their followers did. In the short run, the Liberals were made to seem more divided than the Conservatives. But the future was foreshadowed by the fact that a significant fraction of

English-speaking Liberal MPs also supported the motion; no English-speaking Conservative did.[7]

Similarly diagnostic of the brokerage challenge was debate on an 1890 bill to amend the North-West Territories Act. The intention of the bill was to increase the territories' control of their finances, but it died on the order paper when D'Alton McCarthy used the occasion to attempt to abolish French as an official language in the region. As Thomas (1978, 185) put it, McCarthy's initiative

> touched off one of the most notable debates in Canadian parliamentary history, as well as taxing to the utmost Macdonald's ingenuity in maintaining unity among the divergent elements in his party. The issue was equally embarrassing to Laurier, for anything which appeared to be a concession to McCarthy's position would threaten his still tenuous hold on French-Canadian opinion, while to appear as the supporter of French-Canadian nationalism would damage his position in Ontario and other English-speaking areas.[8]

Honoré Mercier, the electoral beneficiary of the Riel crisis, took up the task of settling the issue of Jesuits' estates. Dissolution of the Society of Jesus in 1773 left large areas of land and many institutions in Quebec in legal limbo. Protestant disapproval, divisions within the Quebec church, and revival of the Jesuit order made settlement of estates a political nightmare. Mercier grasped the nettle and, with the mediation of Leo XIII, produced a settlement. That the Catholic Church – the Society of Jesus in particular – was given anything, and that the Pope played a role in the division of estates, inflamed Protestant opinion, especially in Ontario. Proclamation of the act in July 1888, the bicentennial of the Battle of the Boyne, was a symbolic affront. Although the settlement stirred deep passions in both Quebec and Ontario, neither Macdonald nor Laurier sought to exploit them even covertly.[9]

Much the same was true with the Manitoba schools controversy. In Manitoba, the parties shared an interest in abridging Catholic rights, if from different motives. Manitoba Conservatives did not have a complex coalition to manage, and Manitoba Liberals exemplified their party's Whig legacy (Crunican 1974; Hall 1981, Chap. 5). In national politics, in contrast, the parties converged in trying to mute division. The minority schooling rights in question supposedly enjoyed federal protection under the Manitoba Act of 1870, in that Ottawa was empowered to pass a remedial bill. The Conservative government, which included Hector-Louis Langevin, leader of the Castors (see Chapter 4), and Clarke Wallace, Grand Master of the Orange Lodge of Canada, came close to passing such a bill but fell short at the end. The Liberals opposed the bill but without proposing a concrete alternative. On each side, manoeuvring was subtle and delicate since each party risked being disembowelled from within; ultimately, something like this happened to the Conservatives. This chapter's epigraph from Father Lacombe captures the agony of the situation. Once in power, the Liberals dealt with the issue, assisted by the apostolic delegate, Cardinal Merry del Val. The terms, set in the Laurier-Greenway Agreement, were largely dictated by Manitoba.

The denominational basis of schooling in the North-West Territories episodically intruded into the federal arena in the 1870s, 1880s, and 1890s as the Catholic position alternately strengthened and weakened (Hall 1985; Lupul 1974). Matters came to a head with the Alberta and Saskatchewan autonomy bills in 1905, and this episode is arguably an exception that proves the rule. The Laurier government inserted separate school guarantees over the objections of politicians in the region. Superficially, then, the party system seems to have divided in 1905 right at the denominational boundary. Although it could be styled as a departure from the earlier urge to compromise, close inspection suggests that debate was not over Catholics' access to denominational schools as such but over which denominational privileges to protect given the recent history of flux. Laurier seems clearly to have been moved by the plight of the Catholic minority yet also to have hoped that clarity would prevent a recurrence of the Manitoba crisis. The move induced fissures within the Liberal Party, and they re-emerged six years later. The point stands: domestic contestation over specifically religious questions was toxic for parties, and they strove mightily to quell it.

The parties' success in keeping the lid on is evident in Figure 5.2, which plots time paths for religious division from 1878 to 1921. Because recovery of the early history is possible only with riding-level data, the figure plots

FIGURE 5.2 Emergence of the Catholic-Liberal alignment, 1878-1921

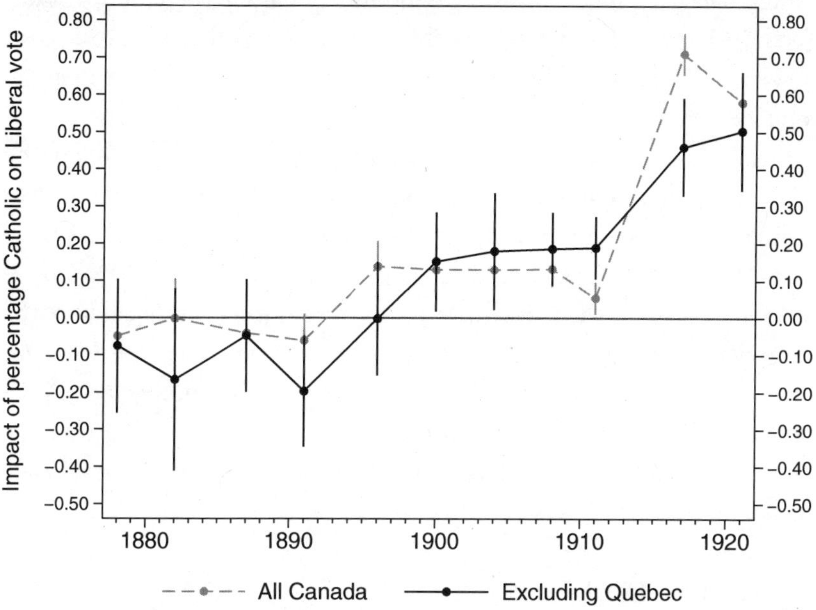

Notes: This figure plots coefficients and confidence intervals for the impact of the percentage Catholic in the riding on the percentage vote for the Liberal party, based on ecological regressions for each election. The coefficients can be interpreted as estimating the Catholic/non-Catholic difference in Liberal support. Where the marker lies above zero, Catholics are more likely than others to vote Liberal. Where the marker lies below zero, they are less likely to vote Liberal.

ecological regression coefficients for the relationship between the district percentage Catholic and the district percentage Liberal and their accompanying confidence intervals. This is an estimation of the Catholic/non-Catholic difference in party share, thus indexing the cleavage itself. Two plots appear, one for all ridings and one for ridings outside Quebec. Parallel estimations offer a check against the possibility that the overall result is simply driven by a Quebec/rest-of-Canada contrast more about language than about religion. It might be more straightforward just to present separate Quebec and non-Quebec estimations, but variation within Quebec in the percentage of Catholics is very small, as Figure 5.1 revealed. Instead, the critical comparison is between the all-Canada plot, which includes Quebec, and the non-Quebec plot, which obviously does not. If the all-Canada coefficient in Figure 5.2 is further away from zero than the non-Quebec one, then the result is being driven by the presence of Quebec in the dataset, and a specifically denominational interpretation is problematic. If the all-Canada coefficient is closer to zero, then the presence of Quebec ridings in that estimate obscures a truly denominational cleavage outside Quebec.

Notwithstanding the bitterness of religious conflict before 1900, the electoral situation in those years is basically indeterminate. Only in 1891 are coefficients significantly different from zero and even then only for the non-Quebec plot. And, in striking contrast to later history, pre-1900 Liberal coefficients tend to be negative. We simply cannot see the divisions of the twentieth century in the early data. The pattern for the rest of the twentieth century does poke through in its first decade, and it is tempting to attribute this to denominational strife, in particular to conflict in 1905 over the Alberta and Saskatchewan autonomy bills. But the decisive shift had already taken place.

Canada in the British Empire

That shift, I argue, reflects activation of Canada's British connection. The turn of the twentieth century saw the connection transformed as Canada reached toward an international personality. The web of implications for party politics was tangled, for rival nationalist visions competed with each other and with sensibilities not so much imperial as colonial. Each party's coalition was ripe for disruption.

The Conservative coalition combined outright colonials with people who saw Canada as being called to a larger role in an empire of self-governing nations. On the colonial side was the Orange Lodge: "Orangeism and Irishmen were especially suited to British North America, for a society was being created there in the image of a British colony, not an independent separate state. Britain's first colony had been Ireland, and out of that tradition of colonial connection Orangeism had emerged" (Houston and Smyth 1980, 185). From this view, Canada was not so much a nation among British nations as British, full stop. This Canada should go to war as a matter of simple loyalty. Most of the time, Conservative colonialists were willing handmaidens of their imperialist co-partisans. However, on the Orange Lodge's original constitutive issue, the Britishness of Ireland, Orangemen could be positively seditious. Canadian Lodges were the largest single overseas source of financial support for the 1914 Ulster resistance, which at its peak involved mutiny in the Curragh barracks and gun-running to private auxiliaries (McLaughlin 2013).

On the imperial side were actors who saw themselves as muscular nationalists. They wanted Canada to act on the global stage, including militarily, and they believed that the appropriate way to do so was as part of an empire conceived as a league of self-governing nations. Extreme elements advocated imperial federation, but most were more pragmatic (Berger 1970). The epigraph from Tennyson, which anticipated the reality of twentieth-century war and looked toward "the Parliament of man, the Federation of the world," eerily foreshadowed this sensibility. For a Conservative such as Robert Borden, the alliance logic of the British Empire led naturally to the League of Nations, which he helped to found. The internationalism of imperialists also surfaced in the Ethiopian crisis of 1935. At the same time, the self-governing side of imperial membership was not meaningless. Canada's interest was not automatically identified with the larger imperial one. A telling example is Arthur Meighen's pragmatism at the 1921 Imperial Conference, when Meighen refused to subsume Canada's interests to a larger imperial one. He particularly objected to Britain's desire (shared by Australia and New Zealand) to renew the Anglo-Japanese Alliance: he did not want Canada to become the Belgium of a war between the United States and a Britain allied with Japan (Graham 1963).

The Liberals also harboured colonialist and nationalist tendencies, and this coalition seems intrinsically to have been more tenuous. The colonial variant saw Canada as a diverse place where different proto-national groups coexisted uneasily. This Canada had overarching interests within North America, and advocacy of those interests could be helped by the British connection (Penlington 1965). But the country was too incoherent internally for national questions to be forced any more than absolutely necessary. This Canada could give sympathetic consideration to aid for the "mother country," especially in its hour of peril, but on terms that would make it less than a full co-belligerent (Cook 1961). Conscription for overseas service would be a dividing line.

Liberal nationalists wanted to loosen the imperial bond, but many also wanted Canada to act on the international stage. This made them potential allies to imperialists as long as the goals in sight were universal. They were potential supporters of conscription but not of gestures that smacked of a blank cheque for imperial adventurism. An example of the latter was the 1922 British call for support in the Chanak Incident. The British proposed to land forces in Turkey to resist Kemalist attacks on Greek communities in Anatolia. Australia and New Zealand heeded the call; Canada, now governed by Mackenzie King and the Liberals, did not. This is commonly seen as the last attempt to create a common imperial foreign policy, with Canada putting the knife in (Graham 1963). Prominent Liberal operatives and supporters who exemplified this sensibility included Clifford Sifton (Hall 1985), earlier a protagonist in the school controversies in both Manitoba and the North-West, and J.W. Dafoe, long-time editor of the *Winnipeg Free Press* (Cook 1963). Both supported conscription but opposed the Chanak venture.

What has all this to do with religion? In this period, an active external policy could be pursued only as part of the British Empire. Foreign policy advocacy reflected the degree to which Canada was idealized as British. To be a British place was to be a Protestant one, at least in certain minds. For instance, the title of the first chapter in Colley's (1992) account of the creation of Britons is "Protestants." Although the rest of her narrative involves a broadening of the conception of Britishness, resistance to such broadening always occurred. Even if arguments for a forward role in war were not couched in ethnic terms, the resonance of such arguments in the electorate was still likely to be mediated by prior religious commitments. The point is no better illustrated than by Irish Canadians, who, as mentioned, were historically cleaved by religion. On the Catholic side before 1914, the leadership was generally supportive of Home Rule, defined at the time as Irish self-government within the United Kingdom, and at odds with Irish Protestants. At that point, Home Rule was still being articulated within an imperial framework, and many Irish Catholics heeded a voluntaristic call to arms at the beginning of the war, as happened in Ireland itself. But as Ireland came apart, so did the Canadian Irish community (McLaughlin 2013).[10] This division within ethnic communities found parallels elsewhere on the denominational landscape.

Reinforcing this external relations pattern, indeed overlapping it, were divisions over civic life within the country. The turn of the century witnessed an efflorescence of officially non-sectarian civil society. On the imperial side, some of these impulses were specifically linked to martial endeavour. The Canadian Red Cross is a case in point. It first emerged during the North-West Rebellion of 1885 to fill a gap in the militia establishment's feeble medical services. It was reinvigorated for similar reasons by the South African War and then languished once that conflict ended, only to be invigorated again by the Great War. The early leadership of the Red Cross was virulently anti-French and anti-Catholic since these groups seemed to be deaf to the call to service (Glassford 2007). And on this view the supreme call to service is war. Some saw the South African War in this light (Miller 1993), and the argument was even more prominent in the Great War. This was not a solely imperialist preoccupation. The same period saw the growth of the social gospel, mainly in churches and colleges founded by Methodists and Presbyterians, denominations whose adherents leaned toward the Liberal Party (Laponce 1969). The social gospel was critical to the creation of welfare institutions, which in turn prefigured the welfare state. Some see this as a response to a theological crisis, the substitution of social action for biblical literalism (Allen 1973; Cook 1985). Others see it as a reinvigoration of a distinctively evangelical engagement with the world (Gauvreau 1991). In any case, as the Great War advanced, social gospel reasoning led to calls for the conscription (Bliss 1968). Foreshadowing later developments, the call increasingly was to conscript not just manpower but also wealth.

All of these tendencies accompanied a desire to transcend the older divisions – to urge abandonment of ethnoreligious passions. But sectarianism can intrude even when the intent is to overcome it. The call to transcendence typically comes from only one side of the sectarian divide. In the Great War, the experience of the trenches undermined the force of arguments for division among Protestants and fed sentiment for church union (Gauvreau 1991, Chap. 7). If union was possible among Protestants, then why not more generally? The period witnessed growing dissatisfaction with both old parties, with their concern to manage sectarian division rather than transcend it, and with their corrupt, patronage-ridden ways (English 1977). As with church union, so with Parliament and the idealization of a union government. If only one side wants to transcend the divide, however, the other side will see the call for transcendence as inherently partial, a call not for understanding but for marginalization.

Even before 1900, the party system seemed to be poised to fracture, and perhaps it was only a matter of time before cracks would appear. Figure 5.2 shows that the first critical election was 1900, when Canada made its first appearance on the global stage: "It was the South African war that produced [the heroic] phase of the imperial movement in Canada ... When it was a question of taking part in the war, by reason of the principles of imperialism, the Ottawa government found behind it a country violently divided" (Siegfried 1966, 201). Laurier resisted Canadian involvement, but his hand was forced. His reluctance, combined with war fever in urban English Canada, provoked intense attack and counterattack (Beck 1968, 94-95; Miller 1993, Chap. 2). Although war fever died down, and the war itself eventually ended, its political legacy endured. Civil-military issues simmered into the new century, including the dismissal of two aggressively imperialist militia commanders (Penlington 1965). Even more divisive, as Chapter 4 showed, was the founding of the navy in 1910.

For the all-Canada plot in Figure 5.2, the significant upward shift occurs in 1896, with no further trend for two decades. Comparison with the non-Quebec plot indicates that the 1896 shift is specific to Quebec. The question was Manitoba schools. Notwithstanding the signal from the Catholic hierarchy that the Conservatives were more trustworthy, voters in Quebec completed the move to the party led by Quebecker Wilfrid Laurier (Neatby 1973). Outside Quebec, 1900 marks the reversal – exactly as Siegfried (1966) argued. Although there is a hint that 1896 sits on a trend of which 1900 is but the culmination, the simplest interpretation is that the key break is in 1900. The next three elections continued the pattern. If there was fallout from the 1905 autonomy bill controversy, it is imperceptible; the new pattern was already in place. The 1911 election shows a dip in the all-Canada relationship, but again this is an artifact: as we know from Chapter 4, Quebec as a whole shifted away from the Liberals in that year. All along the cleavage appears sharper when Quebec ridings are excluded.

All of this was a rehearsal for the Great War. In Parliament, support for a belligerent role in the war was nearly unanimous. Not unanimous was support for conscription. For Borden, conscription was necessary for Canada "to play a full part in the War and the peace that would follow." He saw "a creditable war effort by Canada to constitute a charter of full nationhood" and was already using the word *commonwealth* (Nicholson 2015, 343). For the Liberals, the issue revealed the fault lines between colonials and nationalists. For nationalists, the war was Canada's war; the country was allied with Britain not because of sentiment but because Canadian and British principles were the same. For Laurier, however, the war was Britain's war. This did not preclude direct Canadian military involvement, but it was solely on the basis of sentiment. Canada was not itself a principal belligerent and thus was not obliged to commit its all. Conscription and the union government were suspect as the leading edge of imperial centralization (Cook 1961).

In the immediate background was the 1916 Easter Rebellion in Dublin. The onset of the war temporarily quelled sectarian passion, but the unravelling of Irish unity as the war progressed found parallels in Canada, and the debate in Canada over conscription paralleled that in Ireland. Divisions within the Canadian community continued after the war as the Irish independence drama unfolded (McLaughlin 2013). The story was similar in Australia.

On this basis, the 1917 election split Liberal ranks, to the short-term benefit of the other side. The choice in 1917, strictly speaking, was between "government" and "opposition," where present and former Liberals were often opposing candidates. The Borden government stacked the electoral deck with the Wartime Elections Act, which disenfranchised part of the Liberals' base in the West (Graham 1960, 105). Survival required western and some Ontario Liberal MPs to cross the floor. In 1921, the breach remained, since many Liberals lost to the coalition now appeared as Progressives.

Fracturing of the Liberal elite is fully mirrored in the vote. In Figure 5.2, the "all-Canada" coefficient on the riding percentage Catholic soars to 0.70. In homogeneously Catholic places, 90 percent of the vote went to the Liberals. At the other end of the continuum, where virtually no Catholics were to be found, the party received about 20 percent. This gap between the "all-Canada" and the "excluding Quebec" coefficients indicates that the apparent religious difference is exaggerated. Some of what appears to be generally denominational is also regional and linguistic. Even so, the rise in the cleavage outside Quebec is striking: it jumps from 0.19 to 0.46. What this represents, however, is not so much rallying by Catholics as flight by non-Catholics. In predominantly Catholic places, the Liberals held their ground. The problem in this era, as Figure 5.1 showed, was that outside Quebec such places were rare. In 1911 and before, the Liberals attracted 40 percent support even in wholly Protestant places. In 1917, this share dropped to about 20 percent. In 1921, things only got worse. This is the sociology beneath the Liberal Party's overall weakness in the 1920s. Quebec was able to put the party back in power in 1921 but only barely.

The resumption of peace did not end the old division between Liberals and Conservatives, although subtle modifications were forced on both parties by new global realities. The massive commitment of troops by the overseas dominions moved all the players closer to substantive equality. Against this backdrop, the 1921 election heralded a revolution in Canadian foreign policy, for the Liberal Party now seized the initiative (Stacey 1981).[11] Although Mackenzie King was a nineteenth-century liberal, much like Laurier, staving off further military involvement required his government to act on the international stage. The threat of such involvement was made all the more credible by the sheer scale of troop commitments in 1914-18. Without that precedent, it would have been hard to make sense of the Chanak Incident, mentioned earlier, over which the parties divided. A major fruit of the revolution was the official transformation of empire into commonwealth, at least for the old settler states. The parties were careful in stating their positions but nonetheless were clearly distinct. In the 1926 Imperial Conference that set the stage for full sovereignty, King played a pivotal role.[12] When the report of the committee formed to implement the 1926 conference (the report that led to the Statute of Westminster) was tabled, C.H. Cahan spoke for the Conservatives: "I am persuaded that it is in the best interests of Canada that the British commonwealth of nations, which is commonly known as the British Empire, should remain a subsisting political unit, and not merely a free association of independent states" (119).[13] The Conservatives also opposed the 1927 decision to open a full embassy in Washington (91).

Throughout the interwar period, but especially as the Second World War approached, party divisions remained relevant. Liberal anxiety about being drawn into a global war was evident even in the early 1920s: Mackenzie King resisted Canada's election to the League of Nations Council since it might force great-power responsibilities on the country (65).[14] The Ethiopian crisis of 1935 revealed both parties' tendencies. The crisis began while Conservative R.B. Bennett was still prime minister, and his response illustrates the potential for imperial sentiment to shade into general support for collective security. Canada's representatives to the league, Howard Ferguson and W.A. Riddell, supported sanctions against Italy. King opposed sanctions and forced an about-face in mid-crisis (179).[15] In the following years, he became more involved in British foreign policy, a seemingly ironic turn. In fact, his objective never wavered. Because he knew that, in the event of war, Canada would enter it, he did all he could to postpone it. One route to this objective was to argue for foreign policy coordination, the better to slow down preparations for war (Eayrs 1965, 54).

King's orchestration of the run-up to war was exquisite. On March 30, 1939, King, the Protestant anglophone, committed his government to voluntary enlistment, and Lapointe, the Catholic francophone, declared the inevitability of Canada's involvement (Stacey 1981, 243). For the actual declaration of war, the task of setting out the reasons was also given to Lapointe (262). The Conservatives, for their part, argued for a more aggressive approach all along and for the formation of a coalition, implicitly questioning the legitimacy of the Liberal government in waging total war (Granatstein 1967). They went so far as to present themselves not as the "Conservative Party" but, confusingly, as the "National Government." The war itself re-energized conscription as a central issue, with the Conservatives strongly supporting the measure. This time it fell to the Liberals actually to implement conscription, but they did so without enthusiasm and only after many contortions (Granatstein and Hitsman 1977). The government lost cabinet ministers on both its pro- and its anti-conscription wings (Power 1966). The issue provoked a generals' revolt on the one hand (Roy 1977) and the appearance of the Bloc Populaire Canadien on the other.

Crypto-imperial questions lingered into the 1950s, with the Suez Crisis as a climax. Somewhat against the historical grain, Liberal governments embraced a robust internationalism and presided over the largest peacetime buildup of the armed forces in Canadian history. They sent armed forces to Korea and placed army units on NATO service inside the grandiloquently named British Army of the Rhine (Bothwell 2007). All of this postdated Mackenzie King's retirement, for his postwar impulses remained consistent with his earlier ones. And in both Korea and Europe, Canadian involvement was hesitant and limited (Stairs 1974). If King's retirement was one bookend for this internationalism, then Suez was the other. Hindsight identifies the crisis as a triumph of Canadian diplomacy, but opinion at the time was closely divided.[16] A Gallup Poll reported on November 12, 1956, indicated that more Canadians supported the Anglo-French invasion than opposed it (Hilliker and Donaghy 2005, 30-31).[17] If Suez was the climax, then the foreign policy of John Diefenbaker and Howard Green was the anti-climax. The new government set out to try to align Canada with Britain, only to find that the mother country was no longer interested (Robinson 1989). Perhaps it is fitting that Canada's last attempt to influence British foreign policy was to resist that country's attempt to join the European Union.

Although we do not know how wide the religious cleavage was from the 1920s to the 1940s, survey evidence in Figure 5.3 indicates that it was still wide in 1949 and remained so for many years. The logic of the figure is basically the same as in Figure 5.2, only here the data are from the sample surveys used in Chapter 4.[18] The plot reports marginal impacts derived from underlying bivariate probit estimations between Catholics and others in support for the Liberal Party, along with 95 percent confidence intervals. This is an Alford index de facto (see Chapter 2), the arithmetic gap between Catholics and others. The CES values for 1965 and 2006 are exactly those reported in Table 2.2. This setup facilitates unpacking the cleavage by deducting its regional, linguistic, and ethnic components to see how much intrinsically denominational impact remains. That is a task, however, for later in the chapter. For now, the basic point is clear: for decades, being a Catholic increased the probability of voting Liberal from 20 to 30 points. Evidently, the pattern established early in the twentieth century persisted into the postwar years.

FIGURE 5.3 The religious cleavage in the Liberal vote, 1949-2011

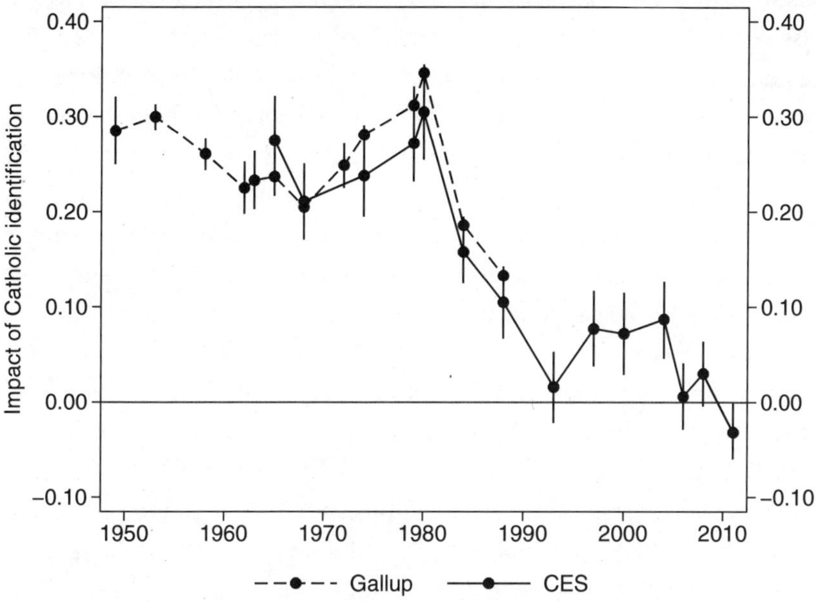

[Figure: Plot of "Impact of Catholic identification" from 1950 to 2010, showing Gallup (dashed) and CES (solid) series. Values start around 0.28-0.30 in the 1950s-1960s, peak near 0.35 around 1980, then decline sharply to near 0.00 by 1990s-2010s.]

Notes: This figure plots coefficients and confidence intervals for the impact of identifying as a Catholic on the likelihood of voting for the Liberal Party. The coefficients can be interpreted as estimating the Catholic/non-Catholic cleavage in Liberal support. Where the marker lies above zero, Catholics are more likely than others to vote Liberal. Where the marker lies below zero, they are less likely to vote Liberal. Entries are estimated marginal effects, with associated 95 percent confidence intervals derived from underlying bivariate probit estimations, in all-Canada Gallup and Canadian Election Studies samples. Dependent and independent variables are dichotomous, whether or not the respondent voted Liberal in the last election and whether or not the respondent is a Catholic. Non-voters and ineligibles are excluded.

The British Empire in Canada

If by 1960 the British connection was no longer vital to Canada's international personality, the decade that followed featured struggle over internal manifestations of the connection. The high point was 1964-65 with the debate over the Maple Leaf flag and its electoral aftermath. As with Suez, hindsight is a fallible guide to contemporary opinion. Opinion was evenly divided, and the balance of party advantage shifted back and forth. Although the Conservative Party lost the debate, the 1965 election brought the party a small net gain in the popular vote (Johnson 2005).[19] Britishness was also a primary driver of resistance to unification of the armed forces accomplished in the late 1960s (Champion 2010, Chap. 8). Echoing 1910, contestation was especially fierce over the navy (Milner 2005, 280 ff.). Issues with explicit or implicit British/anti-British content lingered past 1965, among them metrication, official languages policy, and multiculturalism. But Britishness as such was not the only or even the main pole of resistance to these initiatives, and the latter two drive the narrative of the next section.

Given attenuation of the British connection, it is no surprise that the denominational gap eventually shrank. What is surprising is how long the collapse took. The gap remains wide in both series, especially in the CES, and it appears to persist without diminution until 1980. It is tempting to assign the delay to partisan habit, like the party identification that slowed the political transformation of the US South (Green, Palmquist, and Stickler 2002). But habit cannot account for the full pattern: before 1980, there was no hint of decay, and after 1980 the drop can only be described as precipitous. The gap was cut in half in 1984 and disappeared in 1993. Despite a partial restoration in the later 1990s, it hit bottom in the new century and might have reversed its polarity in 2011.

Multiculturalism and the Shift to Ethnicity

In fact, both the delay in the onset and the suddenness of the drop are statistical artifacts. All along the specifically denominational effect in the cleavage was shrinking, yielding priority to language, region, and ethnicity. But regional politics – specifically Quebec versus the rest of Canada – first masked the shifts and then exaggerated their rate of decay. I show this by a progressive unpacking of Figure 5.3's statistical patterns.

After 1965, the identity margin shifted, and the Liberal Party was the chief protagonist (Igartua 2006). Change in the content of identity politics shifted the mechanisms underlying the cleavage from contextual to compositional. One new pattern was energization of what might be called "the project of French Canada" – with its subtly different manifestations in official languages policy and in Quebec-Canada relations. The other was multiculturalism, including the political incorporation of new Canadians (Black 1982; Triadafilopoulos 2012). In contrast to the consensus among Catholics that might attend a focus on the British connection, later policies sowed division in the ranks: francophones versus non-francophones, prewar versus postwar immigrant groups, and the like. For some groups, Catholic/non-Catholic differences weakened. At the same time, homogeneously Catholic groups became more differentiated from all others. But the basis for the differentiation was ethnic or linguistic, not specifically denominational. Down to 1980, these offsetting forces created a delicate equilibrium that kept the Catholic community as a whole about as sharply differentiated as it had been in 1965. After 1980, this equilibrium unwound. And by the turn of the millennium, lines of force unrelated to the earlier demographic divisions appeared, for example between visible minorities and all others.

Weakening the Impact of Religion

I show attenuation of the religious effect in two stages, by a progressive unpacking of the bivariate setup in Figure 5.3:

- The first stage is to separate Quebec from the rest of Canada to show the extent to which the religious gap is the by-product of an underlying Quebec/rest-of-Canada difference. This is the same strategy as in Figure 5.2, only now translated into survey data. As in Figure 5.2, if the "all Canada" line lies above the "excluding Quebec" line, then Quebec respondents, most of them Catholic, account for a disproportionate share of the apparent cleavage. If the opposite is true, then the cleavage is more broadly based and more a story about the rest of Canada than about Quebec.
- The second stage focuses on Canada outside Quebec and plots the Catholic coefficient when a suite of linguistic and ethnic controls is added to the estimation. At this stage, I also add regional and occupational dummy variables.

At each stage, two plots appear. One is the line from the preceding stage: in the Quebec/rest-of-Canada comparison, this is the plot from Figure 5.3; in the rest-of-Canada comparison, the earlier stage is the line from Panel A with Quebec respondents removed but with no controls. The next line, always bolder, is the product of the current manipulation.

The narrowing of the religious gap appears in Figure 5.4.[20] Panel A shows that before 1970 removing Quebec either has no effect or only

124 *The Canadian Party System*

FIGURE 5.4   Unpacking the cleavage: Impact of controls for region and ethnicity, 1949-2011

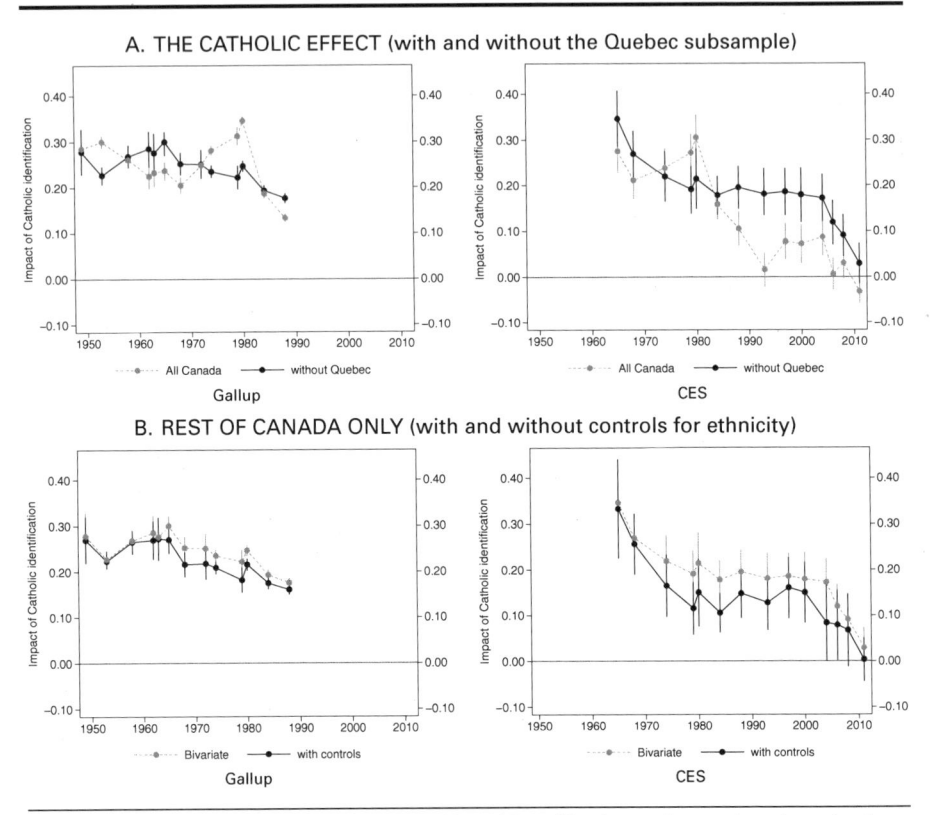

A. THE CATHOLIC EFFECT (with and without the Quebec subsample)

Gallup   CES

B. REST OF CANADA ONLY (with and without controls for ethnicity)

Gallup   CES

Notes: Interpretation of this figure is as for Figure 5.3 but with modifications to the sample or the estimation setup. Panel A shows what happens to Catholic/non-Catholic differences when Quebec respondents are removed from the estimation. Panel B shows what happens to the non-Quebec estimation for the Catholic/non-Catholic difference when controls for ethnicity are added. Entries are marginal effects and associated 95 percent confidence intervals from bivariate estimations in Panel A and multivariate estimations in Panel B. CIPO multivariate estimations control French ancestry and economic and regional terms. Canadian Election Studies estimations also include several ancestry terms (see Figures 5.5 and 5.6).

strengthens the relationship. The gap outside Quebec reaches its postwar peak in the 1960s. This was the moment, captured by Laponce (1972), that seemed to mesmerize subsequent analyses. Outside Quebec, in truth, the gap began to decay immediately after 1965. Over the next two decades, Gallup suggests a shrinkage of about 0.10; the CES reading is closer to 0.15. This drop coexists with a widening of the gap between estimations with and without Quebec; both sources indicate that by 1980 the all-Canada estimate is about 0.10 larger than the non-Quebec one. Over this span,

Quebeckers became more attached to the Liberals, even as their co-religionists elsewhere became less so. The discrepancy is an instance of the pattern identified in Chapter 4: from 1968 to 1984, the Liberal leader – Pierre Trudeau – was from Quebec. In 1984, the party leader from Quebec was a Conservative, Brian Mulroney. Once Trudeau was replaced and Quebec voters fled from the Liberals, the all-Canada line began its precipitous drop.

Mulroney did not further undermine what remained of the Liberals' non-Quebec appeal, however. Both the Gallup and the CES series suggest a tiny retreat after 1980, but the indication from the CES is essentially no movement from 1984 to 2004. The modest 1990s gain in the all-Canada estimation is entirely from the Liberals' similarly modest recovery in Quebec; outside Quebec, nothing happened. The final drop starts in 2006, and the downward trajectory is linear. By 2011, the Catholic effect, strictly speaking, is indistinguishable from zero.

To this point, estimations have been bivariate; the only tweaking has been to drop Quebec respondents. Panel B in Figure 5.4 asks how much of the bivariate impact outside Quebec is properly attributable to other sources, and for this a multivariate setup is appropriate. In the Gallup series, the only ethnolinguistic variable available as a control is mother tongue, the language that the respondent first learned and is still able to speak. The CES makes more ethnic controls possible: ancestry in France, northern Europe, eastern Europe, southern Europe, and outside Europe. Given sample sizes, it is not realistic to slice the sample any more thinly. As mentioned, the dotted grey line repeats the bivariate rest-of-Canada plot from Panel A, and the solid black line plots the multivariate one.

Up to 1965, ethnic controls make little difference: the impact is almost entirely from religious identification. After 1965, however, the lines pull apart, and the impact specific to religion drops. The pattern is clearest in the CES, as it should be. The Gallup representation of ethnicity only pits francophones against all others. Because the CES affords a more elaborate suite of ancestral indicators, the gap captured by the (now *ceteris paribus*) coefficient is between Catholics and non-Catholics of British Isles descent. And the CES indicates that by 1980 controlling ethnicity knocks up to 0.10 off the Catholic–non-Catholic difference in the probability of voting Liberal. In some elections, this meant cutting the religious effect roughly in half. Whereas in 1965 Catholics of British Isles ancestry were indistinguishable from their co-religionists, with about a 0.35 greater likelihood than other British people to vote Liberal, by 1980 that gap had been cut roughly in half. By the 1980s, then, the Catholic community had already lost a lot of its cohesion.

Strengthening the Impact of Language and Ethnicity

After 1965, complementarily, ethnic group differences evolved roughly in line with changes in the focus of identity politics. This is the message of Figures 5.5 and 5.6, which bring out estimated impacts from the ethnolinguistic terms in the equations underlying Figure 5.4B.

The politics of language sharpened after 1965, such that francophones outside Quebec emerged as electorally distinct. In earlier years, language as such rarely drove identity politics, for beyond Parliament and the courts the status of French was weak. In 1969, the Official Languages Act, designed to implement recommendations of the Royal Commission on Bilingualism and Biculturalism, began a revolution in the linguistic competence of the federal government and in the symbolism of the state. This was reinforced by the entrenchment of minority language rights in the Canadian Charter of Rights and Freedoms, 1982, and with enhancement of the federal role by revisions to the act in 1988. This evolution was contested, more sharply in earlier than in later years.

Only after 1960, according to Figure 5.5, does language emerge in sharp outline. The figure reports marginal effects from the language of interview (Gallup) or from ancestry in France (CES). Before 1960, francophones' distinctiveness from the mainstream was mainly a by-product of their Catholicism.[21] After 1965, this ceased to be true. Gallup data suggest that the new distinctiveness was sharp: from 1968 to 1980 (all elections in which the Liberal leader was Pierre Trudeau), French respondents were 20 points more likely to vote Liberal. This distinctiveness was *relative to non–French Catholics*. Over the same period, as Figure 5.4B showed, the greater body of Catholics became less distinct. But the cumulative difference between French Canadians and (by implication non-francophone) non-Catholics was massive. Once Trudeau stepped down, however, the distinctiveness of francophones shrank. It did not disappear, though, and the fact that Liberal leaders from 1993 to 2008 were all from Quebec seems to be relevant. The

FIGURE 5.5 Impact of French language or ancestry: Non-Quebec samples, 1949-2011

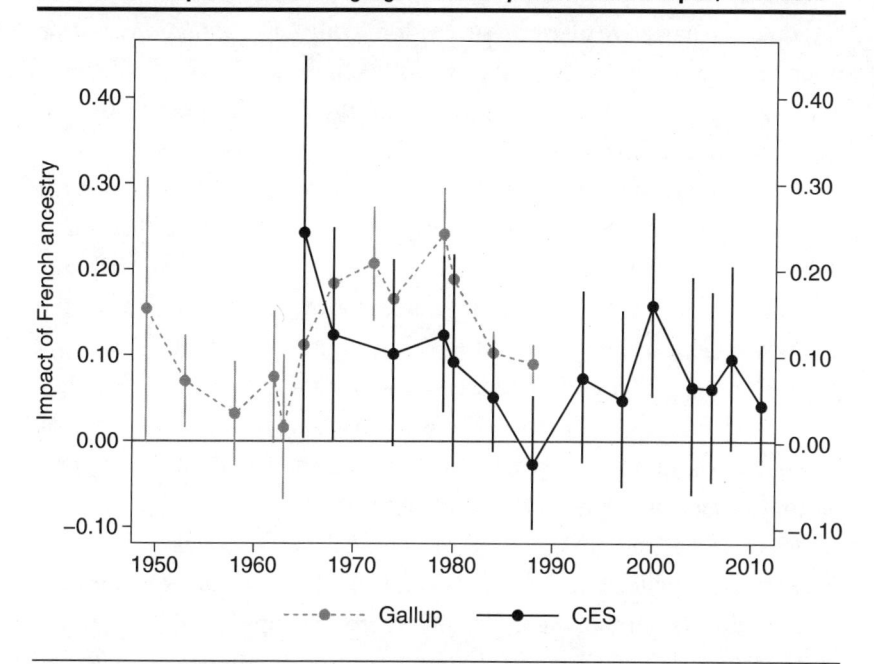

Notes: This figure shows the impact of French language or ancestry on the likelihood of a Liberal vote. Markers above zero indicate that French persons are more likely than others to vote Liberal, controlling for religious denomination and several other factors. Entries are marginal effects from multivariate probit and associated 95 percent confidence intervals from the same estimations as in Figure 5.4 (Panel B). In CIPO estimations, ethnicity is based on language of interview. In Canadian Election Studies estimations, ethnicity is based on ancestry.

pattern for 1988, at least in the CES, is suggestive and reinforces the interpretations of the earlier years. This was the year of the second Official Languages Act, introduced by the Conservatives. The reversion to type in 1993 reflected not retrogression by the Conservatives but their supplanting by the Reformers, who at that point did not support the linguistic consensus of the Mulroney years.

Multicultural policy evolved on a similar timeline. That Canada is a multicultural polity was stated for the record in 1971 by Prime Minister Trudeau. The claim was entrenched in an interpretive clause of the 1982 Charter. As with official languages policy, the next steps were taken by the Mulroney Conservative government. They were the Canadian Multiculturalism Act of 1988 and changes to the Broadcasting Act in 1991. The pattern on the rest of the ethnic field, in Figure 5.6, maps onto this timeline and onto the narrative of group succession. Only CES estimations appear since only these surveys have the requisite ethnic detail. The coefficients have the same meaning as in Figure 5.5, *mutatis mutandis,* and are derived from the same estimations.

Some patterns in the figure are compatible with the policy history. All groups that could, as it were, "see" themselves in the evolving multicultural policy were distinctively Liberal down to 1980. This is not to say that they became so because of the party's initial commitment of 1971. Indeed, the party was already successful with such groups, in some cases as a by-product of the earlier version of identity politics, and multicultural policy could be seen as a payoff to the coalition. Whatever its source, the Liberals' distinctive claim on such groups weakened in the 1980s. Mulroney's attempt to efface his party's ethnic and cultural tilt might have paid off.

It is also possible that the shift in marginal effect reflects shifts in the dependent variable of the Liberals' overall electoral weakness in this decade. But the fine print of the shifts differs across groups in rough conformity to stakes in the policy and shifts in party positioning. Start with the first group to broaden Canada's ethnic mix, northern Europeans, here defined as people with origins in Scandinavia, the Netherlands, and Germany – most of them Protestant monarchies at the time of migration.[22] As a rule, northern Europeans are simply not distinct from the British Protestant reference group, as we might expect from groups that have been on the scene, so to speak, for many decades and who came from places culturally aligned with Britain since the Reformation. The only decade that this group came out of the shadows was the 1990s, when northern Europeans disproportionately supported the culturally conservative Reform Party. This might indicate a backlash against more recent arrivals or against the heightened profile of French Canada.[23]

Up to 1980, eastern Europeans still seemed to be in the Liberal camp. The difference is modest and not always statistically significant. But it is consistent with the earlier record of immigration and exclusion. British Canadians reacted negatively to the arrival of "Galicians" and to the role of Clifford Sifton, Liberal minister of the interior, in championing the new pattern of immigration. It is also consistent with the narrative of official

FIGURE 5.6 Impact of ancestry: Non-Quebec samples, 1965-2011

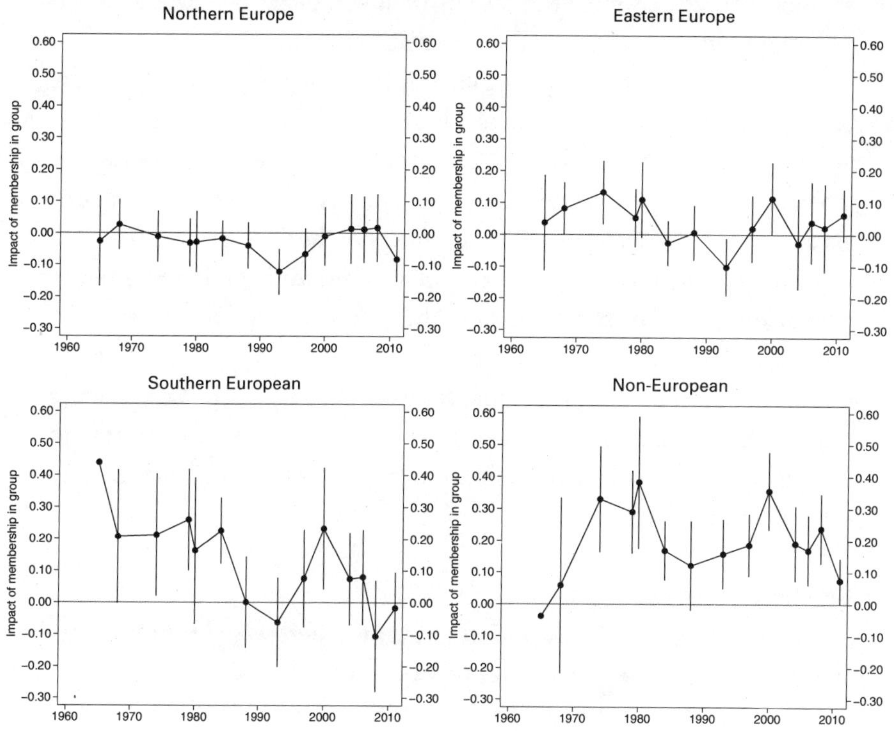

Notes: This figure shows the impact of ancestry on the likelihood of a Liberal vote. Markers above zero indicate that persons of the indicated ethnicity are more likely than others to vote Liberal, controlling religious denomination and several other factors. Entries are marginal effects from multivariate probit and associated 95 percent confidence intervals with Canadian Election Studies data. Estimations include all ancestry terms, Catholic identification, and economic and regional terms.

multiculturalism, itself something of a Ukrainian Canadian invention (Bociurkiw 1978). Be that as it may, the link evaporated in 1984 and has not been restored.

Down to 1984, the group that seemed to be most distinctly Liberal was southern Europeans, most of them Italians. It might be significant that, like French Canadians, this is an almost exclusively Catholic group. This hegemonic Catholicism might in turn have reinforced the groups' sense of ethnic distinctiveness. But the distinctiveness represented by the coefficients, remember, is *relative to other Catholics*. Relative to Protestant

Canadians, southern Europeans (like French Canadians) were even more distinct. This ceased to be the case in 1988, although there was a partial and temporary restoration of the pattern in 2000.

The torch passed to non-Europeans, to "visible minorities," in part because of their growing numbers. One token of this increase is the confidence intervals around the non-European coefficient. In the 1960s, the intervals are massive (so much so that some are suppressed for the sake of visual clarity), a reflection of small numbers in the CES sample. The 1965 pattern is also telling: it is the reverse of later decades. If it is real, and not an illusion created by sampling error, then it testifies to John Diefenbaker as a champion of inclusion. The first Chinese Canadian MP, Douglas Jung, was elected in the initial Diefenbaker surge of 1957. With Diefenbaker's removal from the party leadership, Conservatives apparently reverted to type. As of 2008, non-Europeans were the sole remaining distinctively Liberal group.

Conclusions and Implications

To say that the divide between Catholics and others was anachronistic in the 1950s and 1960s, when it was first observed in survey data, is a misreading of history. In the 1950s, it was still energized by foreign policy debate and the aftermath of global war. In the 1960s, the division turned on wrenching symbolic issues. The issues were not residues of nineteenth-century conflict over schools or the like. Rather, they reflected Canada's ongoing twentieth-century entanglements in imperial and alliance politics. In the late phase, they were about renovation of the symbols of public life. It should be no surprise that many Canadians resisted that renovation.

The place of ethnicity and language in this account is subtle and shifting. At some level, the account is always ethnic. But the level shifts. For most of the twentieth century, the claim is that the ethnic content was *contextual*: being a Catholic, regardless of one's ethnicity, sensitized a person to a non-British conception of the country's identity. Perhaps more to the point, being a Protestant delivered a more Britain-focused conception. This conception might have included other, nominally non-ethnic concomitants, including a republican conception of citizenship. As the claims of the British connection waned, not least because Britain itself changed, the role of ethnicity slipped down a notch on the ladder of aggregation. Religious denomination ceased to be a big tent, and the field was now open for group-specific advocacy, with denominational differences as a by-product.

Yet again the analysis has implications for the normative assessment of the Canadian party system. Cairns (1968) articulates a widely held view that the system encourages division, not cohesion. The record of history is more equivocal. Cairns lays much emphasis on Liberal rhetoric in Quebec in the 1920s, on portrayals of Arthur Meighen as the conscriptionist devil incarnate with designs on the province's young men. Note, however, the context: the moment was the immediate aftermath of the Great War. By this time, the Conservative Party had largely wasted its assets in the province even as it persisted in its imperialist leanings. The tone of the party system in the earlier – no less bitter – conflicts of the 1880s and 1890s was different, and Siegfried (1966) caught both the older pattern and the transition to the new, "heroic" one. In some periods, the party system encourages ethnic and sectional antagonism. In others, it does the opposite. It is reasonable to ask why. This chapter presents no answer, but it puts the question squarely on the table.

The Canadian case suggests a starting point for analyses of comparable party systems. Australia had a Great War conscription crisis of its own, and the electorate rejected the move twice. The labour movement was powerfully implicated in the conflict, but so was the Catholic Church. Although we think of the Australian party system as quintessentially class based, it also has a secondary basis in religious denomination – and, as in Canada, this basis has attenuated (McAllister 2011). Broadly speaking, the same evolution occurred in the United States (Layman 2001). The Canadian case seems to be a clear instance of "the second image reversed" (Gourevitch 1978), of the finding that foreign policy can be a powerful factor in domestic electoral politics. Contrary to the claim in Almond (1950) that foreign affairs are too remote for voters to grasp, US voters have generally stable and differentiated views and commonly act on them (Holsti 1992). These views are not necessarily sophisticated, and everywhere foreign policy is an arena for identity politics.

Although the local cast of characters was transformed over the twentieth century, the specifics of the transformation were incidental for most of the period. The key was the organizational and cultural stability of the overarching umbrella. The Catholic Church was able to gather diverse newcomers to itself and, I surmise, to shape the flow of culturally charged communication. This ongoing denominational structure then had external events and constraints imposed on it, and shifts in those constraints supplied most of the coalitional dynamics, even as these dynamics shaped Canada's response to the world. Had the twentieth century not been one of global war, the denominational basis of Canadian elections would probably have looked very different. When the British Empire faded as the conduit for alliance politics, not to mention for the polity's internal symbolism, the energy went out of the old cleavage.

A further implication is that maintenance of a cleavage requires refreshment through policy conflict, even if mainly in the symbolic domain.[24] Things do not endure merely out of nostalgia, dumb habit, or prepolitical socialization around the family dinner table. The implanting of the denominational difference was not gradual, perhaps constrained by the succession of generations. Rather, it occurred in two bursts, each interpretable in geopolitical terms. No less impressive was the speed with which it unravelled. The same can be said of the rotation of specific ethnic groups through Liberal support from the 1970s through the 2010s.

6

The Life and Death of Insurgents

> Where there is death, there is hope.
>
> – ANON.

Insurgents come in many colours and flavours, but they all have two things in common: sudden appearance and short shelf life. They also tend to be geographically confined, often by the boundaries of an individual province, and are particularly susceptible to discontinuity between provincial and federal arenas. As a body of cases, they are singularly resistant to theoretical explanation.

I begin the chapter with an Olympian overview of all insurgents and both arenas, province by province. This is a chronology of particular parties in particular places. With historical evidence on the table, I turn to the standing body of theory on the statics and dynamics of multipartism. Theory is suggestive but on balance not very helpful. Historical moments that should be particularly promising occasions for new parties to emerge do not have such effects consistently. Particular configurations of political economy and *ex ante* party competition also seem to be candidates for explanation. Here, too, the patterns are not always consistent. In sum, the sheer multiplicity of birth patterns defies even complex theoretical accounts. Theory is all but silent on the other striking pattern: the tendency for insurgents to disappear, sometimes as suddenly as they appear.

The upshot is that history counts, all the more so because Canada is a federation. Provinces, and the federal and provincial arenas within each province, are crucibles for political change. The rhythms of elections diverge among provinces and, within provinces, between arenas. Small differences in timing can yield sharp divergences in insurgent breakthroughs. These early, somewhat accidental timing gaps then constrain future possibilities, such that differences among provinces or between arenas within provinces can reflect not so much current forces as those seemingly no longer relevant. But only some provinces fit this description. In others, the party system resists change and does so in both arenas.

Coexisting with this confusion are simpler patterns more accessible to theory. They have to do mostly with the qualitatively distinct "new" party, the CCF-NDP. Although that party is the central preoccupation of the next chapter, as the twentieth century progressed provincial elections converged. This convergence was not so much in the identities of individual parties as in the general dynamics of the system: the challenge from the left forced anti-socialist interests to coalesce. At a general level, this produced common left-versus-right politics. The impact of history persists in the identity of the party on the right.

Preliminary Empirics

Insurgency is not ubiquitous. It is a feature of certain provinces, certain periods, and certain arenas. It is a story mainly of the West and Quebec, and different provinces become sites for insurgency at different times. The first evidence appears in Figure 6.1. The first great breakthrough, in 1921, is a tale of four provinces: Alberta, Saskatchewan, Manitoba, and Ontario. In Quebec, the critical decade is the 1930s and then only in the provincial arena. British Columbia does not join the pack until 1952-53.

Typically, insurgents do not last. Federal elections were essentially purged of first-generation insurgents by 1980. Indeed, this was true outside Quebec by 1970. Broadly speaking, provincial elections were also purged, although more slowly and with some holdouts. In Alberta, insurgents remained on the provincial map into the 1980s and in British Columbia into the 1990s. Only in Quebec did site-specific parties persist in provincial elections throughout the period.

Trajectories for exit are also province specific. Although the 1921 federal surge receded quickly in most places, in Alberta it did not. The post-1921 provincial decline did not always match the federal one. Alberta and

FIGURE 6.1 Federal and provincial insurgent dynamics by province, 1908-2011

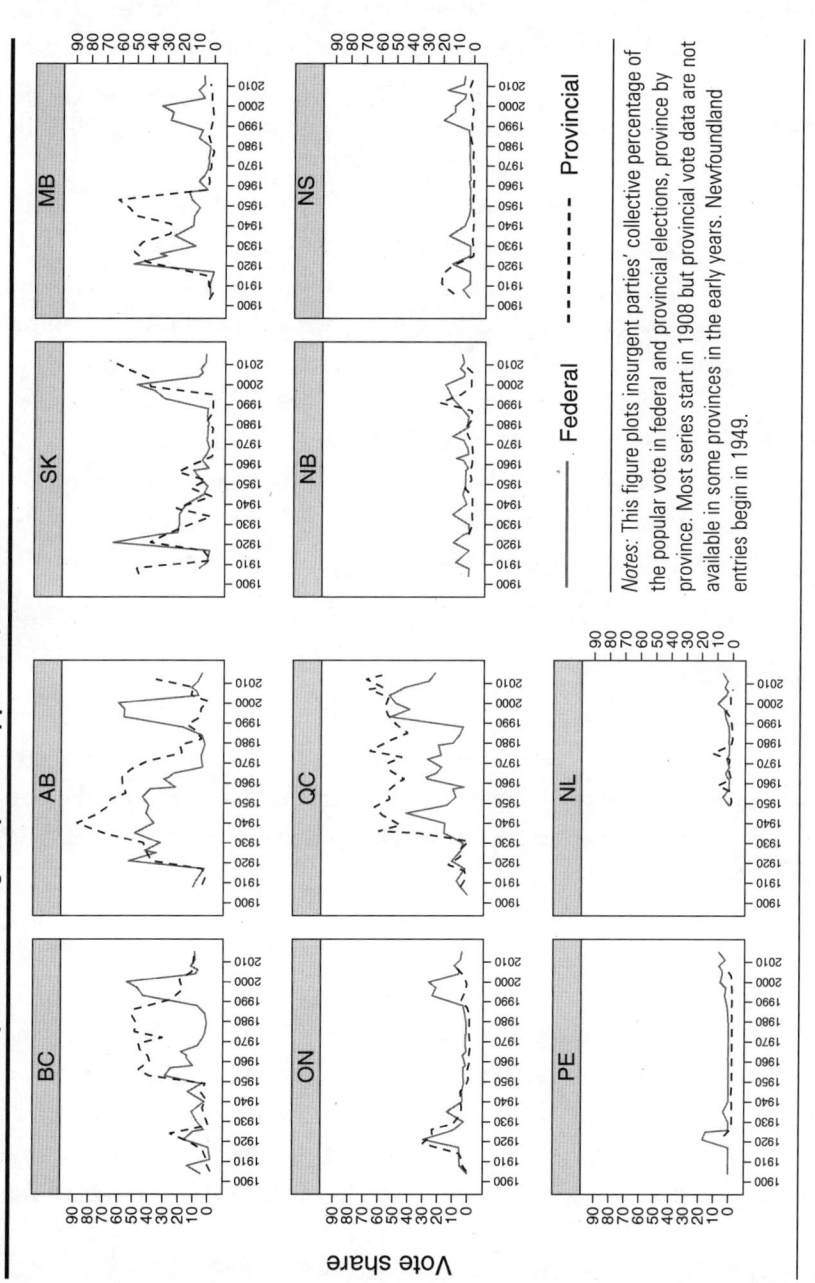

Notes: This figure plots insurgent parties' collective percentage of the popular vote in federal and provincial elections, province by province. Most series start in 1908 but provincial vote data are not available in some provinces in the early years. Newfoundland entries begin in 1949.

Manitoba, where the new party persisted for more than a decade, are cases in point. The legacy of the late surge in British Columbia (1952-53) lasted into the late 1960s federally and the 1990s provincially. In Quebec, federal insurgents have come and gone – swiftly around 1945, more gradually after 1962. In provincial elections, in contrast, the insurgent niche that opened in the 1930s was never vacated.

If by 1980 federal politics seemed to have converged on a "mainstream" logic of domination by parties aspiring to nationwide appeals, the 1993 election sent that apparent equilibrium out the window. For the following decade, the federal insurgent share in the three westernmost provinces approached or exceeded 40 percent, with strong echoes in Manitoba and Ontario (and fainter ones in New Brunswick and Nova Scotia). The same happened in Quebec. For Quebec, the insurgent breakthrough made the two arenas more alike. In the West, the opposite happened since insurgency characterized only the federal arena. That is, it did so initially. Possibly as an echo of the federal pattern and after some lag, new provincial parties appeared in Saskatchewan and Alberta.

Naming Names

The preceding section understates the problem, treating all insurgents in a province as a single entity. Although in any election most of the insurgent vote does go to one party, Figure 6.1 masks the turnover in names. Figures 6.2 to 6.4 plot trajectories for specific parties that elected multiple MPs for more than one election.

The first major insurgent was the agrarian *Progressives*. The critical fact about this 1920s' movement-cum-party is that it mainly contested rural ridings engaged in wheat production for export. Most candidacies were in the prairie provinces and southwestern Ontario. Substantively, the Progressives focused on a single dimension of politics, the conflict between land, on the one hand, and labour and capital, on the other. More than half of the platform was devoted to sectoral issues, half to the tariff alone (Morton 1950, Appendix C). Its more radical elements, mainly in Alberta, also contested the very idea of Westminster politics and championed a functionalist and corporatist model (Macpherson 1953). Some support in Manitoba and Ontario was anti-French (Morton 1950, 83-84, 98-99). But the Progressives also harboured more inclusive elements, which made

FIGURE 6.2 Dynamics for specific insurgents: Federal elections outside Quebec, 1908-2011

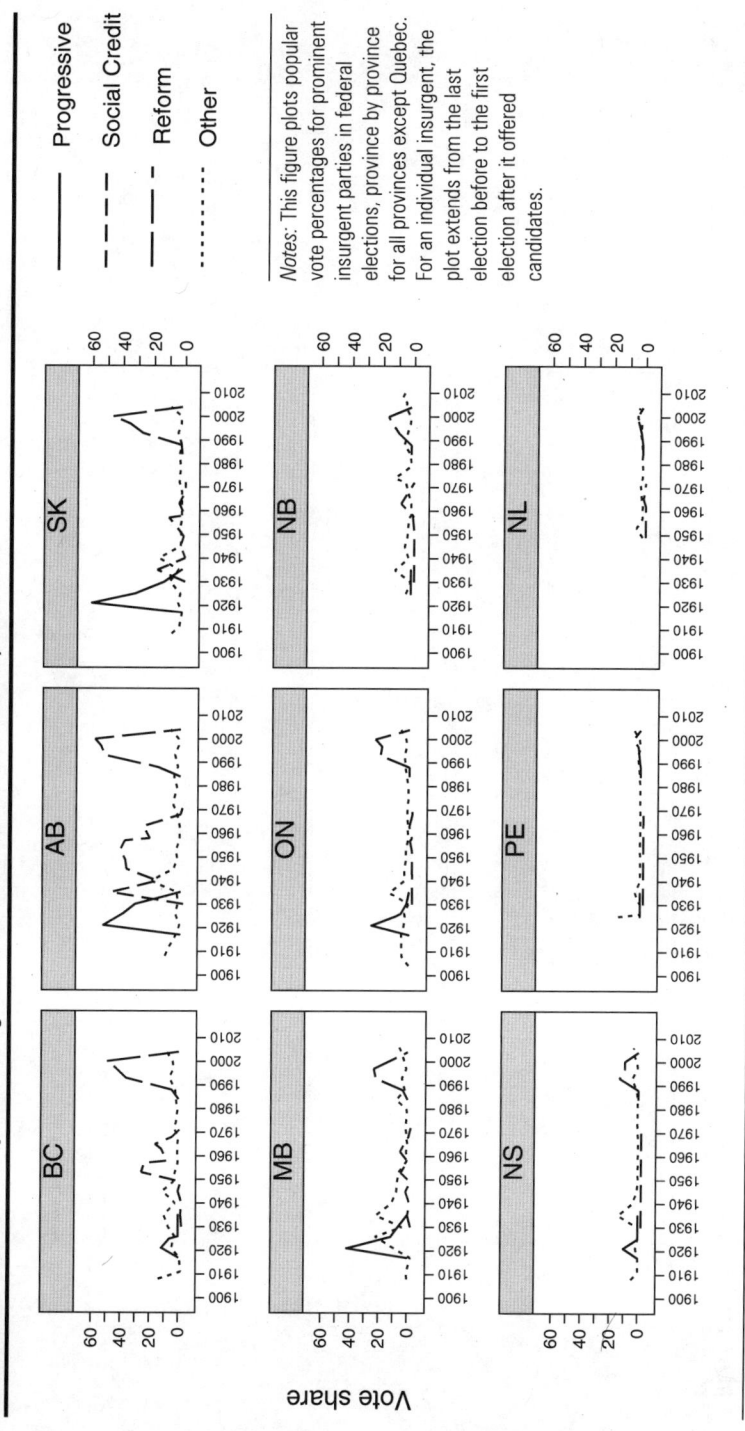

Notes: This figure plots popular vote percentages for prominent insurgent parties in federal elections, province by province for all provinces except Quebec. For an individual insurgent, the plot extends from the last election before to the first election after it offered candidates.

FIGURE 6.3 Dynamics for specific insurgents: Provincial elections outside Quebec, 1908-2011

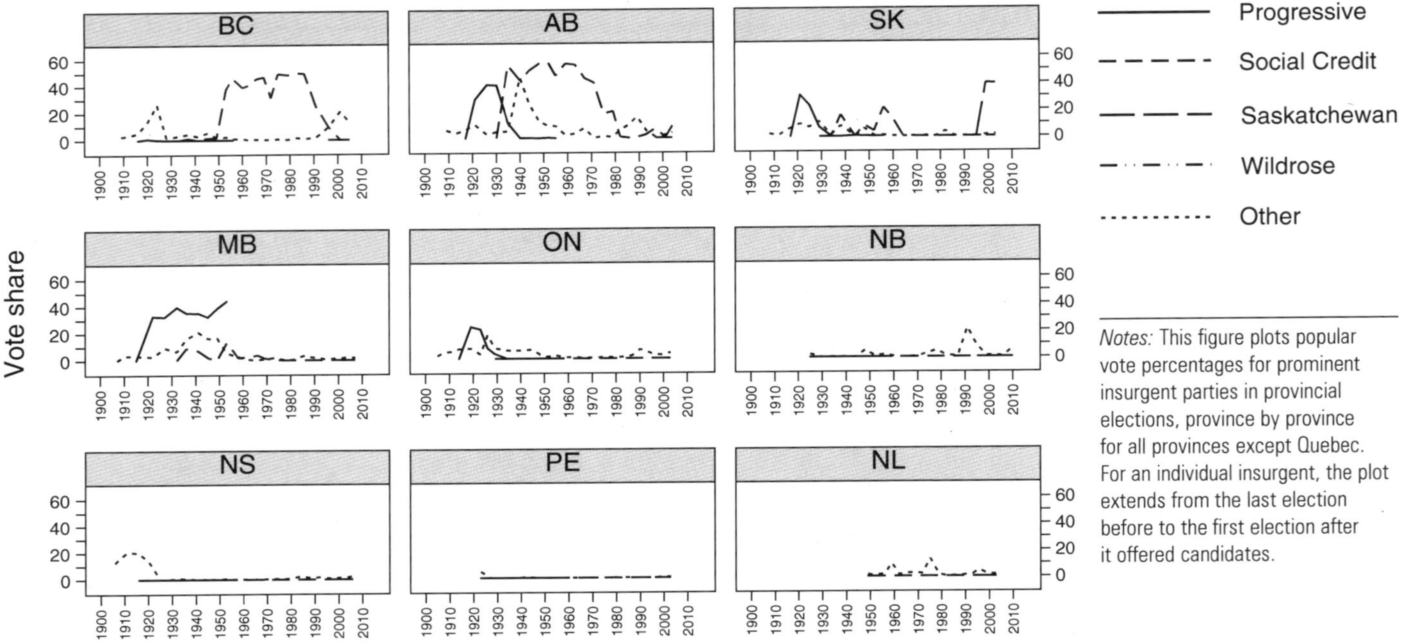

——— Progressive
– – – Social Credit
— - — Saskatchewan
— ·· — Wildrose
········· Other

Notes: This figure plots popular vote percentages for prominent insurgent parties in provincial elections, province by province for all provinces except Quebec. For an individual insurgent, the plot extends from the last election before to the first election after it offered candidates.

them precursors of the CCF and NDP. Their platform advocated collective security through the League of Nations, continuation of the redistributive wartime tax regime, staged demobilization of returned soldiers, gestures toward organized labour, and a wide range of democratic reforms.

The Progressives' federal and provincial trajectories differed twice over. The federal breakthrough in 1921 was uniform across the prairie provinces, ranging from over 40 percent in Manitoba to over 60 percent in Saskatchewan. But the federal share dropped quickly, and the party was basically gone well before 1935. The provincial pattern was less uniform but lasted longer. The party had little provincial traction in Saskatchewan, notwithstanding its stunning federal success in 1921. It was never strong and was susceptible to capture by forces at odds with its original program. It was just visible enough to be critical to the formation of the province's only pre–Second World War Conservative-led government. In Alberta and Manitoba, the party won power and endured. It collapsed in Alberta in 1935 but persisted into the 1950s in Manitoba.[1]

Next up in the West was *Social Credit*, which appeared in 1935 and immediately seized power in Alberta. This party was even more sectionally concentrated than the Progressives, starting in Alberta (although with temporary spillover into Saskatchewan) and later spreading to British Columbia. Notwithstanding superficial similarities in geography, the party inherited little from the Progressives. Where Progressives drew on rural civil society in the West and Ontario, Social Credit began with an appeal both more general (Finkel 1989), possibly with an inverse class bias (Bell 1993), and with little anchoring in civil society (Burnet 1951). Indeed, the party was hostile to intermediary entities, which declined swiftly in Alberta after 1935 (Burnet 1951, 147-48). Its 1935 breakthrough was materially assisted by the radio audience cultivated by its first leader, William Aberhart, and his Prophetic Bible Institute (Bell 1993; Irving 1959). To the extent that the party was animated by ideology, the focus was on money and banking, an ancient agrarian and small-business theme (Macpherson 1953).[2] Eventually, Social Credit morphed into a party of regional defence with a clearly conservative cast.

A second phase began in 1952 with the party's success in British Columbia. The BC variant was never burdened by Social Credit ideology. It swiftly became the electoral instrument for its first leader, W.A.C. Bennett, formerly a Conservative. The party was the unexpected beneficiary of preferential voting in the 1952 provincial election (Elkins 1976),[3] which led to its first (minority) government. Bennett exploited the position to secure a majority result in 1953,[4] and federal candidacies ensued directly (Mitchell 1983).

Federally, Social Credit in the West all but evaporated after 1958, and most of its geography was inherited by the Conservative Party. The party hung on provincially in Alberta and British Columbia. In Alberta, provincial decay started in the 1960s and culminated in its terminal loss of power in 1971. In British Columbia, the party continued to be a central player and usually formed the government. After its loss of power in 1991, however, the party was swiftly marginalized, with all vestiges gone by 2001.

The federal Conservatives might have believed that, after the demise of western Social Credit, they now owned the region. Instead, it was only on loan, and in 1993 much of the region fell to *Reform*. Reform began with echoes of Social Credit, especially in its core geography.[5] In its early years, the party reflected the conflicting objectives of its first leader, Preston Manning (Flanagan 1995). Among its many appeals was an explicit anti-system tendency, the repudiation of party discipline in favour of representation for local majority opinion. By 2000, however, Reform leadership had clearly reconciled itself with mainstream Westminster logic and signalled this by a name change to *Canadian Reform Conservative Alliance*. In itself, the shift failed, but it paved the way for the Alliance's reverse takeover of the Conservative Party in 2003. As an indicator of voters' behaviour, then, the sudden disappearance of Reform/Alliance in 2004 is misleading. Even so, it echoes the earlier disappearance of Alberta Social Credit into a party with a Conservative label. Manning explicitly repudiated taking Reform into the provincial arena, although splinters appeared from place to place.

Among them are two provincial parties currently on the scene. The *Saskatchewan Party* was built from the ruins of the various non-labour elements of the province's landscape. Even more Reform-like is Alberta's *Wildrose Party*. Where the Saskatchewan Party extends toward the political centre, for the Wildrose Party the centre-right is already occupied by the provincial Conservatives. The Wildrose tone is strongly conservative as a result, and its lineage can be traced back to old Social Credit.

Most other parties on the landscape exhibited anti-system tendencies, and only one lasted two or more elections. The 1896 election (not shown here) featured small-scale precursors of 1921. Candidacies by the *Knights of Labour* and by supporters of the anti-French and anti-Catholic publicist-lawyer Dalton McCarthy, sometimes with mutual endorsements, could be seen as anticipating almost all later developments: agrarian and union-based action, anti-Catholicism, and repudiation of party politics as such (Crunican 1974). The *Reconstruction Party* of 1935 was the extended shadow of its leader, H.H. Stevens, a former and future Conservative. Its program exhibited impatience with parliamentarism, and there were dalliances with Social Credit. But it did have a forward-looking program, and it ran candidates nationwide (Wilbur 1964).[6] The most recent entrant, the *Green Party,* seems to have staying power, helped by accommodating party finance legislation. The party is basically a one-dimensional operation, although it is willing to cooperate with other parties, especially the Liberals.

For Quebec, according to Figure 6.4, the narrative begins in the provincial arena. The first entrant was the *Union Nationale* (UN), which emerged in a 1935-36 two-step. The Quebec provincial plot shows a different insurgent in 1935, the *Action Libérale Nationale* (ALN), a left-leaning breakaway from the dominant Liberals. In that year, most of the actors who would soon constitute the Union Nationale were still identified as Conservatives. Their leader, Maurice Duplessis, coopted most of the ALN members into the new UN label, won a resounding majority in 1936, and swiftly buried any reformist impulse. As its name suggests, the UN was committed to a Quebec-specific ethnonational program (Black 1977). Its arrival signalled the final delegitimation of the provincial Conservatives. In contrast to western insurgents, the UN survived for more than three decades and moved in and out of power. When it declined, it yielded to the similarly nationalist *Parti Québécois* in 1970.[7]

The first federal manifestation of Quebec nationalism came in 1942-45. The *Bloc Populaire Canadien,*[8] along with a self-named *Independent Group,* emerged as opponents of conscription. Discontent started with a 1942 plebiscite on relieving the government of its anti-conscription pledge (see Chapter 5). The grouping combined new entrants with defectors from Liberal ranks, but by the time they had an opportunity to seek election the war in Europe was over. Next, in 1962, was the Quebec version of Social

142　*The Canadian Party System*

FIGURE 6.4   Dynamics for specific insurgents: Federal and provincial elections in Quebec, 1908-2011

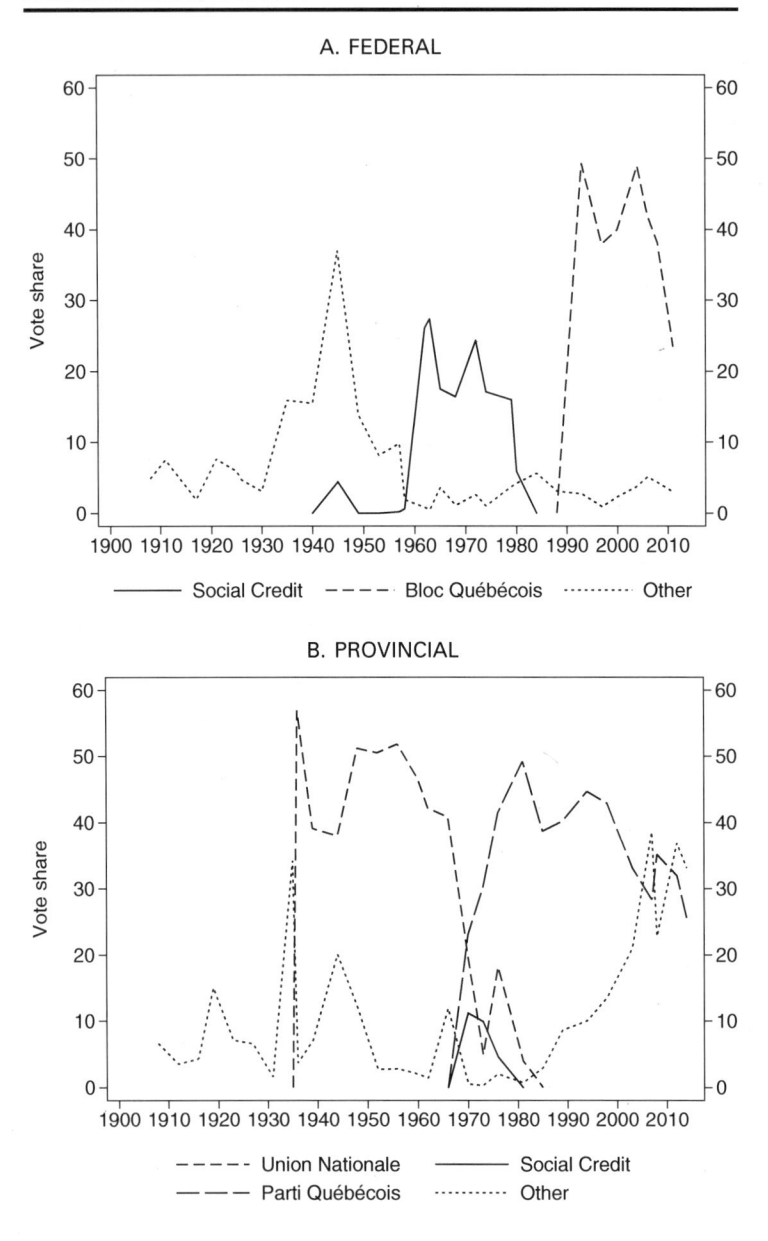

A. FEDERAL

—— Social Credit   – – – – Bloc Québécois   ⋯⋯⋯ Other

B. PROVINCIAL

– – – – Union Nationale   —— Social Credit
— — Parti Québécois   ⋯⋯⋯ Other

Notes: This figure plots percentages of the popular vote for prominent insurgent parties in federal and provincial elections in Quebec. For an individual insurgent, the plot extends from the last election before to the first election after it offered candidates.

Credit. The *Ralliement Créditiste* was effectively separate from the western branch of the movement, and the two existed in tension, alternately breaking apart and reconfederating. Although the religious and linguistic gap between the western and Quebec variants was wide, their support bases were otherwise similar, as was their rhetoric (Pinard 1975). The Créditistes were gone by 1980. Most enduring and most important has been the *Bloc Québécois*, which emerged on roughly the same timetable as Reform and from somewhat similar circumstances. It originated as a breakaway from the inclusive Conservative Party that governed from 1984 to 1993. It helped that the Bloc's first leader, Lucien Bouchard, was a credible presence, a prominent Quebec nationalist and former Conservative cabinet minister. Although the Bloc is a skilled parliamentary presence and claims to sit on the left, at bottom it is a party of ethnoregional defence. Its supporters are ideologically almost indistinguishable from Quebec supporters of the other parties (Johnston 2008, Fig. 2). It does not contest ridings outside the province, and its mere presence can frustrate the Westminster logic in Parliament. Its parliamentary presence evaporated in 2011 and was only modestly enhanced (with a smaller vote) in 2015.

The narrative of insurgents makes generalization hard. The locus of initiative is sometimes federal, sometimes provincial. The breadth of parties' territorial ambition varies considerably: some parties contest one province, whereas others contest several provinces. The bases of insurgency vary qualitatively from episode to episode. And the dynamics of birth and death are remarkably messy. Does theory help?

Multipartism in Theory

Theory comes in two forms, static and dynamic. The distinction is artificial, but little work straddles the boundary. Only a tiny body of work says anything about exits. In general, the theoretical literature is not helpful and often works at cross-purposes.

Statics

This work comes in two distinct flavours. One is an attempt to account for a system's overall fractionalization. This work is silent on the substance of party competition. The other literature attempts to fill this gap by examining substantive differences between party systems in otherwise similar settings.

Given the variety among the provinces, it comes as no surprise that important examples of the latter are by Canadian authors. Some of this work emphasizes factors in political culture and some in political economy.

The Number of Parties

Here two subtly different claims coexist, an inductive one by Taagepera and Grofman (1985) and a deductive one by Amorim Neto and Cox (1997) and Cox (1997).

Taagepera and Grofman (1985) argue that the number of parties is basically the number of issue dimensions plus one. Their evidence for the number of dimensions comes from Lijphart (1999).[9] The relationship between dimensions is basically 1:1 (with an intercept of 1), with an additional lift (but no moderation of the slope) where district magnitude is any number greater than one. This does not get us far. For starters, the formulation falls short of predicting the typical Canadian ENP value for the years before 1993. The number of issue dimensions in Canada according to Lijphart is 1.5, so the predicted ENP is 2.5. But Figure 2.5 shows that the actual ENP for the years covered by Lijphart is 3.0.

Taagepera and Grofman (1985) cannot distinguish cause and effect in the relationship. The deductive literature strongly implies that the number of parties creates – more precisely accommodates – the number of dimensions rather than the reverse. And the electoral system is the key condition: where the district magnitude is one, as in Canada, the predicted ENP is two, full stop.[10] This holds regardless of the complexity of the society – an obvious source of dimensionality. Only if the electoral system is weak – where district magnitudes are greater than one – is social complexity allowed to express itself in party system fragmentation (Amorim Neto and Cox 1997). The prediction for the two-candidate ceiling is the strong form of Duverger's Law. The claim that more parties are permitted but not mandated as the ceiling rises is the law's weak form. But the problem with this thinking was signalled in Chapter 2: notwithstanding a district magnitude of one, Canada has had a multiparty system for decades.

This fact is not lost on deductive theorists and, indeed, helped to move the literature toward the new synthesis, which argues that estimations on the national level are misplaced (Cox 1997). The prediction from Duverger's

Law belongs at the district level. Pressures toward local two-party competition do not guarantee that the same two parties will dominate the contest everywhere, with the result that the national ENP might be larger than the local one. This is the central theme in Chhibber and Kollman (2004), and there is no denying the critical role of sectional breakdown in inflating Canada's total ENP. What is more, Chhibber and Kollman predict – and find – that divergence from the national party system norm is greatest in provinces with the smallest fiscal dependence on the national government. The logic of dependence extends to federal-provincial discontinuities. This might explain the resistance of Atlantic Canada to both insurgency and discontinuity (Chhibber and Kollman 2004, 192 ff.; Thorlakson 2007, 2009).

For my purposes, however, this is about geography as a permissive cause. Because they are less dependent on Ottawa, provinces west of New Brunswick have scope to diverge from the old template. But what would actually drive them to do it? Not all do. The answers might lie in political culture or political economy.

The argument generates a further implication, borne out only spottily. It has always seemed reasonable to suppose that the provincial arena would be the incubator of new parties. The supposition is strongly implied in Chhibber and Kollman (2004), Gerring (2005), and Hug (2001). Although provinces face many common challenges, their respective provincial arenas are more detached from each other than their federal ones. The moving part in the Chhibber-Kollman argument, importance of the federal government, seems to be particularly plausible for the provincial policy landscape. Viewing that landscape through the lens of federal-provincial discontinuity only reinforces the expectation.

Empirically, however, the initiative for new parties is as likely in the federal arena as in the provincial one. Although farmers' candidates appeared in the 1919 Ontario and 1920 Manitoba provincial elections, in neither election was there much coordination among these candidates. The first definite, self-recognized, agrarian bloc arguably was the federal one that emerged in early 1921, composed of defectors from the now-crumbling Unionist government (Morton 1950, 96). Social Credit in Alberta and British Columbia was certainly provincialist at the core, as were most manifestations of Quebec nationalism until 1993. But Quebec Social Credit was essentially a federal phenomenon. And the last great insurgency, Reform, was exclusively federal. Progressives and Reformers had regionally concentrated appeals, and the existence of provincial boundaries probably sharpened discontinuities in their organizations. But it is tempting to conclude that this was something of an epiphenomenon, that the critical factor was simple geography – much of it, indeed, physical geography.

In any case, the locus of initiative is related to breadth of appeal. Outside Quebec, two parties stand out from all other insurgents, and for both the critical arena was the federal one. The Progressives and Reformers were clearly geographically more ambitious – more successful certainly – than the others. At their peaks, they controlled close to half of the vote in all of the West, with non-trivial support in Ontario.[11] This signals that they were not garden-variety insurgents but parties with programs. Their supporters were unlikely to be as programmatic as the parties' elites, especially at first. But commitment to programs enabled these parties to have permanent impacts on the larger party system.

Political Culture

One possibility is provincial variation in political culture. Wiseman (2007) argues that each province has evolved a political culture in some measure prefigured at the founding of the province by the interaction of resource endowment, initial immigration sources, and the economic circumstances of the moment.[12] Wesley (2011) faces the challenge of accounting for the divergent trajectories of the otherwise similar economies and societies of the prairie provinces. The differences, he claims, are the products of party discourse. Initial party divergences might be accidental, but the divergences, once implanted, are self-reproducing. Whatever their merits, neither account is much help in explaining insurgent origins. Wiseman does not pretend to offer an account of party sequences; rather, he presents a more holistic account of practices and sensibilities. Wesley begins his account after the period that this chapter argues to be especially critical, the early 1920s. Indeed, both books are really about the consequences of the heterogeneity in party competition that this chapter tries to explain. Both accounts point toward a conclusion that seems to be inescapable: a large fraction of the pattern reflects powerful path dependencies.[13]

The Political Economy of Grain

By its very nature, conflict between agricultural producers and others leads to geographically differentiated partisan responses. It is arguably significant for a party system whether that differentiation takes place within provinces or among them. Before 1900, the conflict expressed itself mainly within Ontario, pitting southwestern Ontario against the rest of the province. With the rapid development of the West, this issue dimension became more complicated, the agricultural interest became weightier, and the very fact of federalism amplified substantive policy conflict. Notwithstanding the continued importance of export agriculture in southwestern Ontario, by the 1920s such interests both dominated the West and were dominated by it. And they pitted the West – strictly speaking the prairie provinces (plus bits of Ontario and British Columbia) – against the rest. The Canadian pattern of sequential development and institutional amplification of conflict echoed the US pattern of the late 1800s (Lipset 1968). A counterfactual that reinforces this interpretation is Australia. Although relative dependence on commodity exports varies from state to state in Australia – with Western Australia and Queensland being outliers – in comparison with their North American counterparts each Australian state contains similarly structured sectoral conflict within its boundaries. Arguably, this helps Australian sectoral conflict to be encapsulated by the national party system. The Australian example does lend weight to a political economy interpretation of the Canadian pattern and to its US precursor.

In interpreting the events of 1921, the political economy account largely stands. The point is only reinforced by the strength of the Progressives *outside* the prairie West, in the parts of Ontario most like the West. Indeed, western agrarians in many ways were legatees of the older Ontario pattern. Although the Progressives did not remain on the scene long, they did create a legacy for policy. The primary heir was, as already mentioned, the CCF and, to a diminished extent, the NDP.

Another political economy candidate is Reform/Alliance. The most parsimonious way to characterize Reform's appeal, given both its source and its duration, is in policy terms, as described in Chapter 2. On the classic left-right dimension, Reform supporters stood well to the right of the old Conservatives. Reform also drew on anti-French sentiment. It is striking, though, that Reform support was especially deep in communities engaged in primary commodity production. This remains true of the recast Conservative Party, the product of the Alliance reverse takeover of the old Progressive Conservative Party. Like the Progressives, Reform was a midwife to enduring change in the party system.

Dynamics

If these sets of literature are silent or weak on dynamics, the next two bodies of scholarship focus on new-party entry, without saying much about any resultant fragmentation in the party system or about the content of the new parties' appeal. The work is typically multi-country and comparative, but I extract the parts that apply to the Canadian case.[14]

The "Maturity" of the Electorate

In the literature as it currently stands, the factor of most obvious relevance to my account is "maturity" of the electorate. The longer the history of party politics in an electorate, the more resistant that electorate is to new parties (Gerring 2005; Mainwaring and Torcal 2006; Tavits 2006).[15] Lago and Martinez (2011) take this logic to the subnational level, with evidence from Spain. As noted in Chapter 2, Spain has been federalizing since the early 1980s but at different speeds in different regions, such that subnational sequences are like natural experiments. For any emerging subnational community, new-party entry should be most likely early in the sequence of federalization, and this Lago and Martinez find. This has implications, of course, for inter-arena discontinuity.

It is natural to wonder if this is part of the story for Canada. It seems to be intuitively reasonable that the newness of Liberal-Conservative competition in the West was a factor in the region's early susceptibility to insurgency. Although elections in the region go back almost to the middle of the nineteenth century, they did not take on a modern form until early in the twentieth century. In Alberta and Saskatchewan, the Liberal governments were creatures of the Laurier government in Ottawa, and in British Columbia party politics were not established until the turn of the century. Only Manitoba had something resembling conventional electoral politics dating back to the nineteenth century, and even there most of the electorate arrived after 1896.[16]

But the argument faces three difficulties. The first difficulty is that the West was not uniformly prone to insurgency. British Columbia resisted it until 1952-53. It stood aside from the events of 1921, and when it started down the third-party path in 1933-35 its support was focused on the CCF, not on a party with specifically sectional appeal. The province did succumb ultimately to insurgent appeals, but by this time, 1952-53, party politics had been in place for more than half a century. The second difficulty is Reform itself. This most successful of all insurgents arrived on the scene 90 years after the creation of mass electorates in the region and after the apparent reintegration of the region into mainstream parties. And the third difficulty is Quebec and its long history of insurgency. Quebec was slower than other regions to move to effective male suffrage and the last to enfranchise women. But entrenched party politics go back to the nineteenth century. By North American standards, it hardly seems to be an obvious place for electoral novelty.

Adverse Events

Economic factors are ubiquitous in election analysis and regularly included in comparative analyses of new-party entry.[17] For Canada, the historical record is suggestive. The end of the Great War brought a serious slump that produced both agrarian and labour unrest; this was the backdrop to the 1921 election. Recovery such as the 1920s brought was wiped out by the Depression, which began in 1929. Although the first year of the downturn probably helped the Conservatives to win in 1930,[18] the subsequent deepening of the Depression smashed the party system in 1935. The late 1950s brought the "Eisenhower recession," with recovery not starting until the early 1960s; in Pinard's (1966, 1975) account, this was a source of the Social Credit surge. Finally, it is tempting to characterize Reform as a protest movement (Bélanger 2004b). Certainly, its breakthrough election, in 1993, came in the wake of a deep recession, and its support echoed the geography of 1921.

Each of these examples has problematic features, however. In both 1921 and 1935, the places where new parties broke through were economically stricken. But many places no less stricken resisted the new parties, or similarly situated places supported different parties. And some of what appears to be – or is said by observers to be – protest voting does not bear close examination in these terms. Reform is the most problematic case. Notwithstanding superficial parallels with earlier episodes, Reform was not a cry of pain by the dispossessed. Its support came disproportionately from economically comfortable citizens, from people least persuaded that economic times were bad, and overwhelmingly at the expense of one mainstream party, the Progressive Conservatives (Johnston et al. 1996). The party's ultimately smooth reintegration into the mainstream – critically, on its terms – suggests that the distress that drove its 1993 breakthrough was mostly about policy. Indeed, if a 1990s insurgent has prepolitical protest elements, it is the Bloc Québécois (Johnston et al. 1996).

In any case, as channels for economic distress, new parties are hardly necessary. In fact, most analyses of economic voting feature contests among systems' core parties. For economic flux to produce new parties requires the presence of one or more additional moderating factors. Where insurgency is local, we need to consider factors other than geography. One obvious possibility is political economy itself. The broad pattern of insurgency in the prairie West in the face of global economic downturns should not be missed. But economic adversity, even where local, need not produce a new party; it might just lead to punishment of one old party by rewarding the other one.

Dynamics in Context

This suggests that a critical moderator is the party system itself, an early emphasis in the Canadian literature. According to Pinard (1966, 1975), economic adversity represents "structural strain" that creates the impulse for electoral change. For a new party to be the beneficiary, the mainstream alternative must lack credibility. For Pinard, this reflects an earlier history of overweening dominance by the other mainstream party. He offers this as an explanation of the 1962 breakthrough by Social Credit in Quebec. The thesis has been criticized as being more applicable to new parties with vague or non-existent programs than to parties that represent a broad, enduring interest or tendency (White 1973). To be sure, programmatic weakness describes most of the parties considered in this chapter. But a more comprehensive test is not kind to the Pinard thesis (Blais 1973).[19]

Nor have events since 1983 been kind, especially not the 1984-93 sequence. The recession of 1981-83 altered the terms of trade for commodity producers and was so deep that incomes had barely recovered by the time the next recession hit, in 1991. The Liberal government paid a dire electoral price for this (Johnston 1999). But the beneficiary was not a new protest party but the old rival, the Progressive Conservatives. In one sense, this is an exception that proves the Pinard (1975) rule: the old-party alternative to the Liberals was credible, and resort to a third party was not required. Closer inspection raises doubts, however. Most of the 1980-84 shift was in Quebec, in which the Conservative Party of the early 1980s was an even less credible organization than that of the 1950s and 1960s. At least in the earlier period, the party could call on the Union Nationale for help. Part of the story, of course, is Brian Mulroney and his building on the efforts of his immediate predecessors as leader. So why his party's obvious goodwill toward Quebec should produce the punishment of 1993 is not obvious. Although the Bloc Québécois derived credibility from its leader, it was unclear going into the 1993 election that its presence would be nearly fatal for the Conservatives. All of this, in any case, sees us wandering some distance from the original Pinard thesis. The landscape for the thesis seems to be as bleak as in 1973, when Blais wrote his account.

Still, Pinard's intuition is compelling. It comports with recent work that characterizes the entry situation as a strategic game in which established parties are as critical as potential entrants (Hug 2001). Given strategizing on both sides, the fact of entry and the degree of success upon entry cannot be separated. In most systems, successful entrants are usually weak, for potentially strong ones will induce concessions from established parties. Strong parties will be strangled at birth. But the higher the threshold for entry,[20] the stronger any successful entrant: new parties are rare, but when they do appear they are strong; weak parties gain no parliamentary foothold and disappear. On the surface, this still leaves Canada as a conundrum. By conventional indicators (Tavits 2006), Canada has a high threshold. But the country lies off both high-threshold paths: unlike their US counterparts, the old Canadian parties did not crush entrants; in contrast to Britain, Australia, and New Zealand, neither old party was crushed by a newcomer.

The secret might be the intersection of federalism with strong geography. We know from Gerring (2005) that federal systems facilitate party system fragmentation. In Hug's (2001) terms, the existence of subnational units creates the possibility of local rewards for entry that mitigate the daunting character of country-wide FPP. Federalism aside, if interests are highly diversified geographically, then they can turn the anti-entry logic of FPP on its head – locally at least. Insurgents should be drawn disproportionately from interests with spatially focused appeals. This is implicit, of course, in Chhibber and Kollman (2004) and a central theme in Cairns (1968).

Yet many loose ends abide. The dynamics of birth vary across provinces and arenas. Even among provinces with broadly similar sociological circumstances, new-party entry is not uniform. For multi-province parties, entry can be staggered. Sometimes a given province resists a party successful in an adjacent province. Within provinces, party dynamics are not consistently mirrored between federal and provincial arenas. *Contra* Hug (2001), some entrants lacked the unity necessary for strategic behaviour, and some were even surprised at their early success. The years for federal and provincial entry can differ. Even when the party appears simultaneously in both arenas, paths can subsequently diverge, sometimes quickly.

Dynamics of Exit

Death is as ubiquitous a feature of Canadian multipartism as birth. This is hardly a Canadian peculiarity, and scholars are now turning to the question of party disappearance and its close cousin, party fusion. As an example of fusion, the 2003 merger of the Alliance and the Progressive Conservatives has drawn notice (Bélanger and Godbout 2010; Marland and Flanagan 2015; Ware 2009). Most of the carnage on the Canadian landscape is the result not of merger, however, but of simple death. Here, too, the comparative literature, although it captures the gross features of the Canadian party system nicely, is not of much help.

The parties that survive the longest are, not quite tautologically, old and established ones. The key to their survival is their ability to shift policies according to circumstances (Laver and Sergenti 2011; Staniek 2013).[21] This is all the more true for parties operating in relatively consolidated systems, in which the long-lived parties accept the pull of the median voter (Staniek

2013). They need not actually cover the median, but they are unwise to travel too far from it. As far as it goes, this describes the Canadian pattern. Notwithstanding fractionalization of the vote, Canadian parties in Parliament are consolidated. Since the advent of permanent multipartism in 1935, the typical ENP for seats has been 2.5 (slightly higher since 1960). Even at the extreme of parliamentary fractionalization, 2004-11, ENP for seats never exceeded 3.2. And, of course, Canada's old parties wrote the book – or used to – on centrism and mobility.

If in a summary sense Canada is unexceptional for patterns in party life and death, the generalizations in the previous pattern still do not account for the actual chronology. As with the systematic literature on party entry, so with party exit. Some parties last a while; others effectively disappear after one or two elections. Some deaths are sudden; others are gradual. Most parties that die are effectively absorbed (or their labels are absorbed) into older, major parties, with a trend toward the Conservatives. But some insurgents are extinguished by other insurgents. Finally, none of this applies to the party described in the next chapter, the CCF-NDP.

Groping for Patterns through Path Dependency

In sum, mutual scrutiny of narrative by theory and theory by narrative leaves many incongruities. Some of the variety reflects variation across provinces in electoral institutions. The West has been the main site for innovation, and in this western provinces have stood in contrast not just to other regions but also to each other. The pre-existing party context has also differed across provinces, extending beyond the West. Accidents of timing have been critical. Sometimes these accidents reflect the relentless – and occasionally manipulated – operation of the electoral calendar as it acts on political entrepreneurs with varying motivations and skills. The calendar also interacts with international economic flux, such that in some provinces parties and party systems are smashed by forces entirely outside their control even as in other provinces, thanks to fortunate timing, patterns persist largely undisturbed. The overlay of these factors has sent similar provinces down different paths. Increasingly visible through the haze has been an emergent universal functionalism. As the social democratic and labour left took form in the CCF and, with greater force, the

NDP, a common pattern emerged: anti-socialist coordination. Even here, however, history mattered: which party would become the pole of this coordination was often an accident of earlier timing.

Farmers in Politics

The most important instance is the first, around 1921, since it constrained much of the later landscape. This episode featured scattered provincial elections bracketing federal dates, as shown in Table 6.1. Overlaid on this calendar are four factors: electoral institutions, relations among non-farm parties, the strength of farmers' own organizations, and the price of wheat.

Institutional Variation

In contrast to earlier and later periods and to the rest of Canada, the region and period relevant to the Progressive breakthrough featured internal institutional variation. Both district magnitudes and electoral formulas varied across and within the four provinces. In all four, rural votes were counted by FPP in single-member districts. In Ontario and Saskatchewan, this was also true for urban votes. In Manitoba and Alberta, urban voters were consolidated in multi-member districts that encompassed the entire city, one each for Winnipeg, Edmonton, Calgary, and Medicine Hat. In Manitoba, urban votes were counted by the single transferable vote (STV) and in Alberta by the plurality formula. Urban seats were thus allocated more proportionally in Manitoba than elsewhere, to the disadvantage of labour relative to farmers. This fact is all the more critical given that Winnipeg was larger in relation to its province than any other prairie city and had a relatively advanced labour movement.

Party System Factors

Relative sizes of and relations among non-farm parties and between non-farm and farm parties also varied from province to province. Although the Liberals were discredited in the West in 1917, the same was not true in Ontario. Progressive leaders differed across provinces in their attitudes to the old parties. The United Farmers of Ontario enjoyed considerable tactically motivated Conservative cooperation in the 1919 provincial election (Morton 1950, 83). The Liberals were more scandal plagued in Alberta than elsewhere, and their relations with farmers were acrimonious.

TABLE 6.1 Election timing, the price of wheat, and the Progressive/agrarian vote

Month/year of election		Progressive/farmers' share (%) of vote in province				Wheat price (shillings/quarter)
Provincial	Federal	Alberta	Saskatchewan	Manitoba	Ontario	
10/19					21.7	73
6/20				14.1		79
6/21			7.5			90
7/21		28.9				76
	12/21	52.5	61.7	41.9	25.9	45
7/22				32.8		54
6/23					20.9	49
6/25			23.0			57
	10/25	31.5	31.8	25.1	8.8	48
6/26		39.7				62

Notes: Entries under province names are the Progressive share of all votes cast in the province. Boxed cells denote provincial election victories. Federal results are in bold. Wheat price is for the end of the month. For the source on wheat prices, see note 22.

In Manitoba and Saskatchewan, the opposite was true. Nascent socialist and labour parties were important in Alberta, Manitoba, and Ontario, but their relations with farmers varied critically. The two sides had basically friendly relations in Alberta but hostile ones in Manitoba. The Winnipeg General Strike in 1919, a watershed in the political mobilization of the urban left, was anathema to Manitoba agrarians (116-18). In Ontario, farmer-labour relations were complicated by disagreement within the farmers' movement. Its general secretary opposed cooperation with labour, but E.C. Drury, who emerged as the parliamentary leader in 1919, accepted coalition with labour as a matter of necessity. Continuing antagonism along this line was a factor in the ultimate failure of the coalition in 1922 (212 ff.).

Agrarian Coordination

Within the agrarian movement, coordination could not be taken for granted. As Morton (1950, 112) put it, "farmers sought, not power, but representation, and were to be embarrassed by the quite unexpected magnitude of their victory." In Saskatchewan and Manitoba, agrarian leaders negotiated with the governing Liberals even as farmer candidates presented themselves as rivals to the Liberal Party (98-99). Farmers' political resolve generally strengthened from 1919 to 1921 (although it seemed to be strong all along in Alberta). Even so, in the 1921 federal campaign, Progressive and Liberal leaders began by trying to avoid three-way contests. Negotiations unravelled. The Progressive position was undermined by local pressure as agrarian candidates began presenting themselves anyway. In turn, this lowered the Liberals' incentive to cooperate, and then Ontario and Quebec urban interests shifted donations away from the Unionists and toward the Liberals as the best hope of stemming the agrarian tide. There was even some Liberal-Conservative electoral cooperation (122, 125-27).

Price Movements

At the start of the sequence in November 1919, wheat fetched 73 shillings per quarter (eight bushels). It peaked at 90 shillings in June 1921 but by the end of that year had fallen to 45 shillings, and it went lower still in the following months.[22]

Accidents of Timing

The upshot of all this is that, first, agrarian electoral support varied more than would be predicted from background sociology or political economy and, second, the electorate support that did materialize translated imperfectly into strength in parliaments.

- In Ontario, the Progressives achieved a seat plurality with a remarkably small vote. In one sense, this is misleading since agrarian candidates contested only half of the seats in the legislature. But, then, the farm vote was likely to be minuscule where there were no farmers. A big part of the 1919 story is the temporary weakness of the Conservatives, punished after too many years in office. In the next election, in 1923, the United Farmers of Ontario held its ground. But the Conservatives were restored to their former position, helped by movement from the Liberals. Thereafter the United Farmers of Ontario was not a factor in Ontario politics since the internal disagreements that dogged formation of the coalition in 1919 continued.
- In the 1920 Manitoba election, agrarian insurgency blocked the Liberals from retaining a majority but allowed them to hang on to power. Thus, the agrarian movement was spared responsibility for the plunging grain market. The weakness of the Liberal government made it short lived as the 1922 election roughly coincided with the bottom of the wheat market. The Progressive vote went up enough to put the party in power. It was helped by the electoral system since labour candidates received almost as many votes as farmers did. But where, thanks to FPP, the farm vote was amplified, the labour vote, counted under STV, was not. It also helped that the Liberal remnant was sympathetic to farmers, especially in light of the challenge from labour.
- The 1921 Saskatchewan election appears to have been called pre-emptively (Morton 1950, 98). Not only was the farmers' movement hesitant – indeed not ready – to contest the Liberal government's supremacy, but also the election caught the peak in the price of wheat. In terms of votes, the farm interest did well, mainly because several farmer candidates defied the leadership and presented themselves anyway. They were not numerous enough to deny the Liberals their majority, however, and they were able to stay in office until the market for grains improved.

By the next election, the federal Progressives were on the wane, and their provincial counterparts could not borrow credibility from the federal arena. The party hung on for the rest of the decade but with a diminished sense of purpose, such that it became available for co-optation in 1929 by right-wing nativists.

- The last provincial election in the immediate postwar sequence was in Alberta, with a pattern diametrically opposed to that in Saskatchewan. The price of wheat was now plummeting, a full slate of farmer candidates was available in farm constituencies, and labour candidates were strong in Calgary, Medicine Hat, and the mining towns of the southern Rockies. The result was a United Farmers of Alberta (UFA) majority, augmented by labour support. As in Manitoba, the farm vote was not overwhelming, partly because no candidates ran in cities or labour-dominated places. The political situation of labour was unlike that in Manitoba in two ways: labour was an ally of the UFA and supplied a member of cabinet, and the impact of the labour vote was augmented in its urban base by the combination of high district magnitude and FPP. The government was positioned to benefit from recovery in the 1920s.

- In the federal election of December 6, 1921, farmer candidates swept the field. The old parties were all but shut out of the prairie West.[23] In each of the four key provinces (including Ontario), the vote for farmer candidates outran the totals in the preceding provincial elections, even ones that took place mere months before. The highest total of all was in Saskatchewan, the one province in which the Progressives were never to taste power, except much later as the junior partner of a Conservative-dominated coalition.

Divergent Paths

The result was a patchwork quilt, and the movement faded in most places before adjacent provinces could come in line with each other or before federal and provincial arenas could converge. This meant that when the next economic crisis arrived, punishment of incumbents produced yet more incoherence.

- Alberta embarked on 14 years of left-leaning UFA governments, with a party of labour also modestly important. The UFA was a founding

constituent of the CCF, such that, when the UFA was discredited by the economic reverse of the 1930s, so was the CCF. It did not help that, although the UFA organization joined the CCF, the UFA government resisted submergence in the larger movement (Johnson 1979, 96-99). The beneficiary of all this was Social Credit.
- In Saskatchewan, Liberal luck held. In 1929, what was left of the Progressive Party allied with the Conservatives, deprived the Liberals of their majority, and brought the government down. This allowed the Liberals to avoid retribution for the Depression even as the economic collapse marginalized both the Progressives and the Conservatives. Space was thus opened up for an invader, and in 1934 that role was filled by the CCF. Unlike in Alberta, labour in Saskatchewan was not harmed by association with farmers. Although the CCF was rather weak both in 1934 and in 1938, it emerged as the opposition each time and as the only credible alternative to the Liberals.[24]
- In Manitoba, the Progressives continued in power through the 1920s and avoided retribution by coalescing with the Liberal Party. This meant that for the CCF the situation was unlike that in Alberta: in Manitoba, there was no prospect of coalition with farmers and thus no confusion of roles.
- In Ontario, the farmers' party ceased to be a factor in 1922 and thus was not around in the 1930s either to be punished or to sow confusion.

Ethnonationalist Insurgency in Quebec

Quebec was the site of an early path-dependent claim (Pinard 1966, 1975) in relation to the Ralliement Créditiste. Arguably, something like Pinard's logic extends back before the 1930s. The 1917 election and conscription delegitimated the provincial Conservatives along with the federal ones. The responsibility pinned on the federal party for the depth of the Great Depression cannot have helped the provincial party. The Conservatives, therefore, were not a credible vehicle for punishing the provincial Liberals,[25] who had long been in power and had a cumulative record of corruption. Some kind of insurgency was thus arguably in the cards. One possibility leaned left, the Action Libérale Nationale (ALN; Dirks 1991), which entered into an electoral arrangement with what was left of the Conservatives led by Maurice Duplessis. The 1935 election returned a Liberal majority, but the government was immediately engulfed in a corruption scandal. On the opposition side, Duplessis won the politics of manoeuvre in the inter-election year, and the bulk of the ALN delegation shifted to the Union Nationale label. The label genuflected toward the ALN, but the ethos of the new party was conservative and clericalist. Although hindsight suggests that opening a clericalist dimension was inevitable, it is not impossible to imagine a different trajectory. Had the ALN forces prevailed in the period of manoeuvre, the insurgent would have been more forward looking. Its policies would have been informed by Catholic social doctrine, like those adopted by the Godbout Liberals in the 1940s but perhaps less tainted by association with the war policies of the federal Liberals. Such a trajectory would have been less nationalist and probably less clericalist than the one that actually appeared (Behiels 1985).

Anti-Labour Coordination

Although the West has routinely been at odds with the rest of the country, it has also and for the same reason been like the rest of the Anglo-American world. Just as the region was the birthplace of Canadian labour in politics, so too has it been the prime site for anti-labour coordination. Such coordination follows predictable rules, but the exact path of such coordination reflects the earlier history of each system.

Insurgent party activity in British Columbia was not constrained by the complexities of Ontario and prairie farm politics. Developments in British Columbia and later developments in Saskatchewan reflect the growing strength of the CCF and NDP. The socialist threat creates imperatives for consolidation on the centre-right. Under circumstances best characterized as accidental, those pressures can sometimes favour a party specific to the province. More generally, which party is the anti-CCF/NDP pole can be a matter of contingency. Nothing in nature dictated that Social Credit would emerge as even a half-credible alternative in British Columbia in the early 1950s. It did emerge, however, and engaged a politics of manoeuvre that W.A.C. Bennett exploited. Manoeuvre also characterized the mid-1970s, and again Social Credit strategists prevailed. In the 1990s, their skills failed them. Or perhaps Social Credit was swept under by cultural change whose implications had been bottled up. The centrists, mainly urban Liberals, who dominated the Social Credit cabinet in 1975, failed to secure their base inside the party. The party was recaptured by culturally conservative forces that proved to be increasingly unacceptable to the increasingly secular and demographically weighty urban parts of the province. In Saskatchewan, once the CCF became a credible force, Liberals and Conservatives took turns as poles of anti-socialist coordination. Both were singularly incompetent, however, and in the 1990s the task fell to the Saskatchewan Party. In Manitoba, the anti-socialist coalition formed around a traditional party, the Conservatives.[26]

Discussion

Echoes of the various theories of third-party existence, entry, and exit can be detected in the seismology of Canadian insurgents. But the echoes are often faint, and no one theory covers all cases. Indeed, it is not obvious that a matrix combining all of the theories would reach all of the cases. The implication seems to be inescapable: history matters.

This chapter has shown that it matters for the efflorescence of Canadian insurgents. It is the most economical explanation of how Alberta could begin life as Canada's most left-leaning province and then abruptly become the epicentre of the country's political right. The same is true for British Columbia, which featured for decades neither old party as a major player in provincial politics, only for this to cease abruptly in 1991. True also for Saskatchewan's trip in the opposite direction. Even for Quebec it matters, not surprising for a province whose motto is "Je me souviens." That a nationalist dimension would open up and stretch might have been inevitable. But the dimension's particular form was never a given, and Quebec nationalism might have taken on a left-wing cast or been less prominent had the 1935-36 hiatus turned out differently. In short, Johnson's (1979) contention that Alberta's rejection of the CCF at the critical founding moment was an "accident of history" echoes beyond the boundaries of that province.

It also echoes in the divergent outcomes for mainstream parties. At one level, this is just arithmetic: the stronger an insurgent, the weaker one or both of the old parties, and vice versa. But history can also matter for the identity of the old party that does survive. Why, for instance, does the Liberal Party control the right side of the BC space, whereas in Manitoba the right side belongs to the Conservative Party? It does not suffice to object that BC Liberals are a conservative lot. The brand must count for something, and hints of support for the moribund Conservative Party early in the 2013 provincial election campaign suggest that many on the right would rather not support the Liberals – but they feel trapped.

The Canadian provincial pattern reflects a general proposition in the comparative study of party systems and voter alignments: where the left looks similar everywhere – stronger in some places than others but with the same basic social foundations and links to organized labour – the right does not (Lipset and Rokkan 1967). For instance, in some places, the right is secular, in other places Catholic. Even where Catholics are numerous, Catholic parties do not necessarily flourish (Kalyvas 1996). And so on. In the normal politics of the Westminster world, only one non-socialist party survives as a major party. Whatever its origins, the survivor is pushed to the right. But residues of its original base might persist, as might its non-economic policy instincts. Manitoba, British Columbia, and Saskatchewan mimic in the small histories of the other three long-standing Westminster polities. In all three, the left is the fixed point – the NDP in Canada and labour parties elsewhere. In one jurisdiction, the Conservatives control the right, in a second the Liberals, and in the third a party whose name is idiosyncratic and refers to the place.

When historical accident befalls a province, its impact tends to be preserved longer in provincial than in federal elections. Even though federal elections themselves are regionalized – a central theme of this chapter – the federal arena transmits impulses that transcend provincial boundaries. Although I have not spelled it out in detail yet, there is a tendency for mainstream federal parties, in recent years especially the Conservative Party, to absorb sectional insurgents. Notwithstanding the inertia imposed by boundaries, provincial politics are also susceptible to the appeal of the partisan mainstream.

7

Invasion from the Left

> Class was important in Britain because nothing else was.
> – S.E. FINER, *COMPARATIVE GOVERNMENT*

As the narrative in Chapter 6 moved past 1945, it became increasingly necessary to see insurgent parties in relation to a ubiquitous competitor, the CCF-NDP. Although it is also a "new" party, its support differs qualitatively from that for insurgents. The CCF-NDP is a garden-variety party of labour. Its appeal is largely programmatic, and it is linked organizationally to a major part of civil society, the union movement. But until 2011 – and then only temporarily – the CCF-NDP never broke through to major-party status, except in certain provinces and in those provinces more in provincial elections than in federal ones.

I begin this chapter with basic empirics, akin to those in Chapter 6. Where did the party start? On what trajectory did it grow? How did the patterns differ between federal and provincial arenas? The empirics reveal the party's initially confined geography, its evolution beyond its original base, and its general history of weakness. In the rest of the chapter, I walk through alternative explanations of this weakness. The first explanations are "compositional," by analogy to the logic in Chapter 5. An obvious starting point is the historical weakness of organized labour itself, amplified by antagonism between craft and industrial unions, between communists and anti-communists, and between secular unions and Quebec-based confessional unions. Labour mobilization did come late to Canada, and divisions were slow to be resolved, but late and halting mobilization does not provide a satisfactory explanation. This leads to an analysis of the barriers to coordinated labour and partisan mobilization. On the European landscape, ethnic and religious diversity is a major constraint on the left vote, and among the Westminster democracies Canada is easily the most diverse, more so than any European comparator. This diversity accounts for some of the NDP weakness. Even so, if we zero in on the parts of the electorate most like labour party supporters elsewhere, NDP support still seems to be anemic. Accordingly, I conclude the chapter by arguing that left voters in Canada have a peculiar problem of coordination. This explanation is not compositional but "contextual," again as in Chapter 5. It posits that individual-level NDP support is contingent on aggregate circumstances. The problem is the Liberal Party. The explanation of NDP weakness, I argue, is the mirror image of the explanation of Liberal strength. This is not to say that the two parties are mere substitutes, that New Democrats are just Liberals in a hurry, as Mackenzie King famously characterized them, or that Liberal voters are New Democrats begging to be liberated, as NDP strategists sometimes fantasize. The key is that Liberal strength, historically predicated on hegemony in Quebec, set the agenda for many generations of voters, whether they liked it (as many did) or not. Some key evidence of contextual factors in federal elections comes, counterintuitively but counterfactually, from their absence in provincial elections.

Preliminary Empirics

By breaking with the old central Canadian party system, farmers cracked open the door for a labour party to push through. As a result, the early stages of left mobilization shared many of the idiosyncrasies that characterized the agrarian insurgency, including some of its ironies. As the decades advanced, however, the left party acquired its own dynamic, and this in turn made it look more and more like social democratic and labour parties in other countries.

As with farmers, early worker candidacies were sporadic and poorly coordinated. They tended to appear in isolated single-industry towns, especially in Alberta and British Columbia, in a pattern similar to that identified by Lipset (1960, 232-36, 249). The major urban locales were

Winnipeg and Vancouver. The competing fragments of the union movement disagreed over the proper course of action; some of the most important leaders were outright revolutionaries (McCormack 1977). Things began to settle down in the 1920s as farmers' electoral success was accompanied by a handful of labour MPs. As the decade progressed, a critical leavening of Progressives, the "Ginger Group," increasingly aligned themselves with the smaller number of labour MPs. For both groups, the novel experience of actually being inside the corridors of Parliament focused minds and set the stage for a nationwide party (McNaught 1959; Young 1969).

In the 1930s, the fragmented left – some farmers' organizations, unions, socialist societies, various micro-parties, and socialist parliamentarians – began to congeal as a labour party. The full process required a further 29 years, from the initial founding of the CCF in 1932 to its refounding as the NDP in 1961. Although the beginning of the CCF as a federation testifies to the fissiparousness of the early left, by 1937 the CCF was functioning as a unitary entity (Young 1969). Outright marriage with organized labour was delayed by conflicts within the union movement.[1] By 1961, these impediments were no longer in play.

Figure 7.1 plots the chronology for both federal and provincial elections, province by province. Although the trajectory is not always upward, the general picture is of a trend. The breakthrough decade of the 1940s was followed by disappointing results in the 1950s and early 1960s. The solid gains of the 1970s and 1980s were more than reversed in the 1990s; in 1993, the federal party returned shares no better than those in the mid-1930s. But it recovered after 2000, and, if it was not quite to the levels of the 1980s, the 2011 election was a record-setting result. This was almost entirely because of the breakthrough in Quebec; in its areas of historical strength, the party still did not quite reach the 1988 level. For the most part, the pattern has been one of modest flux around an established level or a gradually rising trend. The NDP story is not generally one of boom and bust, of short-run success followed by oblivion. This claim is qualified by evidence from the party's 2008-11-15 surge and decline in Quebec.

Historically, the CCF-NDP stronghold was the West. In one sense, this is not surprising given the role of prairie farmers in breaking the mould

FIGURE 7.1 Federal and provincial CCF-NDP dynamics by province, 1908-2011

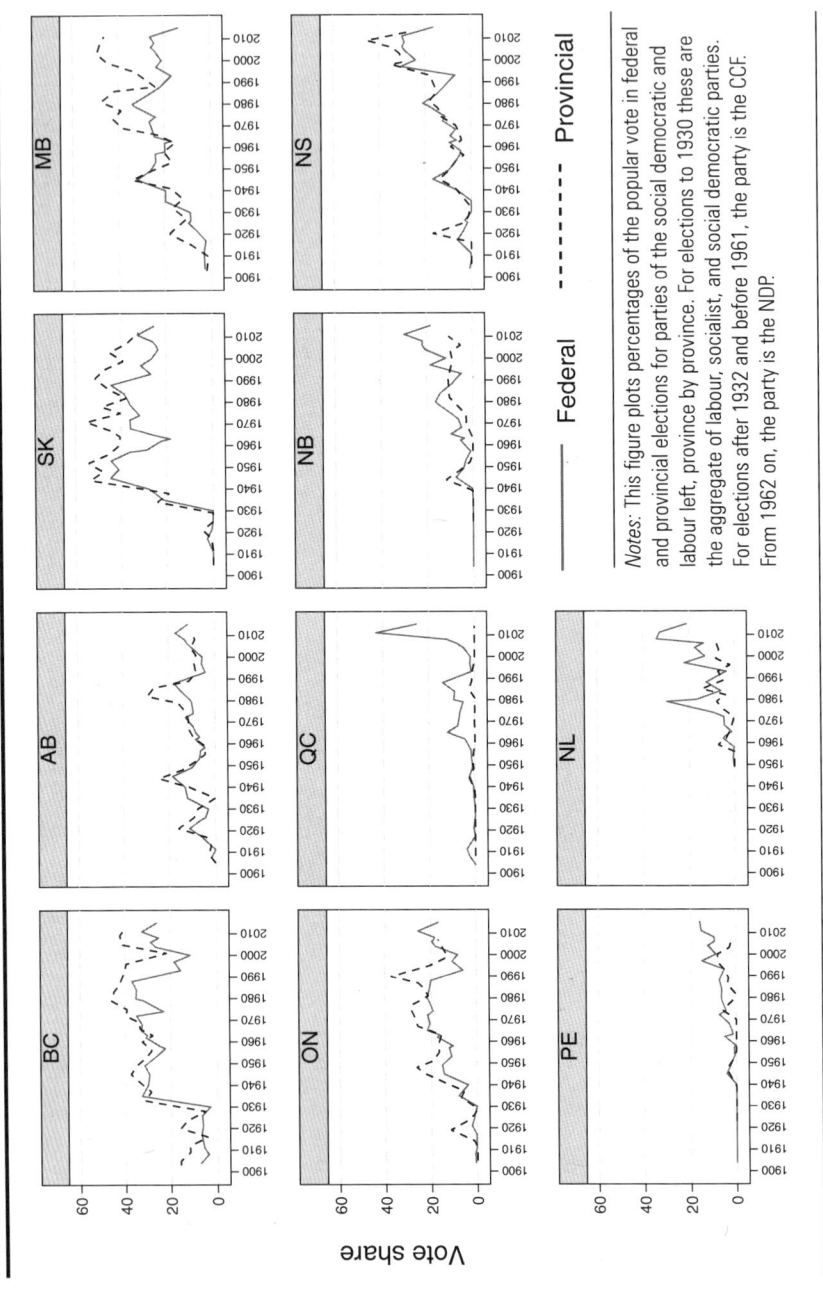

Notes: This figure plots percentages of the popular vote in federal and provincial elections for parties of the social democratic and labour left, province by province. For elections to 1930 these are the aggregate of labour, socialist, and social democratic parties. For elections after 1932 and before 1961, the party is the CCF. From 1962 on, the party is the NDP.

of the old party system and the role of some Progressives in creating the CCF. But the mapping from the Progressives to the CCF is loose. Some of the lack of fit reflects the path dependencies detailed in the preceding chapter. The chief exception, as we already know, is Alberta, where the UFA managed to immolate both itself and the new party in 1935. (Even so, there were many subsequent elections in which the NDP's Alberta share was greater than any share east of Ontario.) The breakthrough was the most complete in Saskatchewan, where the Conservatives and Progressives dragged each other down. That said, the Saskatchewan surge took over a decade to be realized. The same time path prevailed federally in Manitoba, although with a lower ceiling. If the Manitoba NDP ultimately enjoyed greater success provincially than federally, provincial success was a long time coming. And the most important breakthrough of all bore no relationship to earlier events. This was in British Columbia, where the CCF won more than 30 percent of the vote in its first outing, provincially in 1933 and federally in 1935.

Elsewhere the party was usually weak yet rode a modest upward trend. The party enjoyed middling strength in Ontario from fairly early on and is not really stronger now than it was in the 1960s. This generalization must be qualified by noting the party's growth in Ontario that culminated in the NDP government under Bob Rae formed in 1991; it has not recovered from the experience. In Atlantic Canada, the party has strengthened in recent decades, with the 1990s being particularly important. Nova Scotia aside, however, that growth has been mainly a federal phenomenon. In Quebec, the party never really entered the provincial arena and never amounted to much federally – until 2011.

For the CCF-NDP, the contrast between arenas is consistent, unlike the situation with the insurgents. Wherever the NDP is relatively strong – the West and to a lesser extent Ontario and (recently) Nova Scotia – it is stronger provincially than federally. Where the party is historically weak – Quebec and the rest of Atlantic Canada – the opposite is true. (Admittedly, the 2011 federal result in Quebec confuses the pattern.) For the moment, I leave the gap between arenas on the table as a fact. Later in the chapter, it is critical for interpretation.

The party might have started later or hit lower ceilings in some provinces than in others, but everywhere its growth has been secular or at least mainly unidirectional. Its diffusion in federal elections has been especially orderly, notwithstanding the reverse in the 1990s and the sudden shift in Quebec in 2011. The party's Canadian geography resembles the pattern for European social democracy (Bartolini 2000): bigger in some places than others but everywhere similar structurally.

But why is the party not bigger? Majoritarian electoral formulas do discriminate against parties of the left (Iversen and Soskice 2006), but in the other Anglo-American comparators the party of labour is at least the second-place party, the chief competitor to the dominant party of the right. Indeed, as stand-alone entities, these labour parties tend to be larger than their counterparts in proportional representation (PR) systems; they just do not get to participate in broader multiparty coalitions. Only in some provinces and only in provincial elections has such major-party status been true for Canada. The 2011 election seemingly made the NDP the presumptive alternative to one of the mainstream parties, but the election in 2015 erased the gains. What accounts for this prolonged weakness?

The Composition of Canadian Society

It seems reasonable to begin by asking about the makeup of Canadian society. Following the lead of Bartolini (2000), comparative experience suggests that we look, on the one hand, at mobilizational factors – forces that might drive class politics – and, on the other, at constraints and opportunities – variables that might suppress, amplify, or condition the mobilizing factors. Most of the mobilizing factors lie in political economy: industrialization, urbanization, concentration of workers in large firms, and – most critically – numerical mobilization of labour into unions and centralization in union decision making. Among constraints, the obvious starting point is the country's ethnoreligious diversity.

The Mobilization of Labour

At a minimum, class politics seem to presuppose the mobilization of an industrial workforce: the initiation of industrial occupations, the concentration of that workforce in urban places and large firms, and the appearance of labour organizations (Archer 2008; Shalev and Korpi 1980). In all of these trends, Canada was a laggard (Huber and Stephens 2001), so perhaps it should not be surprising that the CCF-NDP had a late start and stunted growth.

Panel A of Figure 7.2 portrays Canada's pattern of late labour mobilization. At the start of the 1930s, less than 10 percent of the labour force was unionized. Among non-agricultural workers, the percentage then began to climb as US industrial unions, mainly affiliated with the Congress of Industrial Organizations (CIO), extended their organizing activity northward.[2] But Canada's continuing agricultural character is shown by the effective stasis in union membership relative to the labour force as a whole; this is shown by the line incorporating data from Kumar (1986). In the 1921 census, 51 percent of the population was defined as rural, and as late as 1941 the percentage was 46. The 1940s, with the industrialization induced by the Second World War, saw the largest percentage point intercensal rural-to-urban shift, a drop to 38 percent rural by 1951.[3] This decade also heralded the start of organized labour's truly consequential growth.

Why was unionization so late even within industrial occupations? One issue might have been the lack of concentration in employment. Large firms are easier to organize, and this seems to be especially important for industrial as opposed to craft unions (Bartolini 2000, 158-59; Lipset 1960, 251, Table 8). So the industrialization of the 1940s might have been as important for its concentration as for its scale. Unionization might also have been inhibited by a hostile regulatory climate. The Industrial Disputes Investigation Act (1907) did acknowledge industrial reality, but its emphasis on postponement, inquiry, and cooling off discouraged strike activity, including strikes for union recognition (Craven 1980). Even though the act was struck down in the 1920s, it remained the basis of provincial labour law.[4] Only with the proclamation of Order-in-Council PC 1003 in 1944 did the regulatory climate become accommodative. As with the older act, PC 1003 became the basic model for provincial action. All of this said, though, the cross-national evidence is equivocal on the relationship between regulatory constraint and union mobilization (Bartolini 2000, 290, Table 6.10, passim). In some countries, the fight for union recognition served as the basis for labour mobilization.

Masked by the figure, however, are three facts critical to forging a link between the labour movement and a political party. First, there was a

170 *The Canadian Party System*

FIGURE 7.2   Labour mobilization and the CCF-NDP vote: The national picture

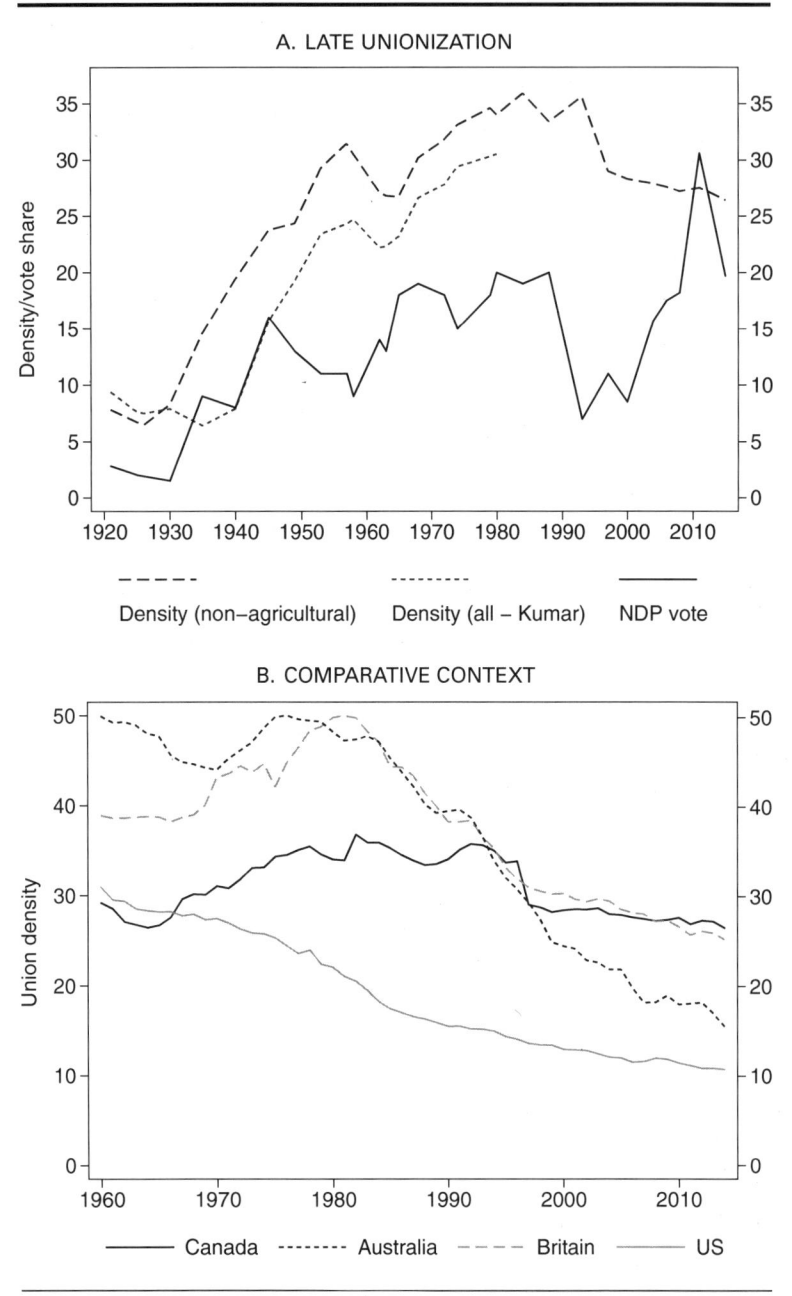

A. LATE UNIONIZATION

[Chart: Density/vote share from 1920 to 2010, showing Density (non-agricultural), Density (all – Kumar), and NDP vote]

Density (non-agricultural)   Density (all – Kumar)   NDP vote

B. COMPARATIVE CONTEXT

[Chart: Union density from 1960 to 2010 for Canada, Australia, Britain, and US]

Canada   ········ Australia   ──── Britain   ──── US

Notes: Panel A plots union density (union members as a percentage of the labour force) for all of Canada along with the NDP percentage of the national popular vote. Panel B compares union densities in Canada with those of the Anglo-American comparators.

division between the craft-oriented Trades and Labour Congress (TLC) and the industry-oriented Canadian Congress of Labour (CCL) (Horowitz 1968). Second, several key CCL unions had communist leaders. Purging communists was critical both to labour unity and to any prospect of affiliation with a mainstream political party (Abella 1973). The purge was accomplished by the early 1950s. This enabled the merger of the two federations in 1956 as the Canadian Labour Congress (CLC). Third, there was a distinct pattern of mobilization in Quebec. Many unions there were confessional, eventually secularized as the Confédération des Syndicats Nationaux. In the 1950s, they were commonly aligned with the Liberal Party and in the 1970s and beyond with the independence movement. Creation of the CLC made possible a formal link with a political party, realized with mutation of the CCF into the NDP in 1961. But this left the Quebec labour movement estranged from the NDP.

After 1961, the trajectory of union density was mainly upward.[5] So, more often than not, was the trajectory of the NDP. Indeed, the NDP vote, also plotted in Figure 7.2A, can be read to echo the pattern of labour mobilization and consolidation. The 1945 election was one critical moment, with a CCF share nearly double that of 1940. Another marker might be 1961, the birth year of the NDP, followed by a rough correspondence in upward trends for both union density and vote share.

However, in the bigger picture, correspondences are weak. On the one hand, the origins of the CCF precede the great surge in labour mobilization. Moreover, the early geography of CCF electoral strength is unrelated to the aggregate position of organized labour. Figure 7.3 juxtaposes the party's federal vote, averaged by decade, with province-level union densities. The picture resembles Figure 7.1 in showing the party's early strength in the West, especially in British Columbia and Saskatchewan. But in those provinces the union movement was less advanced than the party and no more successful than in some provinces where the CCF was weak.

When labour mobilization finally took off, the party did not really follow suit, not even when it morphed into the NDP. From 1945 to 1988, the gap between union density and the NDP vote averaged 10-15 points, depending on the density indicator. The rhythm was not promising: 1945 and 1962 saw the party surge and the gap close; subsequent elections saw the gap widen as labour mobilization continued but the party stagnated

FIGURE 7.3 Labour mobilization and the CCF-NDP vote, by province and decade

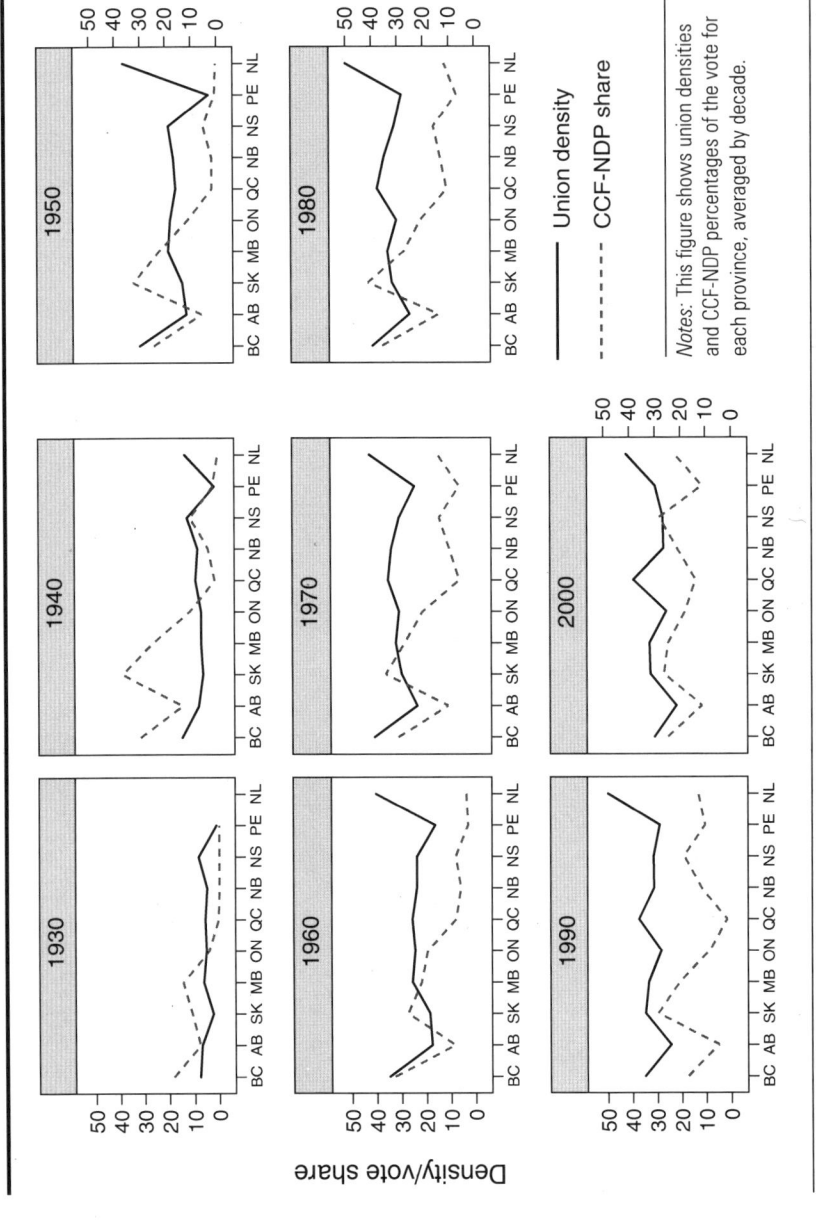

Notes: This figure shows union densities and CCF-NDP percentages of the vote for each province, averaged by decade.

— Union density
--- CCF-NDP share

or grew only marginally. Although the gap closed again after 2000, only in 2011 did the lines intersect. The geographic patterns in Figure 7.3 show a similar disconnect. The party's electoral strength remained distinctly western even as labour mobilization proceeded nationwide. By the 1960s, union density exceeded NDP electoral returns almost everywhere. Only in the 1990s did the NDP vote really nationalize along lines similar to the labour movement – only now the NDP share lagged behind union density almost everywhere.

The Canadian pattern does not seem so peculiar when put in cross-national perspective, however. In Europe, social mobilization works longitudinally but not always cross-sectionally, especially for the late nineteenth and early twentieth centuries. Indeed, "whether one considers the timing of industrialization, the length of industrial-sector predominance, or levels of sector occupation, it does not seem that socialist mobilization was earlier or stronger in the more industrially advanced economies" (Bartolini 2000, 140). This generalization also applies to mobilization of labour in particular: its pace was country-specific and led as often as lagged behind electoral mobilization of the left. Indeed, prior electoral success by a party of the left was often the precondition for the passage of legislation that accommodated drives for union recognition.

The peculiar early position of Saskatchewan and British Columbia illustrates the complexities in getting a labour party off the ground. Much of this mirrors patterns identified in Chapter 6. Some sections of the farming community were initially more supportive of the CCF than others: members of cooperatives (Lipset 1968) and certain crop ecologies (Silverstein 1968, 448-51). In British Columbia, the agrarian vote was not important. Critical there and in Alberta were isolated resource towns (Lipset 1960, 232-36). Producers situated far from population centres and with insecure incomes, even those who owned their means of production (e.g., farmers and fishers), were particularly susceptible to appeals from the left. Also pushing in this direction were communication structures that facilitated internal exchanges even as they screened information from the outside (249). Lipset draws explicit parallels between the Canadian examples and remote locations in Norway.

Similarly, variation in Canada in relations among farmers, labour, and rival parties is hardly peculiar; it echoes patterns observed cross-nationally.

Left parties' early bargains with the agricultural sector are critical to their later success (Bartolini 2000, 466-86). Bargains are not guaranteed to materialize since tensions remain: urban socialists have to make their peace with private owners of agricultural land, the presence of an agricultural proletariat can be an issue (Luebbert 1991, 287ff), and the price of food can be a sticking point. Not surprisingly, alliance patterns diverged within Canada. Manitoba farmers could not countenance an alliance with organized labour, but Alberta farmers could (Morton 1950). Particularly relevant to the Saskatchewan experience was the pattern in which farmers formed cooperatives that then federated. This in turn facilitated bargaining with urban workers. This was true in Alberta a decade earlier but thanks to accidents of timing (Chapter 6) was fatal to both sides of the bargain.

Much of this is mediated through the pre-existing party system. Particularly important is the willingness of non-socialist parties to accommodate labour, and this in turn reflects earlier history. As in Canada, the critical actors are Liberals. Depending on how they fit into pre-class politics, some Liberals are willing to ally with labour, some are radically capitalist, and others vacillate (Luebbert 1992, chaps. 2-5; Bartolini 2000, 420-22). The British example is telling. The party predilection of the early labour leadership was generally Liberal. Although formation of the Independent Labour Party (ILP) proved to be critical, the ILP was not the creature of organized labour; it courted the union movement, not the opposite. Although the ILP heavily populated the Labour Representation Committee, formed in 1900, the committee operated more as a parliamentary lobby group and an adjunct of the Liberals than as a party in its own right (Ball 1981, 44-49). But labour met resistance from elements in the Liberal Party, such that the Liberals effectively kept labour out. Even so, it is not fanciful to posit that had the Liberals held themselves together after 1914, they might have remained the pole of coordination for the labour movement. In Canada, the Liberal Party was often peculiarly hostile to labour (Horowitz 1968), especially in Ontario under Mitchell Hepburn (Saywell 1991). Sometimes Liberal positioning vis-à-vis the CCF reflected its relationship with agrarians. Recall that, where Liberals in Alberta and Saskatchewan were hostile to farmers' political action, in Manitoba (Morton 1950, 122-23, 243) and Ontario (Saywell 1991, 82-83, 96) they were less so. In sum, the Canadian pattern, including its geography, replicates European variation in microcosm.

Whatever the exact trajectory, however, a robust union movement is ultimately a critical prop for the left. In the late twentieth century, parties of the left rarely flourished where organized labour was weak.[6] And by the twenty-first century Canada was no longer a union laggard. To be sure, Canadian union density never reached the stratospheric numbers that formerly prevailed elsewhere. Where the Canadian number barely brushed 40 percent at its peak, more than half of the labour force in Britain and Australia was unionized, as shown by Panel B of Figure 7.2. But Canada has been above the OECD average since 1977 and rivalled Australia and Britain since the mid-1990s. In the new century, Canada has emerged as the most unionized of these four countries even though unionization has fallen in Canada (but not as much as elsewhere; the drops in Australia and the United States are especially striking).[7] Yet in each comparator the party of labour governed for several post-drop years. It seems to be reasonable, then, to ask why the resilience of the Canadian labour movement has not helped the NDP more.

Notwithstanding the growth of the CCF-NDP vote, the history of the union/non-union arithmetic gap is one of trendless fluctuation. This is shown by Figure 7.4, which plots marginal effects and associated 95 percent confidence intervals for all elections since 1940.[8] Key moments in CCF-NDP history are mirrored on the plot. The 1945 election is an early high point, not matched until 2006. The union vote is generally more distinct in the 1960s, 1970s, and 1980s than in the 1950s. The 1990s are a disaster, but the 2000s reveal a generally greater distinctiveness than any earlier decade. There is some correspondence, then, between the arithmetic gap and the party's overall size: 1945 as the breakthrough year; stronger after the organizational renewal of 1961; weak in the 1990s; strong again with the party's recovery in 2004. But overall strength does not account for all of the shifts: although the party surged in 1945 and the 2000s, years with large union/non-union gaps, in none of those years was its strength as great as in the 1980s, and overall growth in the party's share was not obviously mirrored by a secular widening of the union/non-union gap. Also missing in the picture is any immediate impact from the refounding

FIGURE 7.4   Impact of union membership, 1940-2011

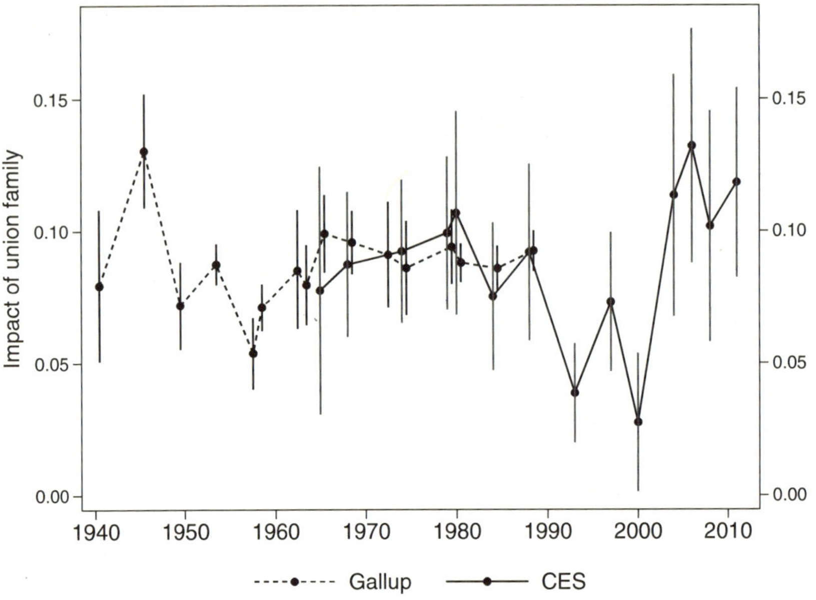

Notes: This figure shows the difference in likelihood of voting for the CCF-NDP between union and non-union families. Markers are point estimates for the marginal effect of union membership derived from bivariate probit estimates. Vertical bars are 95 percent confidence intervals. Non-voters are excluded.

of the CCF as the NDP in 1961. The new party explicitly opened the door to formal affiliation, and where such affiliation occurred it seemed to help (Archer 1985). But such affiliation was slow to build, and the flatter line for the 1960s and 1970s in Figure 7.4 speaks for itself.

On the other hand, union densities were increasing throughout this period. Rather than make total NDP support grow, however, the main effect of this densification was to make union families more important in the party's support base. This is a matter of simple arithmetic. The party was only modestly larger overall in 1988, say, than in 1945. Over the same period, union density roughly doubled, and, given the stable union/non-union difference in Figure 7.4, the union-family/NDP share of the electorate also doubled. Largely offsetting this gain, however, was shrinkage of the initially much larger non-union NDP base. Transformation from the rather eclectic CCF to the union-focused NDP was not without cost. The NDP was not absolutely static in this period, of course, but net growth in the NDP support attributable to increased union density was no more than a few percentage points.

The Competing Claims of Culture

The most obvious barriers are Quebec in particular and the Catholic community in general. Again Europe is instructive. Early in the twentieth century, religion was the chief barrier, most importantly as Catholics resisted the secular force of social democracy. By the end of the century, ethnoregional parties – mostly grounded in language – were the main firewall (Bartolini 2000, Table 4.4, and 184-92 passim). Lijphart (1979) even argues that, where class competes with language and religion, class loses. And, among all rich capitalist countries, Canada is the most diverse, more diverse than the extreme European cases of Switzerland and Belgium (Fearon 2003, 215-16, Appendix): no other rich country with so even a religious split has so large a linguistic minority; no other rich country that has a sharp linguistic divide has so finely balanced a religious one.

The Canadian situation exemplifies the ideological tension inside Catholicism. In the most relevant distillation, the 1931 encyclical *Quadragesimo Anno* by Pius XI, capitalism is condemned for its materialism and inequality, but property is defended as a protection against the state and a basis for private life. Socialism is likewise condemned for its materialist theory of history and its advocacy of class conflict. In the Anglosphere, bishops sometimes evaded the issue by distinguishing an Anglo-style labour party, with its crypto-Christian moral earnestness, from continental Marxism. This cultural pattern also characterized the CCF (Allen 1971; Baum 1980, Chap. 1; McNaught 1963; Young 1969), building as it did on earlier initiatives by Protestant clergy and prominent laity (Cook 1985). But the language of class conflict that accompanied the CCF's founding might have frightened Canadian Catholic clergy (Baum 1980, 99-118). Inside the party, prominent voices (especially in British Columbia, where Marxist tendencies were most pronounced) were publicly equivocal about the wisdom of courting Catholic support (131).

And Canada is only partly in the Anglosphere. If bishops outside Quebec were initially hesitant, the Quebec hierarchy condemned the CCF outright, and this echoed beyond the province. The resonance might have been especially great in the West, to the extent that the Catholic Church there was closely linked to Quebec (Perin 1990). Only in 1943 did the bishops step back, and even then the CCF was not absolved by name.

Early empirical demonstrations are fragmentary but indicate Catholic resistance. Lipset (1968, Chapter 8) shows that the Saskatchewan CCF was initially resisted by non-Anglo-Saxon, especially Catholic, voters. Although Lipset argues that by 1944 ethnoreligious differences were largely effaced, Silverstein (1968, 456-60, 469, Table 10) shows that in the 1960s they had recrudesced – if they had ever really disappeared. We have an indication from Figures 7.1 and 7.3 that Canada followed the European model in that the CCF-NDP vote initially followed Canada's religious geography and then shifted to align with the linguistic map. Until the 1990s, the party's appeal stopped at the Ottawa River (with the occasional exception of heavily unionized Cape Breton). Only in the 1990s did the NDP's geography and that of Catholicism cease to match. Only in 2011 did Quebec drop its resistance.

The aggregate patterns are mirrored in the survey evidence, but only weakly, according to Figure 7.5. I proceed by exclusion, starting with an all-Canada pattern and then seeing what happens to the CCF-NDP share when critical subsets of the electorate are dropped from the sample.[9] As in Chapter 5, I start by dropping Quebec. Whether its early hesitation about the NDP was indeed on religious grounds or on linguistic ones, the province used to be the primary concentration of Catholic religious practice. I then drop Catholics who live outside Quebec. Note that this is a different strategy for the non-Quebec sample from that in Chapter 5. There I controlled for ethnic and other factors that overlap and potentially confound the denominational effect. Here I remove the group most resistant to class-based arguments to see whether or how much the party share grows. For visual clarity, the Gallup and CES data are presented separately, although both are on the 1940-2011 time span.

Setting Quebec aside does make the CCF-NDP look bigger. Taking Quebec out of the calculation makes the party appear to grow about 3 or 4 percent. Taking non-Quebec Catholics out augments the share only slightly, 1 to 2 percent at most, and sometimes not at all. The maximum possible impact of this move would be to inflate the CCF-NDP share by about one-third: that is, by about 5 percent. Nothing on this scale happens.

FIGURE 7.5 Impact on the NDP vote of excluding Quebec residents and Catholics, 1949-2011

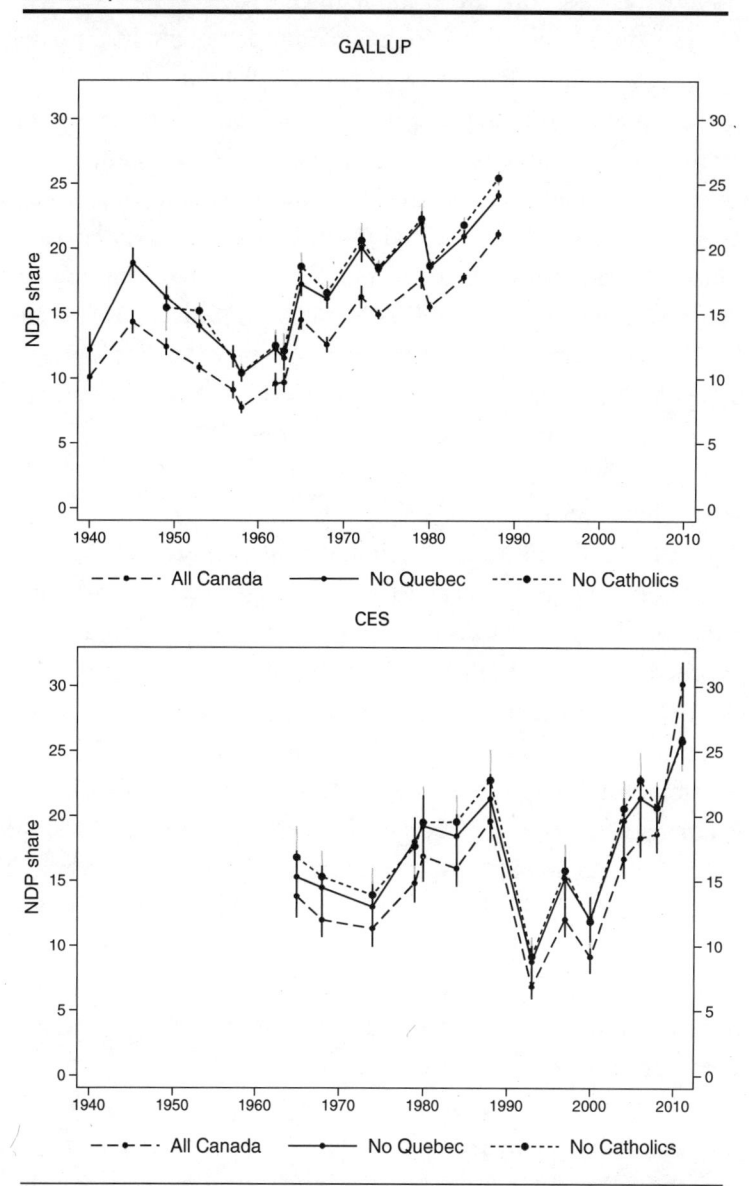

Notes: This figure shows the CCF-NDP vote, according to Gallup and Canadian Election Studies data, in subsets of the electorate, by year. The "All Canada" plot shows the party's percentage share in the total sample. The "No Quebec" plot shows the party's percentage when Quebec respondents are removed from the sample. The "No Catholics" plot shows what happens to the party's share outside Quebec when Catholics are removed from the sample.

In fact, among the pool of Catholics outside Quebec, resistance to the CCF-NDP was never that great, and it quickly waned.

Overall, these hypothetical augmentations do not produce party support on the scale traditionally associated with labour parties elsewhere. Even if we pretend that the electorate consists only of those Canadians culturally the least resistant to the CCF-NDP – less resistant, one might think, than the actual electorates in Australia and Britain – support for the party remains weak. From official returns in its historically strongest provinces, Saskatchewan, British Columbia, and Manitoba, the party's median shares between 1960 and 2011 were, respectively, 31, 29, and 24 percent. So the party was rarely that big a winner even in its sociologically most favourable contexts. To account for the CCF-NDP pattern, then, it does not suffice to focus on compositional issues.

Contexts of Coordination

Elections, especially elections fought under FPP, are exercises in coordination. Parties might be led by elites with clear agendas, but large numbers of voters will be up for grabs, and the subset that coalesces around a given party will do so for a combination of substantive and contingent reasons. Under FPP, a critical contingency is a party's general electoral credibility. The Duvergerian account, as currently conceived (Cox 1997), focuses on credibility at the district level. A central theme in this book is that the local emphasis is insufficient. I argue that voters – at least a critical subset of them – also attend to party prospects in the electorate as a whole. This proposition is hard to substantiate in that the more successful a given party is in exploiting a Canada-wide advantage, the less variance there is to explain. But Canadian voters inhabit (at least) two electorates simultaneously, and one electoral arena can be central to understanding dynamics – or the lack of dynamics – in the other one.

The geography of religion and, even more, the *sui generis* pattern of Quebec's participation in national elections testify to the fragmented character of the polity. But to the extent that federal elections require coast-to-coast coordination, the behaviour of voters in some regions is relevant to the behaviour of voters in other regions. So, if Quebec voters overwhelmingly resist the NDP, then potential NDP voters elsewhere might hesitate.

The same logic applies to cultural variation outside Quebec. Potential New Democrats in the West might notice the historical resistance to the NDP in the east and hesitate to "waste" their votes on a party that is unviable nationally. Some voters in Atlantic Canada might notice the new party's relative credibility in the West and begin to rethink their commitments to old parties. But these ruminations are about federal elections. Provincial elections can be detached from federal ones, as we know from Chapter 2. Their timing is staggered in relation both to federal elections and to provincial elections in other provinces. The relatively long life of federal and provincial parliaments augments the scope for the party in power provincially to detach its electoral rhythms from those in the other arena. Party systems in many provinces are only weakly integrated across arenas. All of this makes the pan-Canadian mutual references that operate in the federal arena much less relevant in the provincial one. The sociology might be the same as in federal elections but not the strategic backdrop. If the sociology of a given province is relatively favourable to the NDP, then the adhesion of Catholics in other provinces to the Liberal Party need not matter for that province's provincial elections.[10] In contrast, where pro-NDP factors are weak, potential supporters might rally to the more acceptable of the old parties.

There are two observable implications of this discontinuity across arenas:

1. The NDP's provincial vote distribution should be geographically more differentiated than its federal one.

    a. The bulk of this extra dispersion should be on the high side: the distribution's positive tail should have higher values for provincial than for federal outcomes.
    b. In the weakest provinces for the NDP, the federal-provincial difference should be reversed (although the fact that all numbers in this range are close to zero almost guarantees that federal-provincial differences will be small).

2. To the extent that it is truly contextual, the pattern should hold even if we exclude Catholics and Quebeckers.

This is an argument by indirection, a form of contraposition.[11] If I cannot definitively prove that NDP strength in a given province is constrained in federal elections by the party's weakness in other provinces and vice versa, I can argue that its differential strength in the provincial arena relative to the federal one reflects the lack of interprovincial connection. Critically, although the electoral context differs, the federal and provincial electorates in a given province comprise essentially the same persons..

FIGURE 7.6   The provincial "counterfactual," I: Official returns

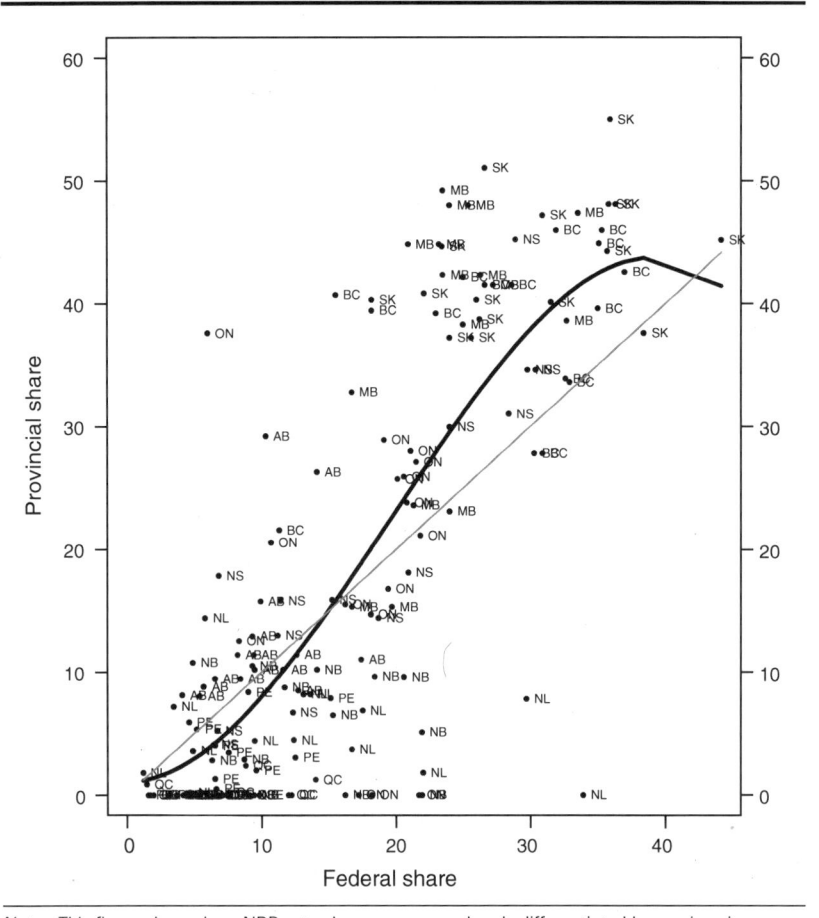

Notes: This figure shows how NDP vote shares are more sharply differentiated by province in provincial elections than in federal ones. Each coordinate represents the NDP share in a federal election in a province and the same party's share in the provincial election closest in time to the federal one. Data points are for federal election years from 1962 to 2008 inclusive. The estimation is for a fractional polynomial. Grey line indicates equality between arenas.

One test is in Figure 7.6. Coordinates are federal and provincial NDP shares, province by province, for each federal election and the temporally closest provincial one (the same election pairs as in Figure 2.8). The relationship is estimated as a fractional polynomial, and the 45 degree line appears to help visual orientation. Points on the scatterplot are labelled by province. The figure focuses on the NDP era, elections since 1960, for which the arguments above make most sense. Before 1960, the CCF commonly declined to run candidates outside the West and Ontario. Additionally, the CCF had a qualitatively distinct relationship with Saskatchewan, such that there was a cluster of very one-sided provincial shares. After 1960, the party moved swiftly to a nationwide appeal (Johnston and Cutler 2009, Fig. 6.3) and Saskatchewan became less distinct.

Over most of its range, the relationship curve lies above the 45 degree line, such that the maximum gap between a given provincial result and its federal equivalent is about 8 percent. This space is basically populated by British Columbia, Saskatchewan, and Manitoba. The polynomial and the 45 degree lines intersect near 10 percent, such that below this value provincial outcomes mainly trail federal ones rather than the reverse. The points in the latter range come mainly from Atlantic Canada and Quebec.

The projection of these arena effects onto individuals appears in Figure 7.7. It combines all Canadian Election Study files, 1965-2011, to show how predicted NDP shares are conditional on the province's percentage of Roman Catholics. Although Catholics as individuals subtract rather little from NDP support (Figure 7.5), the regional pattern is clear: the higher the percentage of Catholics, the weaker the support for the NDP. The figure excludes Catholic respondents so that there can be no leakage from individual differences into the contextual estimation. The analysis is repeated without Quebec to check for the possibility of a language-religion-region confound. The figure glosses over temporal variation to convey a big picture and to maximize power. It concentrates on the years since the founding of the NDP. Finally, the analysis is stacked to enable comparisons between arenas.

The federal-provincial divergence is clear. The east-west gradient is especially sharp in provincial elections and steepens as the Catholic percentage drops. The gradient in federal elections is also visible but much shallower. Above 30 percent Catholic, the provincial line drops below the

FIGURE 7.7 The provincial "counterfactual," II: Conditional impact of religious context, 1965-2011

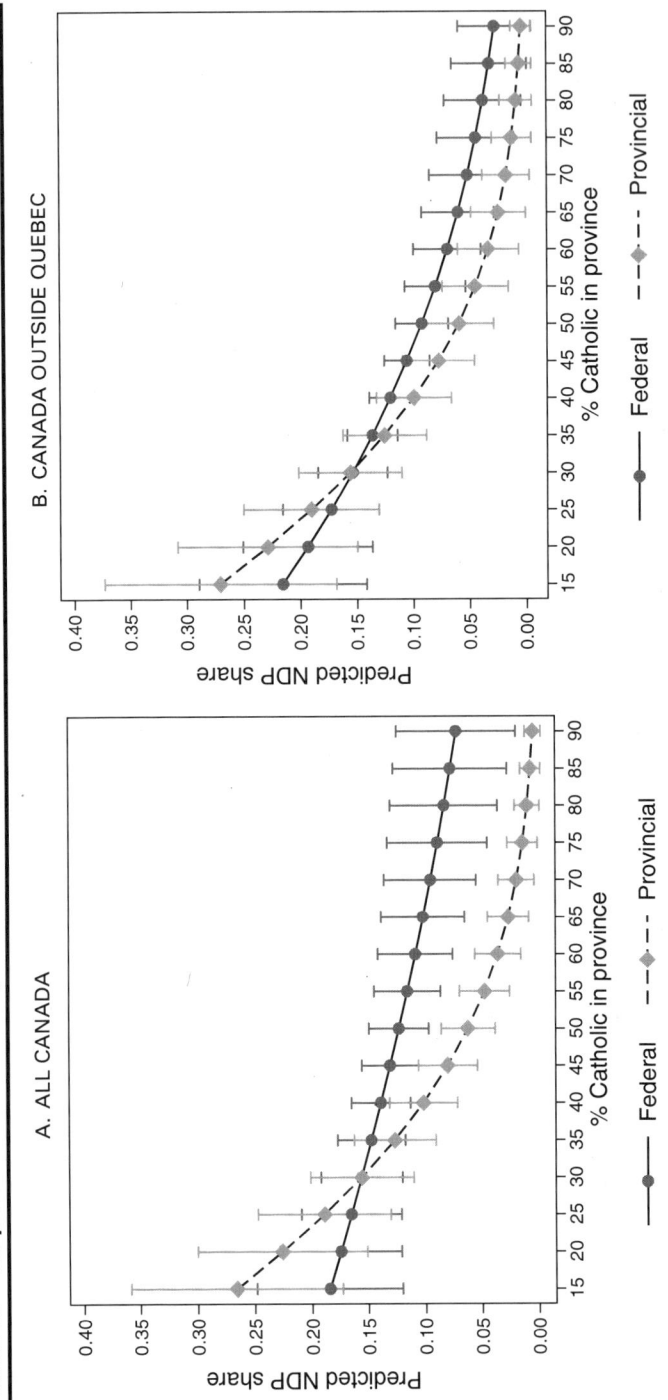

A. ALL CANADA

B. CANADA OUTSIDE QUEBEC

Notes: This figure shows how the NDP vote is more sharply differentiated across provinces in provincial elections than in federal ones. Data are from Canadian Election Studies and from the census in corresponding years. Catholic respondents are excluded. Underlying estimation is by probit with stacked federal and provincial vote data. Vertical bars are 95 percent confidence intervals, based on asymptotic standard errors reflecting clustering of census data by province and duplication of independent variables across stacks.

federal one, and this gap is maximized when the Catholic share hits 70 percent.[12] Thereafter, a floor effect induces a modest convergence, as we also saw in the aggregate data. At the other end, the gap favouring the provincial NDP is about 10 percent; this is the pattern for British Columbia. Panel B takes Quebec out of the estimation, although for visual comparability it maintains the fiction of Catholic percentages above 60 percent. The pattern is basically the same as in the all-Canada estimation but less sharply etched.[13]

Ordering parties by percentage of Catholics elides all sorts of history and even some geography. Simply ordering the provinces from east to west tells much the same story, although with messier graphics. The point, in any case, is not some firm statement about aggregate Catholicism as an ordering principle. The point, rather, is the federal-provincial discontinuity. Whatever the mechanism producing overall NDP strength (or weakness), that mechanism is given freer play in provincial elections than in federal ones. I infer that what is critical in the provincial arena is the absence of a requirement to take the rest of the country into account.

Discussion

Looking beyond the Anglosphere reveals that some of Canada's supposed peculiarities are nothing of the sort. The early appearance of left voting in non-urban – indeed non-industrial – places is not unusual. Fragmentation of initiative, reflecting locally specific relations in the triangle of farmers, workers, and political liberals, regularly characterizes the early history of the left. Canadian federalism creates openings for the logic of cross-national differences to express itself within a single polity. The lack of correspondence over both time and space between union density, on the one hand, and CCF-NDP support, on the other, is also not a peculiarity. By the end of the twentieth century, Canada had a resilient labour movement and a labour party that was an entrenched participant in Westminster-style politics. Indeed, in the early 1990s, the NDP controlled four provincial governments comprising a majority of the country's population. Yet in national politics it could not displace either of its chief competitors, and its appeal to union families remains limited.

An obvious barrier to NDP growth is Canada's ethnoreligious diversity. Canada registers as more diverse than the rest of the Anglosphere, indeed more diverse than the rest of the OECD countries. Canadian diversity maps right onto the shifting logic of the European left (Bartolini 2000), such that religion was critical in early years and ethnicity, language especially, critical in later ones. So merely counting heads gets us some distance toward an explanation.

But it does not get us all the way. The part of the Canadian electorate that should be unencumbered by cultural inertia supports the national NDP at a lower level than its Anglosphere counterparts support their respective Labour parties. In short, diversity as a barrier to growth is not fully captured by an analysis that confines itself to sociological composition. The country's institutional endowment also matters. Canada might be diverse, but it fits this diversity into a firmly majoritarian electoral system. Such a framework might typically increase the electoral shares of left parties,[14] but in Canada the opposite seems to be true.

Making this case is assisted by provincial elections as a rival electoral arena with the same electoral formula as that for federal elections. By compartmentalizing a large part of Canadian diversity, provincial elections suppress cultural factors in some places even as they amplify them in others, all of this relative to a federal baseline. In doing so, provincial elections open windows on the forces at work in federal elections.

As they do, they also highlight problems with received accounts of electoral systems' strategic properties. The existing literature grapples with the fact that electoral action is collective, such that no voter can realistically affect electoral outcomes. The focus is commonly on interventions by strategically placed forward-looking elites in cue giving and party financing. The critical locus is held to be the parliamentary constituency (Cox 1997). The argument in this book, conversely, focuses on collectivities numbering in the millions and sometimes situated on the other side of the continent. The mechanisms might be opaque, but they merit study on their own terms and should not just be assumed away.

8

System Dynamics, Coordination, and Fragmentation

"Provided it does not seem pedantic," the Captain said, "I think I can briefly sum up in the language of signs. Imagine an A intimately united with a B, so that no force is able to sunder them; imagine a C likewise related to a D; now bring the two couples into contact: A will throw itself at D, C at B, without our being able to say which first left its partner, which first embraced the other's partner."

– GOETHE, *ELECTIVE AFFINITIES*

This chapter brings the federal parties together as a system. It covers dynamic relations among the parties and the impacts of these dynamics on the system's overall fractionalization. Dynamics are asymmetrical: insurgents interact mainly with the Conservative Party; the NDP interacts mainly with the Liberal Party. This compartmentalization is greater now than before 1960 and is a reflection of the growth and transformation of the party on the left, as well as of response by the Liberal party. Also asymmetrical is the impact of "new" parties on the system's fragmentation. Insurgents, as creatures of provincial or, at most, regional forces, are especially critical for extra-local fragmentation. The CCF-NDP, in contrast, expanded eastward from its original western niche, and with this expansion came a diffusion of *local* fractionalization similar from riding to riding. The pattern also accelerated with the transformation of the CCF into the NDP. As in Chapter 7, the critical fact is not that the NDP is objectively strong but that its strength is variable over both space and time in analytically telling ways.

Most of the evidence is from federal elections in each province. Although this evidence is aggregated, I present it as diagnostic of flows of individual voters among parties, a claim that I also substantiate with survey evidence. Three recent campaigns – 1988, 1993, and 2011 – are particularly telling. Because these elections featured dramatic shifts within the campaign, they throw especially bright light on patterns of inter-party exchange. For the same reason, they also reveal the extent of contingency underlying seemingly immutable long-standing patterns. Individual-level analyses also show how voters react to forces outside their province and, by extension, beyond their riding. This goes to my general claim about highly aggregated effects of information. For strategic reckoning, as it has come be conceived (i.e., at the level of the electoral district), voters react to inappropriate information. Their decisions incorporate nationwide, as opposed to local or provincial, strategic information, and this can lead them to choices contrary to interest. Even though the motive seems to be coordination among elective affinities, the result is often coordination failure. A background condition for such self-defeating behaviour is local three-party competition.

Why does this situation persist? Earlier chapters made the case for the Liberal Party staying in the game. But the conditions that made that party dominant in the twentieth century no longer hold, and the 2011 election suggested that the party was in extreme peril. Although the Liberals bounced back in 2015, their grip still seems to have loosened, and their survival should not be taken as a given. But the same is true for the NDP.

Historical Dynamics among Parties

Asymmetry is the story in the time series–cross-section estimations in Table 8.1. The table is intended to stake general claims, with almost nothing said about cause and effect. The table portrays the interdependencies of the three main parties' vote shares, with the links between the big old parties suppressed. The latter are strong, unsurprisingly, but of less interest for my thesis than links among each old party and the new ones. I also present an estimation linking the "left" with insurgents. All variables in the estimation are first differences: that is, change in a party's share across

TABLE 8.1 Electoral trade-offs among "old" and "new" parties: Historical patterns

	Conservative	Liberal	"Left" (CCF-NDP)
1908-2015 ($N = 297$, 20-31 observations per province)			
"Left" (CCF-NDP)	−0.45 (0.12)	−0.52 (0.12)	–
Insurgents	−0.85 (0.07)	−0.12 (0.07)	−0.13 (0.04)
R^2	0.58	0.13	0.06
ρ	−0.16	−0.19	−0.26
1908-58 ($N = 127$, 3-14 observations per province)			
"Left" (CCF)	−0.57 (0.28)	−0.35 (0.27)	–
Insurgents	−0.77 (0.12)	−0.20 (0.12)	0.04 (0.05)
R^2	0.57	0.13	0.01
ρ	−0.09	−0.15	−0.05
1962-2015 ($N = 170$, 17 observations per province)			
NDP	−0.44 (0.15)	−0.55 (0.15)	–
Insurgents	−0.95 (0.09)	−0.05 (0.09)	−0.27 (0.05)
R^2	0.61	0.17	0.20
ρ	−0.17	−0.17	−0.25

Notes: Dependent variables are federal Conservative, Liberal, or NDP shares in each province. "Left" is the pre-1935 aggregate of socialist, social democratic, and labour candidacies. Estimation by Prais-Winsten regression in first differences, panel-corrected standard errors in parentheses, and common autocorrelation.

consecutive elections within each province. I interpret a negative link as diagnostic of competition between two parties for the same voters. Certainly, such a coefficient indicates that one party gains at the expense of the other and vice versa. Such aggregate estimations cannot identify definitively that the parties are actually engaging in direct exchange – as opposed to, say, differential turnout or multi-way exchanges – but the patterns can at least be suggestive. Three periods appear: all elections from 1908 to the present, elections from 1908 to 1958, and elections from 1962 to the present. The two subperiod estimations will hold most of my attention since they attest to the structural shift occasioned by the appearance and then the transformation of a party on the left.[1] Each period spans enough elections that it is sensible to talk about temporal dynamics.

The basic pattern persists across the estimations: the Conservatives are more strongly polarized against insurgents than against the left; for Liberals, the opposite is true, and the Liberal vote is more segmented – more specifically polarized against the left – than is the case for the Conservative Party and insurgents. Links between the left and insurgents are weak and might have changed over the twentieth century.

Asymmetries are much sharper after 1960 than before it. Although the Conservatives were polarized against both insurgents and the left all along, the NDP became less polarized against that party after 1960 than before it, even as the Conservatives became more polarized against insurgents. The Liberals were never more than weakly in competition with insurgents, but after 1960 they exchanged almost no voters with them.

Disequilibrium Dynamics within Campaigns

Although I interpret the patterns in Table 8.1 as driven by exchanges of voters among parties, the evidence is indirect at best. For direct evidence, three recent campaigns are particularly diagnostic. Each featured massive flux in a short period, two campaigns with sharp movements on the centre-left and one with big shifts on the centre-right. The dynamics are interesting in their own right, but their key role is as a window on proximity relations among the parties.

Because the story of ideological coordination is mainly about Canada outside Quebec, my analysis excludes Quebec respondents.[2] In each case, Quebec voters were following different dynamics or none at all. My analysis starts with the pre-election wave of the CES, conducted since 1988 as a "rolling cross-section" (Johnston and Brady 2002). The critical feature of the design is that each day's sample is a random subset of the total sample. This facilitates analysis of campaign dynamics.[3] The picture of dynamics in Figures 8.1 to 8.4 involves graphical smoothing to overcome the inevitably large error produced by small daily samples; the point of smoothing is to find the signal in the noise of sampling error (Brady and Johnston 2006). The objective of the dynamic plots is to establish the timing of shifts and to identify which parties move with which shifts. The latter is critical to setting up the second stage, which takes advantage of the fact that each CES also has a post-election wave. This enables analysis of turnover among individual voters from before to after the election. Interpretively, the turnover that matters is among respondents whose first interview took place before the turning point identified by the graphical analysis.

The 1988 Campaign

At the start of this campaign, the Liberals were weak, barely, if at all, ahead of the NDP. This weakness helps to explain why John Turner seized the high ground and placed his party in opposition to the Canada-US Free Trade Agreement (FTA), the precursor to NAFTA. On a left-right axis, this was an aggressive leftward move, closing the gap with the NDP. Turner furthered this gambit by dominating the English-language television debate that took place with four weeks left in the campaign. Although these moves did not deliver victory, they did confirm the Liberal Party's position among the top two finishers. The plot in Figure 8.1 suggests that the party's early gains and late losses mainly reflected exchanges with the

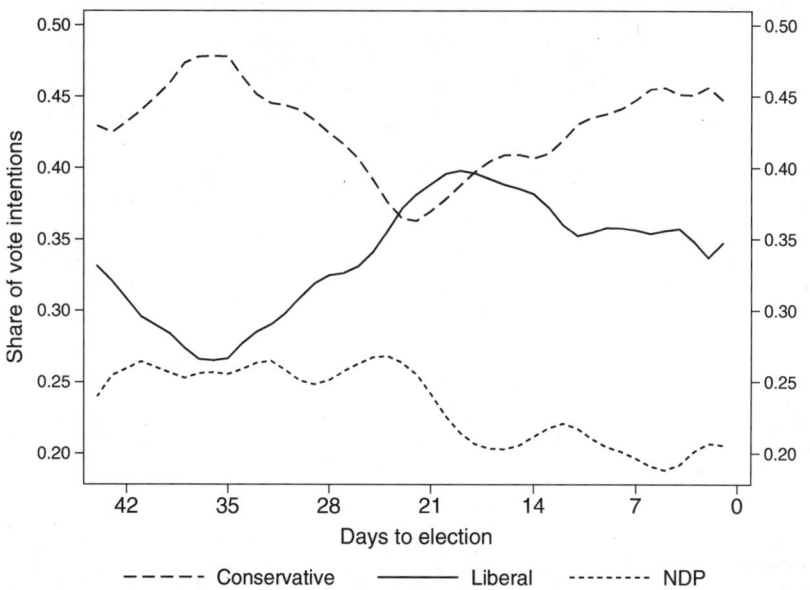

FIGURE 8.1 Dynamics of vote intention, 1988, rest of Canada

Notes: This figure shows the evolution of the vote over the 1988 federal election campaign, with each party's percentage of committed respondents on each day of interviewing for the Canadian Election Study. As daily samples are small, the pattern is smoothed by loess (Cleveland 1993), bandwidth = 0.30.

Conservatives. But once it became clear that the Liberals had recovered their numerical advantage over the NDP, support for the NDP plummeted. Although the 1988 election proved to be the NDP's strongest result to that date, the party was blocked from attaining what seemed at the start to be a realistic objective: to become the official opposition.[4]

Movement by individuals, depicted in Table 8.2, shows that the bases of party choice in 1988 were still complex. Old cultural differences were

Table 8.2 Vote shifts among parties, early campaign to election day, 1988, Canada outside Quebec

Vote intention (October 4-24)	Reported vote (post-election wave)				
	Conservative	Liberal	NDP	Other/none	
	A. Row percentages				N
Conservative	76	10	5	9	*(270)*
Liberal	13	68	6	13	*(180)*
NDP	10	15	67	8	*(155)*
Other/none	21	19	17	43	*(192)*
	B. Diagonal percentages				PRE-ELECTION PERCENTAGE
Conservative	26	3	2	3	34
Liberal	3	15	1	3	23
NDP	2	3	13	2	19
Other/none	5	5	4	10	24
POST-ELECTION PERCENTAGE	36	26	20	18	*(797)*
	C. Support for the FTA				PRE-ELECTION MEAN
Conservative	+0.87	−0.42	−0.56	+0.09	+0.68
Liberal	+0.63	−0.52	−0.90	0.00	−0.32
NDP	+0.67	−0.58	−0.56	−0.75	−0.46
Other/none	+0.73	−0.41	−0.56	+0.09	+0.02
POST-ELECTION MEAN	+0.82	−0.50	−0.52	+0.08	*(797)*

Notes: Rows indicate vote intention for respondents interviewed on or before October 24. Columns indicate votes actually cast on election day. Panels A and B indicate rates and volumes of shifts between parties. Panel C indicates support/opposition to the Canada/US Free Trade Agreement for each pre-post turnover type. Entries in italics are numbers of observations.

still being sorted even as Liberals and Conservatives were shaking off the political economy of the nineteenth century and early twentieth century, when the Conservatives were protectionists and the Liberals free traders. The table includes respondents whose pre-campaign interviews took place before October 24, the date on which the NDP began its retreat. In the top panel appear the *rates* of exchange among parties. For example, among respondents with an early Conservative intention, 76 percent actually voted in line with that intention. Ten percent shifted to the Liberals, 5 percent went to the NDP, and 9 percent went to an "other" party or did not vote. Liberals and Conservatives were more likely to shift to each other than to any other party, in each case about twice as likely as to the NDP.

The *volumes* of Liberal-Conservative exchange were exactly offsetting, as shown by Panel B. Although early Liberal intenders were more likely to shift to the Conservatives than early Conservatives were likely to shift to the Liberals, the smaller Conservative rate of defection was operating on a larger base, and the larger Liberal defection rate was working on a smaller base. Cast as percentages of the total sample, the 3 percent who went from Conservative to Liberal were exactly offset by the 3 percent who went the other way. From Figure 8.1, I infer that such exchange favoured the Liberals at mid-campaign and the Conservatives at the end.

The exchanges were not just weakly motivated movements between almost indistinguishable alternatives. To the contrary, 1988 was a milestone in the differentiation of each party's support base. The left-right gap between the parties' platforms was its widest for the entire postwar period, according to Figure 4.1, and the 1988 election capped a trend dating back to the early 1970s. According to Chapter 5, the traditional ethnoreligious bases of the old parties were also disappearing. One element of this sorting can be seen in Panel C, which gives mean values on a pro-/anti-FTA measure. Liberals who switch to the Conservatives are strongly pro-FTA even as Conservatives who switch to the Liberals are strongly anti-FTA. Each group is much closer to the destination group than to the origin group. Once the campaign got Liberals and Conservatives sorted, the policy gap between the parties' supporters widened dramatically.

Although the location of the NDP in the left-right firmament was never in doubt, movement across the NDP boundary was not simple. An NDP defector was only half again as likely to vote Liberal as Conservative. But

NDP defectors to the Conservatives were exactly offset by Conservative defectors to the NDP (Panel B). In contrast, New Democrats who shifted to the Liberals were not neutralized by Liberals who went to the New Democrats. This made NDP defection critical to the Liberals' ultimate recovery.

The NDP also got caught up in the grand sorting of 1988. New Democrats who defected to the Conservatives were as pro-FTA as defecting Liberals. New Democrats who went to the Liberals were indistinguishable from New Democrats who stayed put. The campaign made NDP supporters slightly more coherent as a group, but it also shrank their numbers.

The 2011 Campaign

In some ways, 2011 was the mirror image of 1988. The long-standing Liberal advantage over the NDP was reversed, and the damage was done inside the campaign. Only in one ironic particular did 2011 reproduce 1988: Liberals' claims to superior electability. In 1988, what ultimately sustained the Liberals was the widely held belief that they were better positioned than the New Democrats to defeat the Conservatives (Johnston et al. 1992, Fig. 8.8). In 2011, Liberal leader Michael Ignatieff invoked the same consideration. In the English-language leaders' debate, NDP leader Jack Layton accosted Ignatieff over the Liberal reputation for breaking promises; Ignatieff replied: "Well, Jack, at least we get into government. You'll be in opposition forever." And in his closing statement, he framed the choice this way: "The choice will be between a Harper government and a Liberal government." Ignatieff never addressed the charge of breaking promises; he relied solely on the strategic argument.[5]

If 1988 still reflected older patterns of cultural differentiation and the recency of the old parties' Canada-US reversal, 2011 was – outside Quebec – a much simpler event. The Quebec pattern remained somewhat mysterious, but the key was that the NDP began to make gains there in early April. The surge in Quebec was phenomenal and gave the party a strong majority of the province's seats.[6] When the Quebec shift registered in Canada-wide poll numbers, it induced further shifts outside Quebec. Now the flow was from Liberal to NDP, reversing the parties' relative overall standings. Figure 8.2 suggests that the NDP surge outside Quebec began

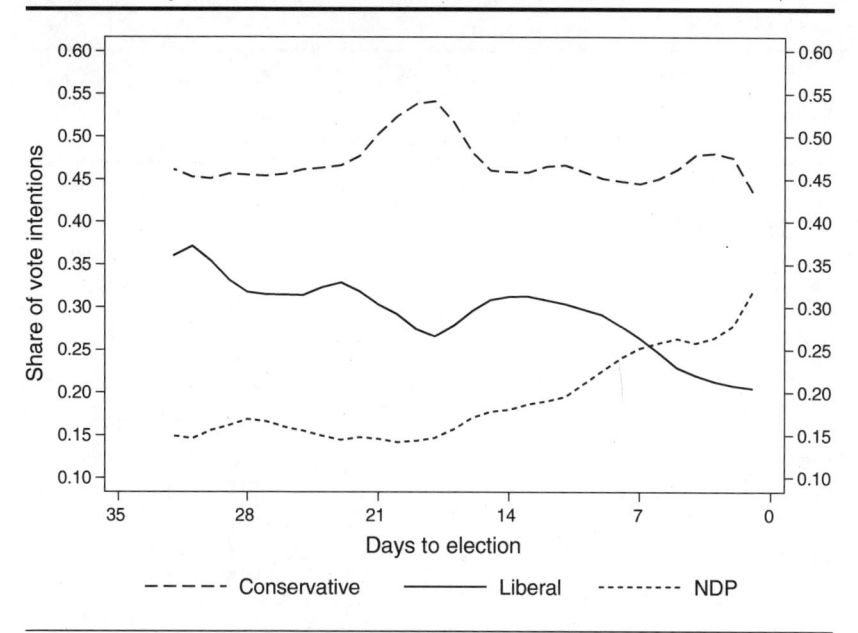

FIGURE 8.2 Dynamics of vote intention, 2011, rest of Canada

Notes: This figure shows the evolution of the vote over the 2011 federal election campaign, with each party's percentage of committed respondents on each day of interviewing for the Canadian Election Study. As daily samples are small, the pattern is smoothed by loess (Cleveland 1993), bandwidth = 0.30.

about two weeks before election day. The Conservative vote was essentially unaffected by the NDP surge.

Individual turnover assumed a simple pattern, especially compared with that of 1988. According to Table 8.3, retention rates in 2011 for the Conservatives and New Democrats were higher than those in 1988; most of the action thus involved erstwhile Liberals. Some Liberals defected to the Conservatives, but this time there was only a weak countervailing shift. (Indeed, defecting Conservatives were more likely to shift to the NDP than to the Liberal Party.) And Liberal supporters were three times as likely to defect to the NDP as to the Conservative Party, again with almost no countervailing shifts.

The ideological character of the shifts is shown in Panel C. Here the indicator is respondents' left-right self-placement, based upon the 11-point scales introduced in Chapter 2.[7] Negative values lean left, and positive values

TABLE 8.3 Vote shifts among parties, early campaign to election day, 2011, Canada outside Quebec

Vote intention (March 26–April 14)	Conservative	Liberal	NDP	Other/none	
	A. Row percentages				*N*
Conservative	85	2	5	8	*(416)*
Liberal	7	58	22	14	*(243)*
NDP	4	2	82	12	*(127)*
Other/none	27	16	22	35	*(249)*

					PRE-ELECTION PERCENTAGE
	B. Diagonal percentages				
Conservative	34	1	2	3	40
Liberal	2	14	5	3	23
NDP	<1	<1	10	1	12
Other/none	6	4	5	9	24
POST-ELECTION PERCENTAGE	43	19	22	17	*(1,035)*

					PRE-ELECTION MEAN
	C. Left-right self-placement				
Conservative	0.26	–0.40	–0.08	0.24	0.25
Liberal	0.13	–0.12	–0.14	–0.17	–0.12
NDP	0.00	–0.20	–0.31	–0.33	–0.30
Other/none	0.09	0.00	–0.09	–0.17	–0.06
POST-ELECTION MEAN	0.24	–0.11	–0.20	–0.12	*(502)*

Notes: Rows indicate vote intention for respondents interviewed on or before April 14. Columns indicate votes actually cast on election day. Panels A and B indicate rates and volumes of shifts between parties. Panel C indicates left-right self-placement for each pre-post turnover type. Entries in italics are numbers of observations.

lean right. The most important line is for respondents who initially indicate Liberal preference. Liberal defectors to the Conservative Party lean right, although not as far as people who start and end the campaign as Conservatives. Defectors to the NDP are the mirror image in that they lean modestly to the left. Indeed, they are indistinguishable from Liberals who stayed home. As in 1988, the election's ideological tone is unidimensionally left versus right. Unlike in 1988, however, the campaign did not widen the gap between the Conservative Party and NDP. In 1988, the big parties exchanged unsorted supporters, and NDP shrinkage reinforced the sorting. As a result, the gap between Liberal and Conservative electoral coalitions widened, as did that between Conservatives and New Democrats. In 2011, in contrast, essentially all defection originated with the centrist Liberals, such that the Conservatives were leavened with centre-right Liberals and the New Democrats with centre-left ones. The gap between Conservative and NDP voters shrank. The system polarized but not in the sense that gaps widened. Rather, the political weight of the party of centre dropped.

The 1993 Campaign

In 1993, the action was on the right. The dynamic evidence is in Figure 8.3. Although the Conservatives plumbed the depths of unpopularity from late 1989 to mid-1992, when the 1993 campaign began their position was difficult but not desperate (Johnston 1999, Fig. 1). At that point, the Conservative share was only slightly smaller than the Liberal one. Victory seemed to be unlikely, but defeat promised to be only a chastening, not a rout. Reform, which ultimately displaced the Conservatives, was polling poorly and received little press coverage (Jenkins 1999, 2002).[8] Five weeks from election day, however, the Conservatives fell off the table. Although Liberal gains were not dramatic, the gap between the parties was now wide. For more than a week, the Conservatives plateaued in the mid-20s. Then, with about three weeks to go, the party began its final descent. Reform, on the other hand, grew gradually over this period. Its slow gain reflected the fact that little was known about the party until late in the campaign (Jenkins 2002). Indeed, the campaign might have revealed too much (Jenkins 1999) given the late drop in Reform support.

The Conservatives bled in two directions. Table 8.4 indicates that there was essentially no return migration; the Conservative bin simply emptied out.[9] Conservatives were equally likely to shift to the Liberal and Reform Parties. Defection to Reform was due to both classic left-right issues and the cultural ones discussed at length in earlier chapters. On left-right issues, the best diagnostic for 1993 was orientation to the deficit. Chronic deficits and mounting public debt were the elephants in the economic policy room

198 The Canadian Party System

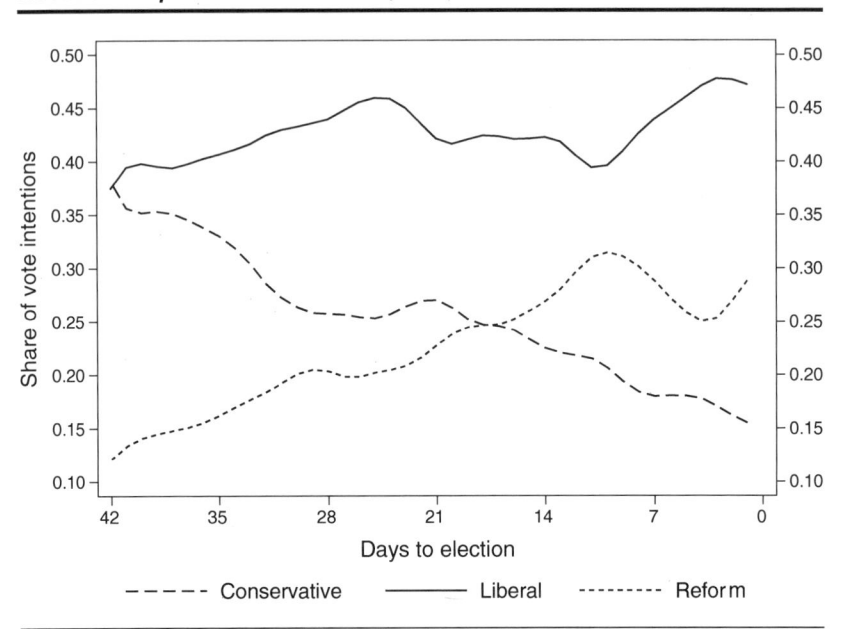

FIGURE 8.3   Dynamics of vote intention, 1993, rest of Canada

Notes: This figure shows the evolution of the vote over the 1993 federal election campaign, with each party's percentage of committed respondents on each day of interviewing for the Canadian Election Study. As daily samples are small, the pattern is smoothed by loess (Cleveland 1993), bandwidth = 0.30.

of the 1990s. So where in 1988 the role of the state was couched in terms of Canadian autonomy versus commercial union, in 1993 it was expressed in terms of how deep the spending cuts would have to be to fight the deficit. Although the Liberal government elected in 1993 would ultimately master the deficit, this future was not visible during the campaign (Greenspon and Wilson-Smith 1996). Among former Conservatives, according to Panel C, deficit orientation clearly differentiated Reformers from Liberals. An even clearer line can be drawn on the national question, however. According to Panel D, Conservatives who defected to Reform were solidly anti-Quebec. Where on the deficit defectors to the Liberals were indistinguishable from Conservatives who stayed home, on the national question defectors to the Liberals were much more pro-Quebec than those left behind. This is a dynamic restatement of the observations in Figure 4.3.

Table 8.4 Vote shifts among parties, early campaign to election day, 1993, Canada outside Quebec

Vote intention (September 10-21)	Reported vote (post-election wave)					
	Conservative	Reform	Liberal	NDP	Other/none	
	A. Row percentages					*N*
Conservative	45	21	21	1	13	*(181)*
Reform	1	69	14	2	14	*(95)*
Liberal	3	6	76	2	13	*(231)*
NDP	0	7	23	48	23	*(61)*
Other/none	7	20	32	4	38	*(138)*

	B. Diagonal percentages					PRE-ELECTION PERCENTAGE
Conservative	11	5	5	<1	5	26
Reform	<1	9	2	<1	2	13
Liberal	1	2	25	1	4	33
NDP	0	1	2	4	2	9
Other/none	1	4	6	1	8	20
POST-ELECTION PERCENTAGE	14	21	40	6	19	*(706)*

	C. Anti-deficit orientation (post-election means)					
Conservative	+0.44	+0.68	+0.47	–	–0.18	*(181)*

	D. Pro-French/Quebec orientation (post-election means)					
Conservative	–0.25	–0.42	–0.03	–	–0.18	*(180)*

Notes: Rows indicate vote intention for respondents interviewed on or before September 10. Columns indicate votes actually cast on election day. Panels A and B indicate rates and volumes of shifts between parties. Panel C indicates support/opposition to deficit cutting for each pre-post turnover type. Panel D indicates support/opposition to doing more for Quebec for each pre-post turnover type. Entries in italics are numbers of observations.

Coordination Failure

All three elections featured behaviour that appears to have been strategic, with voters manoeuvring on the centre-left in 1988 and 2011 and on the centre-right in 1993. Arguments along these lines have pedigrees. The remarkable dynamics in US presidential primaries in the 1970s and 1980s led to innovations in survey sampling and instrumentation that in turn facilitated analysis of voters' expectations. Notable early examples are

Bartels (1988) and Brady and Johnston (1987), who established that primary voters took into account both candidates' "viability" – their odds of winning the nomination – and their "electability" – their odds of winning the general election. Bartels gave a subtle account of possible mechanisms in voters' heads, and Brady and Johnston emphasized the importance of strategic voting in particular. Both pointed to a "momentum" logic that produced a winnowing of the field. Brady and Johnston speculated about the premature forcing of candidate withdrawals – premature in the sense that by the time voters discovered enough about a candidate to dislike him or her, that candidate would be one of the few left standing.

These intuitions bore fruit on many fronts. For the United States, Abramson et al. (1992) confirmed the basic propositions and established that impacts of expectations persist even when voters' projection and wish fulfillment are taken into account. Johnston et al. (1992) extended the logic to the multiparty parliamentary contest in Canada. The logic even extends to proportional representation systems, which often feature thresholds of exclusion for small parties and commonly invite voters to consider alternative combinations of small and large parties in potential governing coalitions (Abramson et al. 2010; Meffert et al. 2011).

But if the manoeuvring is strategic, it is also blinkered. If the point of strategic voting is to improve coordination among elective affinities, the behaviour that actually results is often spectacularly ill advised. In the Canadian case, voters outside Quebec respond to common forces, to events in important provinces, to national polls, or perhaps just to a force no less powerful for being ineffable. In some regions, this might improve coordination within the right or left. This is just a happy accident, however, for in other regions precisely the opposite occurs. Figure 8.4 makes this point by comparing patterns between Ontario and the West, big regions with sharp contrasts in the strength of key parties. The figure focuses on the party making gains, the Liberals in 1988, the NDP in 2011, and Reform in 1993.

In 1988, the Liberals made an especially strong recovery in Ontario, and it was critical to their ability to fight another day. Their gains in the West were smaller (indeed, if we believe the evidence from the early campaign, there might have been no net gain overall). Relative to its early campaign low point, however, the party nearly doubled its share in the

FIGURE 8.4 Common dynamics and divergent outcomes: Coordination failure on the left and right

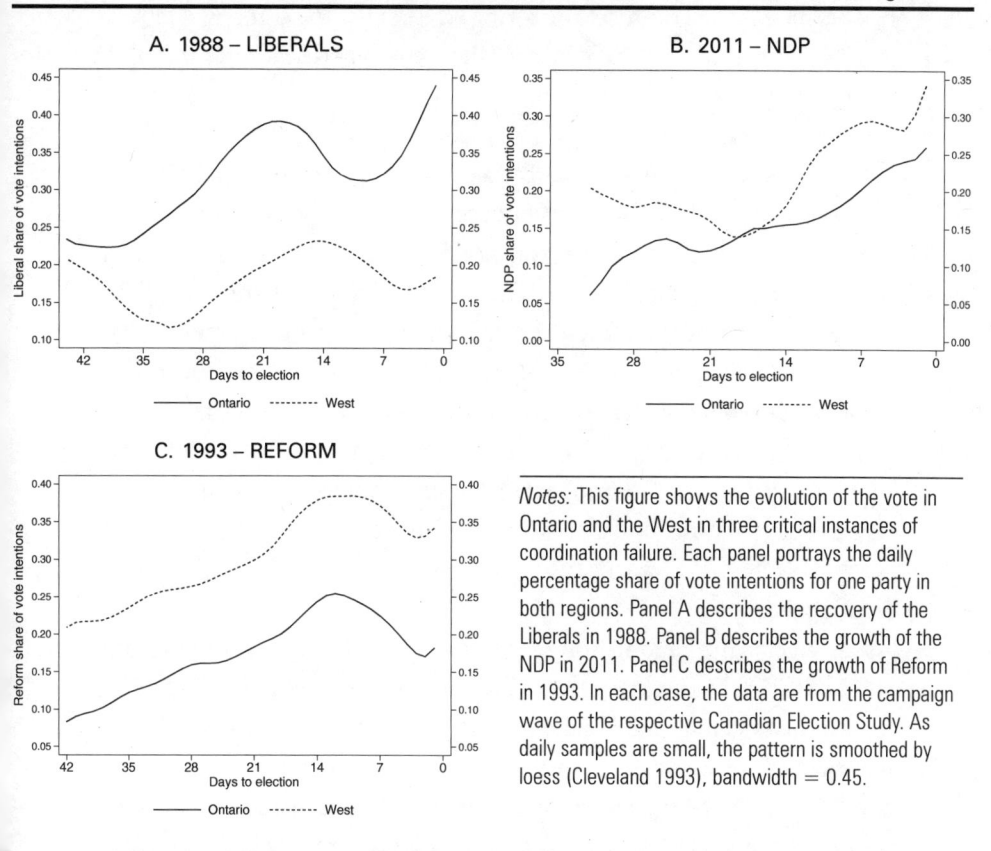

A. 1988 – LIBERALS

B. 2011 – NDP

C. 1993 – REFORM

Notes: This figure shows the evolution of the vote in Ontario and the West in three critical instances of coordination failure. Each panel portrays the daily percentage share of vote intentions for one party in both regions. Panel A describes the recovery of the Liberals in 1988. Panel B describes the growth of the NDP in 2011. Panel C describes the growth of Reform in 1993. In each case, the data are from the campaign wave of the respective Canadian Election Study. As daily samples are small, the pattern is smoothed by loess (Cleveland 1993), bandwidth = 0.45.

West. This might have handed seats over to the Conservatives (Johnston et al. 1992, 224-25).

If the 1988 story is not conclusive, that for 2011 is open and shut. Coordination failure between the Liberal Party and the NDP yielded the difference between a Conservative minority and a Conservative majority. Importantly, this did not happen in the West. NDP gains in that region were in the same range as those in Ontario, but they took the party from the high 10s to the mid-30s. In British Columbia, notably, the Conservatives stalled, winning one fewer seat than in 2008, and the NDP gained three seats at the expense of the Liberals. In Ontario, the effect was the opposite. The common dynamic added some 15 percent to the NDP base, making the party just competitive enough to split the vote with a Liberal Party that had been weakened by losses mirroring NDP gains. The combined Liberal-NDP share shrank by 1 percent, but their combined seat total shrank by 22, exactly the scale of Conservative seat gains.[10]

The 1993 campaign also yielded identical dynamics between Ontario and the West and this time produced a disaster for the centre-right. In each region, the net Reform gain was between 10 and 15 percent. In the West, the initial standing of Reform was much stronger than in 1988 but not strong enough to yield many seats. In Ontario, Reform was all but non-existent. Over the campaign, Reform grew in both regions, but this growth yielded a seat windfall only in the West.[11] In Ontario, the Reform surge produced a disaster. The combined Conservative-Reform vote was almost identical to the Conservatives' 1988 share, but between the two parties they won one Ontario seat. All others went to the Liberals, 98 seats representing one-third of all seats in the House.[12]

Fractionalization

As an electoral phenomenon, coordination failure is meaningful only within districts. As we know from Chapter 2, local sources contribute about half of the system's total breakdown. The other half comes from the system's failure to integrate across Canada's geography. Just as insurgents and the CCF-NDP interact with the other parties in distinct ways, so too they differ in their impacts on fragmentation. Broadly speaking, local fragmentation is mostly the product of gradual growth and diffusion of NDP support. Extra-local fragmentation maps onto the episodic surge and decline of geographically confined insurgents. These patterns shift subtly over the years. Substantiation of these claims requires several steps.

Consider first simple time series analyses for nationally aggregated fractionalization data (the data portrayed graphically in Figure 2.6), with separate regressions for local and extra-local components. The results in Table 8.5 are clear: although each party or party group is relevant to each kind of fractionalization, insurgents are more critical to the extra-local component, whereas the CCF-NDP is more critical to the local one.[13]

The marginal effects in the table are hypothetical (Achen 1983), indicating shifts that would be induced by a unit increment in each independent variable. No less critical is what Achen calls "level" effects, captured by the

Table 8.5 Insurgents and the CCF-NDP as sources of fractionalization, 1908-2015

	All Canada*		Individual provinces
	(1) Extra-local	(2) Local	(3) TSCS†
Insurgents	0.029 (0.002)	0.018 (0.003)	0.024 (0.001)
CCF-NDP	0.013 (0.003)	0.033 (0.004)	0.032 (0.002)
Constant	0.098 (0.049)	1.837 (0.060)	2.020 (0.032)
R^2 adjusted	0.854	0.774	0.69
RMSE	0.112	0.131	–
ρ	0.108	0.161	0.19
N	33	33	307

Notes: This table presents the impact of votes for each kind of "new" party on ENP. Dependent variables in (1) and (2) are the components of total ENP, as in Figure 2.6. The dependent variable in (3) is the federal ENP in each province in each election. Dataset includes all federal elections since 1908 in all provinces.
* Prais-Winsten estimation with AR(1).
† Time series–cross-section estimation with fixed effects.

product of the hypothetical unit effects and the number of units that the independent variable actually shifts. This is the logic of Figure 8.5, which shows how impacts from the rise and fall of party fortunes play out over time. The shape of each plot directly reflects the vote plots in Figure 2.2. At critical moments, insurgents dominate the story, and when they do the bulk of their impact on total fragmentation is by the extra-local route. In the 1920s and 1930s, insurgents accounted for nearly three-quarters of the total gain in fractionalization, and nearly three-quarters of this contribution was extra-local, through the breakdown of cross-regional integration. The pattern was repeated in the 1990s: insurgents – Reform and the Bloc Québécois – contributed about four-fifths of the total breakdown, and over half of it came through the extra-local channel. Dramatic as they were, the insurgent patterns did not endure; each was an episode. Over most decades, insurgent impact is small overall and thus small by either pathway.

Over the full century, the dominant force has been the CCF-NDP, and the enduring pathway has been local. Just by fragmenting local results, NDP growth has typically added 0.6 of an extra "party" to the system. The 1990s were a setback, but it was fully reversed with the NDP recovery in 2004 and after. But CCF-NDP strength was not geographically uniform,

FIGURE 8.5 Sources of federal fractionalization: National level data, 1904-2015

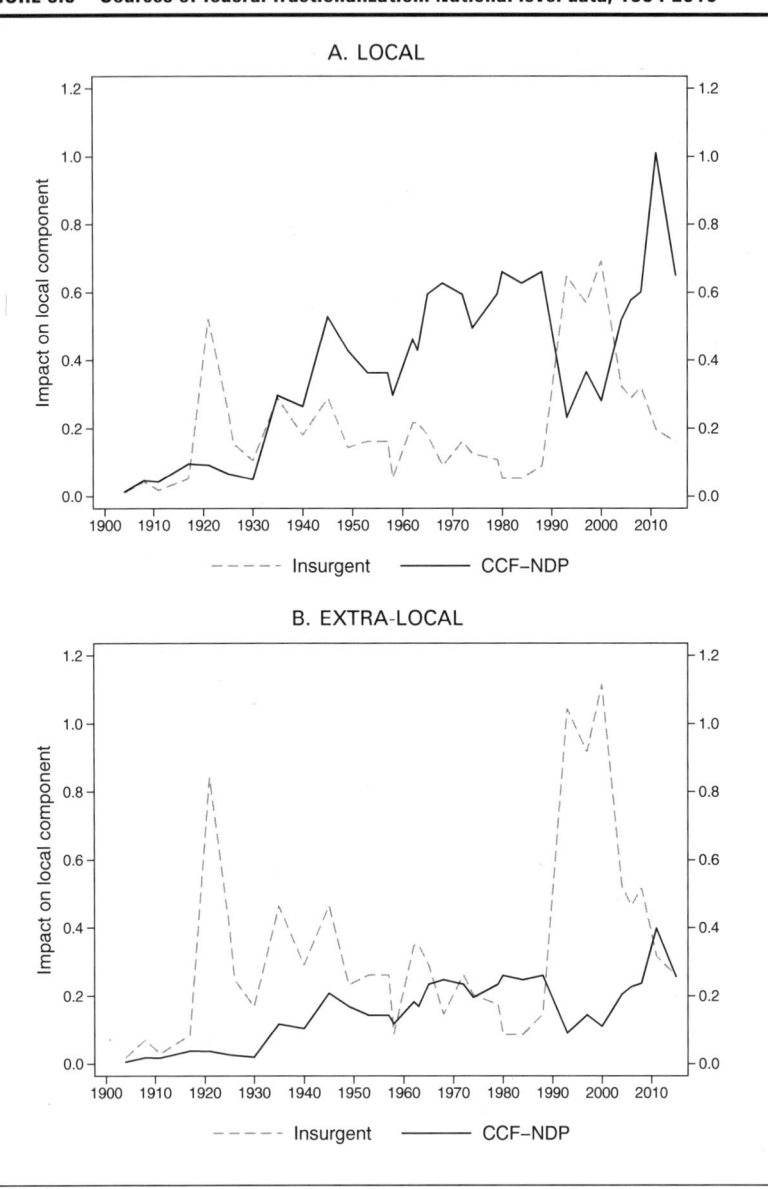

A. LOCAL

[Graph showing Impact on local component from 1900-2010, with Insurgent (dashed) and CCF-NDP (solid) lines]

B. EXTRA-LOCAL

[Graph showing Impact on local component from 1900-2010, with Insurgent (dashed) and CCF-NDP (solid) lines]

Notes: This figure shows the relative contribution of the insurgent and CCF-NDP share of the national popular vote to the two levels at which the federal vote has fractionalized. Panel A shows that the cumulative effect of CCF-NDP growth is greater than that from insurgents on the fractionalization at the riding level. Panel B shows that the insurgent vote is more important than the CCF-NDP vote in the episodes of massive extra-local breakdown. Plots are *ceteris paribus* predicted values, with intercepts zeroed out, from estimations in Table 8.5.

so the party's rise added another 0.25 of a party by the extra-local route. The party's surge in 2011 pushed this close to 0.4 of a party, but the retreat in 2015 brought the number back down to a level typical of the preceding half century.

The estimates in columns (1) and (2) of Table 8.5 are based upon a small number of degrees of freedom, and, most critically, the evidence is aggregated to a level far above where the mechanisms operate. To address this concern, column (3) appears as a robustness check with, in essence, an alternative estimate for the local component: the ENP for the province. Although there is aggregation within provinces, the amount of within-province aggregation is small, much less than the aggregation across provinces that goes into the calculation of the national ENP number.[14] Variation in province-wide ENP is thus mainly driven by the degree of riding-level fractionalization within each province. By implication, the provincial ENP should be driven mainly by CCF-NDP shares. And it is: the coefficient is half again larger for the NDP than for insurgents, broadly in line with the coefficients in column (2). By either estimation, the historical growth of the left vote added the equivalent of 0.66 of a party to the typical local race.

In Table 8.5, all estimations assume that coefficients are stable over the full period. Rather than leave this as an assumption, I break the times series up into four segments that correspond to four obvious breaking points. The first period starts with the arrival of nine-province competition in 1908 and ends in 1930, the last election before the arrival of enduring multipartism. The next sequence starts in 1935, which heralded the arrival of the CCF and a batch of insurgents, notably Social Credit. The system died around 1960, so its last election was in 1958. The next period begins in 1962, the first election contested by the NDP, and ends in 1988. The final period starts in 1993, the electoral landslide that took multipartism to another level.

The evidence appears in Figure 8.6, which presents time series cross-sectional evidence with provinces as the cross-sectional unit, on the model of Table 8.5, estimation (3). Now, however, estimates are conditional on electoral eras.[15] For the NDP and its precursors, there is little to say. Before the founding of the CCF, the "left" appears to have a bigger effect than in later years, but the actual range for the labour and social democratic vote

206 *The Canadian Party System*

FIGURE 8.6   Sources of federal fractionalization: Province-level data, 1904-2015

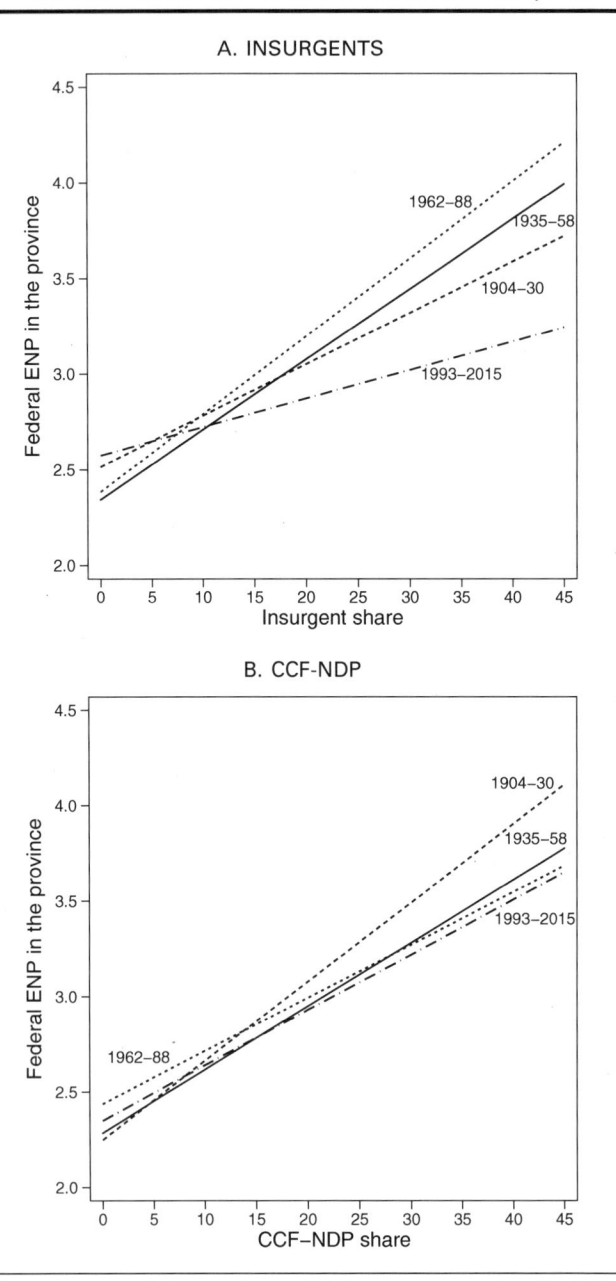

A. INSURGENTS

[Graph showing Federal ENP in the province vs. Insurgent share, with lines for periods 1904-30, 1935-58, 1962-88, and 1993-2015]

B. CCF-NDP

[Graph showing Federal ENP in the province vs. CCF-NDP share, with lines for periods 1904-30, 1935-58, 1962-88, and 1993-2015]

Notes: This figure shows the relative contribution of the insurgent vote and the CCF-NDP vote to electoral fractionalization in each province in each election. The steeper the line, the greater the contribution of the party. Elections are ordered by periods. The figure is based on the estimation in Table 8A.1.

before 1930 is tiny. After 1930, the slope is essentially stable. Its tiny fluctuations are around 0.30, a slightly shallower slope than that in Table 8.5.

For insurgents, there is more to say. The essential fact is that, the larger the scale of insurgency, the smaller its effect on ENP. Between 1962 and 1988, the marginal effect of a gain in insurgent share appears to have dwarfed that for any other period and for the left in any period. But this was a low point in insurgent history, the years when the three Westminster parties seemed to colonize the entire landscape. The next biggest effect seems to have been in 1935-58. In this period, insurgency was not trivial. But it was more nuisance than threat, mostly a story about Alberta with a spasm in Quebec in 1945. The periods in which insurgents really shook the system, raising questions about the viability of one or both of the old parties, seem to have been the years before 1930 and those after 1990. The first period saw the great Progressive breakthrough and a Canada-wide insurgent share to rival the Conservative Party's total vote. When the Progressives surged, the other parties were not obliterated, but they did retreat, so the points toward the right side of the figure are not mere hypotheticals. In the last period, the insurgent advance was more broadly based and enduring. The fact that the slope is so shallow in these years makes the basic point: variation across provinces in ENP was only weakly affected by the insurgent share. Insurgency was so successful that it flattened the shares of both the NDP and the Conservative Party. Across the provinces, ENP varied only modestly, whereas the names of the winners and losers varied immodestly as different parties ran in different provinces.

Recapitulation and Discussion

The Dynamics of Exchange

The Canadian party system is asymmetrical both in the dynamics of exchange among its constituent parties and in the sources of its fragmentation. These asymmetries sharpened over time as the system assumed a left-right ordering. As this happened, party competition fragmented within districts. Ironically, local breakdown reflected extra-local forces.

Early insurgents – most critically the great farmers' movement collectively known as the Progressives – interacted with both old parties. In certain provinces, notably Manitoba and Ontario, Progressives mostly became

Liberals in disguise. Elsewhere they helped to undermine both old parties. Thereafter, insurgents progressively disengaged with the Liberals. With the founding of the CCF, a new dynamic took hold. The growth of the CCF was gradual and, even at its peak, not impressive. Liberals tended to see CCF supporters as heirs to Progressives, as "Liberals in a hurry." The electoral record suggests that the image captures a truth, although the CCF was also, if more weakly, polarized against the Conservatives. The asymmetry sharpened as the CCF morphed into the NDP. As the NDP colonized more and more of the new party space, it also made inroads on the Liberals and largely ceased to do battle with the Conservatives. Insurgents, conversely, increasingly fought over the same turf as the Conservatives and only that turf.

As the system took on an ideological cast, both centre-left and centre-right became vulnerable to coordination failure within districts. In the 1990s, the problem was division on the right. After 2004, the pathology shifted to the left. Three times in the past 30 years the strategic context shifted inside the campaign, and these campaigns – 1988, 1993, and 2011 – were powerfully diagnostic. For each campaign, the CES opened an analytical window on aggregate- and individual-level turnover among the parties. And with each campaign the left-right alignment of the system strengthened. Movement still occurs across interior boundaries – between the Liberal Party and the NDP, between the Liberal and Conservative Parties, between the Conservatives and Reformers. But little movement occurs between now-disconnected parties – neither between Conservatives and New Democrats nor, when Reform existed, between that party and the Liberal Party or NDP.

As voting asymmetries sharpened, so did asymmetries for electoral fragmentation. Insurgents were more important before 1960 than after it, both in that their marginal impact was greater and in that they occupied a larger part of the total landscape. The great exception was Reform, but it, like other insurgents, did not stick around. Marginal impact from the left party did not decline, and, as the NDP supplanted the CCF, the total size of the left grew. Concomitantly, extra-local fragmentation – differences across provinces and regions – became relatively less important. The burden shifted, relatively speaking, to local fractionalization. Mostly, this came about as the NDP gradually moved eastward. In the 1990s, however, local fragmentation was also an issue on the ideological right.

Evidence from campaigns further supports one theme of this book: the relevance in voters' minds of strategic considerations far above – or far removed from – their own electoral district. Consistent with the logic of FPP and the Westminster system, strategic considerations lie at the heart of revealed preferences. Alternative party systems are imaginable – more so, perhaps, in Canada than in the other majoritarian systems. As alternatives pop up in the real time of campaigns, Canadians are forced to think strategically. But the strategic considerations activated by polls do not operate at the level stated by the Neo-Duvergerian Synthesis. In particular, voters do not seem to be driven by the strategic dictates of their local district. More often they respond to structural constraints at the national level. Poll evidence might even accelerate change, a possibility foreseen by Rae (1971). When this happens, however, it can be driven by dynamic indications originating outside their province, and the result can be coordination failure.

Parties as Agents

How has fractionalization become a routine thing? One step in the explanation refers to ideological disconnection:

> The governing logic was always to avoid splitting the vote and allowing a minority to rule ... Why then did the center and the right not coordinate in this way in the rest of Canada? Or why did the center and left not merge? The answer, of course, is that the center-right stratagem has never been necessary in federal politics and the center-left stratagem ... only rarely so. Most of the time, the system is dominated not by either extreme but by the party of the center, the Liberals ... This leaves the principal opponents to the Liberals in a quandary: from a contentless, strategic point of view, the Conservatives and the NDP are each other's obvious partners. Substantively, however, the primary runners-up are even less acceptable to each other than the Liberals are. When Riker (1976) claimed that the key to Canadian multipartism was the presence of localized third-party support, he presented Canada as the easy case. The hard case

was India. Riker argued that the Indian peculiarity was the domination of the system by Congress, a party of the center. This enabled parties on each flank to be both visible and weak. Defeat of Congress required the improbable: a coalition of the ends against the middle. It turns out that the diagnosis Riker made for India also applies to Canada. (Johnston and Cutler 2009, 94)

This describes Canada's form of polarized pluralism, a major theme of this book. Analytically, however, all that it does is redescribe the puzzle. It does not say how a party of the centre persists. Part of the explanation refers to the recurring role of Quebec in putting the Liberals halfway to a single-party majority. I further argue that the Canada-wide implication of Quebec's behaviour induces voters outside Quebec who might otherwise vote for the NDP to vote instead for the Liberal Party. But this just brings up a further puzzle: why does a weak party of the left persist, especially when its growth – by dividing the centre-left – might actually threaten the very project that it champions?

The problem is not that the NDP came into existence. Indeed, its story of origins follows the new-party entry script in Hug (2001, 58, passim). First, the 1956 consolidation of the union movement into the Canadian Labour Congress (CLC) heightened the salience of labour issues. Not only did this solve an abiding strategic problem for the CCF, but also it coincided with a sharp rise in union density (Figure 7.2). Neither old party adjusted to increased union power by becoming pro-labour, however, and documents generated by activists during the three-year transition to the NDP emphasize the unacceptability of the Liberals in particular as a compromise vehicle for labour and the left (CLC-CCF Joint National Committee 1958). Evidence from the Campaign Manifesto Project (Figure 4.1) confirms the correctness of their perception. It helped, ironically, that the CCF was devastated by the 1958 Conservative landslide. The setback stirred the pot inside the party and in the labour movement. But the CCF's momentary weakness also aligns with the logic in Hug: had a CLC combination with the new party seemed like a real threat, one of the old parties itself would have incorporated the left program and effectively strangled the new party in the cradle. Instead, what appeared, as Hug predicts, was a low-threat, weak entrant.

The mystery from the neo-Duvergerian perspective is that the NDP persisted in the struggle indefinitely. The puzzle is only compounded by the setback of the 1990s, which should not be glossed over by hindsight. Events after 2004 could not be foreseen, and the party truly seemed to be on life support. Some in the union movement (notably Buzz Hargrove of the Canadian Auto Workers) entertained the thought that the centre-left was fungible. If outright merger was not in the cards, tactical voting that mostly favoured the Liberals might be.

One possible explanation for the persistence of the NDP is that the matter was endogenized. Certain institutional developments of the 1960s and 1970s made the NDP and other parties agents of the state. It served the interests of Liberal minority governments to co-opt the smaller opposition parties both to support their own programs and to detract from the special place of the Conservatives as the official opposition (Courtney 1978). Some of this was internal to Parliament since official recognition and financial support were extended to the smaller parties. The threshold for eligibility was arbitrary but clearly designed to ensure that the NDP would cross it. Most consequential was a funding mechanism that reimbursed a significant share of party and candidate election expenses. In 2003, support tied to campaigns was augmented by an ongoing quarterly subsidy explicitly reflecting the party's share of the national vote in the preceding election (Aucoin and Bakvis 2015). Even a small party could dangle this tangible incentive before its hesitant supporters.[16]

As an explanation of fractionalization, however, the timing is off. In historical sequence, the mechanisms of party recognition are a consequence, not the cause, of party system breakdown (Courtney 2015). Most importantly, the first elements in the financial regime did not come into force until 1974. By this time, the NDP had been running candidates almost everywhere for more than a decade (Johnston and Cutler 2009, Fig. 6.3).[17] The new law might be credited with prolonging the pattern, but that claim sounds like a just-so story.

A more plausible institutional argument refers to the federal system. Federalism helps with new-party entry, as numerous sources attest. It probably also helps to prolong the life of a weak entrant such as the NDP. It might be critical that the NDP, unlike the other parties, does not have distinct federal and provincial organizations.[18] This imposes an extra burden of loyalty on its supporters, in contrast to the more malleable loyalties permitted by old parties. If this makes the party hard to support, it also makes it hard to abandon. Although the party does not cash out all of its provincial strength in the federal arena, it can at least deliver some of it. In some provinces, the federal party benefits from controlling the provincial government, and even being the official opposition helps it to carry extra weight. In these provinces, the union movement is deterred from dalliance with an old party.

Finally, party elites do not just read back from short-run electoral equilibria. They pursue a mix of electoral, office, and policy goals, with each objective somewhat independent of the others. The exact mix depends on institutional conditions (Strøm 1990). The NDP might be that rare bird, a policy-seeking (as opposed to an office-seeking) party: "Two organizational properties set policy-seeking parties apart from office-seekers: (1) high degrees of intraparty democracy and (2) impermeable recruitment structures. These properties are likely to be favored by labor intensive organization and modest public subsidies" (Strøm 1990, 594).[19] This describes the NDP at least some of the time. Certainly, the NDP (and before it the CCF) embodied a consistent line of policy from the start. As such, its pursuit of office is constrained; it trims its program no more than necessary to be electorally credible. Trimming is more likely in the provincial arena, although only in provinces where the party's chances are greatest. In the federal arena, the party presents itself as an alternative to both old parties, so officially it is also an office seeker. Federally, a breakthrough to major-party status usually seems to be remote, such that the party often emphasizes its policy distinctiveness. In these circumstances, the NDP plays a role like that ascribed by Kedar (2005) to small, flanking parties in multiparty systems with coalition governments: to enable non-centrist voters to pull the median member of the governing coalition toward themselves. The logic can also work within single-party governments. The simplest situations were in 1972-74 and 2004-6, when the Liberal government absolutely required NDP support to survive.[20] In 1963-68, the process was more subtle but with similar effect. Although the Pearson government was not absolutely dependent on the NDP, that party served as a talking point for the left wing inside cabinet (Kent 1988; Smith 1973). It helped that the party was reluctant to treat openly the other small opposition group, the Créditistes, who blocked the restoration of Liberal hegemony in Quebec.[21] The process can even work where the government controls an outright majority. For instance, the modest NDP recovery in 1997 (relative to the 1993 low point) combined with the sharp retrenchment in Liberal seats strengthened the hand of the cabinet's left wing. The sequence of Liberal defeat and victory in 1979-80 also admits such a stylization.[22]

APPENDIX

TABLE 8.A1 Shifts in the relative contribution of support for insurgents and the CCF-NDP to federal fractionalization

	Coefficient	Standard error
"Era"		
1935-58	−0.064	0.068
1962-88	0.470	0.075
1993-2015	0.221	0.100
Insurgent share	0.027	0.002
× "era"		
1935-88	0.010	0.004
1962-88	0.013	0.005
1993-2015	−0.012	0.003
CCF-NDP share	0.041	0.013
× "era"		
1935-88	−0.008	0.013
1962-88	−0.014	0.013
1993-2015	−0.012	0.013
Intercept	1.978	0.045
Overall R^2	0.718	
ρ	0.287	
N	300	

Notes: This table shows the shifting contributions of the insurgent vote and the CCF-NDP vote to electoral fractionalization. The dependent variable is federal ENP in the province, elections since 1908. Estimation is for a time series–cross-section with fixed effects for the province.

9
Federal-Provincial Discontinuity

> Othello: ... what lights come yond?
> Iago: Those are the raised father and his friends.
>   You were best go in.
> Othello: Not I; I must be found.
>   My parts, my title, and my perfect soul
>   Shall manifest me rightly. Is it they?
> Iago: By Janus, I think no.
>
> – SHAKESPEARE, *OTHELLO*, ACT 1, SCENE 2

The Canadian party system is as poorly integrated within provinces as across them, and disintegration appeared early in the twentieth century. But the sources of discontinuity remain obscure. Not all provinces exhibit sharp discontinuities, nor do gaps always persist. Gaps are not simply the result of ambivalence among Quebec francophones about the all-Canada project. Provinces in the West are also critical to the story. For some provinces, arguments in political economy seem to be promising at the start, but for federal-provincial discontinuity – as with differences across regions – they always fall short.

Chapters 6 and 7 point the way, however, and show two of the basic forces in play. The first process involves the appearance of province- or region-specific insurgents, with more depth and staying power in provincial than in federal elections. The second process is more systematic: where the NDP is strong federally, it is stronger still provincially and vice versa. A third process, considered in detail in this chapter, reveals both the power and the limit of Duverger's Law. In contrast to the federal case, provincial party systems remain consolidated. That is, provincial parties and voters behave much as Duverger (1963) predicts. The discrepancy between arenas is especially marked where the CCF-NDP is strong. Growth in the left vote induces strategic consolidation on the centre-right and does so much more efficiently in the provincial arena than in the federal arena. The identity of the centre-right beneficiary has varied over time and place, reflecting historical accident, and this in turn has amplified differences between arenas.

So far as I can push it, my explanation is basically a glorified accounting framework. But why are the gaps in Canada so large? The chapter concludes with a speculative essay on cross-national differences.

Dissimilarity in Space and Time

Overall Pattern

The representation of federal-provincial gaps in Chapter 2 was coarse. Data were grouped by decade, and the identities of individual provinces were masked. Figure 9.1 unpacks the data by identifying each province and, where possible, each federal-provincial election pair from 1900 to the present.[1] Over most of the twentieth century, federal-provincial disconnection was mainly the work of three provinces: British Columbia, Alberta, and Quebec. Other provinces had their moments, but only these three provinces exhibited discontinuity that was both massive and sustained. At times, virtually no reflection of the system in one arena could be found in the other. Yet forces for integration have also been in play. In all three provinces, discontinuities in the twenty-first century are nothing like those in the twentieth century. Quebec and British Columbia are still outliers, but they do not lie as far from other provinces as before. Manitoba and Saskatchewan occupy the middle, with notable punctuations on a rhythm specific to each place. And one decade stands out for widespread fracture: the 1990s.

Partisan Sources

All parties contribute to the discontinuity, but some do so more than others. In Chapter 2, we saw that Liberal and Conservative support is typically

FIGURE 9.1 Federal-provincial dissimilarity, by province and year, 1908-2011

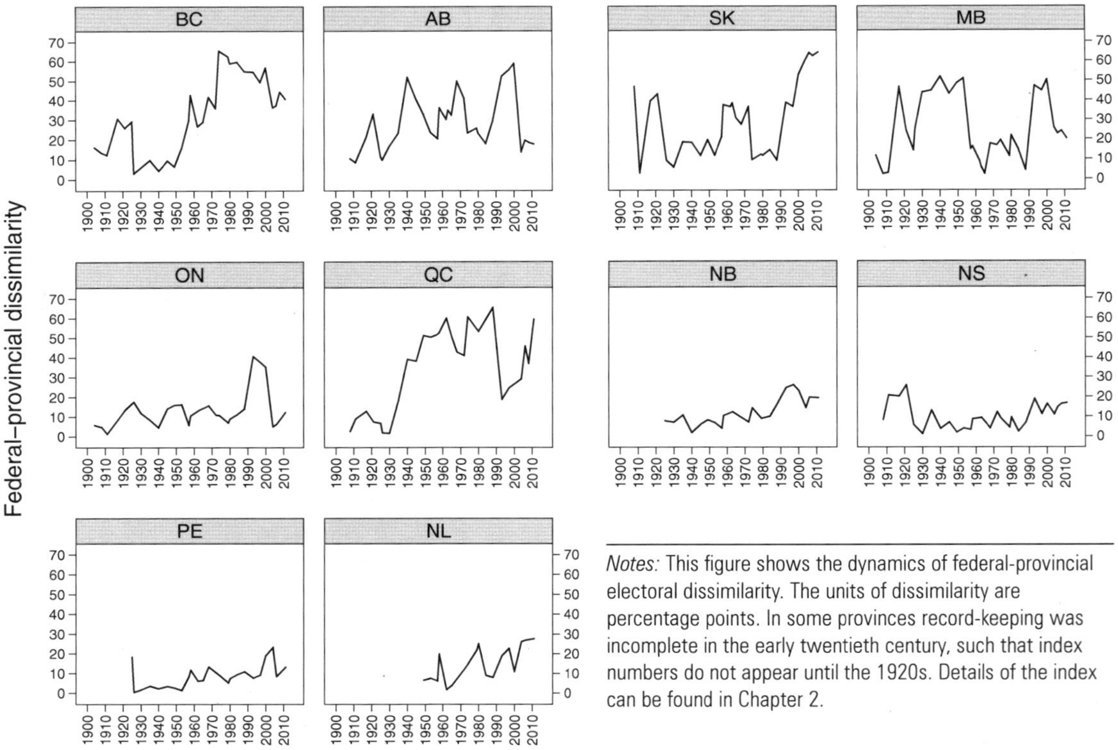

Notes: This figure shows the dynamics of federal-provincial electoral dissimilarity. The units of dissimilarity are percentage points. In some provinces record-keeping was incomplete in the early twentieth century, such that index numbers do not appear until the 1920s. Details of the index can be found in Chapter 2.

deeper federally than provincially, as befits the only two parties ever to govern in Ottawa. For the Conservatives, the 1990s were the exception to this rule. Otherwise, the federal-provincial gap was typically greater for the Conservatives than for the Liberals. The mirror image holds for new parties, since insurgents and the NDP are usually stronger provincially than federally. For the NDP, the gap between arenas is modest. For insurgents, the gap is massive, even when its direction is reversed.

Figure 9.2 amplifies the story by focusing on variation over the landscape. Its data points are standard deviations (SDs) across provinces in vote shares, election by election. SDs are generally larger in the provincial arena. The exceptions are the 1920s (the Progressives) and the 1990s (the Reformers). Gaps in SD have widened for both the Conservatives and the New Democrats. All along the gap has been especially great for insurgents. Moreover, the insurgent estimate understates both magnitudes and gaps, for the underlying value is the combined share for *all* of the parties not accounted for in the other three panels. For individual insurgent parties, sectional differences and between-arena gaps are even greater.

The resultant pattern of provincial party systems appears in Table 9.1. At first glance, it seems like a patchwork quilt. Such an impression is correct for earlier decades, but the table also reveals the emergence of the functionalist logic identified in Chapters 6 and 7. The earliest provincial-arena breaches with the old party system involved agrarian insurgents, as we know, making an insurgent a central player in some provinces as early as the 1920s. In Alberta, the old parties struggled for decades to appear at all. In Manitoba, the Progressive movement had a more complicated and intimate relationship with the old parties – especially with the Liberals – but this too made its party system *sui generis*. The most enduring insurgent pattern has been in Quebec. Not only was the Union Nationale an early entrant, but also the Parti Québécois brings the tradition right down to the present. The table masks the appearance of other Quebec "soft nationalist" insurgents as well. The only other insurgent that survives to the present is the Saskatchewan Party, a recent arrival.[2] In other provinces, the tendency has been for insurgency to fade and for one or the other of the old parties to reassert its presence.

The growing functionalism on the landscape is driven by the advance of the NDP. Crudely put, where the NDP makes a serious beachhead, it

FIGURE 9.2 Variation of party shares across provinces, 1908-2011

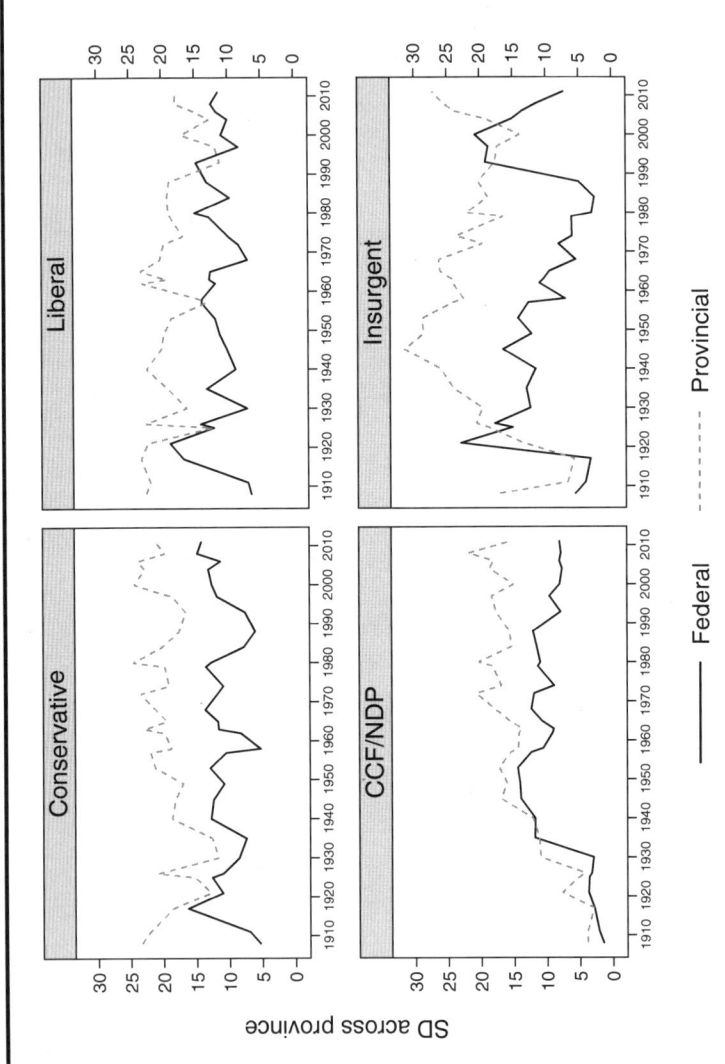

Notes: This figure plots the regional differentiation in each party's vote in both federal and provincial elections. The index of regional differentiation is the standard deviation of the party's vote. The larger the standard deviation, the more concentrated the party's vote is in individual provinces. To put it another way, the larger the standard deviation, the more regionally concentrated the vote.

Table 9.1 Insurgents and the CCF-NDP as major parties in provincial politics, 1900-2010

Decade	BC	AB	SK	MB	ON	QC	NB	NS	PE	NL
1900	Con / Lib	Lib / Con	Lib / PrRt[1]	Lib / Con	Con / Lib	Lib / Con	Lib / Con	Lib / Con	Lib / Con	
1910	Con / Lib	Lib / Con	Lib / Con	Lib / Con	Lib / Con	Lib / Con	Lib / Con	Lib / Con	Lib / Con	
1920	Con / Lib	Lib / UFA	Lib / Con	UFM / Lb:Co	Lib / Con	Lib / Con	Lib / Con	Con / Lib	Con / Lib	
1930	Lib / CCF	SC / UFA	Lib / Con	LPrg[2] / Con	Lib / Con	Lib / UN[5]	Lib / Con	Lib / Con	Lib / Con	
1940	Lb:Co[3] / CCF	SC / Unity[4]	CCF / Lib	LPrg[2] / CCF	Con / Lib	UN / Lib	Lib / Con	Lib / Con	Lib / Con	
1950	SC / CCF	SC / Lib	CCF / Lib	LPrg[2] / Con	Con / Lib	UN / Lib	Con / Lib	Lib / Con	Lib / Con	Lib / Con
1960	SC / NDP	SC / Con	NDP / Lib	Con / Lib	Con / Lib	Lib / UN	Lib / Con	Con / Lib	Con / Lib	Lib / Con
1970	SC / NDP	Con / SC	NDP / Lib	Con / NDP	Con / Lib	Lib / PQ	Con / Lib	Lib / Con	Lib / Con	Con / Lib
1980	SC / NDP	Con / NDP	Con / NDP	Con / NDP	Lib / Con	Lib / PQ	Lib / Con	Con / Lib	Lib / Con	Lib / Con
1990	NDP / Lib	Con / Lib	NDP / Lib	Con / NDP	Con[6] / Lb:ND	Lib / PQ	Lib / Con	Lib / Co:ND	Lib / Con	Lib / Con
2000	Lib / NDP	Con / Lib	NDP / Sask[7]	NDP / Con	Lib / Con	Lib / PQ	Con / Lib	Con / NDP	Con / Lib	Con / Lib

Notes: Entries indicate the two strongest parties in provincial elections in order of strength, by province and decade. Cells outlined in bold feature an insurgent. Shaded cells indicate a strong CCF or NDP presence.
1 Provincial Rights Party, later absorbed into the Conservatives.
2 Liberal-Progressive coalition.
3 Liberal-Conservative coalition.
4 Liberal and Conservative joint slates, 1940 and 1944.
5 The Union Nationale did not congeal until 1936, but many of its elements were visible in the 1935 election.
6 The three parties were near parity in Ontario in the 1990s.
7 Saskatchewan Party, formed in 1997.

does not retreat.[3] This is clearly the pattern in British Columbia, Saskatchewan, and Manitoba. Generally speaking, the party is more of a presence in more places in later periods than in earlier ones. It is also true that polarization of the NDP against an insurgent is not uncommon. Such a pattern persisted for four decades in British Columbia and one decade in Manitoba. In Saskatchewan, this has been the case for nearly two decades.[4]

Differential Pressure for Consolidation

The failure of federal elections to conform to Duverger's Law is not mirrored in provincial elections. Figure 9.3 documents this, along with province-specific elaboration. Its ENP plots are lightly smoothed to heighten the distinctiveness of key features. Begin with the overall pattern in the "total" panel at bottom right. It shows that party system breakdown started earlier in the provincial arena than in the federal one. This is consistent with the standing narrative on the Canadian system as well as with general propositions about imperatives for electorate-wide coordination. Innovation has always been easier in single provinces, even as in federal voting each province's electorate is constrained by coordination imperatives originating outside the province. The federal side caught up, however, and for about five decades the ENP in each arena averaged about 2.6. Late in the twentieth century, the federal party system fractionalized further. But the provincial arena did not follow suit, and the mean provincial ENP is still 2.6. The federal-provincial ENP gap has been as wide as 0.5 of an equivalent party, and recently it has averaged about 0.3. In most provinces, the federal norm has become three-party competition. In the provincial arena, competition is closer to the Duvergerian two-party ideal.

The size of the gap varies widely, as does its time path. Three provinces are *sui generis*. Quebec broadly mirrors the Canada-wide pattern but on its own rhythm, reflecting mainly the ebb and flow of nationalist forces in one or the other arena. Ontario is the only province where the arenas track each other, with matching gains leading to three-party competition in both arenas. Only in Alberta is there a long and still-active run in which the provincial arena is more fragmented.

Elsewhere the gap widened and acquired a systematic form driven by NDP growth and by forces reacting to that growth. A few early iterations were required for the system to take hold. The earliest gaps reflected

FIGURE 9.3 Effective number of parties: Provincial versus federal arenas, 1908-2011

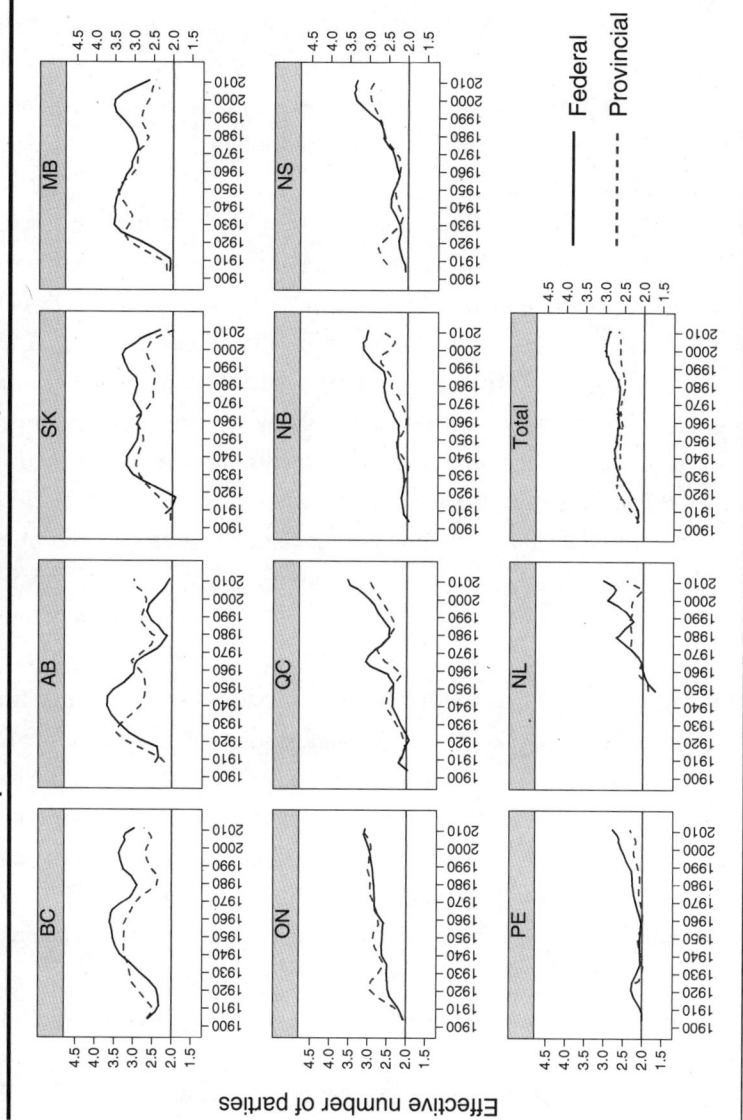

Notes: This figure plots the fractionalization of each province's federal and provincial electorate. Entries are ENP values for federal and provincial elections within each province, election by election. Plots are smoothed for clarity by loess, bandwidth = 0.25.

different players but otherwise had some affinities with the later pattern. In the 1920s, gaps were greatest in the three prairie provinces and reflected agrarian insurgency, which fractionalized the federal vote more completely than the provincial one. Since the 1930s, however, the largest and most persistent gap has been in British Columbia, where the CCF made its first breakthrough. British Columbia was joined in the 1960s by Saskatchewan and in the 1970s by Manitoba, the other main sites of NDP support. Atlantic Canada eventually came to exhibit a weaker version of the pattern, also on the rhythm of NDP growth.

British Columbia, Saskatchewan, and Manitoba differ from all other provinces in one critical particular, however. For these provinces, not only did their federal electorates fractionalize, but also their provincial ones *de*fractionalized; they defied the dominant trend and consolidated. This reflects the fact that NDP growth carries a special charge. Where the NDP grows to major-party status, the rest of the party system reacts just as in other Westminster countries: anti-socialist forces consolidate. In British Columbia, this began as a Liberal-Conservative coalition, which in 1952 and 1953 permitted itself an Australian-style flirtation with a preferential ballot.[5] The move failed, the coalition was supplanted by insurgent Social Credit in 1952, and FPP was restored after 1953. The Liberals and Conservatives were then marginalized for four decades. In 1991, Social Credit was challenged by a resurgent Liberal Party. Once it became clear that the Liberals were now the privileged anti-socialist alternative, Social Credit and its successors were consigned to the dustbin of history. In Saskatchewan, three different parties challenged the NDP – one at a time. In Manitoba, Liberal-Conservative contestation yielded to a Conservative-NDP system. The three provinces now look like the Britain–Australia–New Zealand complex in microcosm, with a standard-issue labour party polarized against a local alternative whose identity is an accident of history.

Figure 9.4 takes these anecdotes and presents a comprehensive estimation. It also presents the contrasting case, the failure of consolidation in the federal arena. For each arena, the independent variable is the CCF-NDP share in the province, and the setup is quadratic. The dependent variable is the second-to-first (SF) ratio (Cox 1997) for the two largest non-NDP parties: that is, the vote share of the second largest non-left party divided by the vote share of the largest one. The indicator is designed to capture

FIGURE 9.4 CCF-NDP strength and centre-right consolidation: Provincial versus federal patterns, 1908-2011

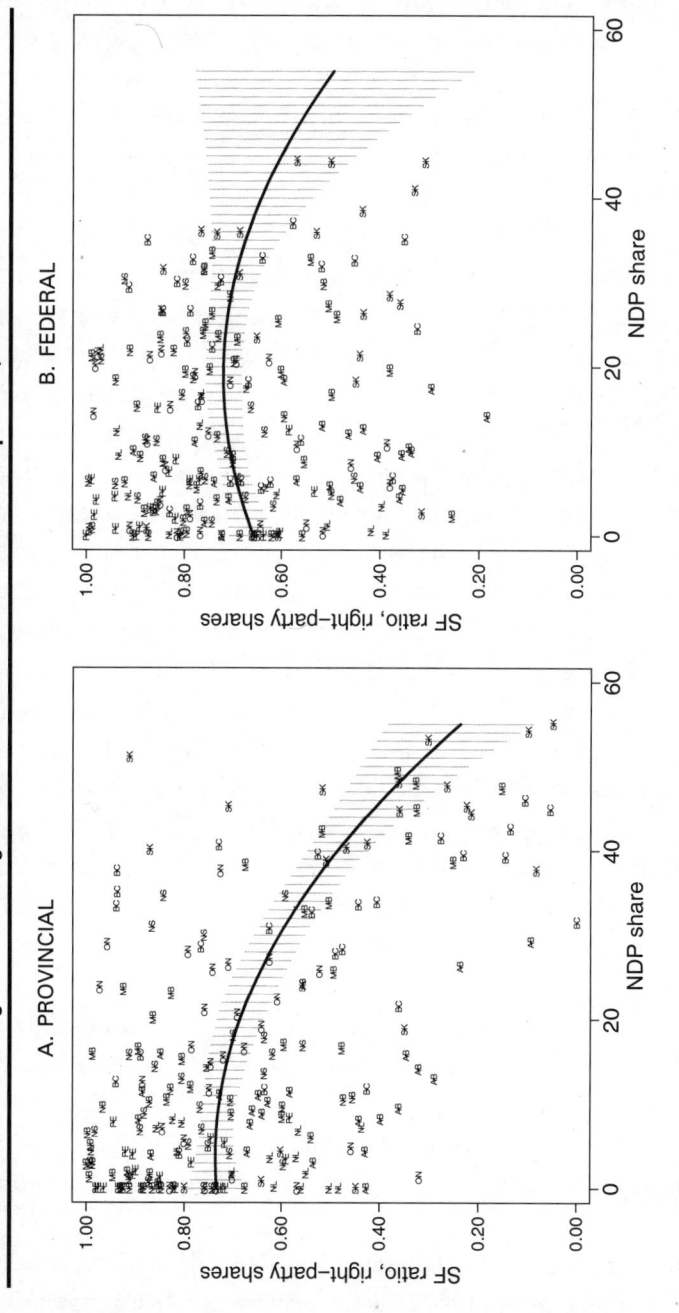

Notes: This figure shows the relationship between the NDP percentage of the vote in the province and the ratio between vote percentages of the second-place non-labour party and the first-place one. The lower that ratio, the more consolidated is the vote of the centre-right. In Panel A, the vote percentages in question are for provincial elections. In Panel B, the votes are for the federal electorate in the province. The figures are based on the estimations in Table 9A.1. Quebec elections are excluded.

the marginalization of a strategically disfavoured alternative.[6] The setup is quadratic because fear of the left should kick in only beyond some threshold.[7] The federal-provincial difference is clear. As the provincial left grows, the centre-right consolidates at an accelerating rate. The marginal effect of the CCF-NDP is nearly twice as great when its share is about 50 percent than when it is about 30 percent. In the federal arena, this pattern is echoed only weakly: there is a hint of curvature but only at extreme values. Part of the story, of course, is that, even in provinces of relative strength, the CCF-NDP's federal share tends to be smaller than its provincial one, and vice versa, as Figure 7.6 showed. There is thus a dearth of observations above 35 percent. If the NDP recovers or enhances the position that it gained in 2011, then the federal relationship might also strengthen. (Indeed, there is a hint of this in Figure 9.3, which shows a late federal ENP drop in the NDP's three historically strongest provinces.) Even so, it is unlikely that the arenas would converge completely since the greater relevance of provincial electorates to each other in the federal arena - perhaps more to the point the greater *irrelevance* of provincial electorates to each other in the provincial arena - would continue as before, even if future elections process a different set of strategic considerations.

Sometimes the strategically preferred provincial party is an insurgent. This happened in 1952 in British Columbia when the collapse of the Liberals and Conservatives made Social Credit the privileged anti-socialist alternative. The same thing happened with the Saskatchewan Party in 1997.[8] More generally, insurgents and the NDP are more likely to coexist in provincial than in federal elections, as shown in Figure 9.5. In provincial elections in which the NDP returns shares in the 40-50 percent range, insurgent shares range up to 50 percent and beyond. The same is true for NDP shares in the 30-40 percent range. For the full set of elections, the relationship between CCF-NDP and insurgent shares is slightly positive, a correlation of +0.12. The ubiquity of such instances and the identities of the players were given in Table 9.1: in province-decade combinations in which the NDP is a major player (the shaded cells), the alternative is an insurgent one time in four.

The federal pattern is very different. For NDP federal shares greater than 40 percent, the maximum insurgent share is barely 6 percent. For NDP shares between 30 and 40 percent, all insurgent observations but one

Figure 9.5 Covariance between NDP and insurgent shares: Provincial versus federal patterns, 1908-2011

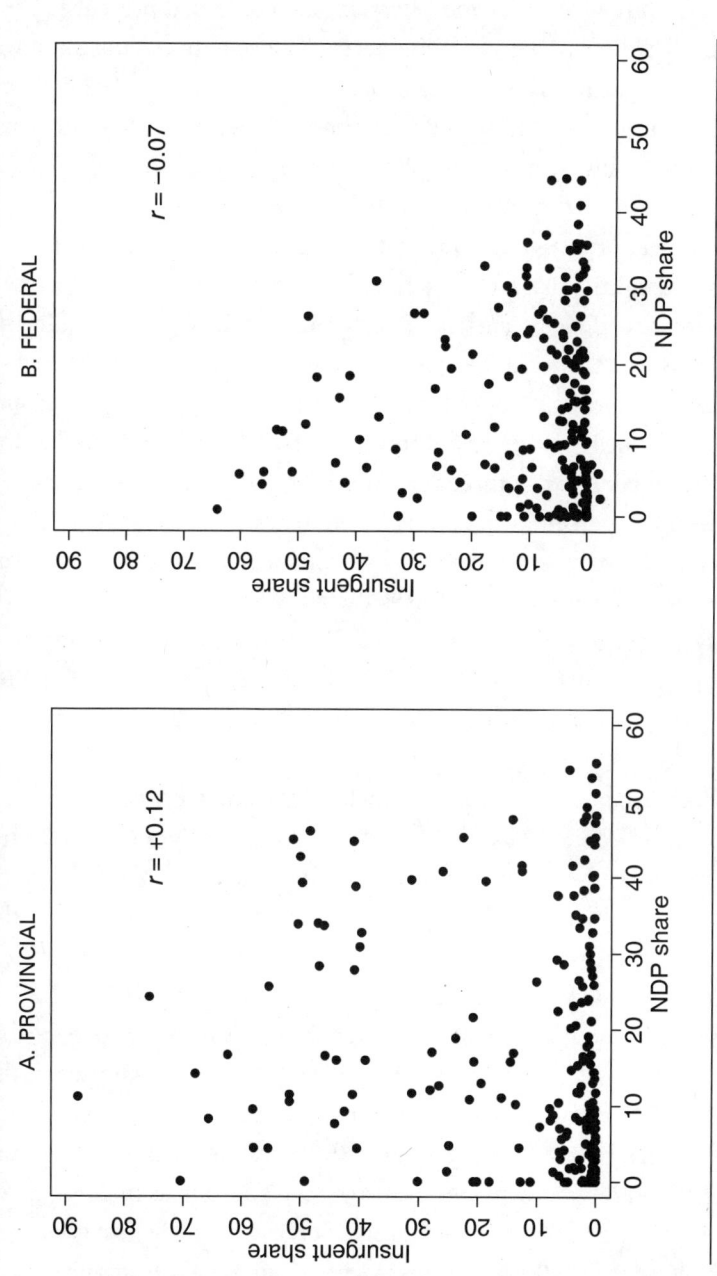

A. PROVINCIAL

$r = +0.12$

B. FEDERAL

$r = -0.07$

Notes: This figure shows how the strength or weakness in the CCF-NDP vote is related to the strength or weakness of insurgents. Markers denote each party's share in a given election. In Panel A, the vote percentages in question are for provincial elections. In Panel B, the votes are for the federal electorate in the province. Quebec elections are excluded.

lie below 20 percent. The overall correlation between NDP and insurgent shares is slightly negative. By implication, the continued presence of the distinctively federal parties, the Liberals and Conservatives, constrains the scope for new parties. This constraint was evident even in the 1920s, when agrarian insurgency ran up against stronger Liberal and Conservative resistance federally than provincially. This resistance is key to the federal side's greater fractionalization shown in Figure 9.3.

The impact of insurgents on the fractionalization of provincial party systems is conditional on NDP strength. This conditionality is weak to non-existent for federal parties. The evidence is in Figure 9.6. On the vertical axis is the ENP for the province, once for the province as part of the federal electorate and once for its own provincial elections. The insurgent share defines the x-axis, and the CCF-NDP share is presented as the conditioning factor, with three representative NDP shares: 0 percent, 20 percent, and 40 percent. Underlying the figures are double quadratic estimations: each party is represented by a quadratic estimation, as is the interaction between the two.[9] This is dictated by the arithmetic of ENP. No party, simply by growing, can increase ENP indefinitely; at some point, it becomes so big that its growth has a consolidating effect. The interaction among parties is necessary to establish the mutual conditionality of effect, the point that I am trying to make.

In both arenas, insurgent and CCF-NDP shares have diminishing marginal effects on ENP, as is arithmetically required. For insurgents, this is shown by the downward concavity of the slopes. For the CCF-NDP, it is best shown by the fact that gaps between intercepts diminish as the party's share increases. By both indicators, though, increments in ENP are smaller provincially than federally. Indeed, when the provincial NDP share is 40 percent, ENP is generally lower across the full range of plausible insurgent shares than when the NDP sits at 20 percent. And when the provincial NDP is at 40 percent, growth in the insurgent share adds *nothing* to ENP. In that context, insurgent growth drives both old parties off the field. The federal pattern echoes the provincial one, but, as mentioned for both insurgents and the NDP, the diminution in marginal effect is weaker. At an NDP share of 40 percent, insurgents seem to have a sharply curvilinear effect, but the massive confidence intervals remind us that this part of the landscape is all but empty.

Figure 9.6 Insurgents, the CCF-NDP, and ENP in the province: Provincial versus federal patterns, 1908-2011

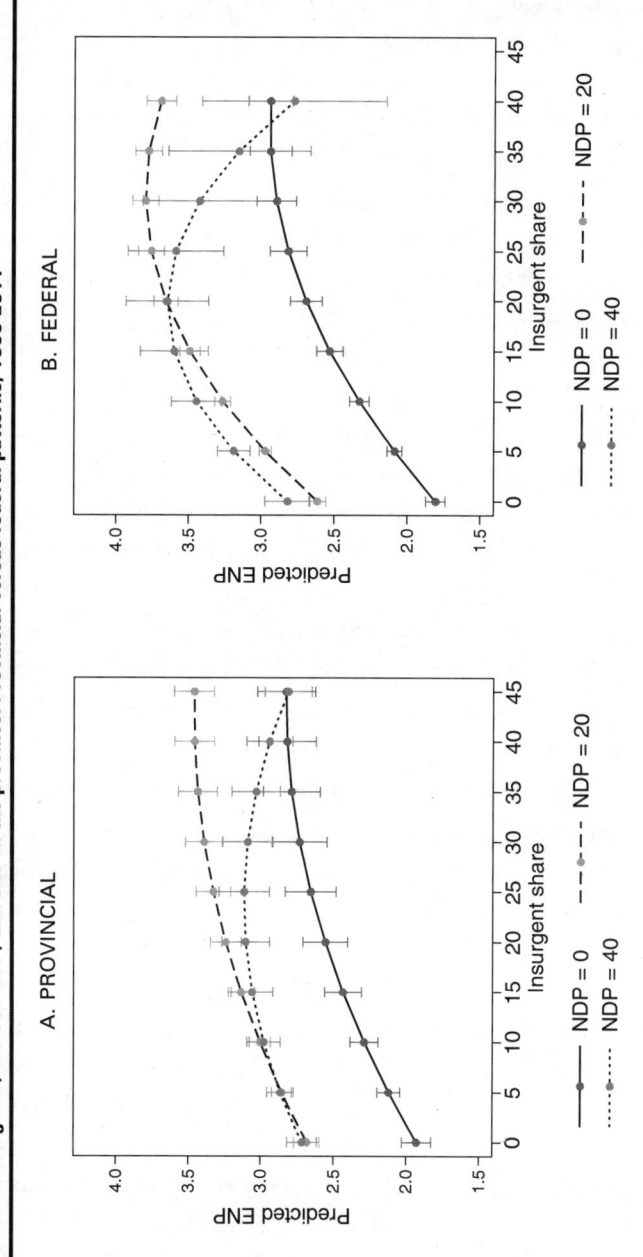

Notes: This figure shows how CCF-NDP vote percentages combine to affect the fractionalization of the vote in a province. The indicator of fractionalization is the ENP. The slopes of the lines show how the strength of insurgents affects ENP, a basically positive relationship. The three separate lines show how the impact of insurgents is conditional on the strength of the NDP. The NDP shares for each line are arbitrarily selected, as the interaction between insurgents and the NDP is continuously defined. All estimations, including the interactions, are quadratic in form to reflect the logic of calculation of ENP. In Panel A, the relationships are for provincial elections. In Panel B, the relationships are for the federal electorate in the province. The figures are based on the estimation in Table 9A.2.

Summary Impact

In sum, federal-provincial divergence has three main sources: insurgency, the CCF-NDP, and counter-coordination against the CCF-NDP threat. The relative weight of these sources has shifted as the functionalist logic of left versus non-left has displaced older idiosyncrasies. These elements are brought together in Figure 9.7, which plots the results of an integrated, time-sensitive estimation of results from 1931 to the present. The founding of the CCF was one critical moment. Although the pre-1931 left vote was critical to the narrative of Chapter 7, the collective share of these scattered micro-parties is too small – zero more often than not – to be useful in the integrated estimation. Also critical was the refounding of the CCF as the NDP. Although the NDP was not an instant success, it quickly signalled its intention to become a coast-to-coast party. Accordingly, the estimation is conditional on the shift from the CCF to the NDP. Each of the three independent variables is measured in the provincial arena. Although both arenas enter into the calculation of federal-provincial dissimilarity, variation in dissimilarity values is driven more powerfully by province-level factors. This reflects the greater sectionalism in the geography of provincial party shares, as shown in Figure 9.2. Although all parties enter into calculation of the dependent variable, the new parties are the dynamic force. To give insurgents their full due, Quebec is included in the estimation. Thus, in contrast to the estimates for centre-right consolidation, all provinces underpin the estimates that produce Figure 9.7.

Insurgents are always important. In the "CCF era," 1931-60, a 1.0 percent increase in the provincial insurgent share yielded a 0.42 percent increase in dissimilarity. In the "NDP era," that impact increased slightly, to 0.50 percent.[10] The continuing impact of insurgency reflects the fact that provincial insurgents often do not have federal counterparts, and when counterparts do exist they are usually weak and marginalized relatively quickly. (This is so notwithstanding the federal success of Reform/Alliance in its moment on the stage.) The contrast here is mostly between Alberta, Quebec, and British Columbia and all other provinces and between Saskatchewan now and Saskatchewan before 1997. One other feature requires comment: across the board, the insurgent line sits on a higher plane after 1960 than before it. For any given insurgent share, the predicted

Figure 9.7 Sources of federal-provincial dissimilarity, 1931-2011

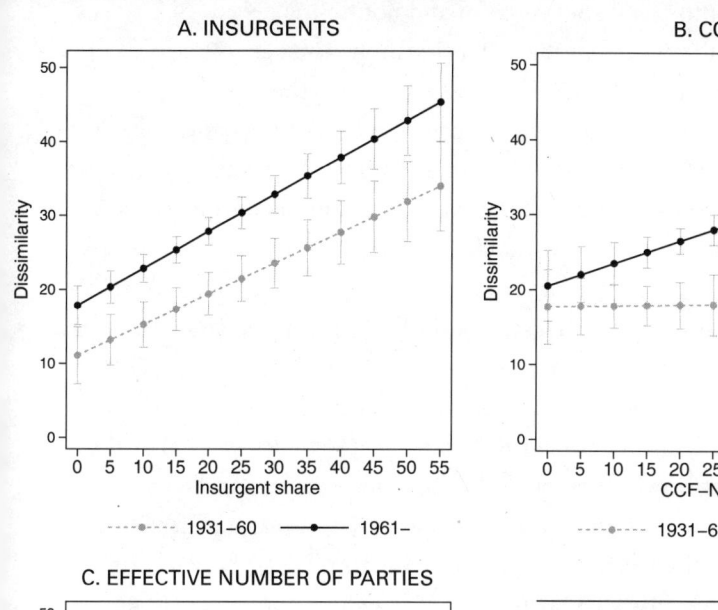

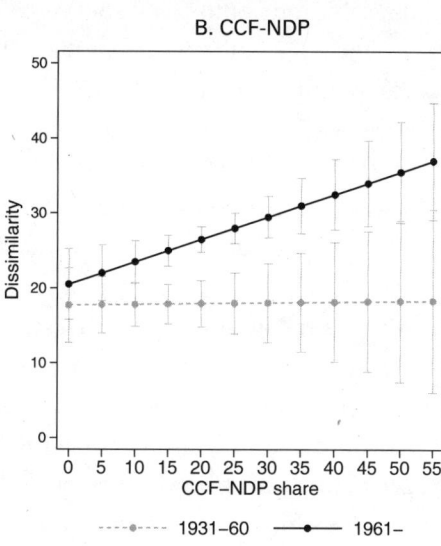

A. INSURGENTS

B. CCF-NDP

C. EFFECTIVE NUMBER OF PARTIES

Notes: This figure shows how insurgent vote percentages, CCF-NDP vote percentages, and the overall fractionalization of the electorate – all in the provincial arena – combine to produce dissimilarity in federal and provincial outcomes. The period is from the founding of the CCF to the present. All relationships are also conditional on the transition from the CCF to the NDP. The figure is based on the estimation in Table 9.A3.

dissimilarity value is about 10 points higher in the later period. This reflects intensification of the battle between left and non-left.

The NDP is the source of that intensification. The party is critical to the overall story in a way that the CCF never was. The size of the CCF was not a direct factor in federal-provincial discontinuity. Where the party was weak, it was weak in both arenas, and in the rare instances in which it was strong it was strong in both arenas. This is implied in Figure 9.2, which shows that the standard deviations for the CCF – the readings before 1960 – are only slightly larger for provincial elections than for federal ones. After its refounding as the NDP, in contrast, the party's geographies diverged. As the party approached power in certain provinces, its SD increased; its provinces of relative strength pulled away from the rest. The federal party, in contrast, spread to almost all provinces, such that the geography became less differentiated. This is also evident in Figure 9.2. This transformation manifests itself in Figure 9.7 as a major shift in estimated power. After 1961, a 1.0 percent gain in NDP provincial share typically translates into a 0.30 percent gain in federal-provincial dissimilarity. Here the contrast is mainly between Manitoba, Saskatchewan, and British Columbia and all other provinces, with Ontario and Nova Scotia occasionally joining the big three.[11]

Party system fragmentation now also plays a role. Before 1960, variation in provincial ENP made no difference to overall dissimilarity. In those years, provincial and federal ENP did not differ much, not in most provinces at least. As Figure 9.3 shows, only after 1960 did a systematic ENP discrepancy emerge, reflecting nearly universal increases in federal fractionalization even as certain provincial electorates went in the opposite direction. As this happened, provincial ENP emerged as a factor in its own right. Panel C in Figure 9.7 shows that after 1960 fractionalization of the provincial vote made the arenas more alike. Fractionalization in the provincial arena reflects the same pressures that operate in the federal one. These pressures include an ongoing "trickle down" of organizational energy from the federal NDP to weak provincial counterparts, as in Atlantic Canada. Also in play are demonstration effects on the political right since the Wildrose and Saskatchewan Parties emulate the exclusively federal Reform Party. Conversely, when the provincial arena consolidates – or reconsolidates – pressures in play federally are not accommodated provincially. Typically, this happens when the NDP poses a threat of becoming the governing party. So the NDP affects the gap between arenas twice over: its mere appearance can increase the gap between arenas, but this effect is then augmented by counter-consolidation.[12] As Figure 9.3 shows, in the western trio with a strong NDP, ENP values have been dropping for decades.

Discussion

The NDP as a Catalyst

Federal-provincial disparities offer a further field for one of this book's main themes: the NDP as a driver of recent patterns in the party system. Directly, this is visible through the increased weight, post-1960, of variation in provincial NDP shares. Indirectly, it is visible in the increased weight of ENP effects (Figure 9.7, Panel C) and in the post-1960 rise in the insurgent line (Panel A). Critical to the argument is that the NDP is a party like labour parties elsewhere in the Anglosphere, both in its programmatic commitments and in the reactions that it provokes when it gets within hailing distance of power. Unlike those counterparts, however, its diffusion and success are incomplete. For analytical purposes, this incompleteness is a godsend. It means that the turning of strategic wheels is visible in real time, usually in slow motion. Just as electorates in different provinces – and in the same provinces at different times – approach the party system differently according to strategic circumstances, so too does a given electorate approach the party system in different ways according to the geographic scale of the total electorate. For the provincial arena, the total electorate is each province by itself. In the federal arena, each province is one among many; the total electorate is Canada.

Deep Division

Of course, the NDP and its entailments are not the whole story. For certain periods and in certain provinces, it is hardly the story at all. Although insurgents have become less important overall, they still populate some of the landscape. They are most of the story for Quebec, and this illustrates a major theme of this book: deep division. For many decades, the Quebec nationalist dimension stretched further in the provincial arena than in the federal arena toward outright secession. Federally, the Quebec electorate settled on one or the other – but not both – of the old parties. Since 1993, the pattern has become more complicated and variable. The appearance of the Bloc Québécois in 1993 narrowed the gap between arenas. Fracturing of the provincial electorate after 2000, with openings toward social conservatism and softer variants of nationalism, reopened the gap. The sudden NDP federal breakthrough in 2011, with no provincial counterpart, widened the gap still further.

The Scale of Discontinuity
What makes Canada's federation so distinctively vulnerable to gaps between arenas? In the absence of usable theory, the way to proceed is to triangulate among the cases in Figure 2.8. The cases vary in terms of ethnoregional diversity, electoral institutions, and what might be called the "history of geography."

Comparing Canada with Germany and Spain points to the electoral formula. All three countries have the parliamentary framework in common. Neither Germany nor Spain is as diverse or geographically massive as Canada, yet both countries harbour serious internal geographic variations. Germany is still relatively young as a unified entity, especially given the disruption occasioned by the Second World War, the postwar division between East Germany and West Germany, and their financially painful and culturally difficult reintegration. Spain is only now becoming federal, but its historically centralized state masks severe subnational differences, in particular the minority nationalities of Basques, Catalans, and Galicians. For Canada, Quebec aside, it is not obvious that subnational pressures are stronger than in either of the European comparators. Yet its electoral gaps dwarf those in Germany and Spain.

What clearly does distinguish Canada from Germany and Spain is the electoral formula. The PR formula in Germany and Spain allows discontinuities to express themselves but does not amplify them. The FPP formula in Canada plays an independent moderating role. Early in the twentieth century, FPP arguably suppressed federal-provincial gaps since discrepant underlying tendencies were bottled up inside the pre-existing parties. But once new parties appeared, FPP amplified their specificity. The so-called psychological effect, the tendency for vote shares to reconsolidate after a party system crisis, took federal and provincial electorates within certain provinces – the same people essentially – in different directions.

The Canada-Australia comparison can be said to reinforce the electoral system emphasis. Here the critical component is not the formula but district magnitude, single-member districts for all Commonwealth House districts and for lower-house districts in all states but Tasmania. Although Australia's majority formula enables fractionalization in first preferences, like under PR, countering this is the logic of single-member districts. Although Australian fractionalization has been quite like that in Canada (Figure 2.5), the two countries are poles apart for federal-state gaps (Figure 2.8). Australia might illustrate the other side in the contingency in the impact of the electoral system: state-level insurgencies might be suppressed and Commonwealth-state discontinuities minimized.

But are the Canadian and Australian cases as comparable as all that? There is no equivalent to Quebec, of course, in Australia. More generally, the countries differ profoundly in the history and geography of settlement. Demographic and institutional development in each Australian state was rapid and simultaneous compared with Canada's multi-century story. All Australian states attained autonomy and "responsible government" before creation of the federation, and all entered the union at the same time. Indeed, all participated in creating it; no state is a creature of the central government. Moreover, each state can be stylized in roughly the same way: a single coastal metropolis controlling access to a state-specific hinterland,[13] with conflict among land, labour, and capital taking roughly the same form. States vary in the importance of export-oriented primary commodity production, but all states have significant primary sectors, and commerce in each state is forced through its own metropolitan choke point, not through the metropolis of any other state. Canada differs in all of these particulars. European occupation required three centuries. Quebec, for instance, was older when British Columbia became a crown colony in 1858 than British Columbia is now. Three provinces – Manitoba, Saskatchewan, and Alberta – are creatures of the federal government and remained colonized, in a manner of speaking, until 1930.[14] British Columbia took on the trappings of responsible government only when required as a condition for admission to Confederation, and it did not adopt party politics until the twentieth century. Most important, arguably, is that the country's historical metropoles, Montreal and Toronto, have hinterlands that include other provinces. This is also true for the smaller metropoles of Winnipeg and Vancouver. Canada's National Policy of tariff protection, railway subsidy, and prairie settlement was explicitly designed to serve the metropolitan interest. Provincial boundaries became expressions of economic (not to mention cultural) difference, with a powerful tendency to organize provincial politics – and sometimes federal politics – in opposition to the federal government. This can happen in Australia too – Western Australia is a case in point – but the primary tension between metropolis and hinterland is still within each Australian state, not among them.

If Canada stands in contrast to Australia as a geographic expression, the same cannot be said for Canada versus the United States. Although the timelines for settlement differ subtly, as do key barriers to the east-west axis of occupation, Canada-US similarities are as striking as the differences. The oldest and the youngest states and provinces are about the same age. Both federations are a mix of pre-existing jurisdictions and creatures of the federal governments. The United States provided the template for the trinity of tariffs, railways, and homesteading that constituted Canada's National Policy. Contention between the resource-rich interior and coastal metropoles has been a recurring feature of US politics. Early American insurgencies were models for Canadian ones and even supplied some of the personnel. And then there is the American South. Although the South and Quebec represent very different social formations, each represents a profound challenge to integration. It is useful to remember, to paraphrase Sniderman et al. (1974), that Canada might look forward to its civil war, but the United States has already had its. And for most of the twentieth century, the fit of the South to the US party system had strong parallels to Quebec in Canada: hegemonic commitment to one party and in a way that set that party, the Democrats, at odds with itself, more even than was true for the Liberals in Canada.

Yet we have long since ceased to think of US politics as a site for third-party activity. Third-party candidates enjoy occasional success in presidential and gubernatorial elections, but not since the Greenbackers in the 1870s and 1880s and the People's Party in the 1890s has there been a notable legislative presence. Figure 2.5 is eloquent on how closely the US

House hews to the Duvergerian two-party ideal. And Figure 2.8 confirms that the dominant pattern for US federal and state arenas is continuity. The median federal-state gap in the United States since 1960 is even smaller than that in Australia. Political careers commonly start in a state's lower house and progress through successive layers of the state and federal hierarchies. Discontinuity, such as it is, mainly reflects lags in realignment. The federal party system underwent a massive postwar nationalization as formerly Republican regions moved toward the Democrats and the South moved – spectacularly – in the other direction. Roughly speaking, the state-level transformation lagged the federal one by a decade or more. Only as intermediate-level politicians progressed through their orderly *cursus honorem* did vacancies, and thus open seats, emerge at lower levels. But the system ultimately did return to close integration across levels everywhere.

If the weakness of third parties accounts for the lack of federal-state gaps – the opposite of the Canadian sequence – then what accounts for the weakness and short life spans of American insurgents? Some of the story must lie in historically great absorptivity of US parties, which in turn reflects the separation of powers (Carey and Shugart 1995; Shugart and Carey 1992). Absence of the requirement for outward cohesion to sustain the political executive permits US parties to internalize dissent, which in turn minimizes the scope for federal-state compartmentalization. In Canada, the parliamentary requirement to sustain (or oppose) the political executive creates an imperative for party cohesion that is difficult to square with the country's diversity. The result is party system fragmentation (Lipset 1954, 1960), which in turn opens the door for federal-provincial gaps.

All of this is conjecture, based upon comparison of Canada with three federations that have little of Canada's history of geography, of which two use PR and one uses an electoral system with strong affinities to that in Canada. This comparison is then coupled to one with the United States, which has strikingly similar geography and history and an identical electoral system but a framework of separated powers with profoundly different implications for the permeability of parties. Comparing so few cases as a correlational exercise gets us only so far. Closer analysis of the cases seems to be critical but is beyond the scope of this book.

APPENDIX

TABLE 9.A1 Left threat and right consolidation, 1908-2011

	Provincial		Federal	
CCF-NDP share				
Linear term	0.0014	(0.0036)	0.0066	(0.0036)
Quadratic term	−0.00019	(0.00008)	−0.00017	(0.00010)
Intercept	0.73	(0.03)	0.66	(0.03)
Overall R^2	0.31		0.01	
ρ	0.17		0.24	
N	204		205	

Notes: This table shows how the vote for rival non-socialist parties shifts toward one party as the CCF-NDP threat (the party's vote share) grows. The relationship is stronger in provincial than in federal elections. The dependent variable is the SF ratio (Cox 1997) in each province at each election for parties of the centre-right. Estimations are for time series–cross-section with fixed effects for the province. Alberta (1921-30) and Quebec are omitted.

TABLE 9.A2   Joint effect of insurgents and the CCF-NDP on ENP, 1908-2011

	Federal		Provincial	
Insurgent share				
Linear term	0.06	(0.006)	0.04	(0.01)
Quadratic term	−0.0007	(0.001)	−0.0005	(0.0001)
CCF-NDP share				
Linear term	0.06	(0.005)	0.06	(0.006)
Quadratic term	−0.008	(0.002)	−0.0009	(0.0001)
Insurgent × CCF-NDP				
Linear	0.0006	(0.0009)	−0.0002	(0.0008)
Ins quad	0.000005	(0.00002)	0.00001	(0.00001)
NDP quad	0.00001	(0.00002)	0.000001	(0.00001)
Both quad	0.000001	(0.0000006)	0.0000004	(0.0000003)
Intercept	1.75	(0.04)	1.93	(0.05)
Overall R^2	0.87		0.72	
ρ	0.28		0.09	
N	211		209	

Notes: This table shows the difference between federal and provincial arenas in how insurgent and CCF-NDP shares interact to affect ENP. The dependent variables are the federal and provincial ENPs in each province for elections since 1908. Estimations are for time series–cross-section with fixed effects for the province. Quebec is omitted.

Table 9.A3 Impact of insurgent votes, CCF-NDP votes, and provincial ENP on federal-provincial dissimilarity, 1930-2011

	Coefficient	Standard error
"Era"	26.8	11.4
Insurgent share	0.417	0.073
× "era"	0.085	0.08
CCF-NDP share	0.011	0.15
× "era"	0.288	0.145
ENP	−0.024	4.53
× "era"	−9.81	5.13
Intercept	10.9	10.5
Overall R^2		0.62
ρ		0.163
N		*218*

Notes: This table shows the impact on federal-provincial electoral dissimilarity from the insurgent vote, the CCF-NDP vote, and overall ENP. The dependent variable is federal-provincial dissimilarity since 1930. Independent variables are measured in the provincial arena. Estimations are for time series–cross-section with fixed effects for the province.

10

Conclusion

The disjointed character of the Canadian party system is both an explanatory challenge and a research opportunity. Elsewhere in the world of majoritarian institutions, two big parties command – or used to command – both the strategic heights and the surrounding lowlands. Alternatives to the party system in place are scarcely imaginable, much less realizable. When we lift the Canadian hood, we see the moving parts, and breakdown often seems to be imminent. Accordingly, my argument has many threads, both in outcomes and in explanatory factors. This chapter draws the threads together, extracts further implications, and identifies new research challenges.

First I line up questions and answers. The questions are as outlined in Chapter 2. The answers come out of the tripartite order in the rest of the book: the foundations of Liberal and Conservative support, the conditions for and patterns of third-party entry and exit, and interactions between old and new parties and between federal and provincial arenas. All of this explanatory effort identifies at least three big research issues – and leaves them hanging.

The first issue is that the Westminster system has not one majoritarian logic but two, and they can be at odds with each other. One logic is electoral, where divergent geographies produce different competitive conditions in different places, differences that the electoral system then amplifies. The system can be particularly kind to small, single-region parties. The other logic is parliamentary, where the Westminster propensity for single-party government favours geographically inclusive parties. The claim that the two logics exist is not original. But the Canadian system indicates that their coexistence has dynamic implications.

The second issue is the place of history in analytic history, which I illustrate in two parts. First, the power of the Catholic cleavage cannot be accounted for other than by reference to history. Some of this involves the rise and fall of contemporaneous factors. But the case also illustrates how party organizations can use pre-existing coalitions and practices to adapt to new issues. Second, within Canada's borders, parties and voters enact the drama that comparativists see as differentiating countries. Just as cross-national comparison, especially of the configuration of forces on the centre-right, requires reference to historical sequences, so too do comparisons among Canadian provinces and, to an extent, between arenas within provinces.

Third, running through much of the analysis are patterns that smack of voters' processing of strategic information. But voters do so at a level of aggregation on which they can have no possible effect. Where does this leave our notions of electoral rationality?

Recapitulation

The Puzzles

One striking fact about the Canadian electorate is its early and enduring fragmentation, as indicated by the effective number of parties or ENP. This came about even though the Canadian electoral system punishes coordination failure savagely and should either discourage new entrants or accommodate them by marginalizing an old party. What it should not do is allow new parties to enter and then limit their growth. In part, the Canadian exception reflects the emergence of different party systems in different regions. But as the century advanced, fragmentation also increased within districts. What is more, the rhythm of fragmentation has differed between the within-district – or local – and the between-district – or extra-local – components. For local fragmentation, growth has been gradual. Extra-local breakdown, in contrast, has surged abruptly and often declined just as abruptly. These extra-local pulses account for much of the system's volatility. All comparable systems exhibit moments of extreme volatility, but the Canadian extremes outrank the others. In other systems, extreme volatility predates the Second World War; in Canada, it recurs even to the present and might be growing in scale. Meanwhile, voters in some provinces are weakly moored between federal and provincial arenas. No single factor accounts for differences across provinces in the scale of this disconnection.

Febrility in outcomes seems to correspond to abiding weakness in the system's social anchoring. In contrast to the rest of the Anglosphere, the Canadian system's class basis is weak. For decades, the strongest anchor – and it truly was strong – was religious denomination, basically Catholics versus Protestants. A denominational base for choice is not unusual in itself, but in Canada its link to specifically religious dimensions of policy is obscure. Most puzzling of all is the system's domination by a party of the centre. This domination is critical to explaining many of the system's other features but itself is contrary to nature. Accordingly, the place to start is with Liberal domination and the dynamics of old-party competition.

Old-Party Dynamics

For most of the twentieth century, Liberal control of government was predicated on the party's strength in Quebec, the historical pivot for government. Quebec voters were efficiently coordinated, with a vote distribution typically one-sided yet mobile. The province presided over the onset of Liberal domination in the 1890s and the possible end of that domination in 1984. From 1896 to 1980, the Liberals swept Quebec 20 times, which they then cashed out for 17 Canada-wide victories. When they failed to sweep Quebec, they won only once.[1] Here, then, is the first proposition.

1. *From the origins of the party system to 1993, control of a bloc of seats from Quebec was the necessary and sufficient condition for Liberal government, a condition routinely fulfilled from 1896 to 1984.*

Outside Quebec, the Liberal Party was sustained by a base that held positions on certain subdomains of Canada's "national question" also held by Quebeckers. For most of the twentieth century, the subdomain was the place of Canada in the British Empire. Catholics, and not just French-speaking ones, were generally resistant to the pro-empire pole of this axis. The Catholic share of the total population grew over the century and became less concentrated in Quebec and the francophone ecumene outside Quebec, so the base became strategically more useful. Energization of the foreign policy agenda in the first decades of the century brought the Catholic/non-Catholic cleavage to the fore. As the empire retreated after 1945, a residue of the British connection persisted in conflicts over symbols of the polity, notably the maple leaf flag. After 1965, the British connection faded, and religious denomination became electorally less encompassing. Outside Quebec, cultural issues became parcelled into ethnically specific components. Into the 1980s, francophones and southern Europeans remained distinctly Liberal, thanks to official language and early stage multicultural policy, but Catholics of British Isles origins fell away. Later the identity margin shifted to people of non-European backgrounds, whose numbers were also growing. In the twenty-first century, this group has been the Liberals' last remaining distinctive pillar. This leads to a second set of propositions.

2. *Liberal support outside Quebec was driven by shifting definitions of identity politics, ranging from the place of Canada in the world, as mediated by membership in the British Empire and Commonwealth, to the ethnic definition of the Canadian nationality.*

   a. *Focus on the British connection enabled an encompassing coalition that included most Catholics.*
   b. *In these years, appeals to francophones, inside and outside Quebec, were encompassed in appeals to Catholics more generally.*
   c. *The diminished relevance of the British connection led to ethnically focused appeals and, ultimately, to a narrowing of the Liberal Party's cultural base.*

Liberal domination of Quebec rarely reflected complete identification of the party with the province's interests. As the national question shifted from the place of Canada in the British Empire to the place of Quebec in (or out of) Canada, such identification became even less likely. What sustained the Liberals in Quebec was the routine absence of an acceptable and electorally viable alternative. Among parties with historical strength in the province, the Liberal Party was often the *least* pro-Quebec

– alternatively put, the most pro-Canada. Outside Quebec, the opposite was true. If the Liberals did not adopt a precisely pro-Quebec position, at least they championed a pro-French (or pro-Catholic) one. Tensions within the party were common, sometimes producing defection, as in 1917, or cabinet crisis, as in 1944-45. For my argument, however, the key point is that the Liberals were vulnerable on both flanks.

Where Liberal electoral coalitions were occasionally tense, Conservative ones could be outright incoherent. On national questions, Conservatives outside Quebec were unsympathetic to Quebec's interests. Inside Quebec, however, the residue of the party's base was nationalist or ultra-Catholic, depending on the era, and when that residue was mobilized and augmented it was wedded to francophobes outside Quebec.[2] This happened in 1911, when anti-imperialists in Quebec rallied to a Conservative Party that campaigned elsewhere on a sharply pro-imperialist platform. It happened again in 1958, when provincial Union Nationale elites made a bet on John Diefenbaker. And it happened spectacularly in 1984, a shift amplified in 1988.[3] Each time the subsequent loss exceeded the preceding gain. Over the twentieth century, the magnitude of swings grew. The third set of propositions follows.

3. *Every time in the twentieth century that the Conservatives ascended to Canada-wide majority status, a large swing – usually the largest – occurred in Quebec.*

   a. *The resulting coalition was distinctly pro-Quebec inside that province and distinctly anti-Quebec elsewhere in Canada. This coalition was unsustainable.*
   b. *Without exception, the Conservative Party lost all – or more – of the ground that it had gained in Quebec. Only once, in 1935, was this not attributable to betrayal of Quebeckers' hopes.*
   c. *Sometimes the Conservatives experienced comparable losses outside Quebec. Usually, this reflected disappointment for economic rather than cultural reasons. The exception was 1993, when Conservative losses inside and outside Quebec were symmetrical.*
   d. *These catastrophic Conservative swings are the most important single component of the party system's pattern of episodic volatility.*

Third-Party Entry and Exit

The early years of third-party strength, the 1920s especially, were a "search" phase as political entrepreneurs and voters alike sought a label for their unease with the old system.[4] New-party proto-elites were still getting themselves sorted out ideologically. At this point, the Liberal Party remained in competition for some of the new-party vote, especially in Manitoba and Ontario. Elsewhere this was not so. Most distinct was Alberta, where the United Farmers of Alberta allied with labour. Much of the vote was simple protest, however, drawn to the most accessible vehicle and unlikely to stay there when conditions improved. The geographical focus of the early parties helped them at first, thanks to the logic of the electoral system, but then it limited their growth.

In the 1930s, there began a clarification of alternatives. Critically, the CCF crafted an appeal to the progressive and programmatic residue of the old agrarian insurgency. No less critically, the party admitted labour supporters and socialist intellectuals into its ranks, and these recruits came to define the party's appeal and modus operandi. Notwithstanding bumps along the way, including resistance within the ranks to identification with the union movement, the party evolved into a conventional party of labour. The culmination was its refounding in 1961 as the NDP. As the CCF's and NDP's interest group and ideological focus sharpened, the political left became less available as a vehicle for protest. If the party was unlikely to benefit from short-term discontent, neither was it vulnerable to boom and bust. Its growth, although not unbroken, was usually gradual. Thus, here is the next proposition.

4. Growth of the CCF-NDP was the primary contributor to long-run fractionalization of the electorate.

This also made the CCF-NDP qualitatively distinct from other new parties. I labelled these parties collectively as "insurgents," a description that focuses on their electoral febrility. From the 1930s to the 1980s, they served mainly as vehicles for varying combinations of short-run protest and more enduring region-specific discontent. But also, somewhat in parallel with ideological clarification that the CCF-NDP brought to the left, other new parties increasingly became vehicles for articulation of programs recognizably on the right. The ultimate expression of this was Reform, later called Alliance. Reform artfully included both regional and ideological elements in its appeal, but the balance shifted toward ideology as the party moved toward merger with the old Progressive Conservatives. Although Reform can be said to have taken over the Conservatives, rather than the opposite, it is significant that the name of the merged party carries no echo of the insurgency. Like its short-lived and programmatically protean insurgent predecessors, Reform disappeared from history. The following general propositions apply.

> 5a. *Insurgents created most of the short-term flux: dramatic entries, often assisted by the logic of the electoral system, and dramatic exits.*
> b. *Insurgents supplied a varying but cumulatively small share of overall electoral fractionalization.*

Interaction among New and Old Parties

Insurgent parties in Canada began as protean entities, with either ambiguous ideological aspirations or none at all. Insurgents evolved in an ideological direction, however, and increasingly became vehicles for debate over definition of the political right. This put them in competition with the Conservative Party, inducing electoral dynamics that became increasingly detached from those of the Liberals or New Democrats. Although the Conservatives themselves remain in competition with their neighbours just to the left, the Liberals, their electoral exchanges with insurgents are more dramatic.

All along, insurgency has been a sectional phenomenon, sometimes expressing discontent in the West, sometimes in Quebec, increasingly in both regions. There has been essentially no trend in this phenomenon. As a result, insurgents have a high level of geographic variance relative to their total share of votes. Thanks to this, they often do well in translating votes into seats. Both statically and dynamically, insurgents are strong where Conservatives are weak and vice versa.

This similarity sets up the final regularity: the insurgent vote is febrile. Insurgents appear suddenly, do not persist indefinitely, and sometimes disappear as quickly as they appear. When an insurgent appears, it does so at the expense of the Conservative Party. This displacement commonly characterizes the bust end of a Conservative boom-bust sequence. When an insurgent disappears, conversely, its supporters are mostly swept up in a Conservative boom.

The upshot of all this is the following.

6. *Insurgents and the Conservatives together generate a disproportionate share of the system's total volatility.*

   a. *When insurgents are strong, they contribute a disproportionate share of the extra-local component of ENP.*
   b. *When insurgents are weak, and the Conservatives displace them, much of the extra-local component of ENP is erased.*

The pattern for the NDP is very different. The western origins of the political left are evident in the weakly positive correlation with insurgency before 1960. This also reflects the fact that both early insurgents, mainly Progressives, and the scattered elements that later congealed as the CCF broke through federally in the 1920s. After 1960, the NDP-insurgent relationship is clearly negative.

The left began in the West, but it did not stay confined there. From its founding, the CCF had serious eastern Canadian support if not a commensurate share of seats. With the refounding of the CCF as the NDP, eastern support and representation increased, especially in the 1990s. Although this was a decade of NDP weakness, the party's recovery began in 1997 in Atlantic Canada. When its western strength began to be restored in 2004, its recently acquired Atlantic base remained in place.[5] Quebec entered the fold with the NDP breakthrough in 2011. This diffusion occurred as the NDP's Canada-wide share trended generally upward, such that the ratio of the party's geographic variance to its overall share moved sharply downward.

The upward trend in NDP support has been gradual, however, and occasionally it has gone in reverse. The dominant upward trend has been the complement of a correspondingly gradual decline of the Liberal Party. When the NDP retreats, as in the 1990s and 2015, the Liberals become the prime beneficiary.

Putting all of this together leads to the following point.

7. *NDP growth is critical to the increasing scale of district-level fractionalization, which in turn is increasingly important as a component of the party system's overall fractionalization.*

This leaves a quandary. The shift from the Liberals to the New Democrats has been gradual and might have been arrested. Nowhere else in the Anglosphere does such a pattern of disjointed and polarized pluralism persist. Either potential labour-left entrants are repelled, as in the United States, or labour breaks through quickly, inducing in turn a painful but ultimately conclusive reshaping of the centre-right, as happened everywhere else. Either way the pressure toward two-party consolidation seems to be irresistible (or it did in the first half of the twentieth century). The Canadian system's resistance to this pressure is a compound of forces keeping the Liberals credible and forces enabling the New Democrats to stave off oblivion. The federal system is critical to the offsetting operation of these forces.

Contrary to a widely held view, the system does not lack ideological content, and Canadian politics is organized along left-right lines, much like in the rest of the world. If the gap between the Liberal Party and NDP has narrowed, the difference between the Liberals and Conservatives has widened, such that the biggest gap is now between the biggest parties. Left versus right is not the only organizing principle, but this too is hardly unique to Canada. In the twenty-first century, the distinctive feature of the Canadian system is not the absence of ideology but the presence of a viable party of the centre. These are distinct propositions, and neither precludes the other. The presence of a centre party can enable more voter mobility than in systems with an empty or unviable centre. Even so, the record shows that most of the volatility for which Canada is justly famous is not about the centre; it is about the right. And mobility on the right is mostly about the system's other dimension, the national question.

Interaction across Arenas

Federal systems facilitate the entry and survival of new parties, and Canada is a case in point: new parties are more successful overall in provincial elections than in federal ones. It is also true that the stronger a new party is provincially the stronger it is federally and vice versa. But its success is more differentiated in the provincial arena than in the federal one. This is a corollary of the fact that, strong or weak, elements of the national party system are present in all provinces' federal electorates. The same is not true for provincial electorates: in some provinces, one of the old parties has been (or both have been) feeble or even non-existent. Thus, a basic proposition follows.

8. *The greater differentiation in new-party shares in provincial electorates than in federal ones is a major source of federal-provincial discontinuity.*

This argument presupposes the existence of underlying forces rooted in geography that motivate resistance to the national party system. Resistance just happens to be more effective in the provincial arena. But the argument has two variants, and they drive a wedge between the two kinds of new party. Most insurgents represent resistance to the old-party system but without a clear sense of an alternative system. Progressives, for instance, were not sure that they even wanted to be a party. Social Credit ultimately became indistinguishable from mainstream Conservatism but also (especially at its origin) embodied antipathy to party politics as such. Critically, none of these entities sought to grow beyond its region of origin. The CCF-NDP, in contrast, represented resistance to the old system but neither to a national system nor to parties as such. The party aspires to reshape that system everywhere and, by implication, aspires to grow. Its growth has reshaped the national system, such that the system is now an amalgam of old and new. This makes resistance to the national system more – not less – ubiquitous. Resistance to the old parties continues in the West and is an established pattern. As such, it poses a standing challenge to the old pattern where the latter is most entrenched, especially in Atlantic Canada. Both patterns of resistance are stronger provincially than federally, which amplifies the general logic captured by proposition 8.

9. *In regions generally resistant to change in the party system, resistance to the NDP in particular is stronger provincially than federally.*[6]

NDP growth also amplified federal-provincial differences by indirect means. In other Westminster systems, the growth of labour parties forced realignment among the older, non-labour alternatives. Recasting of the centre-right is most of the story of Duverger's Law in action. The incomplete diffusion of the NDP illustrates both the logic of the law and its limitations. As just argued, in provinces where the NDP is most successful, its shares are larger in the provincial arena than in the federal one. Given that the provincial arena is an electorate unto itself, NDP strength is a threat of the same order as that in the other Westminster polities, with the same implication for its rivals. As the NDP grows, it induces a drop in the ratio of the second-place rival to the first-place one, and it does so with increasing marginal impact. This serves to keep the provincial arena ENP in the range of the canonical 2.0. Which of the rivals survives the squeeze is an accident of history and can even be an insurgent. This process does not operate federally. Not only is federal NDP growth weaker even in its places of strength, but also the party so far has not threatened to form a federal government. Its growth, as already argued, merely fractionalizes the federal electorate.

Where the NDP is generally weak, the argument goes in reverse but with the same effect on federal-provincial discontinuity. The party remains weak in provinces where vestiges of the system's old cultural logic persist, essentially in provinces with large Catholic populations. In these places, the victim of the squeeze is the NDP itself. Again, the squeeze is more effective in the self-contained provincial arena. Federally, the NDP is present, if weaker than elsewhere, making the federal ENP larger than the provincial one. Putting all of this together, the following propositions hold.

10. *The pattern of NDP growth amplifies federal-provincial discontinuity by revealing differential scope between arenas for the power of Duverger's Law.*

   a. *Where the NDP is relatively strong, all but one of the centre-right alternatives are squeezed in the provincial arena but not in the federal one.*
   b. *If the privileged centre-right alternative is an insurgent, then federal-provincial discontinuity is further amplified.*
   c. *Where the NDP is relatively weak, the party itself is more squeezed provincially than federally.*

Research Challenges

Competing Majoritarian Logics

Westminster parliamentarism has two logics of coordination, electoral and parliamentary, and they operate separately; this was a key intuition in Cox (1997). The Canadian case reveals that not only are these logics separate, but also they can work against each other. The resulting tension underpins the conjunction of one-party domination, chronic multipartism, and episodic volatility.

The key to Liberal longevity was segmentation of the electorate: Quebec versus the rest of Canada. Liberal domination of Quebec, a big province, routinely placed the party halfway to a Canada-wide majority of seats. Modest shares of the vote in the rest of the country sufficed to push the party over the threshold needed for a majority government. Whether to be beaten or to be joined, the Liberals were the recurring focal point for the entire electorate.

Not surprisingly, this generated frustration outside Quebec. The frustration did not necessarily name Quebec and was often couched in terms of the immobility of the entire framework. One expression of frustration was insurgency, which the electoral system encouraged. Here we come to a critical contingency in electoral amplification. Although FPP generally amplifies differences among parties, the degree of amplification is conditional on the interaction between a party's overall size and its geographic concentration. A large party faces a powerful incentive to spread its appeal (Calvo and Rodden 2015; Johnston and Ballantyne 1977). For small parties, the opposite is true: votes yield seats more efficiently when the vote is concentrated. This is one of the central complaints in Cairns (1968). And the small parties that benefit from this contingency are insurgents. So whether the electoral system discourages or encourages invasion by new parties is highly contingent. It specifically encourages them to the extent that geography matters, and the proliferation of sectional parties has been a Canadian commonplace.

Yet small, geographically concentrated parties are as notable for their deaths as for their births. The reason lies in the other logic of majoritarianism. Notwithstanding fractionalization of the vote – indeed partly because of that fractionalization (Calvo and Rodden 2015, Fig. 2) – multiparty systems under FPP still routinely generate single-party governments. This is true even when no single party controls a majority of seats (Strøm 1983). So voting for a third party is not a path to representation in cabinet. It can be a path to influence, such as when a minority government needs support for its programs and when only one small party is realistically able to give that support. But as long as voters out of sympathy for the party in power persist in supporting an insurgent, they will be frustrated. The path to defeating that government lies through electoral consolidation. Thus, the parliamentary and electoral logics can be at odds with each other only for so long – at most, the Canadian case suggests, for two decades. If one side of frustration is fractionalization, the other is episodic – and epic – consolidation as voters abandon insurgents to coalesce around the only nationally viable alternative, the Conservatives.

Consolidation only inverts the rhetoric of frustration, however. In the twentieth century, each moment of Conservative power ended badly. The result was further fractionalization somewhere on the landscape – inside Quebec, outside Quebec, or both. This installed a new disconnect between Parliament and electorate.

For Chhibber and Kollman (2004), this disconnect was not an issue. They took it to indicate the diminished importance of the federal agenda. In my view, they misstate the narrative of power in the federation. More to the point, they do not notice the episodic dynamic in Canadian elections and its link to their key dependent variable. This book identifies that dynamic and offers some narrative on its underlying mechanisms. But the narrative barely scratches the surface and represents a key opening for further research. This is a natural segue to the next research challenge.

The History in Analytic History

This book proclaims itself to be an analytical history. For much of the argument, however, history is just a glorified time series. Certain quantities – electoral volatility, for instance – make sense only with temporally ordered events. More generally, many of the book's claims are driven directly by disruptive moments and indirectly by serially correlated error terms. But unit homogeneity – uniform functionality in the parameters of an estimation model – is presumed. Models are sometimes made conditional on operators with historical referents, as exemplified by the CCF-NDP "eras" of Chapters 8 and 9. Even these conditions are not arbitrary, however, since they represent a sequence in party development that seems to be universal. The NDP might be a late bloomer, but the manner of its blooming has much in common with labour and social democratic parties elsewhere. Indeed, that commonality is one of this book's central themes.

In at least three cases, however, the book stakes stronger historical claims. The first refers to tides in opinion or sentiment powerfully affected by geopolitics. The argument also shows how coalitions built in response to these tides can be cashed out for further purposes. This is the story of the self-reproduction of the denominational cleavage in old-party support. The second is how old parties can make expectations self-reinforcing. The third refers to the sequencing of insurgency, province by province. Sequencing can make otherwise similar provinces diverge in the moment, which in turn shapes each province's responses to later crises. This accounts for some of the texture in the CCF's early history and for variations across the western provinces in the identities of non-socialist alternatives. Each argument involves path dependency (Brady and Collier 2010; Capoccia and Ziblatt 2010).The mechanisms in play are positive feedback (Pierson 2000) and reactive sequences (Mahoney 2000).

Catholics and Protestants

The traditionally dominant religious cleavage in Liberal and Conservative support was substantively religious neither in its origin nor in its perpetuation. That it lacked contemporary content in faith or morals was not in dispute in mid-to-late-twentieth-century scholarship; the lack only contributed to the mystery. It seemed to be reasonable to suppose, however, that the cleavage had nineteenth-century origins with doctrinal content. But this too proves false to the record. Instead, the cleavage is a product of forces outside Canada, of twentieth-century great-power rivalry.

The origin story is consistent with the logic of path dependency in that "early historical events are contingent occurrences that cannot be explained on the basis of prior events or 'initial conditions'" (Mahoney 2000, 511). There was an "initial condition" of a sort: religious denomination was an ongoing factor in acceptance of the claim that Canada was fundamentally a British place and that overseas obligations flowed from this fact. Before the twentieth century, this division mattered little for policy. By the turn of the century, however, Canada was arguably poised for a global role, and opinion leaders associated with the Conservative Party made this case (Berger 1970). The events that activated the division were outside Canadian control. The gold rush on the Rand and the South African War forced the issue onto the agenda, despite the best efforts of the Liberal Party to keep it off. When the Great War amplified the division, the government of Robert Borden made electoral calculations in relation to conscription that worked off pre-existing patterns. Even so, the war itself was a genuinely external shock. Although war might have been widely expected, the nature of British involvement was not easily forecast. It was not a foregone conclusion that there would be a massive British land force, which in turn encouraged participation by expeditionary forces from the overseas dominions. Similarly, it is not a stretch to imagine a different timetable. What if the war had begun in 1916? The Borden government was seen as weak and likely to be defeated in an election expected for 1915 (Willms 1956). How would a government led by Sir Wilfrid Laurier have responded to the call to arms?

Of course, these counterfactuals are just that, and Canada entered the war with a government sympathetic to the imperial perspective, and the country landed in a conscription crisis. The basic mould laid down in 1917 persisted for decades. Does this merely testify to the power of party identification, especially as such identities are transmitted within families across generations? Johnston (1985) attacks the intergenerational component directly, and scepticism about the persistence of party identification is widespread in Canadian scholarship (see, for example, Clarke et al. 1996). Besides, the link between religious denomination and the vote weakened quickly after 1965 and did so along lines that corresponded to contemporary shifts in policy and party leadership. If it ended so quickly, how had it persisted for so long, especially given the massive reshaping of the geopolitical landscape after 1945?

The pre-1945 persistence of the division can be explained by the continuation of the basic 1917 lines of force. Although the United States was slowly displacing Britain as a trading partner and source of investment, this was not immediately obvious to key political actors. The British connection, even if attenuated by the Statute of Westminster, was still the conduit for military impulses. The fierce backlash in Conservative circles to the 1940 Ogdensburg Agreement for defence production sharing with the United States is diagnostic. So, for that matter, is the Conservative Party's reaction to Canada's role in the 1956 Suez Crisis.

But Suez was a spasm, and the official Canadian response was not sympathetic to Britain's late-imperial claims. Indeed, Suez now seems like a turning point in the Liberal Party's willingness to change the ethnic character of the country's key symbols. Critically, doing so did not force the party to confront its sociological foundations. Quite the contrary, the party adapted them to serve the new agenda, and so in opposition did the Conservatives. It is tempting to conclude that each party pointed itself down this road precisely to keep the old coalition intact. This interpretation is broadly consistent with the radical constructionist claim in Brodie and Jenson (1988).

Self-Reinforcing Expectations

An example of positive feedback is the self-reinforcement of expectations for parties' electoral strength or weakness. Events since 1965 align with Boix's (2009, 510) observations on the resilience of old parties:

> Once some parties become established as the main electoral contenders, voters are suddenly much more constrained in their behavior. The main parties constantly appeal to their own electoral viability ... This electoral advantage ... has an additional and very important consequence. It gives the parties the capacity and time to adjust policy promises ... to shifts in the electorate ... so that they can remain strongly competitive in the electoral arena.

The bases of party competition in 2015 were very different from those in 1965. On some questions, the old parties have exchanged positions. Each party had a near-death experience. Yet both survive as recognizable heirs to the organizations that fought the old fights.

Self-enforcing expectations have been especially relevant for the permanently vulnerable party of the centre. One instance was the 1988 election. By degrees, both the old Conservative Party and the new NDP became more of a threat to the Liberal Party, all the more so as globalization forced trade policy to the centre of the national agenda. The Conservatives, helped by the declining relevance of the British connection, moved toward the free-trade pole of debate, an increasingly natural position for a party of the right. The NDP was arguably poised to take over the Conservatives' old role as the party of economic nationalism; this, too, seems to be natural for a party of labour. The Liberal Party risked being squeezed, and pre- and early campaign polls suggested that this was about to come true. Johnston et al. (1992) argue that Liberal leader John Turner's decision to block the Canada-US Free Trade Agreement (FTA) gave doubters a reason to come home. His choice might have been necessary, but would it have been sufficient? Also working for Turner was his party's history. Notwithstanding Liberal weakness in the polls, CES respondents rated the Liberal Party's chances of winning Canada-wide and in their own constituency higher than those of the NDP. The Liberals' expected advantage, unsurprisingly, grew after Turner's success in the debates (Johnston et al. 1992, 200-4). Then, as Conservative counterattacks eroded his personal credibility and the power of his anti-FTA arguments, all that remained was the Liberals' perceived feasibility (see Johnston et al. 1992, Figs. 8.8 and 8.9).

The counterfactual for 1988, so to speak, was 2011. The Liberals remained vulnerable on their left flank. Their opposition to the US FTA did not carry over to NAFTA, of which they became champions. And it was the Liberals who waged an energetic war on the public sector deficit. Their tack to the left in 2000-4-6 (Figure 4.1) might have been motivated by fear of the NDP. Given the 2011 NDP surge, Liberals played the viability card once again. But several years out of power and a progressively weakening position in votes and polls undermined their claim. If the NDP seemed to be an unlikely pretender to victory, so did the Liberal Party.

Accidents of History

Some of the narratives here are also about positive feedback. The most telling ones, however, are about reactive sequences. The collapse in world wheat prices after the First World War presented the three prairie provinces (and western Ontario) with a common challenge. But the response of each province was *sui generis*. Some of this might have reflected background differences in settlement patterns and crop ecology, but much of it reflected immediate political circumstances. The first element was the attitude of the provincial Liberals toward farmers and organized labour. A second element was the electoral institutions in place at the onset: some provinces used only FPP and single-member districts; Manitoba had multi-member urban districts with STV; Alberta also used multi-member districts for its cities but with the plurality formula.[7] A third element was that, since the agrarian initiative was localized, the movement mobilized at different rates in different provinces. This variation intersected with two longitudinal factors out of farmers' control: the timing of drops in the price of wheat and the timing of elections.

The result was a patchwork quilt. In Ontario, a weak farmer-labour coalition formed but could not sustain itself. In Manitoba, an agrarian government formed and lasted, and its claim to stand above party politics hampered effective competition for decades. This government was unsympathetic to organized labour, morphed into an ideologically conservative coalition with the Liberal Party, and ultimately shed its Progressive label. In Saskatchewan, the agrarian movement barely got off the ground in provincial politics, only gaining enough altitude to be worth co-opting by a resolutely reactionary Conservative government later in the decade. In Alberta, a UFA government proved to be resilient and was located further to the left than any other provincial party of government or opposition, with labour representation in the inner circle. In the 1921 federal election, Progressives won massive victories region-wide, with the biggest margins coming in Saskatchewan, where the provincial movement was the weakest.

This variety then shaped further developments. Prospects for a CCF breakthrough in the 1930s reflected the legacy of the 1920s. In Alberta, the CCF ought to have benefited from the high ground occupied by the UFA, whose extra-parliamentary wing was present at the CCF's founding. But the UFA in government was a reluctant partner and, in any case, was swept away in 1935 by a second round of unrest. In Saskatchewan, the weakness and ultimate discrediting of the agrarian party left space on the left for the new CCF. Space existed for the CCF in Manitoba as well, although success was longer in coming there than in Saskatchewan.

That said, with the passage of time, a functionalist reading of the CCF and NDP became more and more plausible. The NDP grew everywhere west of the Ottawa River and eventually began to grow east of that line. If it grew more and faster in some places than in others, its social bases became more similar province to province. At the same time, cultural resistance to it morphed from a denominational basis to a linguistic-cum-Quebec-nationalist one. All of which is to say that the NDP followed a trajectory typical of labour and social democratic parties elsewhere (Bartolini 2000). It just happens that this trajectory is visible within the Canadian federation.

Evidence of path dependency also remains on the right side of the left-right spectrum. Where the NDP is a serious contestant for power, the menu of alternatives is diverse. Variation in these alternatives across the three provinces of historically greatest NDP strength eerily tracks the pattern for the rest of the Anglosphere. In Britain and Manitoba, the chief rival is the Conservative Party. In Australia and British Columbia, the alternative is a party carrying the name Liberal. In New Zealand and Saskatchewan, the anti-socialist label refers to the place itself: the National Party and the Saskatchewan Party.[8] Beyond the amusement value of this parallel is a more general lesson. The pattern in these provinces – and in some measure across most provinces – replicates the asymmetry between left and right in all party systems. In their own social bases, social democratic and labour parties are similar from country to country. Growth in the left vote was not a simple function of prior strength in that demography; often the causal arrow went the other way as left parties in power shaped their own bases. But as the century advanced, these bases converged cross-nationally. Variation in their overall strength reflected, among other factors, the weight of cultural resistance, from Catholics in early decades and from linguistic minorities in later ones. On the other side of the spectrum, no such functionalist story can be told. Rather, the configurations reflect either somewhat accidental wins and losses in showdowns, as is typical of the Anglosphere, or timely deals involving change in the electoral system, the pattern elsewhere (Boix 1999; Cusack, Iversen, and Soskice 2007). The right side of the arena cannot be understood other than historically, with special reference to accidents of timing. The same is true, especially in the provincial arena, for the Canadian party system.

Positive feedback, or self-replication, seems to have been clearly in play with the history of the Liberal Party and that of some provincial insurgents. These parties used the resources of office to gather further resources, recruit ambitious personnel, manipulate the rules of the game in their favour, and appeal to their reputations for viability. And, as Boix (2009) argues, these parties used these advantages to reposition themselves. This seems to have been especially true of the Liberal Party as it retooled its cultural appeals, as it closed the ideological gap with the NDP, and as its leaders repeatedly emphasized the infeasibility of the NDP. But it also accounted for the differential endurance of insurgents. Those that gained power in their first or second opportunity tended to stick around; others faded quickly.

Reactive sequences, in which "early events trigger subsequent development not by reproducing a given pattern, but by setting in motion a chain of tightly linked reactions and counterreactions" (Mahoney 2000, 526-27), are critical to the patchwork quilt of provincial (and occasionally federal) elections in the West. Following are some key examples:

- In Alberta, the UFA victory in 1921 meant that in 1935 blame for the Depression fell on this party. As the UFA defined the left, the avenue for protest in Alberta was, by default, on the right.[9]
- The failure of the original agrarian insurgency in Saskatchewan and the right-wing character of the successful Manitoba insurgency meant that in those provinces vulnerability to invasion was on the left flank.
- The history of success enjoyed by the Saskatchewan Liberal Party meant that it, and not some other party, was forced to the right by the rise of the CCF. The Liberal Party's poor record in office from 1964 to 1971, its weak fit with the federal party, its poor showing in 1970s' provincial elections, and general discrediting of the federal Liberal brand in the region contributed to the provincial party's collapse and replacement by a rejuvenated provincial Conservative Party, a better fit with the circumstances. That party was singularly inept in power, however, and after 1993 might have suffered by association with the now discredited federal Conservative brand. This left the right side of the field open to a provincial insurgent affiliated with neither old party but benefiting from the credibility of the federal insurgent, Reform. This is the Saskatchewan Party.
- In British Columbia, emergence of the CCF in 1933 coincided with dire punishment of the Conservatives, who had the misfortune of being in power when the Great Depression hit. This forced the Liberal Party, against the inclinations of its leader Duff Pattullo (Fisher 1991; Ormsby 1962), to be the main party of the right. The positioning was somewhat

mitigated by the Conservatives' partial recovery later in the decade but was then reinforced by the perceived necessity to coalesce with the same Conservatives in 1941. The 1952 attempt to lower the costs of old-party coordination with a preferential ballot instead facilitated the breakthrough by Social Credit and discredited both coalition partners. In 1972-75, Social Credit survived the electoral confusion that accompanied the NDP's first victory, but by 1991 Social Credit had become a poor fit with the province's increasingly diverse, secular, and urban electorate. Although re-emergence of the Liberal Party in 1991 was a centrist signal from the electorate, the victor in 1991 was the NDP. Once again the Liberals were forced to become the alternative on the right.

These capsule narratives are gleaned from scattered sources and informal observations made over the course of my long academic career. Closer inspection might prove many of them wrong. They are mere sketches, in any case, and much of the narrative needs to be added. Filling it in should take the form of pursuing the facts relevant to testing propositions with analytical content as well as to identification of key break points in analytically problematic sequences. In some cases, as with the narrative of Liberals and Catholics, the challenge might require Bayesian tools to link dataset observations to causal process ones,[10] as suggested by Humphreys and Jacobs (2015).

Strategic Information

A recurring theme in this book is the role of expectations for party performance as conditioned by the country's majoritarian institutions, especially by the electoral system. An additional dimension is the fact of federalism: Canadians simultaneously inhabit two different electorates. It is not a surprise that strategic considerations underpin some of Canada's apparent peculiarities. What is a surprise is how strategy plays out: its operation is not consistent with the essentially local emphasis in neo-Duvergerian rational choice theorizing, nor does it coexist easily with the localism that is a major theme in the study of Canadian party organizations (Carty and Eagles 2005).

In this book, strategic considerations first surface in the account of Quebec's twentieth-century status as the pivot for governments. This was especially critical for the Liberal Party, the usual beneficiary of the Quebec bloc vote. Outside Quebec, voters were typically required to take Liberal strength into account, either to support the party or to manoeuvre to defeat it. This made a party of the centre more powerful than in any comparable system and thus is critical to understanding many – indeed most – of the system's other peculiarities.

The Quebec-centred logic, augmented by enduring conflict over the British connection, is one key to the weakness of the NDP. The mere existence of the Quebec Liberal bloc discouraged prospective New Democrats even as it encouraged actual Liberals. In a similar vein, the geographic distribution of Roman Catholics gave the Liberal Party a base outside Quebec that was usually complementary to the base within the province. This base became more useful, electorally speaking, as the century advanced. The electoral power of Catholics in eastern provinces depressed the prospects for the NDP in western provinces. Yet the strength of the NDP in the West encouraged its prospective supporters in the east. The evidence for these claims lay not in federal elections themselves but in comparisons within provinces between the federal and provincial arenas. A provincial arena need not be affected by patterns in other provinces, so in the West the NDP is stronger provincially than federally. In the east, the opposite is true. This discrepancy is complemented by the greater power of Duverger's Law in the provincial arena.

The final piece of evidence comes from recent campaigns. In 1988, 1993, and 2011, voters in some regions reacted to dynamics in other regions as those dynamics were revealed by polls and attendant media commentary. This worked to salvage the Liberals in 1988 but sink them in 2011. In 1993, campaign dynamics took an initially divided right and made the division worse. In each case, the result was coordination failure. The Liberals' recovery in 1988, helpful in Ontario, drove NDP support down in the West, where the party enjoyed a historical advantage. In 2011, the NDP surge in Ontario, a place of relative weakness, divided the centre-left and handed seats to the Conservatives. This more than offset the increase in efficiency that occurred in British Columbia, where the NDP's starting point was strong.

None of this speculation is consistent with the neo-Duvergerian logic of Cox (1997) and Chhibber and Kollman (2004). Nor, for that matter, is any of the survey-based work on electoral expectations dating from the 1980s (cited in Chapter 8). Something strategic is in play, but the mechanism cannot expect utility maximization of the sort theorized by Riker and Ordeshook (1968) and as extended to multiparty elections by Black (1978) and Cain (1978). That argument squarely underpins the reformulation of Duverger that culminates with Cox (1997). But there is no chance that voters in the situation that this book describes or in situations captured by survey-based work in other countries can have any personal effect on the result. In no sense can their benefit from the outcome be affected by personal choice. A more sensible way to think about viability, perhaps, might be in terms of feasibility of the choices in the set. This still begs the question of why voters would care given their individual impotence. Yet we must infer that they do care. Surely this is a challenge for analytical theorists of the next generation.

Unfinished Business
Many key claims in this book no longer hold. Quebec has ceased to be the pivot for government. The increasing policy divergence between the Liberals and the Conservatives may have reshaped the system's dynamics. In particular, the Conservatives may not be as vulnerable to boom and bust as they once were. This also probably reflects the changed profile of the Quebec electorate: no longer monolithic, more penetrable as a matter of routine by outside forces, and – most critically – with the nationalist pole now occupied by the Bloc. Even in its currently weakened state, the Bloc's mere existence deters Conservatives from yielding to the twentieth century's recurring Faustian temptation.

Quebec aside, the identity politics in this book are also mostly dated. To be sure, Canadian institutions retain much of their outward Britishness and these features remain contested. The restoration of the old names for the army and air force indicates that British symbolism is not always beating a retreat. But now the old issues reverberate mostly as subtext – or they do outside Quebec. Other forms of identity politics, many of them now also dormant, appeared only as they intruded on the party battle, and mainly to unsettle and ultimately help undo the old framework. The substance of the issues that now dominate the landscape had not yet surfaced, or had only begun to emerge. So the book has little to say about New

Canadians (except as part of a highly aggregated ancestry category), First Nations, the north, gender, or sexuality. It hints that the Liberals can cash out their experience with twentieth-century identity politics in mastering the identity politics of the twenty-first. But it is only a hint.

Even though the Liberals have returned to power, the system still seems unsettled. The party has governed for less than one-third of the time since 1984 and roughly half the time since 1993. It does not seem like the natural party of government, just one of the claimants. The logic of the book suggests that having ceased to benefit from domination of Quebec, the party should now face a squeeze between parties with more natural anchors in civil society, as happened in the comparator countries and in some provinces. The 2011 election seemed to herald just such a development. In one sense, the return of the Liberals to major party status simply conforms to a historical regularity. But the most powerful mechanism that underpinned the old regularity no longer operates. If the Liberals resume their traditional place – even if they merely stay competitive – we will have to look for new mechanisms to explain a new anomaly. In some respects, this book's key contribution for the future lies in telling us where not to look.

Appendix: Data Sources

Survey Data

The integrated file of Gallup (Canadian Institute of Public Opinion) data originated with the UBC Data Library, an official Gallup depository. The merging of CIPO files from the UBC Data Library repository was initiated by Jean Laponce, who was interested in a small social group, Jewish Canadians (Laponce 1988), and a small party, the Communists (Laponce and Sekhon 1995). The data file used in this book was brought to completion by Mark Pickup (2005). CIPO documentation is not informative about sampling, but I assume that CIPO made the transition from quota to probability sampling on roughly the same timetable as in the United States (Converse 1987): that is, in the aftermath of the 1948 Dewey-Truman debacle. Robinson (1999) shows that in these years Canadians were closely involved in and attentive to US developments. Since all my uses of CIPO data involve probit estimations of group differences, it is not clear to me that weighting would make much difference. In contrast to Berinsky (2006, 2009), I am not interested in reconstructing the balance of opinion on any question. Like Berinsky, I have no choice but to assume Missing at Random (MAR) for unit non-response, and the labour involved in model-assisted post-stratification seems to be pointless.

The *Canadian Election Study* has been in existence for every election since 1965 except 1972. With one exception, the studies from 1965 to 1984 were all face to face (FTF), geographically clustered, and post-election. The exception was the 1980 study, done by telephone with a proper subset of the 1979 FTF sample. From 1988 on, the main body of the CES has been conducted by telephone on a random-digit dialing (RDD) sample. Response rates in the 1980s and 1990s were over 60 percent. By the 2000s, the rates were in the 40-50 percent range. The main body of data is usually collected during the official campaign period: that is, before election day. The pre-election wave is released as a rolling cross-section, such that the day of interview is a random draw from time. This feature enables the campaign analyses in Chapter 8. Every study since 1988 has also featured a post-election telephone wave linked to the pre-election wave as a panel. Panel attrition in the 1980s and 1990s was about 15 percent. More recently, it has been closer to 25 percent. Along the way, there have been some inter-election panels, such that in some years panel respondents coexist with freshly recruited cross-section respondents. A post-election, self-completion, mail-back component is also a regular feature of the study. All respondents who complete the post-election wave are offered this option, and the take-up rate is high. The resulting sample, however, is a biased subset of the original cross-section. This book uses the mail-back sample in a few places. Creating and updating the CES-merged file were done by Amanda Bittner, John McAndrews, and Grace Lore.

Australian National Political Attitudes (1967) data were kindly furnished by Clive Bean. Data from the 2004 *Australian Election Study* were furnished through the Comparative Study of Electoral Systems (CSES) Module 2. The 2005 *New Zealand Election Study* data were downloaded from http://www.nzes.org/. *British Election Study* data are accessible at http://www.britishelectionstudy.com/data-objects/cross-sectional-data/. American National Election Studies are accessible at http://www.electionstudies.org/studypages/download/datacenter_all_NoData.php.

Election Returns

Wherever possible election returns are based upon official sources, usually the online site of the chief electoral officer or equivalent for the jurisdiction in question. There is simply no denying the utility of Wikipedia and other online sources in speeding up this process, however. Subnational sources can be spotty for earlier years. Research assistants in this venture were Amanda Bittner, Janine van Vliet, Şule Yaylaçi, Andrea Nuesser, and Megan Dias.

Union Density

Consistently measured union data are surprisingly hard to come by. The cross-national data originate with the OECD *StatExtracts* (http://stats.oecd.org/index.aspx?), which usually accepts what national statistical agencies report with an in-house preference for survey data. The OECD methodological document can be found at http://www.oecd.org/employment/emp/UnionDensity_Sourcesandmethods.pdf. I have supplemented data from Labour Canada with data from Kumar (1986). Data on union density by province were gathered through intermittent reports, usually one per decade. In this, assistance from Janine van Vliet and Amanda Bittner was vital.

Notes

Chapter 2: Situating the Case

1 Although Sniderman and his colleagues stylized the traditional arguments to reject them, their synthesis remains the most accessible gloss on an old literature.
2 At least the NDP has accepted the majoritarian system for most of its history. The party's official position has changed in recent years. It remains to be seen if the commitment would survive a period in power. Tellingly, perhaps, provincial NDP actors are less supportive than federal ones of electoral system change.
3 The 1878 election was the first election in modern form, with almost all seats contested on the same day with secret ballots in single-member districts. The preceding system was stacked in the governing party's favour. Balloting was not secret and took place at strategically located hustings. Writs of election were issued district by district in a similarly strategic way (Reid 1932). Archaic features persisted for some years after 1878: acclamations were still common, the franchise still involved property qualifications, writs of election were still delayed in some western districts, and a small number of two-member districts remained.
4 I argue in Chapter 5 that the election in 1900, fought in part over Canada's involvement in the South African War, began the process that the Great War completed.
5 Neatby (1973, Chapter 10) shows that, in fact, the vacuum was already opening up between 1902 and 1910.
6 This is Olympian hindsight, to be sure. An observer in 1925 would have been struck by how sudden and dramatic the Conservative recovery was from the 1921 low point.
7 The 1896 election also featured insurgency that anticipated events in 1921 and later. It has been little studied as a systemic phenomenon, however. But see Blake (1979) and Crunican (1974).
8 Social Credit seems to have hung on longer, but what appears as a single series is really two separate patterns spliced together to avoid visual clutter. Its early strength

was in Alberta and British Columbia, and its later strength was in Quebec; the two wings were sometimes united, sometimes not.

9 Because these are unweighted means across provinces, the federal values do not correspond exactly to those in Figures 2.1 and 2.2. By "adjacent," I mean the closest provincial election to the federal one, whether earlier or later. The focus on adjacent elections originates in Johnston (1980) and seems to have become the norm in the literature on federalism. See, for example, Jeffery and Hough (2003) or Pallarés and Keating (2003).

10 Consistent with this pattern is evidence of increased federal-provincial integration of membership and career paths in recent decades (Pruysers 2014).

11 New Zealand no longer relies exclusively on SMD, but it did so for almost the entire twentieth century. This chapter uses only elections before New Zealand shifted to mixed-member proportional (MMP) in 1996.

12 This is the interpretation in Hirano and Snyder (2007). To anticipate the next few pages, Hirano and Snyder contest the Chhibber-Kollman (2004) interpretation of the US pattern and argue that the class realignment has been the essential cause of the US ENP trajectory.

13 As calculated, variation in turnout is neglected.

14 As noted, it did this by a merger of the Alliance with the Progressive Conservatives rather than by a massive vote swing.

15 Thanks to Canada's peculiar volatility, transitions to and from power are often messy. In the twentieth century, Canada experienced eight minority governments, 15 years in total. Yet, when majorities do appear in Canada, they can be overwhelming. For 22 years of the twentieth century, one or the other Canadian governing party commanded more than two-thirds of all seats. Both oversized and undersized governments reflect fractionalization of the underlying vote. The smaller the largest party, the more likely a minority result; the more fractionalized the other parties, the more likely an overwhelming majority. Modest perturbations of the party size distribution can produce swift alternation between extremes. Such flux occurred in Britain and New Zealand before the Second World War but rarely after it. In Canada, both extremes were as common after the war as before it.

16 Some states are omitted in some years for other reasons. Nebraska state elections are officially non-partisan, so there is no equivalent to a state-level result. The same was true of Minnesota for much of the period. In states with only one member of the House of Representatives, acclamation can wipe out the federal count; Vermont is a notable example.

17 Volatility also inspired early comparative scholarship on voter psychology, particularly on party identification (Converse 1969; Converse and Dupeux 1962), and a psychological emphasis is prominent in Canadian scholarship, with "stable dealignment"

(LeDuc 1984) as a working term of art. This book leaves this psychology aside and emphasizes the sociological variant of the story.
18 The modesty of the Australian result is a bit misleading since the real story in the 1960s was not so much the attraction of Catholics to Labour as the repulsion of Catholics by Liberals (McAllister 2011, Fig. 5.7).
19 They are the British Conservatives, the Australian Liberals, and the New Zealand National Party.
20 The Benoit-Laver fieldwork was conducted in 2003 and 2004, and in the Canadian case reference is back to the 2000 election. Imputations were originally scaled 0 to 20. The data are available for download at http://www.nsd.uib.no/macrodataguide/set.html?id=27&sub=1.
21 The most comprehensively documented CMP source is Volkens et al. (2013). The dataset with standard errors is justified in Benoit, Laver, and Mikhaylov (2009) and is accessible through Lowe et al. (2011a).
22 Left-right data were collected in the post-election mailback wave and originally scaled 0 to 10. Respondents were first asked to place themselves and then to place each party. The battery is part of Comparative Study of Electoral Systems (CSES) post-election Module 2. The availability of these data for 2004 dictated my choice of the same year for the CMP imputation. CSES data are described and available for download at http://www.cses.org/.

Chapter 3: Liberal Dominance, Conservative Interludes
1 This was the title of a series of articles by Laporte in *Le Devoir*, October-December 1956. See Behiels (1985, Chapter 10, passim).
2 Because Atlantic Canada never had the seat numbers – not even in the nineteenth century – to be seriously in play as a pivot for government, it is omitted from this graph. It appears in most of the other figures in the chapter, however.
3 The provincial party, led by Honoré Mercier, was temporarily labelled the Parti National, the better to capture a broad base of nationalist sentiment.
4 Although most claims in this chapter pertain to all elections from 1878 to 1988, for the analysis of popular votes, certain exclusions are warranted. Before 1887, anti-Conservative forces in Quebec had not congealed as a coordinated entity calling itself by one name and with candidates in a majority of the province's ridings. Admitting earlier elections would actually sharpen the claims but not in a way that honestly represents the case. The same would be true for the 1917 election, which polarized Quebec against the rest of the country over conscription. The logic shifts below for the analysis of seats, in which an honest accounting requires that all elections be included.

5 The findings here seem to contradict Sankoff and Mellos (1973), who argue that Quebec's seat-vote relationship is indeed distinct and that the relative homogeneity (Montreal aside) of Quebec's geography (which in turn reflects an underlying social homogeneity) enables modest vote flux to become immodest seat flux. Their evidence is from provincial elections and spans fewer decades than those in Figure 3.3.
6 The figure is a visual rendering of an estimation described in detail in the appendix to this chapter. The appendix includes Wald tests for differences among regions in the responsiveness of seat shifts to vote shifts. The distinctively responsive region is Atlantic Canada, with Ontario in second place.
7 QCA originated with the study of dichotomies but evolved to include less strictly defined alternatives, called "fuzzy sets." This pushed QCA onto turf where regression-type techniques already existed and raised the level of controversy (Ragin 2005; Seawright 2005). Focusing on the dichotomy at the threshold keeps the analysis close to the original qualitative intuitions in QCA.
8 Because this analysis focuses on seats, there is no reason to exclude the 1878 and 1882 elections. The 1917 election is also included since it serves as something of a contrasting case.
9 The 1968 election might be classified as a near landslide.
10 In seven elections, neither party swept the province.
11 In these terms, Cairns (1968) also does not have it quite right for the South. Before 1960, returns were about as one-sidedly Democratic as Quebec ones were one-sidedly Liberal. Some of this reflects the ubiquity of acclamations, but the point stands. The missing ingredient in the South was electoral mobility. In the era of white supremacy, the region was simply never available to Republican candidates. In the presidential arena, this began to change in the 1950s. Transformation in the House and Senate required many decades. On the earlier one-sidedness and the transformation, see Shafer and Johnston (2006).

Chapter 4: Liberal Centrism, Polarized Pluralism

1 I made this claim in Johnston (2008), although it was first made by Dobell (1986).
2 To render shifts in policy proportional to the starting point, the data in Figure 4.1 use logit scales rather than the original additive version presented in Figure 2.9. The logit transformation makes conceptual sense in that it proportionalizes shifts in left-right orientation (Lowe et al. 2011). In truth, shifting to the logit format does not alter relationships in the Canadian series, and the plot in Figure 4.1 closely resembles that in Cochrane (2010), although with confidence intervals added.
3 In 1988, the object was "French Canada." By 1993, this seemed like an obsolete formulation, if it was not already so by 1988. In 1993, "French Canada" and "Quebec"

were randomized for the purpose of calibration, and thereafter "Quebec" has been the cue. Comparison between treatments suggests that "Quebec" is more polarizing, but the difference is slight. Initially, the number of response alternatives was five, and a single query was used. Since 1997, the question has been split into a stem that asks only about direction and branches that elicit distance; the combination is then aggregated back to a seven-point scale.

4 By "party" I mean the one that the respondent supported at the election in question. Using identification rather than vote tells a similar story, but the years covered in the figure are ones of great flux, as Chapter 2 showed. The meaning of identification was correspondingly compromised, and, besides, many respondents expressed none. Focusing on the vote enables me to deploy a larger share of each sample, a major consideration when the sample is being sliced up to 10 ways. Flux in support means that movement among party support groups more often reflects change in their composition than change in party positioning.

5 This is least true for the 1993, 1997, and 2000 elections, in which Reform arguably usurped the Conservatives' position.

6 For details on the CIPO file, see the appendix on data sources.

7 The 1940 result is based upon two polls during the 1945 campaign.

8 In the CIPO series, the distinction is based upon respondents' language. In the CES, this is also true for Quebec residents. Outside Quebec, the indicator is ancestry, which the CIPO did not query. Ancestry is almost as sure a guide to party preference as active use of the language, and it enables assigning many more respondents to the French category than would be possible with language alone. At the same time, it enables expansion of the variance on the right-hand side of the equation, which in turn stabilizes estimates.

9 Census data at the riding level first became available in machine-readable form thanks initially to Blake (1972) and eventually to Elections Canada. Among the early elections, Blake's datasets included the 1908-21 sequence. Data for elections before 1908 were extracted under my auspices from published census records and electoral returns.

10 Estimation of implicitly individual-level relationships with aggregate data is controversial. Strictly speaking, the situation is indeterminate. Among other things, the setup assumes, implausibly, that there is no aggregation bias (Achen and Shively 1995, 82-93). Even without aggregation bias, social gravitation might reinforce individual differences, introducing another dose of positivity into the coefficient. A classic example is the contrast drawn by Butler and Stokes (1969, 144-50) between mining and resort towns. But for the question at hand the method suffices. Alternative estimation strategies either rest on equally implausible assumptions or yield unhelpfully

vague results. King (1997) proposes a solution to the problem, but it has not received universal acceptance, on which see Tam Cho and Gaines (2004).

11 Some of the Quebec/rest-of-Canada contrast is an artifact of treating the rest of Canada as a single electorate. Certain western provinces rival Quebec in both one-sidedness and volatility, but their patterns are masked and sometimes offsetting (Johnston 2013). No such province is as big as Quebec, however.

12 Lagging the dependent variable reveals that the impact of the typical leadership change unfolds over the succeeding tenure, with an asymptotic long-term boost for the Quebec Liberals of 30 points. No one quite fits this description, but Laurier (six elections) and Trudeau (five) come close.

13 Somewhat counterintuitively, the Liberals were better off outside Quebec when their leader was from Quebec, an average boost of about five points. Arguably, the party's ability to recruit leaders from Quebec was tangible evidence for non-Quebeckers of its credibility inside the province.

14 The choice requiring the most justification is the 1911 majority over the more one-sided 1917 result. For the crash of 1921, 1917 seems to be the obvious backdrop. But this second majority was not a consolidation of the 1911 result (as 1988 was for 1984). Rather, the governing coalition changed shape fundamentally with the addition of formerly Liberal MPs and the loss – and then some – of all 1911 gains in Quebec.

15 Using differences finesses a measurement issue that would otherwise be distracting. Before 1988, the party identification indicator did not prime for non-partisanship. Since 1988, the CES has used an identification measure that mimics the induction in the original US version. Thus, the incidence of reported party identification dropped with this change, producing overall identification levels like those in the United States (Johnston 1992). Rather than allow this shift to muddy the graphical waters, it seems best to present the data in a way that minimizes the method variance and focuses on the substantive political difference.

16 Splitting the CES series at 1993 does not mask much within-period variation. Only once before 1993 were the regional differences effectively null, and after 1993 the direction of difference in Figure 4.8 holds every year.

17 Extending the estimation period to 2000 keeps coefficients pretty much as in Figure 4.9. Evidently, the emergence of the Bloc Québécois insulated Quebec against the drop in turnout that appeared elsewhere in Canada. After 2000, however, the relationship fell apart as Quebeckers joined the national trend of declining turnout.

18 Although the Quebec estimate is clearly different from zero, it is also the most unstable. This reflects the fact that the dependent variable, the Liberal share, is more volatile in Quebec than elsewhere. There is thus more overall variance to explain, a fact that leaks into the calculation of the standard error of the coefficient.

19 The contrast with 1911 is interesting. Evidently, Conservative protectionism was linked to the British Empire only when it was useful to do so.

20 Before 1958, Duplessis routinely supported the federal Conservatives but in a rather pro forma way and without much hope of impact (Cohen 1965, 84). There is a suggestion that efforts were stepped up modestly in 1957 as the Union Nationale machine focused on 25 seats (Meisel 1962, 174) and the Conservatives made small gains.

21 By my count from the Gallup source file used earlier in this chapter, polls in five distinct months gave the Conservatives an average of 58 percent of vote intention outside Quebec. Movement inside Quebec seems to have been induced by the Conservatives' success in June 1957, since the party's Gallup share in that province doubled between May and July and never went below 40 percent in the succeeding months.

22 A copy of the full-page ad can be found in Beck (1968, 325).

23 Although John Turner began his parliamentary career as a Quebec MP, he had lived outside the province since his first retirement from politics. In his second parliamentary career, he returned to his BC roots, so to speak, as MP for Vancouver Quadra.

24 Energy battles actually played well in Quebec. I recall ubiquitous signage on Montreal buses emphasizing that Petro-Canada belongs to Quebeckers. This was in 1980, the year of the first sovereignty referendum.

25 With few exceptions, the other pattern was four-way competition in which a New Democrat also appeared. Reflecting NDP national strategy, there were more NDP candidates in 1963 than in 1962. In both years, however, NDP shares were risible, and the party was not competing for Créditiste supporters.

Chapter 5: Catholics and Others

1 Translation: From our friends deliver us, O Lord. Letter to Adélard Langevin, Bishop of Saint Boniface, December 12-13, 1895 (cited in Crunican 1974, 139n11).

2 The early-middle decades of the twentieth century are missing, as mentioned in Chapter 4.

3 Notwithstanding its early history of hegemonic Protestantism, Ontario exerted a special pull for postwar Catholic immigrants, indeed for non-British immigrants in general. The contrast between Ontario and British Columbia in the period 1945-70 is especially striking (George 1970; Kalbach 1970).

4 In the late nineteenth century and early twentieth century, the region was about 33 percent Catholic. Now the share is more like 40 percent.

5 This is a back-of-the-envelope calculation, applying the breakdown in the 1961 census, the last to enumerate specific British and Irish sources, to the CES sample. At that census, people of Irish origin constituted 22 percent of the overall British group. Assuming that 40 percent of them were Catholic (below in text), and assuming that

the CES estimate of 18 percent Catholic among people of British Isles origin was correct, this yields an Irish share of all British Isles Catholics of about 50 percent.
6 It is of interest that four of the five concerned the West. As such, they are part of the background to Chapter 6, much of which deals with the unsettled politics of the region in the first half of the twentieth century.
7 My account is based upon Waite (1985, 162 ff., 473n24).
8 My account is based upon Thomas (1978) and Waite (1985, 259 ff.).
9 This paragraph draws mainly on Miller (1979).
10 To be sure, Protestants had always been vital to the Home Rule effort in Ireland, and the same could be said for opinion in Canada. For instance, Edward Blake, sometime leader of the Canadian Liberals, scion of a transplanted Galway family and kin to the Anglican elite of London, Ontario, ended his career as an Irish MP at Westminster. By the 1910s, however, leadership of Irish nationalism was already shifting in a Catholic and Gaelic direction, and a similar drift might have occurred in Canada. The passages in this section draw heavily on McLaughlin (2013).
11 In this paragraph and the next, all page references are to Stacey (1981) unless otherwise noted.
12 Since King did not want to provoke pro-empire opinion, he declined to deploy the language of independence; his emphasis was on equality of status (85). But this was a rhetorical move.
13 In an interesting parallel to King's rhetoric (note 12), his party did not force a vote on the question.
14 Interestingly, his Quebec lieutenant, Ernest Lapointe, urged the contrary, on the grounds that being in a position to shape events was a better insurance policy. Lapointe's argument had an ironic echo in the late 1930s.
15 Less salient but also diagnostic of the party division was Bennett's initial remedy for the Depression, a move toward empire free trade and the Ottawa Conference (Drummond 1974; Glassford 1992).
16 For brilliant and acerbic critiques of the Liberal reaction to Suez, the Toronto *Telegram* columns of Judith Robinson (1957) are unmatched. Although their tone is unabashedly anglophile and Tory, their content anticipates themes in the left version of Canadian nationalism that emerged a decade later.
17 There is some question about the representativeness of the sample for this poll.
18 The survey series starts in 1949 because Gallup did not query religious denomination before that year.
19 The complexity of the debate and the depth of feeling are captured, if somewhat eccentrically, in Champion (2010, Chapter 7).
20 For visual clarity, Gallup plots to 1988 and CES plots from 1965 appear side by side rather than overlapping.

21 Coefficients for French in 1949 are clearly non-zero, but the point estimates are not credible, given the massive confidence interval.
22 The issue is slightly confused by the inclusion of Austria in this category, but most immigrants from Austria-Hungary appear in the eastern European category. Significant minorities of Dutch and German descendants are Catholic.
23 This is not an artifact of a concentration of such Canadians in the West. The degree of concentration tends to be overstated, and the ethnic coefficients are all estimated in models that include region of residence.
24 This is an underappreciated theme in Zaller (1992).

Chapter 6: The Life and Death of Insurgents

1 The extended duration for the Manitoba Progressives reflected their coalition with the provincial Liberals and, in the Second World War, other parties as well.
2 Most observers see the financial emphasis as essentially conservative. For instance, Smiley (1962) likened Social Credit to Pierre Poujade's Union de Défense des Commerçants et Artisans, the quintessential anti-system party of the French Fourth Republic. But Bell (1993, Chapters 4 and 5) makes a spirited case that both the original Social Credit doctrine and the version adapted to Alberta had genuinely anti-capitalist elements.
3 A Liberal-Conservative coalition attempted to facilitate vote exchange through an Australian-style combination of preferential ballot and majority formula. Instead, Social Credit was the main second choice, even for CCF supporters. For some of the latter, Elkins (1976) argues, populism was part of the CCF's appeal, and on this dimension Social Credit was closer to the CCF than were either of the mainstream parties.
4 Having secured his majority, Bennett then returned the province to FPP.
5 It was no coincidence that Manning's father, Ernest, was the second Social Credit premier of Alberta and heir to Aberhart's Prophetic Bible Institute.
6 Indeed, the party's fate – more votes than for either Social Credit or the CCF but only one seat – made it an exemplary case of the divisive dynamic of FPP (Cairns 1968).
7 The Union Nationale hung around on the fringe of Quebec elections until the 1980s. The assimilation of some of its former operatives into the Parti Québécois helped that party to win the 1976 election.
8 At this point, the "nation" was not so much Quebec as French Canada, and the 1945 Bloc ran two candidates in Ontario.
9 Strictly speaking, the dimensionality data are from the 1984 edition, the data are replicated in Lijphart (1999, Table 5.3), and the Taagepera and Grofman (1985) proposition is retested by Lijphart (1999, Fig. 5.1).

10 The empirical literature is usually a bit more accommodating and usually accepts some number fractionally larger than two as evidence of predictive success.
11 In 1921, for instance, the Progressives' largest single provincial delegation was from Ontario, reflecting the sheer size of that province, to be sure, but the point stands.
12 Wiseman twins some provinces, for example Manitoba with Saskatchewan and Alberta with British Columbia.
13 Wesley (2011) is clear that his is a path-dependent account, in both his argument and his conceptual sources (see especially 245 ff.).
14 Classics of the genre include Harmel and Robertson (1985); Hauss and Rayside (1978); Hug (2001); and Tavits (2006).
15 In Tavits (2006), which seems to be the article of record, the major theme is indeed electoral maturity. She also recognizes the height of the threshold for new-party entry and the strength of pre-existing corporatist institutions.
16 It is further tempting to conjecture that the absorption of regional parties into the national system in the 1960s testifies to the maturation of western electorates. At this point, however, the logic seems to turn back on itself. If the issue is an electorate's psychological susceptibility to novelty, then the very ages of non-mainstream parties in the West would argue against their disappearance.
17 Although economic factors appear, their predictive track record is not good, not for new-party entry. Tavits (2006) is a case in point.
18 The accumulation of scandals also probably contributed to the Liberals' defeat that year.
19 After the flurry of interest in the early 1970s, the study of Canadian third parties as such, as opposed to work on individual new parties, languished until the 2000s. Although Bélanger (2004a, b) has resurrected interest in the general phenomenon, his work is more about overall success than about entry conditions. The comprehensive account in Bélanger (2011) is extremely eclectic, reflecting the theoretical disarray that Blais (1973) identified four decades earlier.
20 The idea of an electoral threshold grows out of attempts to exclude tiny parties from parliaments elected under proportional representation. The concept is now of general application. For a discussion and extension of the concept and an application to party and electoral system comparison, see Lijphart (1994).
21 These findings are broadly consistent with those of Adams et al. (2006), although they examine flux in electoral performance rather than outright party death.
22 For this period, Canadian producers were price takers in the Liverpool market (Marr and Paterson 1980). The price series is from the National Bureau of Economic Research, *NBER Macrohistory: IV. Prices,* http://www.nber.org/databases/macro history/contents/chapter04.html, series m04002, *Great Britain Wheat Prices* 09/1845-10/1934. Coding conventions for this series are at http://www.nber.org/databases/

macrohistory/rectdata/04/docs/m04002.txt. Prices are quotes from the end of the month and not seasonally adjusted.
23 The region elected almost as many labour candidates (three) as old-party ones (four, all Liberals).
24 Social Credit was also conspicuous in the 1938 Saskatchewan election, reflecting the novelty and seeming radicalism of that party in its early days.
25 The provincial Conservative vote in this period was broadly similar to the federal vote but seemingly with little potential to grow.
26 That the Conservative Party became well positioned in Manitoba is a tribute to Duff Roblin, who located his party to the left of the old Progressive-Liberal coalition and absorbed all of the forces to his right.

Chapter 7: Invasion from the Left

1 Also awkward was that the CCF did not countenance affiliation by entities that spanned provinces, disqualifying railway brotherhoods, for example (McNaught 1959, 261).
2 Although commitment of resources to Canada by the CIO grew roughly as union density also grew, the causal link is contested (Abella 1973).
3 Figures are from the Statistics Canada census page *Population, Urban and Rural, by Province and Territory (Canada)* at http://www.statcan.gc.ca/tables-tableaux/sum-som/l01/cst01/demo62a-eng.htm. "Rural" means outside any organized territory with a population of 1,000 or more. Australia is a useful comparison: there the rural percentages, based upon the same criterion as in Canada, in 1933 and 1947 were 36 and 31 (Australia 1949, 709).
4 Riddell (1993) attributes the 5-10-year mobilization lag relative to the United States to this regulatory impediment.
5 Union density did drop after 1990 but not by as much as Figure 7.2 suggests. The seemingly abrupt fall in 1997 reflected the fact that the Corporations and Labour Unions Returns Act (CALURA), which required exact reporting of unionization and collective agreements, was terminated. Estimates are now based upon the Canada Labour Force Survey (LFS), which might be more accurate. In any case, the shift in measurement produced an overnight drop in density as measured (Akyeampong 2004).
6 France, where union density has always been low, is a major exception.
7 Even more striking is the drop in New Zealand, which does not appear in Figure 7.2 so as not to obscure differences among the other cases.
8 The data sources are as described in Chapter 4 and as used there and in Chapter 5. For reasons discussed in Chapter 4, the Gallup series ends with the 1988 election.

9 I use survey data rather than official returns since the ultimate objective is to compare the situations with and without Catholics, so to speak, and the distinction can be made only with information on individuals.
10 In provincial elections, pressures for consolidation might be strong on the other side of the party battle, such that one of the old parties gets squeezed out. This is common in comment on the provincial party system in British Columbia, and it replicates a standard pattern in comparative research, especially in majoritarian systems (Cox 1997; Duverger 1963). For an early distillation of the BC pattern, see Cairns and Wong (1985).
11 If it is difficult to prove that $q \to p$, it might be easier to prove that $\neg q \to \neg p$.
12 In truth, estimates in this range are driven by respondents in Quebec since no other province is 70 percent Catholic. The next highest percentages after Quebec are for New Brunswick, in the mid-50s.
13 Although for many point estimates confidence intervals for one line overlap those for the other, the arena interaction is highly significant in both estimations.
14 But not, as I acknowledged earlier, their time in government (Iversen and Soskice 2006; Rodden 2010).

Chapter 8: System Dynamics, Coordination, and Fragmentation

1 I chose first differences rather than levels since this focuses the mind on dynamics. They also effectively centre the estimation and render the intercept a nullity, thus saving space on the table. Running the setup as a fixed-effects estimation in levels produces essentially the same pattern, although with less sharp differentiation among parties. I also ran the Liberal and Conservative estimations jointly as seemingly unrelated regressions (SUR); here the worry is common errors between the equations given the identical makeup of the right-hand variables. Again, running the setup as SUR does not change the interpretation and, if anything, sharpens the results. Since first-difference coefficients were essentially identical across fixed- and random-effects setups, I decided to focus my worry on correlation in errors among the provinces and thus present panel-corrected standard errors.
2 Johnston (2008, Fig. 2) shows that party supporters in Quebec, in contrast to supporters in the rest of Canada, are almost indistinguishable by ideology. The historical irrelevance of conventional left-right orientations in Quebec is also implicit in the account of that province's peculiar electoral dynamics in Chapter 3.
3 Reassuringly for the credibility of my claims for the diagnostic power of the CES campaign data, party shares of vote intention in the last week of pre-election fieldwork do a good job of forecasting the actual result.
4 The narrative in this paragraph is based upon Johnston et al. (1992).

5 The quotes are extracted from https://www.youtube.com/watch?v=jGYE2d4LJ5M. The first starts at 1:46:57 and the second at 1:56:15. For what it is worth, among the handful of 2011 CES respondents who believed that any party other than the Conservatives would win, many more named the Liberals than the New Democrats.

6 In one sense, Quebec repeated older patterns (Chapter 3) of electoral volatility, with a 2008-11 volatility index value of 25.9. The same was true for electoral consolidation, with an NDP seat bloc fractionally below what I identified in Chapter 3 as the historically critical 20 percent threshold. This time, however, the large seat share did not deliver power to the beneficiary. And the NDP's control of so many seats was truly an electoral system artifact (Cairns 1968) since the party's vote share was only 43 percent.

7 In Figure 2.9, the scales represent respondents' imputations of party positions on the left-right axis. In Table 8.3, respondents are asked to place themselves. Where in Chapter 2 the scale was recalibrated to −100, +100, here (for ease of presentation) the indicator is scaled to the −1, +1 interval. The left-right scales were presented to respondents in the self-administered mail-back portion of the 2011 CES, so respondent numbers are smaller than those in turnover tables of Panels A and B.

8 To avoid visual clutter, Figure 8.3 excludes the NDP. The 1993 election was a low point for the party, as earlier chapters established, but its plight was clear from the start, and the campaign did not make things worse.

9 Table 8.4 does not help much for understanding the collapse of the NDP given that the damage was mostly done before the campaign. Analysis of 1988-93 turnover indicates that in 1993 a 1988 New Democratic voter was about as likely to vote Liberal as stay with the NDP and about 2.5 times as likely to vote Liberal as Reform. These ratios hold for the country as a whole (Johnston 2005, 46, Table 3) as well as for Canada outside Quebec. The overall scale of the flight from the NDP was such that New Democratic defectors were a non-trivial element of the growth of Reform, especially since Reform had its most credible candidates in the West, the region of historical NDP strength. For all that, a New Democratic defector was much less likely to vote Reform than was a Conservative defector. The most powerful factor by far in governing NDP defection was ideological proximity, with the Liberals as the preferred destination.

10 The Conservatives' Ontario vote share did grow by 5.2 points, so the party's advantage was not entirely the result of coordination failure.

11 Only in Alberta and British Columbia in fact. It was in 1997 and 2000 that Reform's seat share expanded into the rest of the West.

12 It also helped the Liberals that the Ontario NDP vote collapsed, a bigger collapse, proportionately speaking, than the Conservative one. Ten Liberal seats were gained at NDP expense. So the story of 1993 is not entirely one of coordination failure, since

the centre-left became better organized even as the right fell apart. But few of the shifts on the centre-left occurred in the campaign.
13 Because of concern that errors are correlated between equations, I also estimated the two equations as a system of seemingly unrelated regressions. Coefficients essentially do not differ between SUR and time series setups. It seemed to be better to use a time series approach for what are, in fact, time series data, so the estimation in the table is by the Prais-Winsten method.
14 If we take elections from 1988 to 2006 to represent the current pattern, then provincial ENP are 0.89 smaller, on average, than the Canada-wide values but only 0.14 larger than within-province average local ENP. Provincial ENP varies from 2.41 (Prince Edward Island) to 3.17 (British Columbia). The range for local average ENP is trivially smaller, 2.39 to 3.05, with only two deviations from the rank order between the distributions. The provincial-local gap tends to be slightly larger where ENP are higher.
15 The figure omits confidence intervals to reduce clutter. The regression setup is linear (as in Table 8.5) even though, on the logic of ENP, effects cannot be linear over the full range of the independent variable. The linear setup is simple interpretively and not misleading over the range of actual variation. As a practical matter, curvilinearity is captured by breaking the analysis up into periods.
16 This has since been rescinded but not on a timeline relevant to my narrative.
17 Courtney (1978, 43n26) recounts an anecdote implying that broadcasting considerations made it necessary to run candidates everywhere or almost everywhere. The arithmetic in the anecdote does not add up, however, nor does the timing. Regulations had been in force since the 1930s and did not suffice to encourage the pre-1961 CCF to run candidates everywhere.
18 The exception is for Quebec, where NDP activists committed to a secessionist stance and forced the national party to disavow them.
19 Strøm (1990) goes on to say that these conditions are difficult to exemplify and offers the Finnish Social Democrats as a possible instance.
20 In the second case, not even the NDP was big enough to sustain the Liberal government. And after 2004 the NDP smelled blood. Its recovery that year strengthened its office orientation (Heath 2007), which seemed to be vindicated in 2011.
21 Why did the NDP and Liberals not just coalesce? The answer seems to be covered by the logic identified in Strøm (1983).
22 The influence of Reform between 1993 and 1997 illustrates a corresponding logic of influence from the political right. Greenspon and Wilson-Smith (1996, 276) argue that Finance Minister Paul Martin based his political case for massive retrenchment upon the electoral strength of Reform.

Chapter 9: Federal-Provincial Discontinuity

1 Party breakdowns for provincial elections are not available for all provinces before the 1920s. Not every provincial election is paired with a unique federal one and vice versa, depending on the timing and relative frequency of elections at each level.
2 Alberta's Wildrose Party should also be mentioned, but the electoral record of this party is chequered, and its future is obscure. Alberta could become like Saskatchewan over the next few electoral cycles.
3 Although Alberta in the 1980s and 1990s, Ontario in the 1990s, and Nova Scotia in the 2010s might be exceptions. In none of those instances – not even the NDP governments in Ontario and Nova Scotia – was the NDP electoral share as large as is typically the case in Manitoba, Saskatchewan, and British Columbia. Alberta post-2015 is an open case; it might well join the other western provinces in the ongoing strength of the NDP.
4 It is also the pattern of the moment in Alberta, with an NDP government and a Wildrose opposition.
5 This was not the only use of the alternative vote based upon a preferential ballot in western Canadian provincial politics, as noted in Chapter 6, but the BC case seems to be the only one in which the protagonists were motivated by fear of the labour left. See also Jansen (2004).
6 In Cox's (1997) original formulation, the SF ratio is among runners-up, with the first-place party out of the calculation. Whereas his intent is to capture a general process of consolidation, mine is to focus on the anti-socialist variety.
7 The estimation, described in detail in Table 9.A1, uses fixed effects for the province and thus concentrates on dynamics – the impacts of over-time shifts within a province. Estimations exclude Quebec, for which the provincial NDP has always been irrelevant. Notwithstanding genuflections to the left by the Parti Québécois, that party is ideologically more ambiguous than the NDP. The same is true for the federal Bloc Québécois. Other nationalist parties in Quebec tend to be conservative. Alberta in the 1920s is also excluded since the UFA was neither itself a party of labour nor an obvious rallying point for anti-socialist forces.
8 It is reasonable to ask if the patterns described in this section are not just about reaction to the challenge from the left but also indicative of the general impact of FPP, as per Cox (1997). Although SF ratios calculated for the entire system are generally higher in federal than in provincial elections, much of this is a by-product of differential coordination against the left in particular. Indeed, although Cox describes the process of consolidation generally, the narrative underpinning of his argument mainly concerns the rise of the labour left.
9 The estimation models are in Table 9.A2.

Notes to pages 228–48   281

10 The shift in slopes does meet the conventional criterion for statistical significance, however.
11 Alberta has now joined the western group, although it remains to be seen how this will play out in future elections.
12 Bear in mind that, on the logic of Figure 9.7C, counter-coordination means movement toward *smaller* ENP values.
13 Once again the island state of Tasmania is a partial exception.
14 By this I mean that Ottawa controlled the disposition on crown lands in each province until that date.

Chapter 10: Conclusion

1 The Liberal Party has regained power twice since 1980, but it no longer dominates the system. It is out of power as often as it is in, and its periods of rule are not strikingly long.
2 The 1917 and 1930 elections were exceptions to the general rule. In 1930, Quebec supplied most of the boost that gave the Conservatives a majority, but the party's expansion in the province built out from an Anglo-Montreal base. In 1917, the party turned its back on Quebec and on the Faustian bargain that it had made in 1911 but was compensated by gains in the rest of the country.
3 On a modest scale, something like this happened in 2006. The shift that year toward the Conservatives was greater in Quebec than elsewhere and yielded a body of supporters slightly less pro-Canada than Liberal supporters in the province (Figure 4.3). Conservative supporters outside Quebec remained firmly opposed to promotion of that province's interests.
4 This description also applies to the still understudied election of 1896.
5 Although in 2015 the NDP lost all of its seats in the region, its losses were on roughly the same scale as elsewhere.
6 Reform might have been a bridge between old and new forms of insurgency. To the extent that it embodied a somewhat contentless "westernism," it echoed the older pattern. As the avatar of a new, harder-edged conservatism, it aspired to grow, much like the NDP. So, although Reform was weaker in the East than in the West, it eventually ran candidates in all predominantly anglophone places. In provincial politics, however, it had no presence. Awkwardly for this part of my argument, neither did Reform have a presence in western provincial politics, with the limited exception of British Columbia and there without the federal party's blessing. Realignment of provincial elections was deemed to be unnecessary and, given the strength of the NDP, unwise. Of course, Reform's exclusively federal focus also contributed to federal-provincial discontinuity. Like other insurgents, Reform (by that name at

least) has disappeared from the scene, so it belongs here in a footnote rather than as a major qualification of the main argument.
7 They were changed to STV in 1926, but that is outside my argument.
8 The situation in Alberta is up for grabs. If the Alberta NDP is now to be a long-lasting member of the inner circle, the Conservative and Wildrose Parties will be forced into either a merger or a showdown. Either way only one of the names can endure.
9 Whether at its origins Social Credit was on the right, as commentators maintain, or on the left, as Finkel (1989) argues, is neither here nor there for my argument. It was not the CCF, and it soon enough moved to the right.
10 The nomenclature for the distinction originates with Brady and Collier (2010).

References

Abella, Irving M. 1973. *Nationalism, Communism, and Canadian Labour: The CIO, the Communist Party, and the Canadian Congress of Labour, 1935-1956*. Toronto: University of Toronto Press.

Abramson, Paul R., John H. Aldrich, André Blais, Matthew Diamond, Abraham Diskin, Indridi H. Indridason, Daniel J. Lee, and Renan Levine. 2010. Comparing Strategic Voting under FPTP and PR. *Comparative Political Studies* 43: 61-90.

Abramson, Paul R., John H. Aldrich, Phil Paolino, and David W. Rohde. 1992. "Sophisticated" Voting in the 1988 Presidential Primaries. *American Political Science Review* 86 (1): 55-69.

Achen, Christopher H. 1983. *Interpreting and Using Regression*. Thousand Oaks, CA: Sage.

Achen, Christopher H., and W. Phillips Shively. 1995. *Cross-Level Inference*. Chicago: University of Chicago Press.

Adams, James, Michael Clark, Lawrence Ezrow, and Garrett Glasgow. 2006. Are Niche Parties Fundamentally Different from Mainstream Parties? The Causes and the Electoral Consequences of Western European Parties' Policy Shifts, 1976-1998. *American Journal of Political Science* 50: 513-29.

Akyeampong, Ernest B. 2004. The Union Movement in Transition. *Perspectives* 5 (8): 5-13. http://www.statcan.gc.ca/pub/75-001-x/10804/7011-eng.pdf.

Alford, Robert R. 1963. *Party and Society: The Anglo-American Democracies*. Chicago: Rand McNally.

Allen, Richard. 1971. *The Social Passion: Religion and Social Reform in Canada, 1914-1928*. Toronto: University of Toronto Press.

Almond, Gabriel A. 1950. *The American People and Foreign Policy*. New York: Harcourt Brace.

Amorim Neto, Octavio, and Gary W. Cox. 1997. Electoral Institutions, Cleavage Structures, and the Number of Parties. *American Journal of Political Science* 41: 149-74.

Archer, Keith. 1985. The Failure of the New Democratic Party: Unions, Unionists, and Politics in Canada. *Canadian Journal of Political Science* 18: 353-66.

Archer, Robin. 2008. *Why Is There No Labor Party in the United States?* Princeton, NJ: Princeton University Press.

Aucoin, Peter, and Herman Bakvis. 2015. Canadian Public Funding of Political Parties and the End of Per-Vote Subsidies. In *Parties and Party Systems: Structure and Context*, edited by Richard Johnston and Campbell Sharman, 222-42. Vancouver: UBC Press.

Australia. Commonwealth Bureau of Census and Statistics. 1949. *Official Yearbook of the Commonwealth of Australia: No. 37 – 1946 and 1947*. Canberra: Commonwealth Government Printer.

Axelrod, Robert M. 1970. *Conflict of Interest: A Theory of Divergent Goals with Applications to Politics*. Chicago: Markham.

Bakvis, Herman, and Laura G. Macpherson. 1995. Quebec Block Voting and the Canadian Electoral System. *Canadian Journal of Political Science* 28: 659-92.

Ball, A.R. 1981. *British Political Parties: The Emergence of a Modern Party System*. London: Macmillan.

Bartels, Larry M. 1988. *Presidential Primaries and the Dynamics of Public Choice*. Princeton, NJ: Princeton University Press.

Bartolini, Stefano. 2000. *The Political Mobilization of the European Left, 1860-1980*. Cambridge, UK: Cambridge University Press.

Bartolini, Stefano, and Peter Mair. 1990. *Identity, Competition, and Electoral Availability: The Stabilisation of European Electorates, 1885-1985*. Cambridge, UK: Cambridge University Press.

Baum, Gregory. 1980. *Catholics and Canadian Socialism: Political Thought in the Thirties and Forties*. Toronto: Lorimer.

Beck, J. Murray. 1968. *Pendulum of Power: Canada's Federal Elections*. Scarborough, ON: Prentice-Hall.

Behiels, Michael D. 1985. *Prelude to Quebec's Quiet Revolution*. Montreal: McGill-Queen's University Press.

Bélanger, Éric. 2004a. The Rise of Third Parties in the 1993 Canadian Federal Election: Pinard Revisited. *Canadian Journal of Political Science* 37: 581-94.

–. 2004b. Antipartyism and Third-Party Vote Choice: A Comparison of Canada, Britain, and Australia. *Comparative Political Studies* 37 (9): 1054-78.

–. 2011. Third Party Success in Canada. In *Canadian Parties in Transition*, edited by Alain-G. Gagnon and A. Brian Tanguay, 83-109. Toronto: University of Toronto Press.

Bélanger, Éric, and Jean-François Godbout. 2010. Why Do Parties Merge? The Case of the Conservative Party of Canada. *Parliamentary Affairs* 63 (1): 41-65.

Bell, Edward A. 1993. *Social Classes and Social Credit in Alberta*. Montreal: McGill-Queen's University Press.

Bennett, Andrew. 2010. Process Tracing and Causal Inference. In *Rethinking Social Inquiry: Diverse Tools, Shared Standards*, 2nd ed., edited by Henry E. Brady and David Collier, 207-19. Lanham, MD: Rowman and Littlefield.

Benoit, Kenneth, and Michael Laver. 2006. *Party Policy in Modern Democracies*. London: Routledge.

Benoit, Kenneth, Michael Laver, and Slava Mikhaylov. 2009. Treating Words as Data with Error: Estimating Uncertainty in Text Statements of Policy Positions. *American Journal of Political Science* 53: 495-513.

Berger, Carl. 1970. *The Sense of Power: Studies in the Ideas of Canadian Imperialism, 1867-1914*. Toronto: University of Toronto Press.

Berinsky, Adam J. 2006. American Public Opinion in the 1930s and 1940s: The Analysis of Quota-Controlled Sample Survey Data. *Public Opinion Quarterly* 70: 499-529.

–. 2009. *In Time of War: Understanding American Public Opinion from World War II to Iraq*. Chicago: University of Chicago Press.

Black, Conrad. 1977. *Maurice Duplessis*. Toronto: McClelland and Stewart.

Black, Edwin R. 1975. *Divided Loyalties: Canadian Concepts of Federalism*. Montreal: McGill-Queen's University Press.

Black, Jerome H. 1978. The Multicandidate Calculus of Voting: Application to Canadian Federal Elections. *American Journal of Political Science* 22 (3): 609-38.

–. 1982. Immigrant Political Adaptation in Canada: Some Tentative Findings. *Canadian Journal of Political Science* 15: 3-28.

Blais, André. 1973. Third Parties in Canadian Provincial Politics. *Canadian Journal of Political Science* 6: 422-38.

–. 2005. Accounting for the Electoral Success of the Liberal Party in Canada. *Canadian Journal of Political Science* 38: 821-40.

Blake, Donald E. 1972. The Measurement of Regionalism in Canadian Voting Patterns. *Canadian Journal of Political Science* 5: 55-81.

–. 1979. 1896 and All That: Critical Elections in Canada. *Canadian Journal of Political Science* 12: 259-79.

Bliss, J.M. 1968. The Methodist Church and World War I. *Canadian Historical Review* 49: 213-33.

Bociurkiw, Bohdan. 1978. The Federal Policy of Multiculturalism and the Ukrainian-Canadian Community. In *Ukrainian Canadians, Multiculturalism, and Separatism: An Assessment*, edited by Manoly R. Lupul, 98-128. Edmonton: University of Alberta Press.

Boix, Carles. 1999. Setting the Rules of the Game: The Choice of Electoral Systems in Advanced Democracies. *American Political Science Review* 93: 609-24.

–. 2009. The Emergence of Parties and Party Systems. In *The Oxford Handbook of Comparative Politics*, edited by Carles Boix and Susan Stokes, 499-521. Oxford: Oxford University Press.

Bothwell, Robert. 2007. *Alliance and Illusion: Canada and the World, 1945-1984*. Vancouver: UBC Press.

Brady, Henry E., and David Collier, eds. 2010. *Rethinking Social Inquiry: Diverse Tools, Shared Standards*. Lanham, MD: Rowman and Littlefield.

Brady, Henry E., and Richard Johnston. 1987. What's the Primary Message: Horse Race or Issue Journalism? In *Media and Momentum: The New Hampshire Primary and Nomination Politics*, edited by Gary R. Orren and Nelson W. Polsby, 127-86. Chatham, NJ: Chatham House.

–. 2006. The Rolling Cross-Section and Causal Attribution. In *Capturing Campaign Effects*, edited by Henry E. Brady and Richard Johnston, 164-95. Ann Arbor, MI: University of Michigan Press.

Brodie, Janine, and Jane Jenson. 1988. *Crisis, Challenge, and Change: Party and Class in Canada Revisited*. Ottawa: Carleton University Press.

Brym, Robert J., Michael W. Gillespie, and Rhonda L. Lenton. 1989. Class Power, Class Mobilization, and Class Voting: The Canadian Case. *Canadian Journal of Sociology* 14: 25-44.

Burnet, Jean R. 1951. *Next-Year Country: A Study of Rural Social Organization in Alberta*. Toronto: University of Toronto Press.

Butler, David E., and Donald E. Stokes. 1969. *Political Change in Britain*. London: Macmillan.

Cain, Bruce E. 1978. Strategic Voting in Britain. *American Journal of Political Science* 22: 639-55.

Cairns, Alan C. 1968. The Electoral System and the Party System in Canada, 1921-1965. *Canadian Journal of Political Science* 1: 55-80.

Cairns, Alan C., and Daniel Wong. 1985. Socialism, Federalism, and the B.C. Party Systems 1933-1983. In *Party Politics in Canada*, edited by Hugh G. Thorburn, 468-506. Toronto: Prentice-Hall.

Calvo, Ernesto, and Jonathan Rodden. 2015. The Achilles Heel of Plurality Systems: Geography and Representation in Multiparty Democracies. *American Journal of Political Science* 59: 789-805.

Capoccia, Giovanni, and Daniel Ziblatt. 2010. The Historical Turn in Democratization Studies: A New Research Agenda for Europe and Beyond. *Comparative Political Studies* 43 (8-9): 931–68.

Carey, John M., and Mathew Søberg Shugart. 1995. Incentives to Cultivate a Personal Vote: A Rank Ordering of Electoral Formulas. *Electoral Studies* 14: 417-439.

Carty, R. Kenneth. 2015. *Big Tent Politics: The Liberal Party's Long Mastery of Canada's Public Life*. Vancouver: UBC Press.

Carty, R. Kenneth, and Munroe Eagles. 2005. *Politics Is Local: National Politics at the Grassroots*. Don Mills, ON: Oxford University Press.

Champion, C.P. 2010. *The Strange Demise of British Canada: The Liberals and Canadian Nationalism, 1964-1968*. Montreal: McGill-Queen's University Press.

Chappell, Henry W. Jr., and William R. Keech. 1986. Policy Motivation and Party Differences in a Dynamic Spatial Model of Party Competition. *American Political Science Review* 80 (3): 881-99.

Chhibber, Pradeep K., and Ken Kollman. 2004. *The Formation of National Party Systems: Federalism and Party Competition in Canada, Great Britain, India, and the United States*. Princeton, NJ: Princeton University Press.

Clarke, Harold D., Jane Jenson, Lawrence LeDuc, and Jon H. Pammett. 1996. *Absent Mandate: Canadian Electoral Politics in an Era of Restructuring*. Toronto: Gage.

CLC-CCF Joint National Committee. 1958. *A New Political Party for Canada*. Ottawa: CLC-CCF Joint National Committee.

Cleveland, W.S. 1993. *Visualizing Data*. Summit, NJ: Hobart.

Cloutier, Édouard, Jean H. Guay, and Daniel Latouche. 1992. *Le virage: L'évolution de opinion publique au Québec depuis 1960*. Montréal: Québec/Amérique.

Cochrane, Christopher. 2010. Left/Right Ideology and Canadian Politics. *Canadian Journal of Political Science* 45 (3): 583-605.

Cohen, Ronald I. 1965. *Quebec Votes: The How and Why of Quebec Voting in Every Federal Election since Confederation*. Montreal: Saje.

Colley, Linda. 1992. *Britons: 1707-1837*. New Haven, CT: Yale University Press.

Converse, Jean N. 1987. *Survey Research in the United States: Roots and Emergence, 1890-1960*. Berkeley: University of California Press.

Converse, Philip E. 1969. Of Time and Partisan Stability. *Comparative Political Studies* 2: 139-71.

Converse, Philip E., and Georges Dupeux. 1962. Politicization of the Electorate in France and the United States. *Public Opinion Quarterly* 26: 1-23.

Cook, Ramsay. 1961. Dafoe, Laurier, and the Formation of Union Government. *Canadian Historical Review* 42: 185-208.

–. 1963. *The Politics of J.W. Dafoe and the Free Press*. Toronto: University of Toronto Press.

–. 1985. *The Regenerators: Social Criticism in Victorian Canada*. Toronto: University of Toronto Press.

Cornell, Paul G. 1962. *The Alignment of Political Groups in the Province of Canada*. Toronto: University of Toronto Press.

Courtney, John C. 1978. Recognition of Canadian Political Parties in Parliament and in Law. *Canadian Journal of Political Science* 11 (1): 33-60.

–. 2015. Canada's National Parties: From Private to Public Institutions. In *Parties and Party Systems: Structure and Context*, edited by Richard Johnston and Campbell Sharman, 202-21. Vancouver: UBC Press.

Cox, Gary W. 1987. *The Efficient Secret: The Cabinet and the Development of Political Parties in Victorian England*. Cambridge, UK: Cambridge University Press.

–. 1990. Centripetal and Centrifugal Incentives in Electoral Systems. *American Journal of Political Science* 34 (4): 903-35.

–. 1997. *Making Votes Count: Strategic Coordination in the World's Electoral Systems*. Cambridge, UK: Cambridge University Press.

Craven, Paul. 1980. *"An Impartial Umpire": Industrial Relations and the Canadian State*. Toronto: University of Toronto Press.

Crunican, Paul. 1974. *Priests and Politicians: Manitoba Schools and the Election of 1896*. Toronto: University of Toronto Press.

Cusack, Thomas R., Torben Iversen, and David Soskice. 2007. Economic Interests and the Origins of Electoral Systems. *American Political Science Review* 101: 373-91.

Dirks, Patricia G. 1991. *The Failure of L'Action Libérale Nationale*. Montreal: McGill-Queen's University Press.

Dobell, W.M. 1986. Updating Duverger's Law. *Canadian Journal of Political Science* 19: 585–95.

Downs, Anthony. 1957. *An Economic Theory of Democracy*. New York: Harper and Row.

Drummond, Ian M. 1974. *Imperial Economic Policy 1917-1939*. London: Macmillan.

Dunleavy, P., and F. Boucek. 2003. Constructing the Number of Parties. *Party Politics* 9: 291-315.

Duverger, Maurice. 1963. *Political Parties: Their Organization and Activity in the Modern State*. Translated by Barbara North and Robert North. New York: Wiley.

Eayrs, James. 1965. *In Defence of Canada: Appeasement and Rearmament*. Toronto: University of Toronto Press.

Elkins, David J. 1976. Politics Makes Strange Bedfellows: The B.C. Party System in the 1952 and 1953 Provincial Elections. *BC Studies* 30: 3-26.

English, John. 1977. *The Decline of Politics: The Conservatives and the Party System 1901-20*. Toronto: University of Toronto Press.

Erikson, Robert S., and Mikhail G. Filippov. 2001. Electoral Balancing in Federal and Subnational Elections: The Case of Canada. *Constitutional Political Economy* 12: 313–31.

Erikson, Robert, and John H. Goldthorpe. 1992. *The Constant Flux: A Study of Class Mobility in Industrial Societies.* Oxford: Clarendon Press.

Fearon, James D. 1999. What Is Identity (as We Now Use the Word)? Unpublished manuscript, Stanford University.

–. 2003. Ethnic and Cultural Diversity by Country. *Journal of Economic Growth* 8: 195-222.

Filippov, Mikhail, Peter C. Ordeshook, and Olga Shvetsova. 2004. *Designing Federalism: A Theory of Self-Sustainable Institutions.* Cambridge, UK: Cambridge University Press.

Finer, S.E. 1970. *Comparative Government.* London: Allen Lane.

Finkel, Alvin. 1989. *The Social Credit Phenomenon in Alberta.* Toronto: University of Toronto Press.

Fisher, Robin. 1991. *Duff Pattullo of British Columbia.* Toronto: University of Toronto Press.

Flanagan, Thomas. 1995. *Waiting for the Wave: The Reform Party and Preston Manning.* Toronto: Stoddart.

Frizzell, Alan Stewart, and Anthony Westell. 1985. *The Canadian General Election of 1984: Politicians, Parties, Press, and Polls.* Ottawa: Carleton University Press.

Gauvreau, Michael. 1991. *The Evangelical Century: College and Creed in English Canada from the Great Revival to the Great Depression.* Montreal: McGill-Queen's University Press.

George, M.V. 1970. *Internal Migration in Canada: Demographic Analyses.* Ottawa: Dominion Bureau of Statistics.

Gerring, John. 2005. Minor Parties in Plurality Electoral Systems. *Party Politics* 11: 79-107.

Glassford, Larry A. 1992. *Reaction and Reform: The Politics of the Conservative Party under R.B. Bennett.* Toronto: University of Toronto Press.

Glassford, Sarah Carlene. 2007. Marching as to War: The Canadian Red Cross Society, 1885-1939. PhD diss., York University.

Goethe, Johann Wolfgang von. 1971. *Elective Affinities.* Translated by R.J. Hollingdale. London: Penguin.

Goldthorpe, John H. 1980. *Social Mobility and Class Structure in Britain.* Oxford: Clarendon Press.

Gourevitch, Peter. 1978. The Second Image Reversed: The International Sources of Domestic Politics. *International Organization* 32 (4): 881-912.

Graham, Roger. 1960. *Arthur Meighen, a Biography: I. The Door of Opportunity.* Toronto: Clarke, Irwin.

–. 1963. *Arthur Meighen, a Biography: II. And Fortune Fled.* Toronto: Clarke, Irwin.

Granatstein, J.L. 1967. *The Politics of Survival: The Conservative Party of Canada, 1939-1945*. Toronto: University of Toronto Press.

Granatstein, J.L., and J.M. Hitsman. 1977. *Broken Promises: A History of Conscription in Canada*. Toronto: Oxford University Press.

Green, Donald, Bradley Palmquist, and Eric Stickler. 2002. *Partisan Hearts and Minds: Political Parties and the Social Identities of Voters*. New Haven, CT: Yale University Press.

Greenspon, Edward, and Anthony Wilson-Smith. 1996. *Double Vision: The Inside Story of the Liberals in Power*. Toronto: Doubleday.

Hall, D.J. 1981. *Clifford Sifton: The Young Napoleon, 1861-1900*. Vancouver: UBC Press.

–. 1985. *Clifford Sifton: A Lonely Eminence, 1900-1929*. Vancouver: UBC Press.

Harmel, Robert, and John Robertson. 1985. Formation and Success of New Parties: A Cross-National Analysis. *International Political Science Review* 6: 501-23.

Hauss, Charles, and David Rayside. 1978. The Development of New Parties in Western Democracies since 1945. In *Political Parties: Development and Decay*, edited by Louis Maisel and Joseph Cooper, 31-57. Beverly Hills: Sage.

Heath, Jamie. 2007. *Dead Centre: Hope, Possibility, and Unity for Canadian Progressives*. Toronto: Wiley.

Hechter, Michael. 1987. *Principles of Group Solidarity*. Berkeley: University of California Press.

Heer, David M. 1962. The Trend of Interfaith Marriages in Canada: 1922-1957. *American Sociological Review* 27: 245-50.

Hilliker, John, and Greg Donaghy. 2005. Canadian Relations with the United Kingdom at the End of Empire, 1956-73. In *Canada and the End of Empire*, edited by Phillip Buckner, 25-46. Vancouver: UBC Press.

Hirano, Shigeo, and James N. Snyder. 2007. The Decline of Third-Party Voting in the United States. *Journal of Politics* 69: 1-16.

Holsti, Ole R. 1992. Public Opinion and Foreign Policy: Challenges to the Almond-Lippmann Consensus. *International Studies Quarterly* 36: 439-66.

Horowitz, Gad. 1968. *Canadian Labour in Politics*. Toronto: University of Toronto Press.

Houston, Cecil J., and William J. Smyth. 1980. *The Sash Canada Wore: A Historical Geography of the Orange Order in Canada*. Toronto: University of Toronto Press.

–. 1990. *Irish Emigration and Canadian Settlement: Patterns, Links, and Letters*. Toronto: University of Toronto Press; Belfast: Ulster Historical Foundation.

Huber, Evelyne, and John D. Stephens. 2001. *Development and Crisis of the Welfare State: Parties and Policies in Global Markets*. Chicago: University of Chicago Press.

Hug, Simon. 2001. *Altering Party Systems: Strategic Behavior and the Emergence of New Political Parties in Western Democracies*. Ann Arbor: University of Michigan Press.

Humphreys, Macartan, and Alan M. Jacobs. 2015. Mixing Methods: A Bayesian Approach. *American Political Science Review* 109: 653-73.

Igartua, José E. 2006. *The Other Quiet Revolution: National Identities in English Canada, 1945-71*. Vancouver: UBC Press.

Irving, John A. 1959. *The Social Credit Movement in Alberta*. Toronto: University of Toronto Press.

Iversen, Torben, and David Soskice. 2006. Electoral Institutions, Parties, and the Politics of Class: Why Some Democracies Distribute More Than Others. *American Political Science Review* 100: 165-81.

Jansen, Harold J. 2004. The Political Consequences of the Alternative Vote: Lessons from Western Canada. *Canadian Journal of Political Science* 37: 647-69.

Jeffery, Charlie, and Dan Hough. 2003. Regional Elections in Multi-Level Systems. *European Urban and Regional Studies* 10: 199-212.

Jenkins, Richard W. 1999. How Much Is Too Much? Media Attention and Popular Support for an Insurgent Party. *Political Communication* 16 (4): 429-45.

–. 2002. How Campaigns Matter in Canada: Priming and Learning as Explanations for the Reform Party's 1993 Campaign Success. *Canadian Journal of Political Science* 35: 383-408.

Johnson, Gregory A. 2005. The Last Gasp of Empire: The 1964 Flag Debate Revisited. In *Canada and the End of Empire*, edited by Phillip Buckner, 232-50. Vancouver: UBC Press.

Johnson, Myron. 1979. The Failure of the CCF in Alberta: An Accident of History. In *Society and Politics in Alberta*, edited by Carlos Calderola, 87-107. Toronto: Methuen.

Johnston, Richard. 1980. Federal and Provincial Voting: Contemporary Patterns and Historical Evolution. In *Small Worlds: Provinces and Parties in Canadian Political Life*, edited by David J. Elkins and Richard Simeon, 131-78. Toronto: Methuen.

–. 1985. The Reproduction of the Religious Cleavage in Canadian Elections. *Canadian Journal of Political Science* 18: 99-113.

–. 1992. Party Identification Measures in the Anglo-American Democracies: A National Survey Experiment. *American Journal of Political Science* 36: 542-59.

–. 1999. Business Cycles, Political Cycles, and the Popularity of Canadian Governments, 1974-1998. *Canadian Journal of Political Science* 32: 499-520.

–. 2005. Canadian Elections at the Millennium. In *Strengthening Canadian Democracy*, edited by Paul Howe, Richard Johnston, and André Blais, 19-61. Montreal: Institute for Research on Public Policy.

–. 2008. Polarized Pluralism in the Canadian Party System. *Canadian Journal of Political Science* 41: 815-34.

–. 2013. Alignment, Realignment, and Dealignment in Canada: The View from Above. *Canadian Journal of Political Science* 46: 245-71.

Johnston, Richard, and Janet Ballantyne. 1977. Geography and the Electoral System. *Canadian Journal of Political Science* 10: 857-66.

Johnston, Richard, André Blais, Henry E. Brady, and Jean Crête. 1992. *Letting the People Decide: Dynamics of a Canadian Election*. Montreal: McGill-Queen's University Press.

Johnston, Richard, André Blais, Elisabeth Gidengil, Neil Nevitte, and Henry E. Brady. 1996. The 1993 Canadian Election: Realignment, Dealignment, or Something Else? Paper presented at the 1996 Annual Meeting of the American Political Science Association, San Francisco, 28 August–1 September.

Johnston, Richard, and Henry E. Brady. 2002. The Rolling Cross Section Design. *Electoral Studies* 21: 283-95.

Johnston, Richard, and Fred Cutler. 2009. Canada: The Puzzle of Local Three-Party Competition. In *Duverger's Law of Plurality Voting: The Logic of Party Competition in Canada, India, the United Kingdom, and the United States*, edited by Bernard Grofman, André Blais, and Shaun Bowler, 83-96. New York: Springer.

Jones, Richard. 1980. *Vers une hégémonie libérale: Aperçu de la politique canadienne de Laurier à King*. Cahiers d'histoire politique 1. Québec: Librairies des Presses Université Laval.

Kalbach, Warren E. 1970. *The Impact of Immigration on Canada's Population*. 1961 Census Monograph. Ottawa: Dominion Bureau of Statistics.

Kalyvas, Stathis N. 1996. *The Rise of Christian Democracy in Europe*. Chicago: University of Chicago Press.

Kedar, Orit. 2005. When Moderate Voters Prefer Extreme Parties: Policy Balancing in Parliamentary Elections. *American Political Science Review* 99: 185-99.

Kent, Tom. 1988. *A Public Purpose*. Montreal: McGill-Queen's University Press.

King, Gary. 1990. Electoral Responsiveness and Partisan Bias in Multiparty Democracies. *Legislative Studies Quarterly* 15 (2): 159-81.

–. 1997. *A Solution to the Ecological Inference Problem: Reconstructing Individual Behavior from Aggregate Data*. Princeton, NJ: Princeton University Press.

King, Gary, and Robert X Browning. 1987. Democratic Representation and Partisan Bias in Congressional Elections. *American Political Science Review* 81 (4): 1252-73.

Kumar, Pradeep. 1986. Union Growth in Canada: Retrospect and Prospect. In *Canadian Labour Relations*, edited by W. Craig Riddell, 95-160. Toronto: University of Toronto Press.

Laakso, Markku, and Rein Taagepera. 1979. "Effective" Number of Parties: A Measure with Application to West Europe. *Comparative Political Studies* 12: 3-27.

Lago, Ignacio, and Ferran Martínez. 2011. Why New Parties? *Party Politics* 17: 3-20.

Laponce, Jean A. 1969. Ethnicity, Religion, and Politics in Canada: A Comparative Analysis of Survey and Census Data. In *Quantitative Ecological Analysis in the Social Sciences*, edited by Mattei Dogan and Stein Rokkan, 187-216. Cambridge, MA: MIT Press.

–. 1972. Post-Dicting Electoral Cleavages in Canadian Federal Elections, 1949–68: Material for a Footnote. *Canadian Journal of Political Science* 5: 270-86.

–. 1988. Left or Centre? The Canadian Jewish Electorate, 1953-1983. *Canadian Journal of Political Science* 21: 691-715.

Laponce, Jean A., and Jas Sekhon. 1995. Ethnicity or Class? The Canadian Communist Party's Electorate. *Nationalism and Ethnic Politics* 2: 270-83.

Laver, Michael, and Ernest Sergenti. 2011. *Party Competition: An Agent-Based Model*. Princeton, NJ: Princeton University Press.

Layman, Geoffrey. 2001. *The Great Divide: Religious and Cultural Conflict in American Party Politics*. New York: Columbia University Press.

LeDuc, Lawrence. 1984. Canada: The Politics of Stable Dealignment. In *Electoral Change in Advanced Industrial Democracies: Realignment or Dealignment?*, edited by Russell J. Dalton, Scott C. Flanagan, and Paul Allen Beck, 402-24. Princeton, NJ: Princeton University Press.

Lieberson, Stanley. 1970. *Language and Ethnic Relations in Canada*. New York: Wiley.

Lijphart, Arend. 1979. Religious vs. Linguistic vs. Class Voting: The "Crucial Experiment" of Comparing Belgium, Canada, South Africa, and Switzerland. *American Political Science Review* 73: 442-58.

–. 1994. *Electoral Systems and Party Systems: A Study of Twenty-Seven Democracies, 1945–1990*. Oxford: Oxford University Press.

–. 1999. *Patterns of Democracy: Government Forms and Performance in Thirty-Six Countries*. New Haven, CT: Yale University Press.

Lipset, Seymour Martin. 1954. Democracy in Alberta. *Canadian Forum* (November-December): 175-77, 196-98.

–. 1960. Party Systems and the Representation of Social Groups. *European Journal of Sociology* 1: 50-85.

–. 1968. *Agrarian Socialism: The Cooperative Commonwealth in Saskatchewan. A Study in Political Sociology.* 1950; reprinted, New York: Doubleday.

Lipset, Seymour Martin, and Stein Rokkan. 1967. Cleavage Structures, Party Systems, and Voter Alignments: An Introduction. In *Party Systems and Voter Alignments*, edited by Seymour Martin Lipset and Stein Rokkan, 1-64. New York: Free Press.

Lowe, William, Kenneth Benoit, Slava Mikhaylov, and Michael Laver. 2011a. Replication Data for The Manifesto Project Data Extended to Include the Logit Scales and Standard Errors. http://hdl.handle.net/1902.1/17073.

–. 2011b. Scaling Policy Preferences from Coded Political Texts. *Legislative Studies Quarterly* 26: 123-55.

Luebbert, Gregory. 1991. *Liberalism, Fascism, or Social Democracy: Social Classes and the Political Origins of Regimes in Inter-war Europe*. Oxford, UK: Oxford University Press.

Lupul, Manoly R. 1974. *The Roman Catholic Church and the North-West School Question*. Toronto: University of Toronto Press.

Macdonald, Stuart Elaine, Ola Listhaug, and George Rabinowitz. 1991. Issues and Party Support in Multiparty Systems. *American Political Science Review* 85: 1007-31.

Macpherson, C.B. 1953. *Democracy in Alberta: Social Credit and the Party System*. Toronto: University of Toronto Press.

Mahoney, James. 2000. Path Dependence in Historical Sociology. *Theory and Society* 29: 507-48.

Mainwaring, Scott, and Mariano Torcal. 2006. Party System Institutionalization and Party System Theory after the Third Wave of Democratization. In *Handbook of Political Parties*, edited by Richard S. Katz and William Crotty, 204–27. London: Sage.

Mainwaring, Scott, and Edurne Zoco. 2007. Political Sequences and the Stabilization of Interparty Competition: Electoral Volatility in Old and New Democracies. *Party Politics* 13: 155-78.

Manza, Jeff, and Clem Brooks. 1999. *Social Cleavages and Political Change: Voter Alignments and US Party Coalitions*. Oxford: Oxford University Press.

Marland, Alex, and Tom Flanagan. 2015. From Opposition to Government: Party Merger as a Step on the Road to Power. *Parliamentary Affairs* 68 (2): 272-90.

Marr, William L., and Donald G. Paterson. 1980. *Canada: An Economic History*. Toronto: Macmillan.

McAllister, Ian. 2011. *The Australian Voter: 50 Years of Change*. Sydney: University of New South Wales Press.

McCormack, A. Ross. 1977. *Reformers, Rebels, and Revolutionaries: The Western Canadian Radical Movement, 1899-1919*. Toronto: University of Toronto Press.

McLaughlin, Robert. 2013. *Irish Canadian Conflict and the Struggle for Irish Independence, 1912-1925*. Toronto: University of Toronto Press.

McNaught, Kenneth. 1959. *A Prophet in Politics: A Biography of J.S. Woodsworth*. Toronto: University of Toronto Press.

Meffert, Michael, Sascha Huber, Thomas Gschwend, and Franz Urban Pappi. 2011. More Than Wishful Thinking: Causes and Consequences of Voters' Electoral Expectations about Parties and Coalitions. *Electoral Studies* 30 (4): 804-15.

Meguid, Bonnie M. 2005. Competition between Unequals: The Role of Mainstream Party Strategy in Niche Party Success. *American Political Science Review* 99: 347-59.

Meisel, John. 1962. *The Canadian General Election of 1957*. Toronto: University of Toronto Press.

Mendelsohn, Matthew. 2003. Rational Choice and Socio-Psychological Explanation for Opinion on Quebec Sovereignty. *Canadian Journal of Political Science* 36 (3): 511-37.

Miller, Carman. 1993. *Painting the Map Red: Canada and the South African War, 1899-1902*. Montreal: McGill-Queen's University Press.

Miller, J.R. 1979. *Equal Rights: The Jesuits' Estates Act Controversy*. Montreal: McGill-Queen's University Press.

Milner, Marc. 2005. More Royal than Canadian? The Royal Canadian Navy's Search for Identity, 1910-68. In *Canada and the End of Empire*, edited by Phillip Buckner, 272-84. Vancouver: UBC Press.

Mitchell, David J. 1983. *W.A.C. Bennett and the Rise of British Columbia*. Vancouver: Douglas and McIntyre.

Morton, W.L. 1950. *The Progressive Party in Canada*. Toronto: University of Toronto Press.

Neatby, H. Blair. 1973. *Laurier and a Liberal Quebec: A Study in Political Management*. Toronto: McClelland and Stewart.

Nicholson, G.W.L. 2015. *Canadian Expeditionary Force, 1914-1919: Official History of the Canadian Army in the First World War*. 1962; reprinted, Montreal: McGill-Queen's University Press.

Nieuwbeerta, Paul, and Nan Dirk de Graaf. 1999. Traditional Class Voting in Twenty Postwar Societies. In *The End of Class Politics? Class Vote in Comparative Context*, edited by Geoffrey Evans, 23-57. Oxford: Oxford University Press.

Oliver, Peter. 1977. *G. Howard Ferguson: Ontario Tory*. Toronto: University of Toronto Press.

Ormsby, Margaret A. 1962. T. Dufferin Pattullo and the Little New Deal. *Canadian Historical Review* 43: 277-97.

Pallarés, Francesc, and Michael Keating. 2003. Multi-Level Electoral Competition: Regional Elections and Party Systems in Spain. *European Urban and Regional Studies* 10: 239-55.

Pederson, Mogens. 1979. The Dynamics of European Party Systems: Changing Patterns of Electoral Volatility. *European Journal of Political Research* 7: 1-26.

–. 1983. Patterns of Electoral Volatility in European Party Systems: Explorations in Explanation. In *Western European Party Systems: Continuity and Change*, edited by Hans Daalder and Peter Mair, 29-66. London: Sage.

Penlington, Norman. 1965. *Canada and Imperialism, 1896-1899.* Toronto: University of Toronto Press.

Perin, Roberto. 1990. *Rome in Canada: The Vatican and Canadian Affairs in the Late Victorian Age.* Toronto: University of Toronto Press.

Pickup, Mark A. 2005. Examining Electoral Accountability through the Dynamics of Government Support: Party Popularity, the Economy, and Political Context. PhD diss., University of British Columbia.

Pierson, Paul. 2000. Increasing Returns, Path Dependence, and the Study of Politics. *American Political Science Review* 94 (2): 251-67.

Pinard, Maurice. 1966. La faiblesse des Conservateurs et la montée du Crédit Social en 1962. *Recherches sociographiques* 7: 360-63.

–. 1975. *The Rise of a Third Party: A Study in Crisis Politics.* Montreal: McGill-Queen's University Press.

–. 1997a. Les quatre phases du mouvement indépendantiste québécois. In *Un combat inachevé*, edited by Robert Bernier, Vincent Lemieux, and Maurice Pinard, 29-50. Sainte-Foy: Presses de l'Université du Québec.

–. 1997b. Les fluctuations du mouvement indépendantiste depuis 1980. In *Un combat inachevé*, edited by Robert Bernier, Vincent Lemieux, and Maurice Pinard, 69-99. Sainte-Foy: Presses de l'Université du Québec.

Power, Charles Gavan. 1966. *A Party Politician: The Memoirs of Chubby Power.* Toronto: Macmillan.

Prang, Margaret. 1960. Clerics, Politicians, and the Bilingual Schools Issue in Ontario, 1910-1917. *Canadian Historical Review* 41: 281-307.

Pruysers, Scott. 2014. Reconsidering Vertical Integration: An Examination of National Political Parties and Their Counterparts in Ontario. *Canadian Journal of Political Science* 47 (2): 237-58.

Rabinowitz, George, and Stuart Elaine Macdonald. 1989. A Directional Theory of Issue Voting. *American Political Science Review* 83: 93-121.

Rae, Douglas W. 1969. *The Political Consequences of Electoral Laws.* New Haven, CT: Yale University Press.

–. 1971. *The Political Consequences of Electoral Laws.* 2nd ed. New Haven, CT: Yale University Press.

Ragin, Charles C. 2005. Core versus Tangential Assumptions in Comparative Research. *Studies in Comparative International Development* 40: 33-38.

Reid, Escott M. 1932. The Rise of National Parties in Canada. *Papers and Proceedings of the Canadian Political Science Association* 4: 187-200.

Reif, Karlheinz, and Hermann Schmitt. 1980. Nine Second-Order National Elections: A Conceptual Framework for the Analysis of European Election Results. *European Journal of Political Research* 8: 3-44.

Riddell, W. Craig. 1993. Unionization in Canada and the United States: A Tale of Two Countries. In *Small Differences That Matter: Labor Markets and Income Maintenance in Canada and the United States*, edited by David Card and Richard B. Freeman, 109-47. Chicago: University of Chicago Press.

Riker, William H. 1976. The Number of Political Parties: A Reexamination of Duverger's Law. *Comparative Politics* 9: 93-106.

–. 1982. The Two-Party System and Duverger's Law: An Essay on the History of Political Science. *American Political Science Review* 76: 753-66.

Riker, William H., and Peter C. Ordeshook. 1968. A Theory of the Calculus of Voting. *American Political Science Review* 62: 25-42.

Robinson, Daniel J. 1999. *The Measure of Democracy: Polling, Market Research, and Public Life, 1930-1945*. Toronto: University of Toronto Press.

Robinson, H. Basil. 1989. *Diefenbaker's World: A Populist in Foreign Affairs*. Toronto: University of Toronto Press.

Robinson, Judith. 1957. *This Is on the House*. Toronto: McClelland and Stewart.

Rodden, Jonathan. 2010. The Geographic Distribution of Political Preferences. *Annual Review of Political Science* 13: 321-40.

Roy, Reginald H. 1977. *For Most Conspicuous Bravery: A Biography of Major-General George R. Pearkes, V.C., through Two World Wars*. Vancouver: UBC Press.

Rumilly, Robert. 1953. *Henri Bourassa: La vie d'un grand Canadien*. Montréal: Les Éditions Chantecler.

–. 1973. *Maurice Duplessis et son temps*. Montréal: Fides.

Sankoff, David, and Koula Mellos. 1973. La régionalisation électorale et l'amplification des proportions. *Canadian Journal of Political Science* 3: 380-98.

Sartori, Giovanni. 1966. European Political Parties: The Case of Polarized Pluralism. In *Political Parties and Political Development*, edited by Joseph LaPalombara and Myron Weiner, 137-76. Princeton, NJ: Princeton University Press.

–. 1976. *Parties and Party Systems: A Framework for Analysis*. Cambridge, UK: Cambridge University Press.

Sawatsky, John. 1991. *Mulroney: The Politics of Ambition*. Toronto: McClelland and Stewart.

Saywell, John T. 1991. *Just Call Me Mitch: The Life of Mitchell F. Hepburn*. Ontario Historical Studies Series. Toronto: University of Toronto Press.

Scott, F.R. 1957. *The Eye of the Needle: Satires, Sorties, Sundries*. Montreal: Contact Press.

Seawright, Jason. 2005. Qualitative Comparative Analysis vis-à-vis Regression. *Studies in Comparative International Development* 40: 3-26.

Shafer, Byron E., and Richard Johnston. 2006. *The End of Southern Exceptionalism: Class, Race, and Partisan Change in the Postwar South.* Cambridge, MA: Harvard University Press.

Shalev, Michael, and Walter Korpi. 1980. Working Class Mobilization and American Exceptionalism. *Economic and Industrial Democracy* 1: 31-61.

Shugart, Matthew S., and John Carey. 1992. *Presidents and Assemblies: Constitutional Design and Electoral Dynamics.* Cambridge, UK: Cambridge University Press.

Siegfried, André. 1966. The Race Question in Canada. Carleton Library No. 29. 1906; reprinted, Toronto: McClelland and Stewart.

Silverstein, Sanford. 1968. Occupational Class and Voting Behavior: Electoral Support of a Left-Wing Protest Movement in a Period of Prosperity. In *Agrarian Socialism: The Cooperative Commonwealth in Saskatchewan. A Study in Political Sociology,* edited by Seymour Martin Lipset, 435-79. 1950; reprinted, New York: Doubleday.

Smiley, Donald. 1962. Canada's Poujadists: A New Look at Social Credit. *Canadian Forum* 42: 121-23.

Smith, Denis. 1973. *Gentle Patriot: A Political Biography of Walter Gordon.* Edmonton: Hurtig.

Sniderman, Paul M., H.D. Forbes, and Ian Melzer. 1974. Party Loyalty and Electoral Volatility: A Study of the Canadian Party System. *Canadian Journal of Political Science* 7: 268-88.

Stacey, C.P. 1981. *Canada and the Age of Conflict.* Vol. 2. Toronto: University of Toronto Press.

Stairs, Denis. 1974. *The Diplomacy of Constraint: Canada, the Korean War, and the United States.* Toronto: University of Toronto Press.

Staniek, Magdalena. 2013. Predicting Party Failure: Party Policy and Longevity of Legislative Parties in New and Established Democracies, 1945-2010. Prepared for presentation at the Political Studies Association Annual Conference, March 25-27, Cardiff, UK.

Strøm, Kaare. 1983. *Minority Government and Majority Rule.* Cambridge, UK: Cambridge University Press.

–. 1990. A Behavioral Theory of Competitive Political Parties. *American Journal of Political Science* 34: 565-98.

Taagepera, Rein, and Bernard Grofman. 1985. Rethinking Duverger's Law: Predicting the Effective Number of Parties in Plurality and PR Systems – Parties Minus Issues Equals One. *European Journal of Political Research* 13: 341-52.

Tam Cho, Wendy K., and Brian J. Gaines. 2004. The Limits of Ecological Inference: The Case of Split-Ticket Voting. *American Journal of Political Science* 48: 152-71.

Tavits, Margit. 2006. Party System Change: Testing a Model of New Party Entry. *Party Politics* 12: 99-119.

Thomas, Lewis Herbert. 1978. *The Struggle for Responsible Government in the North-West Territories, 1870-1897*. 2nd ed. Toronto: University of Toronto Press.

Thomsen, Søren R. 1987. *Danish Elections, 1920-79: A Logit Approach to Ecological Analysis and Inference*. Aarhus: Politica.

Thorlakson, Lori. 2007. An Institutional Explanation for Party System Congruence: Evidence from Six Federations. *European Journal of Political Research* 46: 69-95.

–. 2009. Patterns of Party Integration, Influence, and Autonomy in Seven Federations. *Party Politics* 15: 157-77.

Triadafilopoulos, Triadafilos. 2012. *Becoming Multicultural: Immigration and the Politics of Membership in Canada and Germany*. Vancouver: UBC Press.

Tukey, J. 1977. *Exploratory Data Analysis*. Reading, MA: Addison-Wesley.

Volkens, Andrea, Pola Lehmann, Nicolas Merz, Sven Regel, and Annika Werner. 2013. *The Manifesto Data Collection, Manifesto Project (MRG/CMP/MARPOR), Version 2013a*. Berlin: Wissenschaftszentrum Berlin für Sozialforschung (WZB).

Waite, P.B. 1985. *The Man from Halifax: Sir John Thompson, Prime Minister*. Toronto: University of Toronto Press.

Ware, Alan. 2009. *The Dynamics of Two-Party Politics: Party Structures and the Management of Competition*. New York: Oxford University Press.

Wesley, Jared J. 2011. *Code Politics: Campaigns and Cultures on the Canadian Prairies*. Vancouver: UBC Press.

White, Graham. 1973. One-Party Dominance and Third Parties: The Pinard Theory Reconsidered. *Canadian Journal of Political Science* 6: 399-421.

Wilbur, J.R.H. 1964. H.H. Stevens and the Reconstruction Party. *Canadian Historical Review* 45 (1): 1-28.

Willms, A.M. 1956. Conscription, 1917: A Brief for the Defence. *Canadian Historical Review* 37: 338-51.

Wiseman, Nelson. 2007. *In Search of Canadian Political Culture*. Vancouver: UBC Press.

Wrong, Dennis H. 1957. The Pattern of Party Voting in Canada. *Public Opinion Quarterly* 21 (2): 252-64.

Young, Walter D. 1969. *The Anatomy of a Party: The National CCF, 1932-1961*. Toronto: University of Toronto Press.

Zaller, John R. 1992. *The Nature and Origins of Mass Opinion*. Cambridge, UK: Cambridge University Press.

Index

Note: Page numbers in *italics* refer to figures or tables.

Aberhart, William, 139
Abramson, Paul R., 200
Achen, Christopher H., 202-3
Action Libérale Nationale (ALN), 141, 159-60
agrarian electoral support, 153-59; coordination, 156; divergent paths, 158-59; election timing, *155t*, 157-58; farmer candidates, 145, 158; institutional variation, 154; party system factors, 154-56, *155t*, 255; political economy of grain, 147-48, *155t*, 156-58
agrarian insurgency: electoral history, 19, 26, 141, 149, 164, 174-75, 244; failure, 258; and labour mobilization, 164-77; provincial arena, *155t*, 156, 157-58, 217, 222, 226, 256, 258; Western region, 147, 157, 173, 174, 256, 258. *See also* agrarian electoral support; Progressive movement; Social Credit Party
Alberta: agrarian electoral support, 153-59, *155t*; autonomy bill, 110; CCF-NDP, 164-68, *166f*; CCF party, 159; Conservative Party, 282n8; effective number of parties (ENP), *221f*; federal-provincial discontinuity, 215, *216f*, 220-27, *221f*, *223f*, *225f*, *227f*; insurgent parties, *24f*, 134-43, *135f*, *137f*, *142f*, *219t*; labour mobilization, 164-68, *166f*; Liberal Party, 50; NDP, 280n4, 282n8; Social Credit Party, 267n8; United Farmers of Alberta (UFA), 158-59, 256, 258; Wildrose Party, 140, 280n2, 282n8
Alford, Robert R./Alford index, 39-42, 40, *41t*, *42t*, 120
Alliance Party, 19
Alliance/Progressive Conservative, 152, 267n14
Almond, Gabriel A., 131
Amorim Neto, Octavio, 144
ancestry: geography and demography, 103-7, *105f*, *127t*; impact of, 104, 105, 112-22, *127f*, *129f*, 262; multiculturalism and shift to ethnicity, 122-31, *124f*, *127f*, *129f*; party preference,

106-7, 122, 125-30, *127f*, *129f*, 270n8. *See also* ethnicity
Atlantic Canada: Catholic population, 104, 105; Conservative Party support, 97, 99; election turnout, 88, *89f*; federal-provincial discontinuity, 145, 248; insurgent parties, 145; interaction among new and old parties, 246; Irish ancestry, 107; NDP strength, 167, 181, 183, 222, 230, 246, 281n5; popular votes by region, 54-56, *55f*, *57f*, *66t*; regional coalitions, *96t*, 97; seat-share distributions, 56-60, *57f*, *58f*, *59f*, *66f*, 268n2, 269n6; third-party entry and exit, 248. *See also* regions
Australia: Catholics and the party system, 42-43, *42t*, 131, 268n18; conscription crisis, 131; effective number of parties (ENP), *27f*, 31; electoral formula, 25, 233; electoral system comparisons, 233-34; electoral volatility, *32-33f*, *33f*, 34; federalism, 28, 37; federal-provincial discontinuity, 35-37, *36f*; foreign policy, 113, 114, 117; fragmentation, 25-28, *27f*, 233; labour mobilization, *170f*; left-right axis, 235; party system foundations, 131; political economy of grain, 147; rural population, 276n3; union movement, 40-41, *41t*, 131, *170f*, 175

Bakvis, Herman, 98
Ballantyne, Janet, 98
Bartels, Larry M., 200
Bartolini, Stefano, 168
Bélanger, Éric, 275n19
Bell, Edward A., 274n2

Bennett, Andrew, 30
Bennett, R.B., 119, 273n15
Bennett, W.A.C., 139, 160
bilingualism, 18, 126
Black, Conrad, 91
Blais, André, 151, 275n19
Blake, Donald E., 266n7
Blake, Edward, 108, 273n10
Bleus, 89
Bloc Populaire Canadien, 86, 119, 141
Bloc Québécois: electoral history, *21f*, 86, 87-88, 143, 150, 151, 271n17; federal/provincial elections dynamics, *142f*; fractionalization source, 203; left-right orientation, 280n7; in1993 election, 53; support for Quebec, *72f*, *73f*
Boix, Carles, 254, 257-58
Borden, Robert, 113, 117, 253
Bouchard, Lucien Bouchard, 143
Bourassa, Henri, 85-86, 90, 93-94
Bracken, John, 16
Brady, Henry E., 200
British Army of the Rhine, 120
British Columbia: anti-labour coordination, 160-61; CCF-NDP, 164-68, *166f*, 180, *219t*; CCF party, 258-59; Conservative Party, 52; effective number of parties (ENP), *221f*; federal-provincial discontinuity, 215, *216f*, 220-27, *221f*, *223f*, *225f*, *227f*; insurgent parties, *24f*, 134-43, *135f*, *137f*, *142f*, *219t*; labour mobilization, 164-68, *166f*, 173-75; party consolidation pressures, 276n10; regional coalitions, *96t*, 97; Social Credit Party, 160-61, 267n8
Broadcasting Act (1991 revisions), 127-28

Brodie, Janine, 254
"butter not guns," 90-91

Cahan, C.H., 118-19
Cairns, Alan C., 65, 98, 131, 152, 250, 269n11, 274n6, 278n6
Calvo, Ernesto, 98
Campaign Manifesto Project (CMP), 45, 69-70, 210, 268n22
Canada-US Free Trade Agreement (FTA), 191, *192t*, 193, 255
Canadian Auto Workers, 211
Canadian Charter of Rights and Freedoms, 92, 126, 127
Canadian Congress of Labour (CCL), 171
Canadian Journal of Political Science, 65
Canadian Labour Congress (CLC), 171, 210
Canadian Multiculturalism Act (1988), 127-28
Canadian Red Cross, 115
Canadian Reform Conservative Alliance party, 140
Canadian society, 168-80; Anglo-American settler society, 6; Catholic/non-Catholic gap, 41-43, *42f*, 107-12, *111f*, 123-26, *124f*, 130; competing claims of culture, 177-80; globalist views, 253-54; manual/non-manual workers gap, 39, 40; rural population definition, 276n3
Caouette, Réal, 94-95
Castors, 89, 110
Catholics and others, 101-32; analytic history, 252-54; and the British Empire, 112-22; Catholic-Liberal alignment, 10, 41-43, *42t*, 110-12, *111f*, 116, 117-18, 120, *121f*, *124f*, 131, 260; Catholic/non-Catholic gap, 41-43, *42f*, 107-12, *111f*, 123-26, *124f*, 130, 242; Catholic population percentages, 277n12; competing claims of culture, 177-80; education rights, 18, 108, 109-10, 116; geography of religion and language, 103-7, *105f*; multiculturalism and shift to ethnicity, 122-31; *Quadragesimo Anno* (Pius XI), 177; religious identity and the party system, 41-43, *42t*, 46, 107-12, *111f*, 122, 123-26, 240
CCF (Cooperative Commonwealth Federation): competing claims of culture, 177-80; labour mobilization, 171, *172f*; party/electoral history, *20f*, 22, 30, 183, 208, 210, 244, 256, 258-59, 276n1. *See also* CCF-NDP
CCF-NDP: anti-labour coordination, 160-61; competing claims of culture, 178-80, *179f*; effective number of parties (ENP), *237f*; electoral/party history, 11-12, *20f*, 22, 23, 35, 187; federal-provincial discontinuity, 217-20, *218f*, *219t*, *229f*, *238f*; fractionalization, 202-7, 203-7, *203t*, *204f*, *206f*, 208, *213t*; labour mobilization, 39, 164-68, *166f*, *170f*, *172f*, 175-77, *176f*; left-right axis, 163, *223f*, *236f*; liberal centrism, 69; "old"/"new" party dynamics, *189t*; provincial strength, 164-68, *166f*, *218f*, *219t*; seats and votes, *20f*, *24f*, *166f*, *176f*, *218f*; third party entry and exit, 244-45, 248; vote shift dynamics, 190-207, *191f*, *192t*, *195f*, *196t*, *198f*, *199t*. *See also* insurgent parties

centre-left, 7-8, 190, 197, 199, 208, 210-11, 260, 278n12
centre-right: consolidation, 11, 26, 160, 215, *223f*, 224, 228, *236f*, 247; coordination failure, 208; cross-national comparison, 240; disequilibrium dynamics, 190; election campaigns, 197, 199, 202; federal-provincial discontinuity, 249
Chanak Incident (1922), 114, 117
Chappell, Henry W. Jr., 68
Chhibber, Pradeep K., 4, 28-30, 145-46, 152, 251, 260, 267n12
Clarke, Harold D., 86
class politics: Canadian society composition, 168, 174; electoral history, 26, 34, 46; federal-provincial discontinuity, 11; weakness of, 5, 39-41, 46
Cloutier, Édouard, 94
coalition governments: majority and minority governments, *96f*; Quebec as pivot for government formation, *62t*; regional coalitions by province and party, 95-97, *96f*, *100f*; single-party governments, 12; Unionist coalition, *62t*
Cohen, Ronald I., 90-91, 94
Colley, Linda, 114
Confédération des Syndicats Nationaux, 171
Congress of Industrial Organizations (CIO), 169, 276n2
conscription: Australian crisis, 131; election impact, 30, 50, 63, 88, 117, 159, 268n4; Great War, 79, 85, 115, 131, 253; Quebec nationalism, 141; Second World War, 30, 50, 85-86, 94, 113-14; Unionist Coalition, 16, 18

Conservative Party: agrarian electoral support, 153-59, *155t*; boom and bust cycles, 10, 18-19, 34-35, 83-84, *84f*, 243, 246; "butter not guns," 90-91; campaign/election coordination failures, 201-2; conditions for power, 60-65, *62t*; electoral coalitions, 95-97, *96f*, *100f*; electoral history, 15-19, *17f*, 23, 31, 52-54, *80f*, 82-84, *84f*, 281nn2-3; farmers and politics, 154-56; federal-provincial discontinuity, 217-20, *218f*, *219t*; globalist views, 253-54; language politics, *78f*, 92-93; left-right axis, 4-5, 69, *70f*; multiculturalism, 122-30; 1958 election, 91-92; 1984 election, 91-95; "old"/"new" party dynamics, *189t*, 245-47; Ontario support, 278n10; party history, 10, 49-52, 243; popular-vote distribution, 54-56, *55f*, *57f*, *66t*; Quebec support for, 60-65, *62t*, *80f*, 82-84, *84f*, 88-95, 243; regions as brokers of government, *51f*, 52-53, 278n10; seats/seat shares, 56-60, *57f*, *58f*, *59f*; sociology of the vote, 74-79, *78f*; support for Quebec, 70-74, *72f*, 73, *73f*, 131; vote-share trajectories, *24f*; vote-shift dynamics, 190-207, *191f*, *192t*, *195f*, *196f*, *198f*, *199t*; West region, *51f*, 52, 54, 97-98, 99
Corporations and Labour Unions Returns Act (CALURA), 276n5
Courtney, John C., 279n17
Cox, Gary W.: electoral consolidation, 25, 280n6, 280n8; number of parties, 144; rethinking Duverger's Law, 4, 28-29, 180, 260-61; vote share, 222; Westminster parliamentarism, 250
Crunican, Paul, 266n7

cultural politics and patterns, 3, 43
Cutler, Fred, 22, 29, 183, 209-11

de Graaf, Nan Dirk, 39
Democratic Party (US), 40, *41t*, *42t*
Diefenbaker, John: Conservative Party boom or bust, 34-35, 83, 92, 99; electoral history, 19, 34, 52, 243; inclusive policies, 94, 120, 130
Downs, Anthony, 67-68
Drury, E.C., 156
Duplessis, Maurice, 91-92, 94, 141, 159-60, 272n20
Duverger's Law: federal-provincial discontinuity, 11-12, 28, 215, 220, 235, 249; local/extra-local fragmentation, 28-30, *29f*, 31; provincial arena, 260; theory, 3, 4, 144-45, 180, 261

Eastern Europe ancestry, *129f*, 274n22
effective number of parties. *See* ENP (effective number of parties)
1878 election, 266n3
1896 election, 266n7
elections. *See under year of election*
electoral consolidation/coordination, 13, 278n6
electoral formulas: federal-provincial discontinuity, 232-33; fractionalization, 10-11, 25, *29f*, 202-7; nature of, 4; rural/urban vote counts, 154. *See also* electoral systems
electoral history, 13-47; centrist domination, 43-45, *44f*; cross-national patterns, 25-39, 257; early elections, 266n3, 266n7, 268n4, 269n8; foundations of party systems, 39-43, 46; language/religion impact, 18; moving forward, 45-47; party system history, 14-22, *17f*; secular growth, 22; strength of religion, 41-43; weakness of class, 39-41
electoral systems: Canada-Australia comparisons, 233-34; federal-provincial discontinuity, 235; and party system, 97-98; preferential ballot, *2805t*; proportional representation (PR), 6-7, 200, 232, 235, 275n20; provincial arena, 255-56
electoral threshold, 275n20
electoral volatility. *See* episodic volatility
electorate, segmentation of, 10, 250-51
ENP (effective number of parties): cross-national comparisons, 26-28, *27f*, 31; extra-local component of, 246; federal/provincial discontinuity, *229f*, *238f*; fractionalization, *29f*, 205, 207, 240; fragmentation, 26; insurgent parties, 144-46; interaction among new and old parties, 246; joint effect of insurgents and CCF-NDP, *237f*; provincial arena, *221f*, 249, 279n14; single-member district systems, *27f*; typical ENP for seats in Parliament, 153
episodic volatility: Anglo-American cross-national SMD electoral volatility, *32-33f*; Canadian electoral history, 13, 31-35, 46, 240-41; contributing factors, 6, 9, 34, 243, 267n15, 267n17; federal-provincial electoral divergence, *36f*; interaction among new and old parties, 246; in single-member district systems, *32-33f*; volatility index, 34, 278n6
Ethiopian crisis, 113, 119

ethnicity, 122-31, *124f, 127f, 129f,* 130-31, 185-86
ethnonationalism, 85-86, 93-95, 141, 143, 146, 159-60, 161, 231-32

farmers in politics. *See* agrarian electoral support
federalism: Australia, 37; cross-national patterns, 25, 185; as disruptive force, 28, 147, 152, 259; federal-provincial discontinuity, 259, 269n9; new parties, 7, 211-12; Spain, 148; US as prototype, 35-36
federal-provincial discontinuity, 214-38; Canada's National Policy, 234; CCF-NDP strength and centre-right consolidation, 215, *223f, 225t,* 228-31, *236f, 237f;* cross-national electoral divergence, 35-38, *36f,* 232-35, 241; deep division, 231-32; dissimilarity in space and time, 215-20; effective number of parties (ENP), 220, *221f,* 226, *227f, 229f,* 230-31, *237f, 238f,* 281n12; electoral systems, 232-33, 235; insurgent parties, 11, *225t,* 228-31, *229f, 237f, 238f;* interaction among new and old parties, 247-49; main sources, 228-31, *229f,* 233-35, *238f;* NDP as catalyst, 228-32, *229f;* overall pattern, 215, *216f;* partisan impact, 215-20, *218f, 219t,* 228-31, *229f;* party system fragmentation, 230; pressure for consolidation, 220-27, *221f, 223f, 225f, 227f,* 247, 251, 276n10; provincial history, 233-34; rural/urban vote patterns, 153-59, *155t;* scale of discontinuity, 232-35; vote-share patterns, *225f. See also* agrarian

electoral support; Duverger's Law; provincial arena
Ferguson, Howard, 119
Filippov, Mikhail, 38
Finer, S.E., 163
Finkel, Alvin, 282n9
first-past-the-post (FPP) vote counts: CCF-NDP, 22; electoral history, 14, 65, 180, 209; federal-provincial discontinuity, 222, 232-33, 256, 280n8; fragmentation, 25, 28, 47, 54, 250-51; impact on rural SMD districts, 154, 157; insurgent parties, 152, 154, 157-58, 274n4, 274n6; single-party governments, 251; vote-to-seat translations, 38
First World War. *See* Great War
Forbes, H.D., 14
fractionalization: electoral history, 26-28, *29f;* federal-provincial patterns and ENP, *227f;* insurgent parties/ CCF contributions to, *213t;* local/extra-local fragmentation, 202, 203, *204f,* 208-9, 240; parties as agents, 209-13, 211; source of, 202-7, *203t, 204f, 206f*
fragmentation: asymmetrical nature, 207, 208-9; causal factors, 6-7, 9, 207-9, 267n12; cross-national contexts, 25-31, *27f;* federal-provincial discontinuity, 230; local/extra-local components, 28-30, *29f,* 202, *204f,* 208-9, 240; neo-Duvergian predictions, 13
France, union density, 276n6
francophones. *See* language politics
French Canada, 5, 93, 122, 128-30, 274n8. *See also* Quebec
French language, 103-7, *105f, 127t*

geography: regional coalitions, 95-97, 96f, 100f; religion and language, 105f, 127t
Germany, 35-37, 36f
Gerring, John, 25, 28, 145, 152
Ginger Group, 165
globalization, 253, 254-55
Godbout Liberals, 160
grain, political economy, 147-48
Great Britain: Catholic/non-Catholic gap, 42-43, 42t; electoral volatility, 32-33f, 34; ENP in single-member district systems, 27f; labour mobilization, 39, 40, 41t, 170f
Great Depression, 149, 159, 258, 273n15
Great War, 16, 115, 117, 119, 131, 253, 255-56, 266n4
Green, Howard, 120
Green Party, 141
Greenspon, Edward, 279n22
Grofman, Bernard, 144
Groulx, Lionel, 94
Guimont, Ernest, 90

Hargrove, Buzz, 211
Hepburn, Mitchell, 174
Hirano, Shigeo, 267n12
Home Rule, 114
House of Commons: Ontario as pivot, 53-54; popular votes by region, 54-56, 55f, 57f, 65, 66t; Quebec as pivot for government formation, 62t; regions as brokers of government, 49-53, 51f, 60-65, 66t; Riel execution, 108; seats/seat-share distributions, 56-60, 57f, 58f, 59f, 65, 66f; typical ENP for seats, 153
Hug, Simon, 145, 152, 210

identity politics: British identity, 112-22, 242, 254, 260, 261-62; ethnic conception of nationality, 101-3, 273n16; intergenerational component, 253; multiculturalism, 122-31, 124f, 127f, 129f, 130-31; national question, 69-70, 86; and the party system, 10, 87f, 107-12, 131; Quebec, 87f, 88; religious identity and the party system, 41-43, 42t, 46, 107-12, 111f, 123-26; sociology of the vote, 74-79, 76f, 78f. See also language politics
Ignatieff, Michael, 194
Imperial Conference (1926), 118
imperialism, 112-21, 243
Independent Group (Quebec), 141
Independent Labour Party (ILP), 174
India, 209-10
Industrial Disputes Investigation Act (1907), 169
insurgent parties, 133-62; anti-labour coordination, 160-61; conditions for, 7; cyclic nature, 9, 10-11, 161, 208; economic factors, 147-51, 275n22; effective number of parties (ENP), 144-46, 153, 227f; 1896 election, 266n7; electoral history, 10-11, 14-15, 19-22, 20f, 21f, 23, 35; federal-provincial discontinuity, 217-20, 218f, 219t; federal-provincial dynamics, 24f, 134-43, 135f, 137f, 142f, 229f, 238f; fractionalization patterns, 202-7, 203t, 204f, 206f, 213t, 227f; fragmentation theories, 144-48, 207-8; new and old parties, 148-53, 245-47; party fusion, 152; party histories, 136-43; patterns and path dependency, 12, 153-59; provincial arena,

11, 23, *138f,* 154-61, *218f, 219t*; seats and votes, *20f,* 153, *225f*; third-party entry and exit, 7, 10-11, 16, 244-45, 247-49, 275n21
Ireland, Home Rule, 273n10
Irish descent, 104, 106-7, 114

Jenson, Jane, 254
Jesuit estates disposition, 108, 109
Johnston, Richard, 22, 29, 98, 183, 200, 209-11

Kedar, Orit, 212
Keech, William R., 68
Knights of Labour party, 141
Kollman, Ken, 4, 28-30, 145-46, 152, 251, 260, 267n12
Kumar, Pradeep, 169

Labor Party (Australia), *41t, 42t*
labour mobilization, 164-77; anti-labour coordination, 160-61; CCF-NDP vote, *170f, 172f*; communism, 171; electoral/party system history, 14, 22, 26, 164-68, 210. *See also* CCF/NDP; union movement
Labour Party (Great Britain), *41t, 42t,* 174
Labour Party (New Zealand), *41t, 42t*
LaCombe, Albert, 101
Lago, Ignacio, 148
Langevin, Hector-Louis, 110
language politics: Conservative Party, 92-93; geography and demography, *76f, 78f,* 103-7, *105f, 127t*; language and ethnicity, 85, 102, 126-30, *127f*; multiculturalism and shift to ethnicity, 122-31, *124f, 127f, 129f,* 130-31; North-West Territories and language rights, 108; Regulation 17 (1912), 106; sociology of the vote, 74-79, *76f, 78f. See also* identity politics; religion and politics
Lapointe, Ernest, 273n14
Laponce, Jean A., 124
LaPorte, Pierre, 48, 268n1
Laurier, Wilfrid: Canada and the British Empire War, 116-18, 253; Liberal Party, 49, 81-82, 92, 148, 271n12; Naval Bill, 90; religious conflict, 108-10
Laurier-Greenway Agreement, 110
Layton, Jack, 194
League of Nations, 113, 119
LeDuc, Lawrence, 267n17
left-right orientation, 163-86; campaigns, 193, *196t, 201f,* 208, 255; composition of Canadian society, 177-80; definition of "left," 39; growth of left vote, 11-12, 164-68, *166f,* 185-86, *189t,* 205, 206-7, 208, 215, 228, 258; insurgent parties, 141, 143, 147-48, 158-60, 188-89, *189t,* 207-8, 230; left-right locations of parties, 4-5, 14, 45, 79, 97, 147-48, 163-64, 187, 191, 193, 195-97, *196t,* 273n26, 278n7; left threat and right consolidation, 134, 190, 224, *236f*; liberal centrist domination, 43-45, *44f,* 67-69, *70f*; party coordination and consolidation, 200-1, *201f,* 209-10, 280n8; party interactions, 244-46; party organizing principle, 4-5, 8, 9, 11, 69, 153-54, 200, 207, 247, 257, 277n2; path dependency, 257-58; Pearson government cabinet, 213-14; provincial arena, 11-12, 161-62, 164-68, *166f, 189t,* 224; regional

support, 246; third party dynamics, 244-45. *See also* labour mobilization; liberal centrist domination; polarized pluralism

liberal centrist domination, 67-100; and CCF-NDP, 69; Conservative party and Quebec, 82; electoral history, 43-45, *44f*, 89-95; electoral system and party system, 68, 98-99, 241, 247; left-right orientation, 43-45, *44f*, 67-69, *70f*; Liberal Party role, 82, 85-88; national question and support for Quebec, 9-10, 68, 69-74, *72f*, *73f*; partisanship, 86-87, *87f*; political centre defined, 67-69; Quebec and rest of Canada, *80f*, 82-84, *84f*; regional coalitions, 95-97, *96f*, *100f*; sectionalism, 9, 95, *96f*, 97-98; segmented dynamics, 68, 79-84; sociology of the vote, 74-79, *76f*, *78f*; turnout, 88, *89f*; underlying mechanisms, 85-95. *See also* polarized pluralism

Liberal Party: agrarian electoral support, 153-59, *155t*; ancestry impact, *129f*; campaign/election coordination failures, 199-202, *201f*; Catholic-Liberal alignment, 10, 41-43, *42t*, 110-12, *111f*, 116-18, 120, *121f*, *124f*, 131; electoral coalitions, 95-97, *96f*, *100f*; electoral history, 15-19, *17f*, 23, 30, 43-46, 49-52, *80f*, 81-82, 257-58, 262, 281n1; farmers and politics, 154-56; federal-provincial discontinuity, 217-20, *218f*, *219t*; federal-provincial relations, 92; government formation, 60-65, *62t*, 241-42; key to longevity, 250-51; labour mobilization, 171, 174; language politics, *78f*; left-right axis, 5, 14, 69, *70f*, 164; multiculturalism, 122-30; new/old party dynamics, *189t*, 241-47; Ontario, 278n12; party history, 9-10, 18-19, 49-52, 85-88, 99; popular votes, 54-56, *55f*, *57f*, *66t*; Quebec, 5-6, 9, 70-74, *72f*, *73f*, *80f*, 81-82, 88-95, 250-51, 271n11, 271n13; regions as brokers of government, 49-52, *51f*; religious cleavage, *121f*, *124f*; seats/seat shares, 56-60, *57f*, *58f*, *59f*, *66f*; sociology of the vote, 74-79, *78f*; vote-share patterns, 19, *24f*, 88, *89f*, 190-207, *191f*, *192t*, *195f*, *196t*, *198f*, *199t*. *See also* regions

Lijphart, Arend, 43, 144, 177, 274n9, 275n20

Lipset, Seymour Martin, 98, 164, 173, 178, 235

local districts: Duverger's Law, 28-29; federal-provincial discontinuity, 188; insurgent parties, 145, 150, 152, 156, 222, 246, 256; invasion from the left, 180, 185; language politics, 74; religious denomination, 131-32; strategic role, 8, 11-12, 140, 207, 209-10, 259

local/extra-local fragmentation: episodic volatility, 35; fractionalization, 29-31, *29f*, 187, 202-5, *203t*, *204t*, 208-9, 240; insurgent parties, 246; provincial ENP figures, 279n14

Macdonald, John A., 15, 109
Mackenzie King, William Lyon, 61, 114, 118-19, 120, 164, 273nn12-13
Macpherson, Laura G., 98
Mainwaring, Scott, 31

majoritarian institutional contexts: Canadian electoral history, 3, 5-7, 14, 93, 259, 266n2; Catholic/non-Catholic gap, 42-43, 65; competing majoritarian logics, 250-51; federal-provincial discontinuity, 168, 186, 209, 277n10; fractionalization, 250-51; labour parties, 168; majoritarian electoral formula, 14, 168; party systems, 239; Quebec as pivot for government formation, *62t*; regional coalitions, 95-97, *96f*; Westminster parliamentarism, 8, 14, 239-40. See also Duverger's Law

Manitoba: agrarian electoral support, 153-59, *155t*; CCF-NDP, 164-68, *166f*, 180, *219t*; Conservative Party, 52, 276n26; effective number of parties (ENP), *221f*; federal-provincial discontinuity, 215, *216f*, 220-27, *221f*, *223f*, *225f*, *227f*; insurgent parties, *24f*, 134-43, *135f*, *137f*, *142f*, *219t*; Progressive Party, 274n1; regional coalitions, *96t*, 97

Manitoba Act (1870), 110

Manitoba schools controversy, 108, 109-10, 116

Manning, Ernest, 274n5

Manning, Preston, 140

Maple Leaf flag debate, 121, 242

Martin, Paul, 279n22

Martinez, Ferran, 148

McCarthy, D'Alton, 109, 141

Meighen, Arthur, 61, 113, 131

Mellos, Koula, 269n5

Melzer, Ian, 14

Mercier, Honoré, 109, 268n3

Merry del Val, Cardinal Rafael, 110

minority governments, 53, *62t*, 95-97, *96f*, 267n15

Morton, W.L., 156

Mulroney, Brian, 86, 92-93, 125, 127-28, 151

multiculturalism: Canadian Multiculturalism Act (1988), 127-28; language policy, 102, 122; official narrative of, 129-30; shift to ethnicity and language, *124f*, *127f*, *129f*, 130-31, 242

multipartism, 143-53; electoral history, 14, 28; episodic volatility, 31-38, 46; maturity of electorate, 148-49; new parties, 148-53; number of parties, 144-46; party system fragmentation theories, 144-48; party systems history, 45-46, 209-10; political economic/cultural factors, 146, 147-51; provincial elections, 11-12; statics of, 143-48. See also insurgent parties

National Government, 16, 119

nationalism. See ethnonationalism; identity politics

National Party, 257

national question, 9-10, 68-70, 73-74, 97, 113, 198, 241-43, 247

Naval Bill, 89-90

NDP: Alberta, 280n4; competing claims of culture, 178-80, *179f*; election coordination contexts, 180-85, *182f*, *184f*, 201-2, *201f*; electoral history, *20f*, 22, 69, *179f*, 255, 259-60, 272n25, 279n17; ethnodiversity, 185-87; federal-provincial dynamics, *223f*, 280n3; fractionalization patterns, *227f*; history, 7-8, 9, 11, 14,

208, 256-57, 279n20, 281n5; labour mobilization, 171, *172f*; left-right axis, 4-5, *70f*, 163-64; majoritarian electoral formula, 14, 266n2; new/old party dynamics, 245-47; 1988 election, 191-94, *191f*, *192t*; 1993 election, *199t*, 278nn8-9; party system history, 14, 39, 208-13; Quebec, 70-74, *72f*, *73f*, 278n6, 279n18; religious context of electoral returns, 181-85, *182f*, *184f*; third-party entry and exit, 248-49; 2011 election, 194-97, *199t*; union movement, 39-41, *41t*; vote-share patterns, *191f*, *192t*, 194-207, *195f*, *196t*, *199t*, *225f*. *See also* CCF-NDP; insurgent parties
Neatby, H. Blair, 266n5
neo-Duvergerian logic, 4, 8, 209, 211, 260-61
New Brunswick: Catholic population percentages, 277n12; CCF-NDP, 164-68, *166f*, *219t*; effective number of parties (ENP), *221f*; federal-provincial discontinuity, 215, *216f*, 220-27, *221f*, *223f*, *225f*, *227f*; insurgent parties, *24f*, 134-43, *135f*, *137f*, *142f*, *219t*
Newfoundland and Labrador: CCF-NDP, 164-68, *166f*, *219t*; effective number of parties (ENP), *221f*; federal-provincial discontinuity, 215, *216f*, 220-27, *221f*, *223f*, *225f*, *227f*; insurgent parties, *24f*, 134-43, *135f*, *137f*, *142f*, *219t*
new parties. *See* "old"/"new" party dynamics
New Zealand: Anglo-American cross-national SMD electoral volatility, 32-*33f*, 34; butter, 91; Catholics and the party system, *42t*; effective number of electoral parties in single-member district systems, *27f*; electoral volatility in single-member district systems, *32-33f*; union density, 276n7; union movement and party system, *41t*; union/non-union gap, 39, 40
Nieuwbeerta, Paul, 39
1911 election, 50, 243, 271n14
1916 Easter Rebellion, 117
1917 election, 159, 268n4, 269n8, 281n2
1921 election, 149-50, 158, 266n6
1921 Imperial Conference, 113
1930 election, 149, 281n2
1935 election, 50, 149-50, 159-60
1958 election, 91-92
1968 election, 269n9
1984 election, 91-95
1988 campaign/election, 188, 191-94, *191f*, *192t*, 199-201, 254-55, 260
1993 campaign/election, 53-54, 151, 197-99, *198f*, 199-201, *199t*, 260, 278n12, 278nn8-9
non-European ancestry, *129f*
Northern Europe ancestry, *129f*
North-West Rebellion (1885), 18, 115
North-West Territories, education, 110
North-West Territories Act, 109
Nova Scotia: CCF-NDP, 164-68, *166f*, *219t*; effective number of parties (ENP), *221f*; federal-provincial discontinuity, 215, *216f*, 220-27, *221f*, *223f*, *225f*, *227f*; insurgent parties, *219t*
number of parties. *See* ENP (effective number of parties)

Official Languages Act, 126, 127

Ogdensburg Agreement (1940), 254
"old"/"new" party dynamics, 241-47;
economic factors, 147-51, 149-50,
275n17; electoral maturity, 148-49,
275nn15-16; electoral trade-offs,
189t; fractionalization, *203t*; insurgent parties, 148-53; interaction
among parties, 245-47; party system
history, 14, 15-19, 46, 148-53; self-reinforcing expectations, 254-55;
third-party entry and exit, 244-45,
247-49, 275n15; Westminster parliamentarism, 8. *See also* insurgent
parties
Ontario: agrarian electoral support,
153-59, *155t*; Catholic population,
103-4, 272nn3-4; CCF-NDP, 164-68,
166f, *219t*; Conservative Party, *51f*,
52, 53-54, 278n10; coordination,
201f, 278n10; effective number of
parties (ENP), *221f*; election turnout,
88, *89f*; federal-provincial discontinuity, 215, 220-27, *221f*, *223f*, *225f*,
227f; by year, *216f*; insurgent party
dynamics, *24f*, 134-43, *135f*, *137f*,
142f, *219t*; Liberal/Conservative
conditions for power, 63-64; Liberal
Party, 50-53, *51f*, 278n12; pivot role
status, 53-54, 99; popular vote distribution, 54-56, *55f*, *57f*, *66t*; Progressive Party, 275n11; Reform Party,
201-2; regions as brokers of government, 49-53, *51f*, 60-65, *66t*; Regulation 17 (1912), 106; seat-share
distributions, 56-60, *57f*, *58f*, *59f*, *66f*
Orange Lodge of Canada/Orangemen,
108, 110, 112-13, 114
Order-in-Council PC 1003 (1944), 169
Ordeshook, Peter C., 38, 261

Paré, Charles-Guy, 91-92
Parti Québécois, 93, 141, *142f*, 274n7,
280n7
party systems: accidents of history,
255-59; centrist domination, 43-45;
exchange dynamics, 207-9; foundations, 39-43, 46; identity of the "left,"
39; majoritarian institutions, 239;
multipartism, 45-46; Parliament
financial support for smaller parties,
211; parties as agents, 209-13; party
identification, 271n15. *See also*
Canadian society; class politics; electoral history; religion and politics
Pattullo, Duff, 258-59
Pearson, Lester, 91, 212
Pederson, Mogens, 34
Petro-Canada, 272n24
Pinard, Maurice, 149, 150, 151, 159
Pius XI, 94
plurality formula, rural/urban vote
counts, 154
polarized pluralism: Canadian pattern,
5-6, 8, 68, 97, 210, 247; electoral dynamics, 8, 97-99; episodic volatility,
6; segmented dynamics, 79-81;
SMD-based party systems, 97
political culture, 146
political economy, 16, 133, 147-48, 150,
157, 168, 193, 214
Poujade, Pierre, 274n2
presidentialism, 25, 28
Prince Edward Island: CCF-NDP,
164-68, *166f*, *219t*; effective number
of parties (ENP), *221f*; federal-provincial discontinuity, 215, *216f*,
220-27, *221f*, *223f*, *225f*, *227f*; insurgent parties, *24f*, 134-43, *135f*, *137f*,
142f, *219t*

Progressive Conservative party, 16, 148, 150, 151, 152
Progressive movement, 18, 30, 38, 117, 165, 167, 207-8. *See also* union movement
Progressive Party: agrarian electoral support, 153-59, *155t*; electoral history, *21f*, 136-39, *137f*, *138f*, 146, 147, 154-56, *155t*, 157, 246, 256; federal/provincial election timing and the price of wheat by province, *155t*; 1921 election, 275n11; third-party entry and exit, 248
Prophetic Bible Institute, 139, 274n5
proportional representation (PR), 6-7, 200, 232, 235, 275n20
Protestantism, 42, 46, 114, 252-54, 273n10
provincial arena: agrarian electoral support, 153-59, *155t*; CCF electoral support, 183; CCF-NDP, *166f*, *219t*; consolidation/coordination contexts, 180-85, 277n10; cross-arena integration, 23, 267n10; Duverger's Law, 260; effective number of parties (ENP), *221f*, 249, 279n14; electoral coalitions, *100f*; electoral history, 22-24, *155t*, *182f*; electoral institutions, 255-56; federal-provincial discontinuity, 215, *216f*, *229f*, *238f*; fractionalization, *206t*, *227f*; insurgent parties, 11, 23, *138f*, 162, *218f*, *219t*; labour mobilization, 164-68, *166f*, *172f*; "old"/"new" party electoral trade-offs, *189t*; provincial/federal party systems, 217-20, *218f*, *219t*; religious conflicts and party politics, 108-12; third-party entry and exit, 244-45, 247-49; vote-share trajectories, *24f*, 181-85, *182f*. *See also* federal-provincial discontinuity

Quadragesimo Anno (Pius XI), 177
Quebec: Canada survey, 70-74, 269n3, 270n4; Catholic-Liberal alignment, 10, 43, 110-12, *111f*, *121f*, *124f*; Catholic population percentages, 277n12; CCF-NDP, 164-68, *166f*, *219t*; competing claims of culture, *124f*, 177-80; Conservative Party, *51f*, 52-54, 82, *84f*, 88-95, 243, 276n25, 281n3; consolidation/coordination, 278n6; effective number of parties (ENP), *221f*; election turnout, 88, *89f*; electoral history, *80f*, 81-84, *84f*; electoral volatility, 278n6; ethnonationalism, 85-86, 93-95, 141, 143, 146, 159-60, 161, 231-32; federal-provincial discontinuity, 215, *216f*, 220-27, *221f*, *223f*, *225f*, *227f*; geography of religion and language, *76f*, *78f*, *105f*; insurgent parties, *24f*, 134-43, *135f*, *137f*, *142f*, *219t*; labour mobilization, 171; left-right orientation, 277n2; Liberal party, 5-6, 9, 81-82, 88-95, 210, 241-42; national party support, 70-74, *72f*, *73f*; NDP, 278n6, 279n18, 280n7; "old"/"new" party dynamics, 149, 241-43, 245-47; as pivot for government formation, 48-49, 60-65, *62t*, 261; popular votes, 54-56, *55f*, *57f*, *66t*, *80f*; regions as brokers of government, 49-53, *51f*, 60-65, *62t*, *66t*; seat-share distributions, 56-60, *57f*, *58f*, *59f*, 65, *66f*, 269n5, 278n6; Social Credit Party, 267n8; sociology of the vote, 74-79, *76f*, *78f*. *See also* French Canada

Rae, Bob, 167
Rae, Douglas W., 28, 209
Ralliement Créditiste, 76, 76-77, 94-95, 143, 159, 213, 272n25
Réal Caouette, 94
Reconstruction Party, *21f,* 141
Reform/Alliance Party, *21f,* 69, 99, 140, 147-48
Reform Party: campaign/election coordination failures, *201f;* coordination failure on the left and right, 201-2, *201f;* electoral history, 19, 54, 69, 128, 146, 149-50, 270n5; federal/provincial elections dynamics by province, *137f, 139f,* 140; fractionalization source, 203, 208; history, 278n9, 278n11, 279n22; language politics, 127; left-right axis, *70f;* nation-wide support for Quebec, 70-74, *72f, 73f;* 1993 election, 197-99, *198f199t;* West region, 278n11, 281n6
regions, 48-66; brokers of government, 49-54, *51f,* 60-65, *62t;* conditions for power, 9, 60-64; contexts of coordination, 180-85; 1993 landslide and aftermath, 53-54; popular votes by region, 54-56, *55f, 57f,* 65, *66t;* Quebec as pivot for government formation, 48-49, 60-65, *62t;* regional blocs in Parliament by party, *59f;* religious cleavage, *124f;* rural/urban federal-provincial vote patterns, 153-59, *155t;* seats/seat-share-distributions, 56-60, *57f, 58f, 59f,* 65, *66f,* 269n11; third-party politics, 48. *See also* Atlantic Canada; Ontario; Quebec; West region

religion and politics: Canadian electoral history, 10, 41-43; Catholic-Liberal alignment, *111f, 121f, 124f;* competing claims of culture, 177-80; cross-national Catholic/non-Catholic gap, 42-43, *42t;* foundation of party systems, 41-43, *42t,* 241; geography of religion and language, 103-7, *105f,* 111, *127t,* 180-81; religious context of NDP federal/provincial electoral returns, 181-85, *182f, 184f;* religious conflicts and party politics, 108-12; religious identity and the party system, 41-43, *42t,* 46, 107-12, *111f, 121f,* 123-26, *124f*
Riddell, W.A., 119
Riddell, W. Craig, 276n4
Riel, Louis, 18, 49, 89, 108, 109
Riker, William H., 28, 209-10, 261
Robinson, Judith, 273n16
Roblin, Duff, 276n26
Rodden, Jonathan, 98, 250
Royal Commission on Bilingualism and Biculturalism, 126

Sankoff, David, 269n5
Sartori, Giovanni, 6
Saskatchewan: agrarian electoral support, 153-59, *155t;* anti-labour coordination, 160-61; autonomy bill, 110; CCF-NDP, 164-68, *166f,* 180, *219t;* CCF party, 159, 161, 178; effective number of parties (ENP), *221f;* federal-provincial discontinuity, 215, *216f,* 220-27, *221f, 223f, 225f, 227f;* insurgent parties, *24f,* 134-43, *135f, 137f, 142f, 219t;* labour mobilization, 173-75; Liberal Party,

50, 276n23; regional coalitions, *96t*, 97; Social Credit Party, 275n24
Saskatchewan Liberal Party, 258
Saskatchewan Party, *138f*, 140, 161, 217, 224, 257, 258
Sauvé, Paul, 94
Scott, F.R., 67
seats/seat shares: distributions by region, 56-60, *57f*, *58f*, *59f*, 65, *66f*; electoral history, *17f*; insurgent parties and CCF-NDP seats and votes, *20f*; Quebec as pivot for government formation, *62t*
Second World War, 119, 169, 232, 241, 274n1
sectarianism, 115-16
sectionalism, 9, 95, *96f*, 97-98, 228
Shvetsova, Olga, 38
Siegfried, André, 107-8, 116, 131
Sifton, Clifford, 114, 128
single-party governments, 12
single transferable vote (STV), 154, 157
SMD (single-member districts): cross-national electoral volatility, *32-33f*, 267n11; effective number of electoral parties, *27f*; electoral history, 25; impact of FFP vote counts, 154, 157; polarized pluralism, 97
Sniderman, Paul M., 14, 69, 234, 266n1
Snyder, James N., 267n12
Social Credit Party: electoral history, *21f*, 30, 149, 159-61, 205, 222, 224, 248, 259, 267n8; federal and provincial elections dynamics in Quebec, *142f*, 146, 150; federal/provincial elections by province, *137f*, *138f*, 139-40; party history, 76, 86, 95, 205, 266n8, 274n6, 274nn2-3,

282n9; third-party entry and exit, 248; West region, 139-40, 145, 274n5, 276n24
social gospel, 115
socialism, 177
South African War, 115, 116, 253, 266n4
Southern Europe ancestry, impact on Liberal vote, *129f*
Spain, 35-37, *36f*, 148
Statute of Westminster (1931), 38, 253
Stevens, H.H., 141
Strøm, Kaare, 212, 279n19
Suez Crisis, 120, 254, 273n16
system dynamics, coordination, and fragmentation, 187-213; asymmetrical contexts, 11; coordination failure, 199-202, *201f*, 278nn10-12; disequilibrium dynamics within campaigns, 190-207, *191f*, *192t*, *195f*, *196t*; dynamics of exchange, 207-9; fractionalization, 11, 202-7, *203t*, *204f*; historical dynamics among parties, 188-90, *189f*; parties as agents, 209-13

Taagepera, Rein, 144
Tavits, Margit, 275n15, 275n17
third parties. *See* insurgent parties
Thomas, Lewis Herbert, 109
Thomsen, Søren R., 40, 42-43
Thomsen index, 40, *41t*, 42-43, *42t*
Trades and Labour Congress (TLC), 171
Trudeau, Pierre, 52, 76, 95, 125, 126, 127, 271n12
Turner, John, 93, 191, 255, 272n23
turnout, *89f*, 271n17

2006 election, 281n3
2011 campaign/election, 191-201, 194-97, *195f*, *196t*, 260, 262

Unionist coalition, 16, *62t*, 63, 156
union movements: cross-national comparisons, 14, 39-41, *41t*, 276nn6-7; history, 169-73, *170f*, *172f*, 210, 211, 276n2, 276n5; impact on votes, *170f*, 175-77, *176f*; and party system, 39-41, *41t*; union/non-union gap, 39, 40, 175-77, *176f*
Union Nationale (UN), 85-86, 91, 141, *142f*, 151, 160, 243, 272n20, 274n7
United Farmers of Alberta (UFA), 158-59, 256, 258
United Farmers of Ontario, 154, 157
United States: Catholic/non-Catholic gap, 42-43, *42t*; civil rights revolution, 35; effective number of parties (ENP), *27f*; electoral volatility, *32-33f*, 34; federal-provincial electoral discontinuity, 35-37, *36f*; identity politics, 131; labour mobilization, *170f*; regional party alignment shifts, 37; state elections, 267n16; union movement and party system, 39, 40, *41t*

volatility index, 34, 278n6. *See also* episodic volatility
votes: ancestry/language impact, *78f*, *127t*, *129f*; Canadian party system history, *17f*; Conservative Party surge, *84f*; election timing, *155t*; fractionalization, 10-11, 202-7, 250-51; fragmentation, 9, 208-9; insurgent parties, *20f*, 22; left and right contexts, *201f*; protest voting, 149-50; religious cleavage, *121f*, *124f*; rural/urban vote patterns, 153-59, *155t*; turnout, *89f*
vote-share patterns: CCF-NDP, *166f*; federal-provincial discontinuity, *229f*, *238f*; federal-provincial patterns, 153-59, *155t*; fractionalization patterns and ENP, *227f*; insurgent parties, *24f*, 134-43, *135f*, *137f*, *138f*, *142f*, *225f*; labour mobilization, *170f*, *172f*; Liberal Party pattern, 19, *89f*; NDP, *179f*, *225f*; popular votes by region, 54-56, *55f*, *57f*, 65, *66t*; Quebec, *80f*; vote shifts in federal elections, *192t*, *196t*, *199t*

Wallace, Clarke, 110
Wartime Elections Act, 117
Wesley, Jared J., 146, 275n13
Westminster systems, 8, 12, 14, 34, 250
West region: agrarian electoral support, 153-59, *155t*; anti-labour coordination, 160-61; Catholic population, 104; CCF-NDP party strength, 165, 167; Conservative Party, *51f*, 52, 54, 97-98, 99; coordination failure, *201f*; election turnout, 88, *89f*; farmer candidates, 145; labour mobilization, 173-75; Liberal/Conservative conditions for power, 63-64; NDP strength, 228-31, 281n11; new party dynamics, 148-49, 245-47; political economy of grain, 147-48, 150, *155t*, 156-58; popular votes by region, 54-56, *55f*, *57f*, *66t*; Reform Party history, 278n11, 281n6; regional coalitions,

96t, 97; regions as brokers of government, 49-53, 51f, 60-65, 66t; rural/urban federal-provincial vote patterns, 153-59, 155t; seat-share distributions, 56-60, 57f, 58f, 59f, 66f; Social Credit Party, 139-40; third-party politics, 48, 248

wheat prices, 155t, 156, 156-58, 158, 275n22

Whiggism, 108, 109-10
Wildrose Party, 138f, 140, 280n2, 280n4, 282n8
Wilson-Smith, Anthony, 279n22
Winnipeg General Strike (1919), 156
Wiseman, Nelson, 146
Woodsworth, J.S., 94

Zoco, Edurne, 31